CRIMINAL PROCEDURE AND THE CONSTITUTION

Paralegal Titles from Delmar Publishers

Legal Writing, 2nd ed., Steve Barber, 1997
Administration of Wills, Trusts, and Estates, 2nd ed., Gordon W. Brown, 1997
Basics of Legal Document Preparation, Robert R. Cummins, 1997
Constitutional Law: Cases and Commentary, Daniel E. Hall, 1997
Criminal Procedure and the Constitution, Daniel E. Hall, 1997
Survey of Criminal Law, 2nd ed., Daniel E. Hall, 1997
California Estate Administration, Zella Mack, 1997
Torts and Personal Injury Law, 2nd ed., Cathy J. Okrent, William R. Buckley, 1997
The Law of Corporations, Partnerships, and Sole Proprietorships, 2nd ed., Angela Schneeman, 1997
Texas Legal Research, 2nd ed., Pamela R. Tepper, Peggy N. Kerley, 1997

Legal Research, Steve Barber, Mark A. McCormick, 1996
Wills, Estates, and Trusts, Jay H. Gingrich, 1996
Criminal Law and Procedure, 2nd ed., Daniel E. Hall, 1996
Introduction to Environmental Law, Harold Hickok, 1996
Civil Litigation, 2nd ed., Peggy N. Kerley, Joanne Banker Hames, Paul A. Sukys, 1996
Client Accounting for the Law Office, Elaine M. Langston, 1996
Law Office Management, 2nd ed., Jonathan S. Lynton, Terry Mick Lyndall, Donna Masinter, 1996
Foundations of Law: Cases, Commentary, and Ethics, 2nd ed., Ransford C. Pyle, 1996
Administrative Law and Procedure, Elizabeth C. Richardson, 1996
Legal Research and Writing, David J. Smith, 1996

Legal Research and Writing, Carol M. Bast, 1995
Federal Taxation, Susan G. Covins, 1995
Everything You Need to Know About Being a Legal Assistant, Chere B. Estrin, 1995
Paralegals in New York Law, Eric M. Gansberg, 1995
Ballentine's Legal Dictionary and Thesaurus, Jonathan S. Lynton, 1995
Legal Terminology with Flashcards, Cathy J. Okrent, 1995
Wills, Trusts, and Estate Administration for Paralegals, Mark A. Stewart, 1995
The Law of Contracts and the Uniform Commercial Code, Pamela R. Tepper, 1995
Life Outside the Law Firm: Non-Traditional Careers for Paralegals, Karen Treffinger, 1995

An Introduction to Paralegal Studies, David G. Cooper, Michael J. Gibson, 1994
Administrative Law, Daniel E. Hall, 1994
Ballentine's Law Dictionary: Legal Assistant Edition, Jack G. Handler, 1994
The Law of Real Property, Michael P. Kearns, 1994
Ballentine's Thesaurus for Legal Research and Writing, Jonathan S. Lynton, 1994
Legal Ethics and Professional Responsibility, Jonathan S. Lynton, Terri Mick Lyndall, 1994
Criminal Law for Paralegals, Daniel J. Markey, Jr., Mary Queen Donnelly, 1994
Family Law, Ransford C. Pyle, 1994
Paralegals in American Law: Introduction to Paralegalism, Angela Schneeman, 1994
Intellectual Property, Richard Stim, 1994

CRIMINAL PROCEDURE AND THE CONSTITUTION

Daniel E. Hall

Delmar Publishers

an International Thomson Publishing company

Albany • Bonn • Boston • Cincinnati • Detroit • London • Madrid
Melbourne • Mexico City • New York • Pacific Grove • Paris • San Francisco
Singapore • Tokyo • Toronto • Washington

NOTICE TO THE READER

Publisher does not warrant or guarantee any of the products described herein or perform any independent analysis in connection with any of the product information contained herein. Publisher does not assume, and expressly disclaims, any obligation to obtain and include information other than that provided to it by the manufacturer.

The reader is expressly warned to consider and adopt all safety precautions that might be indicated by the activities herein and to avoid all potential hazards. By following the instructions contained herein, the reader willingly assumes all risks in connection with such instructions.

The publisher makes no representations or warranties of any kind, including but not limited to, the warranties of fitness for particular purpose or merchantability, nor are any such representations implied with respect to the material set forth herein, and the publisher takes no responsibility with respect to such material. The publisher shall not be liable for any special, consequential, or exemplary damages resulting, in whole or in part, from the reader's use of, or reliance upon, this material.

Cover Design: Linda DeMasi
Background by: Jennifer McGlaughlin

Delmar Staff:
Acquisitions Editor: Christopher Anzalone
Editorial Assistant: Judy A. Roberts
Developmental Editor: Jeffrey D. Litton
Project Editor: Eugenia L. Orlandi
Production Coordinator: Linda J. Helfrich
Art & Design Coordinator: Douglas J. Hyldelund

Printed in the United States of America

For more information, contact:

Delmar Publishers
3 Columbia Circle, Box 15015
Albany, New York 12212-5015

International Thomson Publishing–Europe
Berkshire House
168-173 High Holborn
London WC1V 7AA
England

Thomas Nelson Australia
102 Dodds Street
South Melbourne, 3205
Victoria, Australia

Nelson Canada
1120 Birchmount Road
Scarborough, Ontario
Canada M1K 5G4

International Thomson Editores
Campos Eliseos 385, Piso 7
Col Polanco
11560 Mexico D F Mexico

International Thomson Publishing GmbH
Königswinterer Strasse 418
53227 Bonn
Germany

International Thomson Publishing Asia
221 Henderson Road
#05 - 10 Henderson Building
Singapore 0315

International Thomson Publishing–Japan
Hirakawacho Kyowa Building, 3F
2-2-1 Hirakawacho
Chiyoda-ku, Tokyo 102
Japan

1 2 3 4 5 6 7 8 9 10 XXX 02 01 00 99 98 97 96

Library of Congress Cataloging-in-Publication Data

Hall, Daniel (Daniel E.)
Criminal procedure and the Constitution / Daniel E. Hall.
p. cm.
Includes bibliographical references and index.
ISBN 0-8273-7516-6
1. Criminal procedure—United States. 2. United States—Constitutional law. 3. Legal assistants—United States—Handbooks, manuals, etc. I. Title.
KF9619.3.H28 1997
345.73'05—dc20
[347.3055]

96-7044
CIP
AC

CONTENTS

CHAPTER 9: The Pretrial Process: Initiation Through Formal Charge 174

CHAPTER 10: Pretrial Process: Arraignment Through Trial 198

CHAPTER 11: Trial 222

IIII Appendix

AM JUR PLEADING AND PRACTICE FORMS, REV: MODEL PRACTICE FORMS FOR EVERY STAGE OF A LEGAL PROCEEDING.

AM JUR PROOF OF FACTS: A SERIES OF ARTICLES THAT GUIDE THE READER IN DETERMINING WHICH FACTS ARE ESSENTIAL TO A CASE AND HOW TO PROVE THEM.

AM JUR TRIALS: A SERIES OF ARTICLES DISCUSSING EVERY ASPECT OF PARTICULAR SETTLEMENTS AND TRIALS WRITTEN BY180 CONSULTING SPECIALISTS.

UNITED STATES CODE SERVICE: A COMPLETE AND AUTHORITATIVE ANNOTATED FEDERAL CODE THAT FOLLOWS THE EXACT LANGUAGE OF THE STATUTES AT LARGE AND DIRECTS YOU TO THE COURT AND AGENCY DECISIONS CONSTRUING EACH PROVISION.

ALR AND ALR FEDERAL: SERIES OF ANNOTATIONS PROVIDING IN-DEPTH ANALYSES OF ALL THE CASE LAW ON PARTICULAR LEGAL ISSUES.

U.S. SUPREME COURT REPORTS, L ED 2D: EVERY REPORTED U.S. SUPREME COURT DECISION PLUS IN-DEPTH DISCUSSIONS OF LEADING ISSUES.

FEDERAL PROCEDURE, L ED: A COMPREHENSIVE, A-Z TREATISE ON FEDERAL PROCEDURE—CIVIL, CRIMINAL, AND ADMINISTRATIVE.

FEDERAL PROCEDURAL FORMS, L ED: STEP-BY-STEP GUIDANCE FOR DRAFTING FORMS FOR FEDERAL COURT OR FEDERAL AGENCY PROCEEDINGS.

FEDERAL RULES SERVICE, 2D AND 3D: REPORTS DECISIONS FROM ALL LEVELS OF THE FEDERAL SYSTEM INTERPRETING THE FEDERAL RULES OF CIVIL PROCEDURE AND THE FEDERAL RULES OF APPELLATE PROCEDURE.

FEDERAL RULES DIGEST, 3D: ORGANIZES HEADNOTES FOR THE DECISIONS REPORTED IN FEDERAL RULES SERVICE ACCORDING TO THE NUMBERING SYSTEMS OF THE FEDERAL RULES OF CIVIL PROCEDURE AND THE FEDERAL RULES OF APPELLATE PROCEDURE.

FEDERAL RULES OF EVIDENCE SERVICE: REPORTS DECISIONS FROM ALL LEVELS OF THE FEDERAL SYSTEM INTERPRETING THE FEDERAL RULES OF EVIDENCE.

FEDERAL RULES OF EVIDENCE NEWS

FEDERAL PROCEDURE RULES SERVICE

FEDERAL TRIAL HANDBOOK, 2D

FORM DRAFTING CHECKLISTS: AM JUR PRACTICE GUIDE

GOVERNMENT CONTRACTS: PROCEDURES AND FORMS

HOW TO GO DIRECTLY INTO YOUR OWN COMPUTERIZED SOLO PRACTICE WITHOUT MISSING A MEAL (OR A BYTE)

JONES ON EVIDENCE, CIVIL AND CRIMINAL, 7TH

LITIGATION CHECKLISTS: AM JUR PRACTICE GUIDE

MEDICAL LIBRARY, LAWYERS EDITION

MEDICAL MALPRACTICE—ALR CASES AND ANNOTATIONS

MODERN APPELLATE PRACTICE: FEDERAL AND STATE CIVIL APPEALS

MODERN CONSTITUTIONAL LAW

NEGOTIATION AND SETTLEMENT

PATTERN DEPOSITION CHECKLISTS, 2D

QUALITY OF LIFE DAMAGES: CRITICAL ISSUES AND PROOFS

SHEPARD'S CITATIONS FOR ALR

SUCCESSFUL TECHNIQUES FOR CIVIL TRIALS, 2D

STORIES ET CETERA—A COUNTRY LAWYER LOOKS AT LIFE AND THE LAW

SUMMARY OF AMERICAN LAW

THE TRIAL LAWYER'S BOOK: PREPARING AND WINNING CASES

TRIAL PRACTICE CHECKLISTS

2000 CLASSIC LEGAL QUOTATIONS

WILLISTON ON CONTRACTS, 3D AND 4TH

FEDERAL RULES OF EVIDENCE DIGEST: ORGANIZES HEADNOTES FOR THE DECISIONS REPORTED IN FEDERAL RULES OF EVIDENCE SERVICE ACCORDING TO THE NUMBERING SYSTEM OF THE FEDERAL RULES OF EVIDENCE.

ADMINISTRATIVE LAW: PRACTICE AND PROCEDURE

AGE DISCRIMINATION: CRITICAL ISSUES AND PROOFS

ALR CRITICAL ISSUES: DRUNK DRIVING PROSECUTIONS

ALR CRITICAL ISSUES: FREEDOM OF INFORMATION ACTS

ALR CRITICAL ISSUES: TRADEMARKS

ALR CRITICAL ISSUES: WRONGFUL DEATH

AMERICANS WITH DISABILITIES: PRACTICE AND COMPLIANCE MANUAL

ATTORNEYS' FEES

BALLENTINE'S LAW DICTIONARY

CONSTITUTIONAL LAW DESKBOOK

CONSUMER AND BORROWER PROTECTION: AM JUR PRACTICE GUIDE

CONSUMER CREDIT: ALR ANNOTATIONS

DAMAGES: ALR ANNOTATIONS

EMPLOYEE DISMISSAL: CRITICAL ISSUES AND PROOFS

ENVIRONMENTAL LAW: ALR ANNOTATIONS

EXPERT WITNESS CHECKLISTS

EXPERT WITNESSES IN CIVIL TRIALS

FORFEITURES: ALR ANNOTATIONS

FEDERAL LOCAL COURT RULES

FEDERAL LOCAL COURT FORMS

FEDERAL CRIMINAL LAW AND PROCEDURE: ALR ANNOTATIONS

FEDERAL EVIDENCE

FEDERAL LITIGATION DESK SET: FORMS AND ANALYSIS

PREFACE

This text is written primarily for the legal studies student. However, it may be used successfully in any undergraduate criminal procedure class.

The fields of criminal law and procedure are dynamic. Recent years have seen significant movements and changes in these areas. State legislatures have acted quickly and with considerable consistency in regard to such things as victims' rights, stalking, and hate crimes. Courts continue to adapt the law to meet these and other new challenges.

In the past ten years, the Supreme Court has revisited issues, and in some instances revisited them again. *Blockburger* was the law, then it was not, and then it was again. Victim impact evidence was a part of sentencing in many states until the Court invalidated its use in *Booth v. Maryland* in 1987. Then, only four years later, in *Payne v. Tennessee,* the Court reopened the door to victim impact evidence. Several other decisions of the Court likewise represent either a retreat or a divergence from prior jurisprudence.

Until recently, litigants looked almost exclusively to federal law for protection of individual rights. We are witnessing, however, a small revolution, or a rebirth, in state constitutional law. This book includes a discussion of the importance of state constitutionalism in the preservation of individual rights.

In Chapter 1 the student is exposed to basic structural information. Federalism, separation of powers, and a special examination of the judicial branch are included. This chapter also briefly introduces the student to criminal law and procedure, including such topics as sources of criminal law and the power of government to control behavior.

Chapter 2 introduces the parties to a case, including the prosecutor, defense attorney, legal assistants, police officers, judges, and victims. The role each plays, as well as ethical constraints, is discussed. The victims' rights movement is included in this overview, which closes with a brief look at the liability and immunity of judges, police officers, and prosecutors.

Chapters 3 and 4 examine the history and impact of both federal and state constitutions on criminal procedure, particularly in regard to the establishment and expansion of individual rights and liberties. Following chapters discuss searches and seizures; arrest; interrogations, confessions, and surveillance; and identification of suspects and defendants. Chapter 5, covering search and seizure, includes a comprehensive examination of automobile searches and stops. The use of profiles to stop persons and vehicles is also considered and the new "plain feel" exception to the warrant requirement is examined. Chapter 6 includes a discussion of the Fourth Amendment rights of prisoners.

Chapters 9 through 12 cover the pretrial process, trial, sentencing, and appeal. Thorough discussion of forms of punishment appears in Chapter 12, including distinctions among various forms of sentencing and incarceration, boot camps, and corporal and capital punishments. The material on restitution, fines, and forfeitures examines Eighth Amendment and due process developments, as well as the use of victim impact statements.

Several "sidebars" detail the actual effect of the exclusionary rule on the criminal justice system, statistics on use of the death penalty, and data on felony case disposition in the United States, among other things. Throughout the book, important legal terms are highlighted in boldfaced type, and a running glossary drawn from *Ballentine's Legal Dictionary and Thesaurus* (Delmar/LCP, 1994) aids students in comprehension. (Terms marked with a dagger are more subject-specific definitions supplied by the author.)

One complaint I have heard (and had) about other texts designed for legal studies students is the absence of cases. Cases serve several important functions. First, they expose students to case analyses. Second, cases increase reader interest in the material because they involve real people and genuine conflicts; most students are intrigued by this fact. Third, cases reinforce the legal principles discussed in the text. Therefore, many case excerpts have been provided. (Cases have been heavily edited, and citations omitted, for improved utility and comprehensibility.) I considered many factors when determining which cases would be included, such as how engrossing the facts were, the age of the case, readability, understandability, and clarity. In short, I selected the most recent, pedagogically valuable cases I could find. Should an instructor wish to omit some or all of the cases from the student readings, this may be done without loss of material, as the text stands alone. The cases simply illustrate the subject matter discussed.

Each chapter ends with two question sections: "Review Questions" and "Review Problems." Generally, the questions sections require students to define terms or explain basic concepts covered in the chapter. The problems sections require more of the student; that is, the student must apply facts to a legal problem.

An Instructor's Manual with a Testbank is available to assist the instructor in preparing for course lecture and discussion. Objective style test questions are provided for each chapter.

I hope that everyone who uses this text, whether student or educator, finds it useful, current, and thought-provoking.

Daniel E. Hall

TABLE OF CASES

F

G

H

I

J

K

L

M

N

O

CHAPTER 1

INTRODUCTION TO CRIMINAL PROCEDURE

CHAPTER OUTLINE

The judicial system is the most expensive machine ever invented for finding out what happened and what to do about it.

Irving R. Kaufman, Judge
United States Court of Appeals
Second Circuit

§ 1.1 Criminal Procedure Defined

Criminal procedure is a field of law that defines the methods used to bring alleged criminal wrongdoers to justice. This is different from *criminal law,* which defines acts and omissions that are criminal and what defenses may be asserted to accusations of criminality. Criminal procedure puts substantive criminal law into action. For reasons you will learn in this text, much contemporary criminal procedure is defined by constitutional law. The United States Constitution establishes a floor—a safety net—of procedures that must be followed by the states and federal government alike. Thus, federal constitutional law receives significant treatment in this text.

That said, do not forget that each state has a constitution that plays a role in criminal procedure. Similarly, common law, statutory law, and court rules are also important.

Each state and the federal government has its own procedural rules. In some instances, the variation is significant. For the purpose of this text, most references are to federal procedure. Many federal procedural rules can be found in the United States Code. A good number of procedures are judicially created (and approved by Congress) and are found in the Federal Rules of Criminal Procedure (Fed. R. Crim. P.). Finally, the constitutions of the national government and the states play a major part in defining the procedures of criminal adjudications.

What follows is a discussion of the constitutional aspects of criminal procedure; the process, from investigation to appeal; searches and seizures; arrests; confessions and admissions; and the right to counsel.

§ 1.2 A Common-Law, Adversarial, and Accusatorial System

The colonists brought with them the common law of England. Today, all states, except Louisiana, which is of the civil law family, are common-law.

> The common law, as it exists in this country, is of English origin. Founded on ancient local rules and customs and in feudal times, it began to evolve in the King's courts and was eventually molded into the viable principles through which it continues to operate. The common law migrated to this continent with the first English colonists, who claimed the system as their birthright; it continued in full force in the 13 original colonies until the American Revolution, at which time it was adopted by each of the states as well as the national government of the new nation.[1]

But what exactly is this common law? Simply stated, the common law is judge-made law. It is law that has been developed by the hands of the judges of both England and the United States. To comprehend how common law developed, you must understand the concepts of precedence and **stare decisis**. When a court renders a legal decision, that decision becomes binding on that court itself and its inferior courts, whenever the same issue arises again in the future. The decision of the court is known as a **precedent**. The principle that inferior courts will comply with that decision when the issue is raised in the future is known as "stare decisis et non quieta movera" (a Latin phrase meaning "stand by precedents and do not disturb settled points"). The Supreme Court of Indiana expressed its view of stare decisis:

> Under the doctrine of stare decisis, this Court adheres to a principle of law which has been firmly established. Important policy considerations militate in favor of continuity and predictability in the law.

TERMS

stare decisis [Latin for] "standing by the decision." Stare decisis is the doctrine that judicial decisions stand as precedents for cases arising in the future. It is a fundamental policy of our law that, except in unusual circumstances, a court's determination on a point of law will be followed by courts of the same or lower rank in later cases presenting the same legal issue, even though different parties are involved and many years have elapsed.

precedent Prior decisions of the same court, or a higher court, which a judge must follow in deciding a subsequent case presenting similar facts and the same legal problem, even though different parties are involved and many years have elapsed.

> Therefore, we are reluctant to disturb long-standing precedent which involves salient issues. Precedent operates as a maxim for judicial restraint to prevent the unjustified reversal to a series of decisions merely because the composition of the court has changed.[2]

During the feudal years in England, there were few formal criminal laws. Rather, local customs and practices developed into rules that governed the behavior of people. The concepts of fairness, justice, and equity were the guiding principles behind these rules. Eventually the courts began to recognize these rules. With that recognition came judicial decisions enforcing them. As precedent, each of those decisions began to establish a body of law, both civil and criminal in nature. The whole of those decisions is known as the common law.

> The common law, as frequently defined, includes those principles, usages, and rules of action applicable to the government and security of persons and property which do not rest for their authority upon any express or positive statute or other written declaration, but upon statements of principles found in the decisions of courts. The common law is inseparably identified with the decisions of the courts and can be determined only from such decisions in former cases bearing upon the subject under inquiry. As distinguished from statutory or written law, it embraces the great body of unwritten law founded upon general custom, usage, or common consent, and based upon natural justice or reason. It may otherwise be defined as custom long acquiesced in or sanctioned by immemorial usage and judicial decision ... .
>
> In a broader sense the common law is the system of rules and declarations of principles from which our judicial ideas and legal definitions are derived, and which are continually expanding. It is not a codification of exact or inflexible rules for human conduct, for the redress of injuries, or for protection against wrongs, but is rather the embodiment of broad and comprehensive unwritten principles, inspired by natural reason and an innate sense of justice, and adopted by common consent for the regulation and government of the affairs of men.[3]

As stated, the common law is fluid and dynamic, changing to meet societal values and expectations. As one court put it, "The common law of the land is based upon human experience in the unceasing effort of an enlightened people to ascertain what is right and just between men."[4]

What happened historically is that courts defined crimes, as there was usually no legislative enactment determining what acts should be criminal. As time passed, established "common-law crimes" developed. First the courts determined what acts should be criminal, and then the specifics of each crime developed; that is, what exactly had to be proved to establish guilt, what defenses were available, and what punishment was appropriate for conviction. Although there is great similarity between the common laws of the many jurisdictions, differences exist because judicial decisions of one state are not binding precedents on other states and because customs and practices vary among communities. However, a court may look outside its own jurisdiction for opinions to guide it in its decision making if no court in its jurisdiction has addressed the issue under consideration. Each state, as a separate and sovereign entity, has the power to decide whether to adopt the common law, in whole or in part, or to reject it.

Initially, the thirteen original states all adopted the common law. Most did so through their state constitutions. Today, only Louisiana has not adopted the common law in some form. However, for reasons you will learn later, approximately half of the states no longer recognize common-law crimes.[5] Even in those states, though, the civil common law and portions of the criminal common law (i.e., defenses to criminal charges) continue in force. Most states have expressly adopted the common law either by statute or constitutional authority. Many states adopted only parts of the common law.

Generally, there is no federal common law; rather, federal courts, in civil cases, apply the common law of the states in which they sit. For example, a United States district court in New Jersey will apply New Jersey common law. Even though this may appear strange to you, it is common practice for federal courts to apply state law. Further discussion of this topic is beyond the scope of this text.

Finally, be aware that common law has been modified and even abolished in some jurisdictions. The modifications to, and nullifications of, common law have come about in many different manners. In some instances, courts have decided that the common law must be changed to meet contemporary conditions. In extreme situations, parts of the common law have been totally abolished. Because legislatures are charged with the duty of making the laws, they have the final word, unless there is a state constitutional provision stating otherwise, on the status of the common law. Some legislatures have expressly given their judiciaries the authority to modify the common law, often with limitations. State legislatures are free to modify, partially abolish, or wholly abolish the common law as long as their own state constitution or the United States Constitution is not violated by so doing. The common law normally is inferior to legislation. This means that if a legislature acts in an area previously dealt with by common law, the new statute controls, absent a statement by the legislature to the contrary. For example, assume that under common law adultery was a crime in State Y. The legislature of State Y can change this by simply enacting a statute that provides that adultery is not criminal. The legislature may also amend the common law by continuing to recognize common-law adultery, but change the penalty for violation. If a state constitution, statute, or judicial decision has not abrogated the common law, presume that it continues in effect.

In addition to being common-law in nature, the legal system is **adversarial.** Adversarial adjudications resemble sporting events. There are two opposing parties and a neutral umpire. In criminal adjudications, these roles are played by the defendant, prosecutor, and judge. The judge in criminal adjudications is a passive participant, usually becoming involved only as needed by the parties or as required by law. Of course, the approach of judges varies and some are more proactive than others. A pure adversarial system is not employed in the United States and judges are expected to supervise the proceedings to assure fairness. The adversary system is built upon the foundation theory that the truth is more likely to be discovered when there are two competing parties, each conducting its own investigation, asserting differing theories of law, and presenting its own case to the court. From this adversarial stance, it is expected that all theories and facts will be discovered and developed.

Also, the role of the judge as impartial, neutral, and detached is believed to increase the fairness of the proceedings, unlike in an inquisitorial system, where the judges sometimes develop an opinion or theory and then work toward proving that theory to be true. In the adversarial system, the parties are largely responsible for development of the case, that is, discovery of the evidence and, accordingly, the issues of law as well.

The adversarial system has its critics. Opponents contend that the truth is not found because the system encourages the opposing parties to present a distorted, misleading, and sometimes untruthful account of the facts. The factfinder, who is not part of the investigative process, is often left to choose between polarized versions of the same event. The adversarial system is also challenged as being unfair because it rests upon the theory that there will be two equally competent competing parties. However, because of differences in the ability of counsel and the respective powers of the parties, this premise is questionable.

In addition to being adversarial, the criminal justice system is **accusatorial**. This means that the government, as the accuser, bears the burden of proving a defendant's guilt. If the government fails in its burden, then a defendant is entitled to a directed verdict or a judgment of acquittal. The accusatorial nature of the system extends beyond placing

TERMS

adversary (adversarial) system The system of justice in the United States. Under the adversary system, the court hears the evidence presented by adverse parties and decides the case.

accusatory (accusatorial) system The system of criminal justice in the United States. Under the accusatory system, the government must formally accuse a person of having committed a crime and must prove the accusation.

the burden of proof on the government at trial. The entire process is designed to minimize the risk of convicting an innocent person. The belief that it is better to free several guilty persons than to convict one innocent person is a major theme of the criminal justice system. Accordingly, the system is designed so that the accused enjoys several advantages, the most critical being the presumption of innocence, the freedom from self-incrimination, the right to a jury trial, and the right to counsel.

The fact that a defendant enjoys a few advantages does not mean that the defendant has the advantage on the whole. The government, whether state or federal, can commit substantial resources to a prosecution.

§ 1.3 The Due Process Model

Criminal justice systems are commonly characterized as adhering to either a *crime control model* or a *due process model*. The repression, detection, and efficient prosecution of crime is central to the crime control model. Failure to detect and successfully prosecute criminals is perceived as a failure of government. This failure leads to a loss of individual liberties because citizens live in constant fear of, and are actually subject to, criminal conduct. A secondary consequence is a loss of confidence in government by the public, thereby further hindering its ability to detect and prevent crime. Prosecution in such systems tends to be bureaucratic, that is, a form of "assembly-line" justice. Some civil law and socialist law nations employ the crime control model.

The due process model focuses on the integrity of individual rights, not the rights of the community to be free from crime. Because of the importance afforded individual rights, legal guilt is at issue, as opposed to factual guilt in the crime control model. *Factual guilt* refers to whether a defendant has in fact committed a crime. *Legal guilt* is concerned not only with factual guilt, but also with whether the defendant's rights have been observed and respected by the government in the processes of investigation and prosecution. It is possible, under the due process model, for there to be sufficient evidence to prove a defendant factually guilty, but because of a civil rights violation the defendant must be declared legally not guilty. The due process model has little tolerance for conviction of the innocent; the crime control model equally abhors crimes going unsolved and offenders unpunished. The investigation and adjudication of defendants is less efficient and more costly under the due process model than under the crime control model.

This is a simplification of the two models.[6] No system falls squarely into one of the two models, although most systems can generally be characterized as adhering to the principles of one more than the other. The United States follows the due process model. Individual rights and fair procedures are the hallmark of the U.S. system of criminal justice. All individuals are innocent until proven guilty. The process itself presumes innocence, and deprivations of liberties are sharply limited and regulated before guilt is found.

Also, as the severity of the government's intrusions or deprivations increases, so must the evidence of guilt. For example, less evidence is required to establish probable cause to support a search of an automobile than to bind a defendant over to trial. This is because binding a defendant over to trial entails greater losses of liberty (possible pretrial detention and the cost and humiliation of being publicly tried) than does the search. You will learn many procedures that support the conclusion that the United States adheres to the due process model. Attempt to identify these characteristics as you read the following chapters. Chapters 2 through 12 examine the basic procedures and constitutional aspects of bringing criminals to justice. First, however, you must become familiar with the legal and criminal justice systems and with the participants in these processes.

SIDEBAR

How to Brief a Case

Decisions of courts are often written and are called *judicial opinions* or cases. These cases are published in law reporters so that they may be used as precedent. Many cases appear in this text for your education. Your instructor may also require that you read other cases, often from your jurisdiction. The cases included in this book have been edited, citations have been omitted, and legal issues not relevant to the subject discussed have been excised.

Most judicial opinions are written using a similar format. First, the name of the case appears with the name of the court, the cite (location where the case has been published), and the year. When the body of the case begins, the name of the judge, or judges, responsible for writing the opinion appears directly before the first paragraph. The opinion contains an introduction to the case, which normally gives you the procedural history of the case. This is followed by a summary of the facts that led to the dispute, the court's analysis of the law that applies to the case, and the court's conclusions and orders, if any.

Most opinions used in this text are from appellate courts, where many judges sit at one time. After the case is over, the judges vote on an outcome. The majority vote wins, and the opinion of the majority is written by one of those judges. If other judges in the majority wish to add to the majority opinion, they may write what is known as a *concurring opinion.* Concurring opinions appear after majority opinions in the law reporters. When a judge who was not in the majority feels strongly about his or her position, he or she may file a dissenting opinion, which appears after the concurring opinions, if any. Only the majority opinion is law, although concurring and dissenting opinions are often informative.

During your legal education, you may be instructed to "brief" a case. Even if your instructor does not require you to brief cases, you may want to, as many students understand a case better after they have completed a brief. Here are suggestions for reading and understanding cases.

1. Read the case. On your first reading, do not take notes; simply attempt to get a feel for the case. Then read the case again and use the following suggested method of briefing.
2. State the *relevant* facts. Often cases read like little stories. You need to weed out the facts that have no bearing on the subject you are studying.
3. Identify the issues. *Issues* are the legal questions discussed by the court.
4. State the applicable rules, standards, or other law.
5. Summarize the court's decision and analysis. Why and how did the court reach its conclusion? Note whether the court affirmed, reversed, or remanded the case.

§ 1.4 The United States Legal and Criminal Justice Systems

Federalism

Before one can undertake learning criminal law or criminal procedure, a basic understanding of the legal system of the United States is necessary. This can be a complex task, as criminal law and procedure are significantly influenced by federal and state constitutional law, the common law, and statutory law at both the federal and state levels. It will be easier to understand how these areas of law affect criminal law if we first explore the basic structure of American government.

The United States is divided into two sovereign forms of government—the government of the United States and the governments of the many states. This division of power is commonly known as **federalism**. It is also common to refer to this division as a vertical division of power, because the national government rests above the state governments in hierarchy. The framers of the Constitution of the United States established these two levels of government in an attempt to prevent the centralization of power, that is, too much power being vested in one group. The belief that "absolute power corrupts absolutely" was the catalyst for this division of governmental power.

TERMS

federalism The system by which the states of the United States relate to each other and to the federal government.

SIDEBAR

At trial, a *sidebar* is a meeting between the judge and the attorneys, at the judge's bench, outside the hearing of the jury. Sidebars are used to discuss issues that the jury is not permitted to hear. In this text, sidebars will appear periodically. These features contain information relevant to the subject being studied.

In theory, the national government, commonly referred to as the *federal government,* and the state governments each possess authority over citizens, as well as over particular policy areas, free from interference by the other government (dual sovereignty).

Determining what powers belong to the national government, as opposed to the states, is not always an easy task. The framers of the Constitution intended to establish a limited national government. That is, most of governmental powers were to reside in the states, with the national government being limited to the powers expressly delegated to it in the federal Constitution. This principle is found in the Tenth Amendment, which reads, "The powers not delegated to the United States by the Constitution, nor prohibited to it by the States, are reserved to the States respectively, or the people."

What powers are delegated to the United States by the Constitution? There are several, including, but not limited to the power:

1. To coin money, punish counterfeiters, and fix standards of weights and measures.
2. To establish a post office and post roads.
3. To promote the arts.
4. To punish piracy and other crimes on the high seas.
5. To declare war and raise armies.
6. To conduct diplomacy and foreign affairs.
7. To regulate interstate and foreign commerce.
8. To make laws necessary and proper for carrying into execution other powers expressly granted in the Constitution.

The last two of these powers—the regulation of interstate commerce and the making of all necessary and proper laws—have proven to be significant sources of federal power. Also important is the "supremacy clause" of Article VI, which provides that

> This Constitution, and the Laws of the United States which shall be made in Pursuance thereof; and all Treaties made, or which shall be made, under the Authority of the United States, shall be the supreme Law of the Land; and the Judges in every State shall be bound thereby, any Thing in the Constitution or Laws of any State to the Contrary notwithstanding.

Simply stated, the supremacy clause declares national law, if valid, to be a higher form of law than state law. Of course, if the national government attempts to regulate an area belonging to the states, its law is invalid and the state law is controlling. But if the national government possesses **jurisdiction** and a state enacts a conflicting law, the state law is invalid. This is not a common issue in criminal law, because state and federal laws rarely conflict; rather, they are more likely to be parallel or complementary. In such cases, a state and federal government have **concurrent jurisdiction** (see Figure 1-1).

Keep in mind that the United States Constitution is the highest form of law in the land. It is the national constitution that establishes the structure of our government. You will learn later the various duties of the judicial branch of government. One duty is the interpretation (determining what written law means) of statutes and constitutions. The highest court in the United States is the United States Supreme Court; as such, that Court is the final word on what powers are exclusively federal or state, or concurrently held. However, once the Supreme Court decides that an issue is exclusively under the control of state governments, then each state has the final word on that issue.

During the past 200 years, the Supreme Court has differed in its approach to federalism. Two general approaches can be identified, though. *Dual federalism* refers to an approach under which the states and federal government are viewed as coequals. Under this approach, the Tenth Amendment is interpreted broadly and the commerce clause and the necessary and proper clause are read narrowly. The Tenth Amendment is interpreted as an independent source of state powers, staking out policy areas within which the national government cannot encroach.

Another theory, *cooperative federalism,* asserts that the national government is supreme. Under this approach, the commerce and necessary and proper clauses are construed broadly. The Tenth Amendment becomes a truism, that is, it reserves to the states only those powers the national government does not possess.

TERMS

jurisdiction A term used in several senses: 1. In a general sense, the right of a court to adjudicate lawsuits of a certain kind. 2. In a specific sense, the right of a court to determine a particular case; in other words, the power of the court over the subject matter of, or the property involved in, the case at bar. 3. In a geographical sense, the power of a court to hear cases only within a specific territorial area.

concurrent jurisdiction Two or more courts having the power to adjudicate the same class of cases or the same matter.

STATE JURISDICTION	CONCURRENT JURISDICTION	NATIONAL JURISDICTION
1. States may regulate for the health, safety, and morals of their citizens	1. Those acts that fall into both federal and state jurisdiction	1. Crimes that are interstate in character
2. Those acts that involve a state government, its officials and property		2. Crimes involving the government of the United States, including its officials and property
Example: murder; rape; theft; driving under the influence of a drug; gambling	*Example:* bank robbery of a federally insured institution	*Example:* murder of a federal official or murder on federal land; transportation of illegal items; interstate flight of a felon

FIGURE 1-1 Federal and State Criminal Jurisdiction

Another characteristic of cooperative federalism is increased interaction between the states and federal government (and local forms of government) in an effort to effectively regulate and administer laws and programs. This aspect of cooperative federalism is a product of the political branches, the executive and legislative. The increased cooperation between state and federal law enforcement agencies to fight the war against drugs during the 1980s and early 1990s is a good example of cooperative federalism.

The Court has vacillated between the two approaches, and the current approach is cooperative federalism. This is not to say that the states are powerless. In fact, one policy area over which the states have maintained considerable control is criminal law. More than 90 percent of all crimes fall within the jurisdiction of the states, not the federal government. However, the sphere of federal government power in criminal law is increasing. This is because more acts are taken in, or are committed using an item that has traveled in, interstate commerce. Acts that have traditionally been state-law crimes may today be federal crimes as well, if there is an interstate component to the act. For example, carjacking, which is the state crime of robbery, if committed with a gun that has travelled in interstate commerce, is also a federal crime.

For a long period of time, it appeared that federal criminal jurisdiction was unlimited. Through the affectation and cumulative effects doctrine, the Supreme Court permitted federal jurisdiction to extend beyond acts directly affecting interstate commerce when considered in aggregate. For example, the Court upheld the federal government's authority to prosecute a farmer for raising wheat in excess of a legal quota because the cumulative effect of all farmers engaging in similar conduct would affect interstate commerce. There was no question in the case that this farmer's individual harvest would have no effect on interstate commerce.[7]

In fact, no federal criminal statute was invalidated by the Supreme Court as exceeding federal jurisdiction from the late 1940s until 1995. *Lopez* was the first case since the 1940s in which a statute was invalidated as extending federal power under the commerce clause too far. It teaches that there must be a genuine connection between commerce and a regulation before Congress may act. The Court's decision was limited to finding that possessing a gun near a school is simply not a commercial activity. Therefore, Congress has no authority to regulate it. Remember, this decision does not forbid the states from creating gun-free school zones. States have the authority to enact such laws under their general police powers. The *Lopez* Court identified when Congress may exercise jurisdiction under the commerce clause:

1. The channels of interstate commerce are affected
2. The instrumentalities of interstate commerce, or persons or things in interstate commerce, are affected, even though the threat may come only from intrastate activities
3. Those activities having a substantial relation to interstate commerce —that is, activities that substantially affect interstate commerce— are affected.

Lopez was concerned with the third category and the Court made it clear that the activity in question could not be regulated unless it *substantially* affected interstate commerce. The cumulative effect an intrastate activity has on interstate activity can continue to be the basis of federal power.

Congressional power under the commerce clause is broad. As the nation and world grow closer together, more activities will be subject to federal regulation. *Lopez* teaches, however, that a true nexus between commerce and a regulated activity must exist. If an activity is not commercial and is entirely intrastate in character, its regulation belongs entirely to the state. The impact of *Lopez* on federal jurisdiction remains

UNITED STATES v. LOPEZ
____ U.S. ____ (1995)

Chief Justice Rehnquist delivered the opinion of the Court.

In the Gun-Free School Zone Act of 1990, Congress made it a federal offense "for any individual knowingly to possess a firearm at [a] place that the individual knows, or has reasonable cause to believe, is a school zone. ... The Act neither regulates a commercial activity nor contains a requirement that the possession be connected in any way to interstate commerce. We hold that the Act exceeds the authority of Congress "[t]o regulate Commerce ... among the several states ... ." U.S. Const., Art. I, 8, cl. 3.

On March 10, 1992, respondent, who was than a 12th-grade student, arrived at Edison High School in San Antonio, Texas, carrying a concealed .38 caliber handgun and live bullets. Acting upon an anonymous tip, school authorities confronted respondent, who admitted that he was carrying the weapon. He was arrested and charged under Texas law with firearm possession on school premises. ... The next day, the state charges were dismissed after federal agents charged respondent by complaint with violating the Gun-Free School Zone Act of 1990. ... [The defendant was indicted and moved to dismiss the indictment on the ground that the statute was beyond congressional powers. The district court denied the motion and the appellate court reversed the trial court conviction.]

We start with first principles. The Constitution creates a Federal Government of enumerated powers. ... As James Madison wrote, "[t]he powers delegated by the proposed Constitution to the federal government are few and defined. Those which are to remain in the State governments are numerous and indefinite." *The Federalist* No. 45 ... . This constitutionally mandated division of authority "was adopted by the Framers to ensure protection of our fundamental liberties." ... [The Court then summarized the history of its commerce clause decisions].

Consistent with this structure, we have identified three broad categories of activity that Congress may regulate under its commerce power. ... First, Congress may regulate the use of the channels of interstate commerce. ... Second, Congress is empowered to regulate and protect the instrumentalities of interstate commerce, or persons or things in interstate commerce, even though the threat may come only from intrastate activities. ... Finally, commerce authority includes the power to regulate those activities having a substantial relation to interstate commerce, ... i.e, those activities that substantially affect interstate commerce. ...

Within the final category, admittedly, our case law has not been clear whether an activity must "affect" or "substantially affect" interstate commerce in order to be within Congress' power to regulate it under the Commerce Clause. ... We conclude, consistent with the great weight of our case law, that the proper test requires an analysis of whether the regulated activity "substantially affects" interstate commerce.

We now turn to consider the power of Congress, in the light of this framework, to enact [the Gun-Free School Zone Law]. The first two categories of authority may be quickly disposed of: [the statute] is not a regulation of the use of the channels of interstate commerce, nor is it an attempt to prohibit the interstate transportation of [a] commodity through the channels of commerce; nor can [the statute] be justified as a regulation by which Congress has sought to protect an instrumentality of interstate commerce or a thing in interstate commerce. Thus, if [the statute] is to be sustained, it must be under the third category as a regulation of an activity that substantially affects interstate commerce.

First, we have upheld a wide variety of congressional Acts regulating intrastate economic activity where we have concluded that the activity substantially affected interstate commerce. Examples include the regulations of intrastate coal mining ... intrastate extortionate credit transactions ... restaurants utilizing substantial interstate supplies ... and production and consumption of home-grown wheat. These examples are by not means exhaustive, but the pattern is clear. Where economic activity substantially affects interstate commerce, legislation regulating that activity will be sustained.

Even *Wickard,* which is perhaps the most far reaching example of Commerce Clause authority over intrastate activity, involved economic activity in a way that the possession of a gun in a school zone does not. ...

[The Gun-Free School Zone law] is a criminal statute that by its terms has nothing to do with "commerce" or any sort of economic enterprise, however broadly one might define those terms. [The statute] is not an essential part of a larger regulation of economic activity, in which the regulatory scheme could be undercut unless the intrastate activity were regulated. It cannot, therefore, be sustained under our cases upholding regulations of activities that arise out of or are connected with a commercial transaction, which viewed in the aggregate, substantially affects interstate commerce. ...

Second, [the statute] contains no jurisdictional elements which would ensure, through case-by-case inquiry, that the firearm possession in question affects interstate commerce. For example, ... 18 U.S.C. § 1202(a), ... made it a crime for a felon to "receive[e], posses[s], or transpor[t] in commerce or affecting commerce ... any firearm." ... The Court interpreted the possession component of § 1202(a) to require an additional nexus to interstate commerce both because the statute was ambiguous and because "unless Congress conveys its purpose clearly, it will not be deemed to have significantly changed the federal-state balance." ... The [Court in a case arising under § 1202(a)] set aside the conviction because although the Government had demonstrated that [the defendant] had possessed a firearm, it had failed "to show the interpreted the statute to reserve the constitutional question whether Congress could regulate, without more, the "mere possession" of firearms. ... Unlike the statute in [this prior case], [the Gun-Free School Zone statute] has no express jurisdictional element which might limit its reach to a discrete set of firearm possessions that additionally have an explicit connection with or effect on interstate commerce. ...

The Government argues that possession of a firearm in a school zone may result in violent crime and that violent crime can be expected to affect the functioning of the national economy in two ways. First, the costs of violent crime are substantial, and, through the mechanism of insurance, those costs are spread throughout the population. ... Second, violent crime reduces the willingness of individuals to travel to areas within the country that are perceived to be unsafe. ... The Government also argues that the presence of guns in schools poses a substantial threat to the educational process by threatening the learning environment. A handicapped educational process, in turn, will result in a less productive citizenry. That, in turn, would have an adverse effect on the Nation's economic well-being. ...

We pause to consider the implications of the Government's arguments. The Government admits, under its "costs of crime" reasoning, that Congress could regulate not only all violent crime, but all activities that might lead to violent crime, regardless of how tenuously they relate to interstate commerce. ... Similarly, under the Government's "national productivity" reasoning, Congress could regulate any activity that it found was related to the economic productivity of individual citizens: family law ... for example. Under the theories that the Government presents in support of [the statute], it is difficult to perceive any limitation on federal power, even in areas such as criminal law enforcement or education where States historically have been sovereign. Thus, if we were to accept the Government's arguments, we are hard-pressed to posit any activity by an individual that Congress is without power to regulate. ...

For instance, if Congress can, pursuant to its Commerce Clause power, regulate activities that adversely affect the learning environment, then, a fortiori, it also can regulate the educational process directly. Congress could determine that a school's curriculum has a "significant" effect on the extent of classroom learning. As a result,

Congress could mandate a federal curriculum for local elementary and secondary schools because what is taught in local schools has a significant "effect on classroom learning" ... and that, in turn, has a substantial effect on interstate commerce. ...

We do not doubt that Congress has authority under the Commerce Clause to regulate numerous commercial activities that substantially affect interstate commerce and also affect the educational process. That authority, though broad, does not include the authority to regulate each and every aspect of local schools.

Admittedly, a determination whether an intrastate activity is commercial or noncommercial may in some cases result in legal uncertainty. But, so long as Congress' authority is limited to those powers enumerated in the Constitution, and so long as those enumerated powers are interpreted as having judicially enforceable outer limits, congressional legislation under the Commerce Clause will always engender "legal uncertainty." ...

These are not precise formulations, and in the nature of things they cannot be. But we think they point the way to a correct decision of this case. The possession of a gun in a local school zone is in no sense an economic activity that might, through repetition elsewhere, substantially affect any sort of interstate commerce. Respondent was a local student at a local school; there is no indication that he had recently moved in interstate commerce, and there is no requirement that his possession of the firearm have any concrete tie to interstate commerce.

To uphold the Government's contentions here, we would have to pile inference upon inference in a manner that would bid fair to convert congressional authority under the Commerce Clause to a general police power of the sort retained to the States. Admittedly, some of our prior cases have taken long steps down that road, giving great deference to congressional action. ...The broad language in these opinions have suggested the possibility of additional expansion, but we decline here to proceed any further. ...

For the foregoing reasons the judgment of the Court of Appeals is Affirmed.

to be seen. As of the close of 1995, most lower courts that examined existing federal statutes upheld them. For example, the federal carjacking statute, which criminalizes the forcible taking of an automobile that has been transported, shipped, or received in interstate commerce, was upheld[8], as was the drug-free school zone law.[9] The latter was justified on the basis of the substantial connection between drugs and interstate commerce.

Regardless of the expansion of federal jurisdiction, most crimes continue to fall within the exclusive jurisdiction of the states. This is because one of the responsibilities of the states is to regulate for the health and safety of its citizens. This is known as the **police power**.

TERMS

police power 1. The power of government to make and enforce laws and regulations necessary to maintain and enhance the public welfare and to prevent individuals from violating the rights of others. 2. The sovereignty of each of the states of the United States that is not surrendered to the federal government under the Constitution.

Most murders, rapes, and thefts are state-law crimes. A few policy areas belong exclusively to the federal government. Punishing counterfeiters is an example.

Many crimes fall within the jurisdiction of both state and federal governments. In these situations, state and federal authorities share jurisdiction to bring charges against the accused. Drug dealers are subject to federal law if they transport or sell drugs in interstate commerce and are also subject to the laws of the states where the transaction occurred. Robbing a federally insured bank, interstate transportation of a crime victim, and violating a person's civil rights (i.e., police brutality) are other examples. Which government will bring charges in these situations is more a political question than a legal one. It is not a violation of double jeopardy for an individual to be tried and punished by both federal and state governments, even for the same act.

Note that local governments have not been mentioned so far. This is because the Constitution does not recognize the existence of local governments. However, state constitutions and laws establish local forms of government, such as counties, cities, and districts. These local entities are often empowered by state law with limited authority to create criminal law, usually in the form of ordinances.

The result of this division of power is that the states (as well as other jurisdictions, such as the District of Columbia), the federal government, and local governments each have a separate set of criminal laws. For this reason, you must keep in mind that the principles you will learn from this book are general in nature. It would be both impossible and pointless to teach the specific laws of each jurisdiction of the United States.

Separation of Powers

Another division of governmental power is known as **separation of powers**. This is the division of governmental power into three branches, the executive, legislative, and judicial, making a horizontal division of power, just as federalism is the vertical division. (See Figure 1-2.) Each branch is delegated certain functions that the other two may not encroach upon. The executive branch consists of the

TERMS

separation of powers A fundamental principle of the Constitution, which gives exclusive power to the legislative branch to make the law, exclusive power to the executive branch to administer it, and exclusive power to the judicial branch to enforce it. The authors of the Constitution believed that the separation of powers would make abuse of power less likely.

	LEGISLATIVE BRANCH	EXECUTIVE BRANCH	JUDICIAL BRANCH
The Government of the United States (federal government)	United States Congress	President of the United States	Federal Courts
State Governments	State Legislatures	Governors	State Courts

FIGURE 1-2 Division of Governmental Power

president of the United States, the president's staff, and the various administrative agencies that the president oversees. Generally, it is the duty of the executive branch to enforce the laws of the national government. In criminal law, the executive branch investigates alleged violations of the law, gathers the evidence necessary to prove that a violation has occurred, and brings violators before the judicial branch for disposition. The president does this through the various federal law enforcement and administrative agencies.

The legislative branch consists of the United States Congress, which creates the laws of the United States. Congressionally created laws are known as **statutes**. Finally, the judicial branch comprises the various federal courts of the land. That branch is charged with the administration of justice. A more comprehensive discussion of the judicial branch follows later in this chapter.

In a further attempt to diffuse governmental power, the framers designed a system of checks and balances that prevents any one branch from exclusively controlling a function. Several checks can be found in the Constitution.

For example, Congress is responsible for making the law. This function is checked by the president, who may veto legislation. The president is then checked by Congress, which may override a veto with a two-thirds majority. The president is responsible for conducting foreign affairs and making treaties, and is the Commander-in-Chief of the military. Congress, however, must approve treaties and declare war, and it establishes the rules that regulate the military.

Through the power of judicial review, the judiciary may invalidate actions of the president or Congress that violate the Constitution.

TERMS

statute A law enacted by a legislature; an act.

In contrast, the political branches select federal judges through the nomination (president) and confirmation (Senate) process. Unpopular judicial decisions may be changed either by statute, if the issue is one of statutory interpretation, or by constitutional amendment, if the issue is one of constitutional interpretation.

Keep in mind that two levels of government exist, excluding local entities. Even though the United States Constitution does not establish three branches of government for the many states (the United States Constitution only designates the structure of the federal government), all state constitutions are, in varying forms, modeled on the federal constitution. The result is a two-tiered system with each tier split into three parts.

What should be gleaned from this is that the legislatures are responsible for defining what acts are criminal, what process must be used to assure that a wrongdoer answers for an act, and what punishment should be imposed for the act.

It is the duty of the executive branch to enforce and implement the laws created by the legislature, as well as to enforce the orders of courts. For example, if a state legislature prohibits the sale of alcohol on Sundays, it is the duty of the appropriate state law enforcement agencies, such as the police or alcohol, firearm, and tobacco agents, to investigate suspected violations and take whatever lawful action is necessary to bring violators to justice. Law enforcement, in the criminal law context, is accomplished through law enforcement agencies and prosecutorial agencies. At the federal level, there are many law enforcement agencies. The Federal Bureau of Investigation, Drug Enforcement Administration, United States Marshal Service, and Department of the Treasury are only a few. State law enforcement agencies include state departments of investigation, state police departments, and local police departments. These and other enforcement agencies are responsible for investigating criminal conduct and for gathering evidence to prove that a criminal violation has occurred. When the law enforcement agency has completed its investigation, the case is turned over to a prosecutor. The prosecutor is the attorney responsible for representing the people. The prosecutor files the formal criminal charge, or conducts a grand jury, and then sees the prosecution through to fruition. In the federal system, the prosecutor is called a United States Attorney. In the states and localities, prosecutors are known as *district attorneys, county attorneys, state attorneys, city attorneys,* or simply *prosecutors.*

Finally, the judicial branch is charged with the administration of justice. The courts become involved after the executive branch has arrested or accused an individual of a crime. This is explored further in the next section of this chapter. Lawyers, legal assistants, and law enforcement officials are likely to have significant contacts with state and federal courts; therefore, it is important to understand the structure of the court system.

§ 1.5 The United States Judiciary

The Structure of the Court System

Within the federal and state judiciaries, a hierarchy of courts exists. All state court systems, as well as the federal court system, have at least two types of courts, trial courts and appellate courts. However, each state is free to structure its judiciary in any manner; hence, significant variation is found in the different court systems. What follows are general principles that apply to all states and the federal system.

Trial courts are what most people envision when they think of courts. Trial courts are where a case begins, where witnesses are heard and evidence is presented, often to a jury as well as to a judge. In the federal system, trial courts are known as United States District Courts. The United States is divided up into 94 judicial districts, using state boundaries to establish district limits. Each state constitutes at least one district, although larger states are divided into several districts. For example, Kansas has only one district, and the federal trial court located in Kansas is known as the United States District Court for the District of Kansas. California, in contrast, is made up of four districts, the Northern, Eastern, Central, and Southern Districts of California.

State trial courts are known by various names, such as *district, superior, county,* and *circuit courts*. Despite variations in name, these courts are very similar.

The court system is actually many court systems comprised of the federal system and the many state systems. As of 1990, there were 28,658 state court judges in the United States sitting in 15,642 state courts. By 1988, there were 280 bankruptcy judges, 284 magistrates, 575 district judges, 168 circuit judges, and 9 Supreme Court Justices.

Source of state statistics: Judicial Council of California, National Center for State Courts.
Source of federal statistics: R. Katzmann, *Judges and Legislators* 60 (Washington, D.C.: Brookings, 1988)

TERMS

trial court A court that hears and determines a case initially, as opposed to an appellate court; a court of general jurisdiction.

Appellate courts review the decisions and actions of trial courts (or lower appellate courts, as discussed later) for error. These courts do not conduct trials, but review the **record** from the trial court and examine it for mistakes, known as *trial court error.* Usually, appellate courts will hear argument from the attorneys involved in the case under review, but witnesses are not heard nor other evidence submitted. After the appellate court has reviewed the record and examined it for error, it renders an opinion. An appellate court can reverse, affirm, or remand the lower court decision. To *reverse* is to determine that the court below has rendered a wrong decision and to change that decision. When an appellate court affirms a lower court, it is approving the decision made and leaving it unchanged.

In some cases an appellate court will remand the case to the lower court. A *remand* is an order that the case be returned to the lower court and that some action be taken by the judge when the case is returned. Often this involves conducting a new trial. For example, if an appellate court decides that a judge took an action that prevented a criminal defendant from having a fair trial, and the defendant was convicted, an appellate court may reverse the conviction and remand the case to the trial court for a new trial with instructions that the judge not act in a similar manner.

In the federal system and many states, there are two levels of appellate courts, an intermediate and highest level. The intermediate level courts in the federal system are the United States Courts of Appeal.[10] There are eleven judicial circuits in the United States, with one court of appeal in each circuit. Additionally, there is a court of appeal for Washington, D.C., and for the Federal Circuit. Therefore, there are thirteen United States Courts of Appeal in total (see Figure 1-3). Appeals from the district courts are taken to the circuit courts. The highest court in the country is the United States Supreme Court. Appeals from the circuit courts are taken to the Supreme Court. Also, appeals of federal issues from state supreme courts are taken to the United States Supreme Court. Although appeal to a circuit court or a state supreme court is generally a right anyone has, the Supreme Court is not required to hear most appeals, and it does not. In recent years the Supreme Court has denied review of approximately 97 percent of the cases appealed.[11]

TERMS

appellate court A higher court to which an appeal is taken from a lower court.

record 1. A memorial that evidences something written, said, or done. 2. A copy of a document or instrument filed or deposited with a public officer to have it preserved as a public record. 3. An official record.

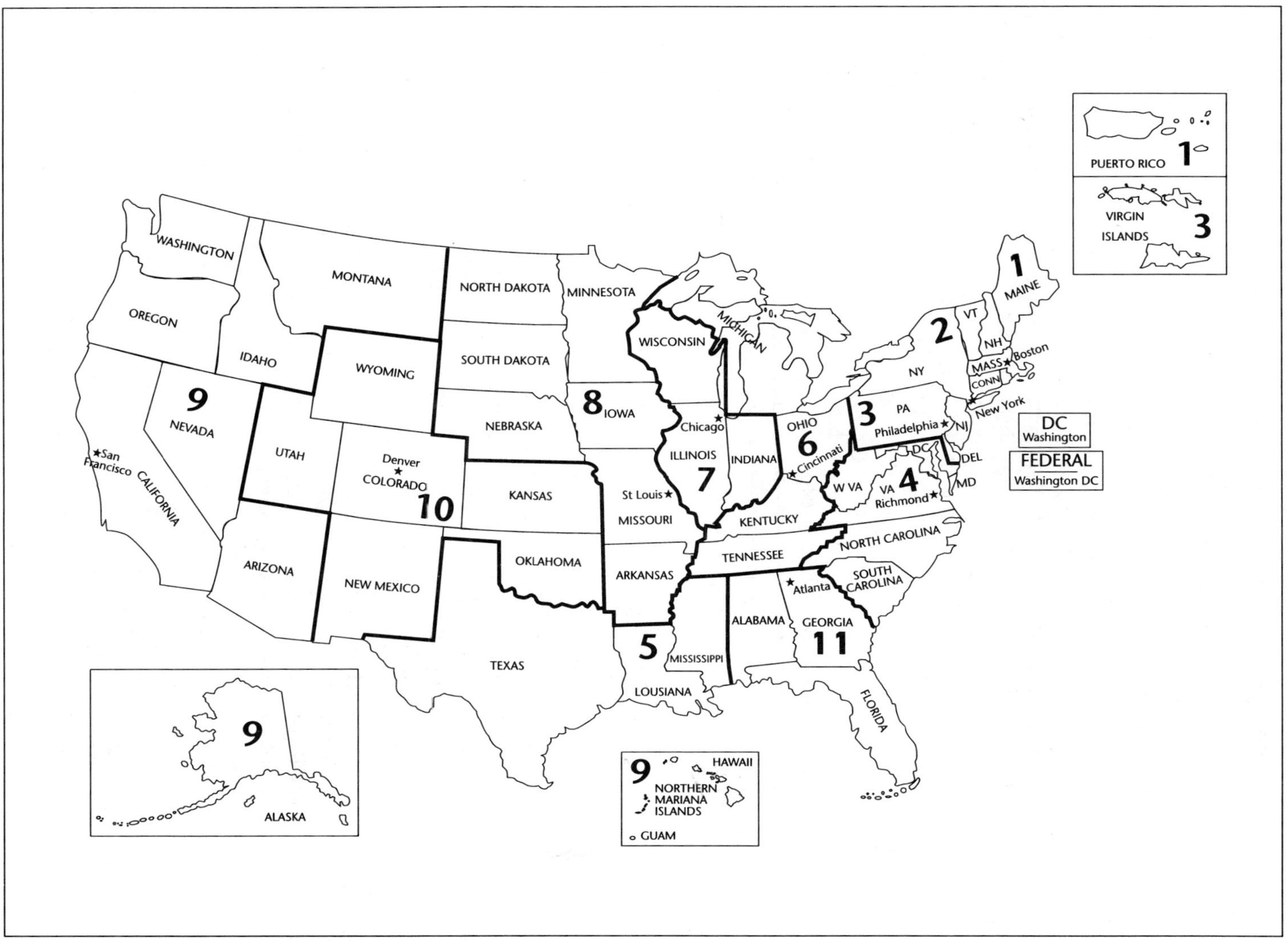

FIGURE 1-3 The Thirteen Federal Judicial Circuits

Therefore, the circuit courts are often a defendant's last chance to have his or her case heard.

Many states also have intermediate-level appellate courts, as well as a high court, although a few states have only one appellate court. Most states call the high court the supreme court of that state and the intermediate level court the court of appeals. An exception is New York, which has named its highest court the Court of Appeals of New York and its lower-level courts supreme courts.

In states that have only one appellate court, appeals are taken directly to that court. New Hampshire is such a state, so appeals from New Hampshire's trial courts are taken directly to the Supreme Court of New Hampshire. Note that in most instances a first appeal is an appeal of right. That means that one has a right to appeal, and the appellate court is required to hear the case. However, second appeals are generally not appeals of right, unless state law has provided otherwise. To have a case heard by the United States Supreme Court and most state supreme courts, the person appealing must seek *certiorari,* an order from an appellate court to the lower court requiring the record to be sent to the higher court for review. When "cert." is granted, the appellate court will hear the appeal, and when certiorari is denied it will not.

Finally, be aware that a number of **inferior courts** exist. These are courts that fall under trial courts in hierarchy. As such, appeals from these courts do not usually go to the intermediate level appellate courts, as described earlier, but to the trial-level court first. Municipal courts, police courts, and justices of the peace are examples of inferior courts. An appeal from one of these courts is initially heard by a state trial-level court before an appeal is taken to a state appellate court. The federal system also has inferior courts. The United States Bankruptcy Courts are inferior courts, as appeals from the decisions of these courts go to the district courts, in most cases, and not to the courts of appeals. Only after the trial court has rendered its decision may an appeal be taken to an appellate court.

Most inferior courts in the state system are not **courts of record**. No tape recording or stenographic recording of the trial or hearing at the inferior court is made. As such, when an appeal is taken to the trial level court, it is normally ***de novo***. This means that the trial-level court conducts a new trial, rather than reviewing a record as most appellate courts do. This is necessary because there is no record to review, because

TERMS

inferior court 1. A court of original jurisdiction, as distinguished from an appellate court; a trial court. 2. A court of limited jurisdiction.

court of record Generally, another term for trial court.

de novo 1. Anew; over again; a second time.

the inferior court is not a court of record. Federal district courts do not conduct new trials, as all federal courts, including bankruptcy courts, are courts of record. State inferior courts have limited jurisdiction; for example, municipal courts usually hear municipal ordinance violations and only minor state law violations. The amount of money that a person may be fined and the amount of time that a defendant may be sentenced to serve in jail are also limited. Generally, no juries are used at the inferior court level.

Figure 1-4 is a basic diagram of the federal and state court systems. The appellate routes are indicated by lines drawn from one court to another.

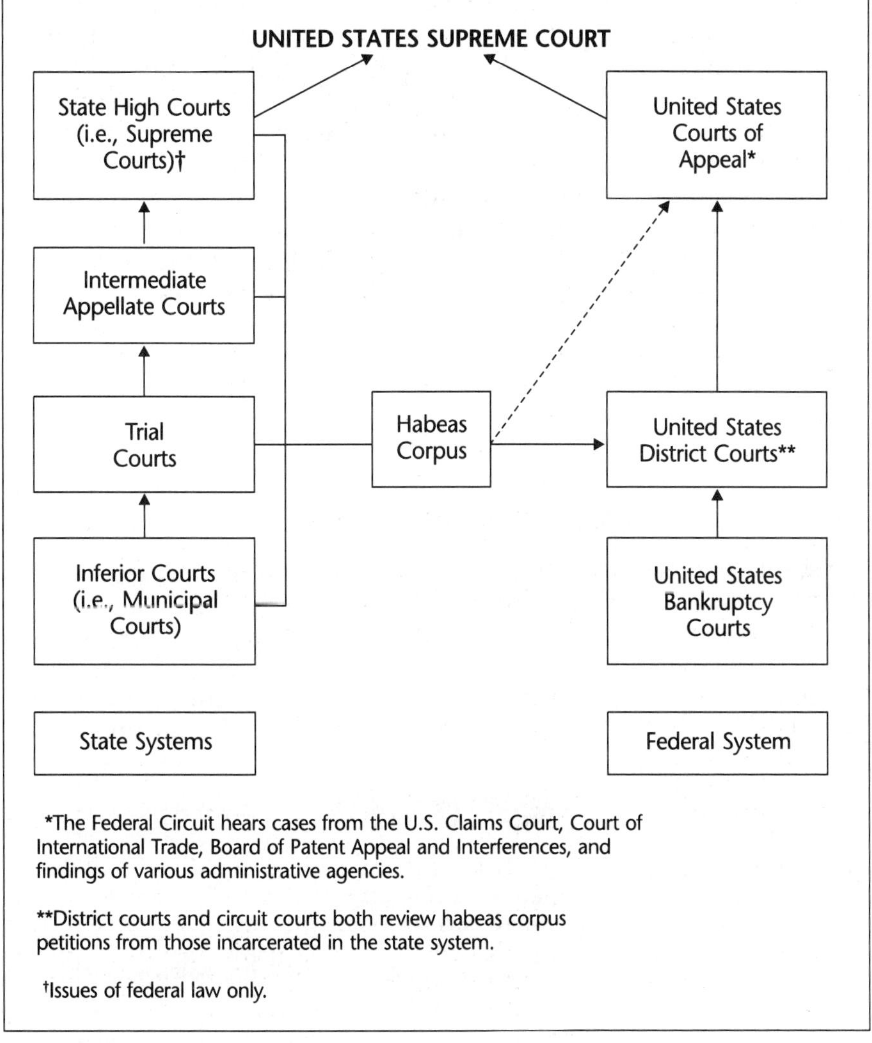

FIGURE 1-4 State and Federal Court Structures

Later in this book you will learn how the appeals process works and how the federal and state systems interact in criminal law. Note where this diagram is located so that you may refer to it later.

Most state trial courts are known as **courts of general jurisdiction.** Courts of general jurisdiction possess the authority to hear a broad range of cases, including civil law as well as criminal. In contrast, **courts of limited jurisdiction** hear only specific types of cases. You have already been introduced to one limited jurisdiction court, municipal courts. Inferior courts, such as municipal courts, are always courts of limited jurisdiction. Some states employ systems that have specialized trial courts to handle domestic, civil, or criminal cases. These may be in the form of a separate court (e.g., Criminal Court of Harp County), or may be a division of a trial court (e.g., Superior Court of Harp County, Criminal Division). Appellate courts may also be limited in jurisdiction to a particular area of law, such as the Oklahoma Court of Criminal Appeals.

The federal government also has special courts. As previously mentioned, a nationwide system of bankruptcy courts is administered by the national government. In addition, the United States Claims Court, Tax Court, and Court of International Trade are part of the federal judiciary, and each has a specific area of law over which it may exercise jurisdiction. Often the cases over which they have jurisdiction are exclusive of district courts. However, the jurisdiction of those courts is outside the scope of this book, as they deal only with civil law. Criminal cases in federal court are heard by district courts, and criminal appeals are heard by the United States Courts of Appeals.

Judicial Review and Other Judicial Functions

Of the three branches of government, attorneys and paralegals have the most interaction with the judicial branch. For that reason, we single out the judicial branch for a more extensive examination of its functions.

First, it must be emphasized that all courts, local, state, and federal, are bound by the United States Constitution. The effect of this is that

TERMS

court of general jurisdiction Generally, another term for trial court; that is, a court having jurisdiction to try all classes of civil and criminal cases except those which can be heard only by a court of limited jurisdiction.

court of limited jurisdiction A court whose jurisdiction is limited to civil cases of a certain type or which involve a limited amount of money, or whose jurisdiction in criminal cases is confined to petty offenses and preliminary hearings. A court of limited jurisdiction is sometimes called a court of special jurisdiction.

all courts have a duty to apply federal constitutional law. This is important in criminal law because it allows defendants to assert their United States constitutional claims and defenses in state court, where most criminal cases are heard. Of course, defendants may also assert applicable state defenses as well.

As previously stated, the judicial branch is charged with the administration of justice. The courts administer justice by acting as the conduit for dispute resolution. The courts are the place where civil and criminal disputes are resolved, if the parties cannot reach a resolution themselves. In an effort to resolve disputes, courts must apply the laws of the land. To apply the law, judges must **interpret** the legislation and constitutions of the nation. To *interpret* means to read the law in an attempt to understand its meaning. This nation's courts are the final word in declaring the meaning of written law. If a court interprets a statute's meaning contrary to the intent of a legislature, then the legislature may later rewrite the statute to make its intent more clear. This has the effect of "reversing" the judicial interpretation of the statute. The process is much more difficult if a legislature desires to change a judicial interpretation of a constitution. At the national level, the Constitution has been amended twenty-six times. The amendment process is found in Article V of the Constitution and requires not only action by the federal legislature but also action by the states. To amend a constitution is simply a more cumbersome and time-consuming endeavor than amending legislation.

The judicial branch is independent from the other two branches of government. Often people think of the courts as enforcers of the law. Though this is true in a sense, it is untrue in that the judicial branch does not work with the executive branch in an attempt to achieve criminal convictions. It is the duty of the courts of this nation to remain neutral and apply the laws in a fair and impartial manner. The United States Constitution establishes a judiciary system that is shielded from interference from the other two branches. For example, the Constitution prohibits Congress from reducing the pay of federal judges after they are appointed. This prevents Congress from coercing the courts into action under the threat of no pay. The Constitution also provides for lifetime appointments of federal judges, thereby keeping the judicial branch from being influenced by political concerns, which may cause judges to ignore the law and make decisions based on what is best for their political careers. Judicial independence permits courts to make decisions that are disadvantageous to the government, but required by law, without fear of retribution from the other two branches.

TERMS

interpret To construe; to explain; to draw out meaning.

The need for an independent judiciary is most important when considering the power of **judicial review**. Judicial review is a power held by the judicial branch, which permits it to review the actions of the executive and legislative branches and of the states and to declare acts that are in violation of the Constitution void. Alexander Hamilton wrote of the power of judicial review, and of the importance of an independent judiciary, in the *Federalist Papers,* wherein he stated:

> Permanency in office frees the judges from political pressures and prevents invasions on judicial power by the president and Congress.
>
> * * *
>
> The Constitution imposes certain restrictions on the Congress designed to protect individual liberties, but unless the courts are independent and have the power to declare the laws in violation of the Constitution null and void these protections amount to nothing. The power of the Supreme Court to declare laws unconstitutional leads some to assume that the judicial branch will be superior to the legislative branch. Let us look at this argument.
>
> Only the Constitution is *fundamental* law; the Constitution establishes the principles and structure of the government. [To a]rgue that the Constitution is not superior to the laws suggests that the *representatives of the people* are superior *to the people* and that the Constitution is inferior to the government it gave birth to. The courts are the arbiters between the legislative branch and the people; the courts are to interpret the laws and prevent the legislative branch from exceeding the powers granted it. The courts must not only place the Constitution higher than the laws passed by Congress, they must also place the intentions of the people ahead of the intentions of the representatives ... [emphasis in original].

The landmark case dealing with judicial review is *Marbury v. Madison.*[12] Chief Justice Marshall wrote the opinion for the Court and determined that, although the Constitution does not contain explicit language providing for the power of judicial review, Article III of the Constitution implicitly endows the power in the judiciary. It is now well established that courts possess the authority to review the actions of the executive and legislative branches and to declare any law, command, or other action void if such violates the United States Constitution. The power is held by both state and federal courts. Any state or federal law that violates the United States Constitution may be struck

TERMS

judicial review† 1. Review by a court of a decision or ruling of an administrative agency. 2. Review by an appellate court of a determination by a lower court.

down by either federal or state courts. Of course, state laws that violate state constitutions may be stricken for the same reason.

The power to invalidate statutes is rarely used, for two reasons. First, the judiciary is aware of how awesome the power is, and this causes courts to be reluctant to use it. Second, many rules of statutory constructions exist, which have the effect of preserving legislation. For example, if two possible interpretations of a statute are possible, one that violates the Constitution and one that does not, one rule of statutory construction requires that the statute be construed so that it is consistent with the Constitution. Although rarely done, statutes are occasionally determined invalid. In the chapter on defenses, you will learn many constitutional constraints on government behavior. These defenses often rely on the power of the judiciary to invalidate statutes or police conduct to give them teeth.

Review Questions

1. What is the common law? How do the concepts of stare decisis and precedent relate to the common law?
2. The common law is different in every state. Why?
3. What is the primary duty of the executive branch of government in criminal law?
4. Define the phrase "court of record."
5. Define jurisdiction and differentiate between a court of general jurisdiction and a court of limited jurisdiction.

Review Problems

1. In 1973 the United States Supreme Court handed down the famous case, *Roe v. Wade,* 410 U.S. 113 (1973), wherein the Court determined that the decision to have an abortion is a private decision that is protected from government intervention, in some circumstances, by the United States Constitution. Suppose that a state legislature passes legislation (a state statute) that attempts to reverse the *Roe* decision by prohibiting all abortions in that state. Which is controlling in that state, the statute or the decision of the United States Supreme Court? Explain your answer.

2. Same facts as in problem 1, except the state supreme court has determined that the state constitution protects the life of fetuses from abortion, except when the life of the mother is endangered. Which is controlling when a mother seeks to have an abortion and her life is not endangered to any greater amount than the average pregnancy, the state constitutional provision protecting fetuses or the decision of the United States Supreme Court? Explain your answer.
3. Assume that the United States Supreme Court has previously determined that regulation of traffic on county roads is a power reserved exclusively for the states. In reaction to this opinion, the United States Congress enacts a statute providing that the regulation of county roads will be within power of the United States Congress from that date forward. Your law office represents a client who is charged with violating the federal statute that prohibits driving on all roads while intoxicated. Do you have a defense? If so, explain.

Notes

1 15 Am. Jur. 2d *Common Law* 6 (1976).

2 *Marsillett v. State,* 495 N.E.2d 699, 704 (Ind. 1986) (citations omitted).

3 15 Am. Jur. 2d *Common Law* 1 (1976).

4 *Helms v. American Security Co.*, 22 N.E.2d 822 (Ind. 1986).

5 T. Gardner, *Criminal Law: Principles and Cases,* 4th ed. (Criminal Justice Series; West 1989).

6 For more information concerning the due process and crime control models, *see* N. Gary Holten & Lawson Lamar, *The Criminal Courts* ch. 1 (McGraw-Hill 1991).

7 *Wickard v. Filburn,* 317 U.S. 111 (1942).

8 *United States v. Oliver,* 60 F.3d 547 (9th Cir. 1995); *United States v. Carolina,* 61 F.3d 917 (10th Cir. 1995).

9 *United States v. Garcia-Salazar,* 891 F. Supp. 568 (D. Kan. 1995). The statute reviewed can be found at 21 U.S.C. §§ 860.

10 28 U.S.C. §§ 41 *et seq.*

11 According to the Office of the Deputy Clerk, Supreme Court of the United States, there were 6,232 cases on the Supreme Court docket in 1994. The Court granted review and rendered decisions in 104 cases, 1.5 percent of the total.

12 1 Cranch 137, 2 L. Ed. 60 (1803).

CHAPTER 2

THE PARTICIPANTS

CHAPTER OUTLINE

The trial of a case [is] a three-legged stool—a judge and two advocates.

Warren E. Burger, Chief Justice
United States Supreme Court

§ 2.1 Introduction

Besides the accused and witnesses, there are five primary participants in criminal adjudications: law enforcement officers, prosecutors, judges, defense attorneys, and victims.

§ 2.2 Law Enforcement Officers

The front line of law enforcement in the United States is what the public commonly refers to as the *police*. Law enforcement officers exist at the national, state, and local levels.

Federal law enforcement agencies include the Federal Bureau of Investigation, the Drug Enforcement Administration, Customs, the Coast Guard, U.S. Marshals, the Secret Service, and the Bureau of Alcohol, Tobacco, and Firearms, to name only a few.

Each state has a police department and many have a counterpart to the FBI, such as the Kansas Bureau of Investigation (KBI). In addition, within each state, county sheriffs and municipal police departments enforce the laws of the state, as well as the laws of their locality. There are more than 20,000 local law enforcement agencies in the United States. This includes 12,502 local police departments; 3,086 sheriffs' offices; 49 state police departments; and more than 600,000 sworn police officers and 200,000-plus civilian personnel. There are approximately 22 officers per 10,000 people in the United States.[1]

Discretion

Law enforcement personnel are expected to keep the peace, investigate possible wrongdoing, enforce the laws, and further crime prevention. Although it is generally held that the police must enforce the laws, it is also recognized that not all the laws can be or should be enforced. Consequently, officers exercise much discretion when performing their daily duties. Deciding whether to conduct an investigation, whether to arrest an offender, or whether a search is necessary, all usually fall within the individual officer's discretion. However, the conduct of police officers must comply with constitutional, statutory, and departmental policy standards.

Ethics

As is true of prosecutors and defense attorneys, the police officer's paramount ethical code is the Constitution. Police officers have a legal and ethical obligation to keep themselves within constitutional limits when performing their duties.

More specifically, the International Association of Chiefs of Police (IACP) has formulated a set of ethical principles intended to guide the law enforcement officer in the performance of his or her duties. The IACP has actually issued two documents, the "Law Enforcement Code of Ethics" and the "Police Code of Conduct." The Code of Ethics is a general statement of ethical responsibility which may be used as an oath of office. The first paragraph of that Code reads:

> As a law enforcement officer, my fundamental duty is to serve the community; to safeguard lives and property; to protect the innocent against deception, the weak against oppression or intimidation and the peaceful against violence or disorder, and to respect the constitutional rights of all to liberty, equality and justice.

The Code of Ethics continues by recognizing that police officers hold a special public trust and that they have an obligation not to violate that trust.

Although substantially the same, the Police Code of Conduct is more specific than the Code of Ethics. The Code of Conduct prohibits: discriminatory treatment of individuals based upon status, sex, religion, political belief, or aspiration; the unnecessary use of force; the infliction of cruel, degrading, or inhuman treatment; violation of confidences, except when necessary in the performance of duties or as required by law; bribery; the acceptance of gifts; refusals to cooperate with other law enforcement officials; and other unreasonable and inappropriate behavior. The Code of Conduct further qualifies the necessary force requirement by stating that force should be used "only with the greatest restraint and only after discussion, negotiation and persuasion have been found to be inappropriate or ineffective."

Officers are expected to behave in a manner that inspires confidence and respect for law enforcement officials. Further, police officers are to attempt to obtain maximum public cooperation and to enforce all laws with courtesy, consideration, and dignity. Although the IACP has no enforcement authority, the Codes do provide an excellent standard for adoption by law enforcement agencies, as well as by individual officers.

For the remainder of this book, references to police or law enforcement officers are to any one of the previously mentioned agencies.

§ 2.3 Prosecutors

Prosecutors are also central to the administration of justice. *Prosecutors* are government attorneys responsible for prosecuting violators. This role includes preparing and filing documents; engaging in pretrial activity, such as discovery; and appearing in court. Prosecutors also act as legal counsel to law enforcement officers, rendering advice on the law of searches, seizures, arrests, surveillance techniques, and similar matters. Prosecutors appear at grand jury hearings, where they present evidence and assist the jury in other ways. Finally, in some jurisdictions, prosecutors act in a supervisory capacity as the head of a law enforcement agency, such as the Attorney General of the United States, who is the head of the Department of Justice.

At the federal level, the highest law enforcement official and prosecutor is the Attorney General, who undergoes the presidential nomination and senatorial confirmation process. The Attorney General is a Cabinet member who heads the Department of Justice.

Within each judicial district is one United States Attorney, a subordinate of the Attorney General, who also is selected through the nomination and confirmation process. United States Attorneys, with the aid of several Assistant United States Attorneys (AUSAs), are responsible for most federal prosecutions. In rare cases, however, another attorney from the Department of Justice may travel to a district to handle a case. Federal law also provides for the appointment of an independent counsel (special prosecutor) when government officials are suspected of violating the law.

Similar to the federal government, each state has an attorney general. The states vary in the structure of their prosecutorial agencies, but most have locally elected prosecutors, who may be titled *prosecutor*, *district attorney*, or *state attorney*. The degree to which these individuals answer to the state attorney general differs greatly. Additionally, local forms of government have attorneys. In some localities, these attorneys prosecute ordinance violations.

Discretion

Prosecutors enjoy considerable discretion when making the decision of whether to prosecute. This is one aspect of prosecutorial **discretion.** This decision must be made by a prosecutor in most cases. In a small number of cases, however, the prosecutor may not be in a position to make this decision, such as when a traffic ticket acts as the charging instrument and the case proceeds directly to court without the prosecutor's involvement. However, most cases are initiated directly by a prosecutor, grand jury, or, as is usually the case, the police (through the arrest and complaint procedure). A case may not proceed under a complaint; rather, the prosecutor must file an information (or an indictment issued by a grand jury) which replaces the complaint. If a prosecutor refuses, or files a ***nolle prosequi***, the case proceeds no further.

There are two general reasons that discretion must be exercised. First, the prosecutor's ethical obligation requires that he or she seek justice, not convictions. Prosecutors are not to maintain a prosecution simply because there is a probability of prevailing. Rather, the totality of the facts must be examined and it must be determined that a prosecution will further justice. The justice obligation continues through the entire adjudicative process. The *Wayte* case involved a challenge to prosecutorial discretion.

Economics is the second reason why prosecutors cannot pursue every case. The resources of the prosecutor and law enforcement agencies are limited. Not every case can be prosecuted because there are inadequate investigators, police officers, prosecutors, and other resources. Prosecutors must prioritize cases for prosecution. The decision of whether to prosecute is influenced by many factors. The facts of the case; the accused's criminal, social, and economic history; the likelihood of success; the cost of prosecution, including the probable time investment; public opinion; the seriousness of the crime; the desires of the victims; police expectations and desires; political concerns; and whether the prosecution will further the administration of justice are all considered.

Although prosecutorial discretion is broad, it is not absolute.

First, the authority to file a *nolle prosequi* or dismissal may be limited. The further along a case is in the process, the more involved the

TERMS

discretion The power conferred upon an official to act according to his or her own judgment and conscience, within general rules of law only, uncontrolled by the judgment or conscience of others.

nolle prosequi [Latin for] "unwilling to pursue." In a criminal case, an entry of record by the prosecutor by which he or she declares his or her intention not to prosecute the case further.

WAYTE
v.
UNITED STATES
470 U.S. 598 (1985)

JUSTICE POWELL delivered the opinion of the Court.

* * *

[Wayte refused to register with the Selective Service System, as required by federal law. At the time of the case, approximately 700,000 men had not registered who were required to by the Selective Service Act. The federal government followed a "passive enforcement" plan whereby it prosecuted only those individuals who announced that they would not comply with the law. Wayte had written several letters to the President and other government officials stating that he would not register and that he intended to encourage others to resist registration. Wayte and 133 individuals were singled out for action. Before prosecutions were initiated, however, an FBI agent was sent to each individual's home in an attempt to persuade the nonregistrant to comply. Only if the nonregistrant refused was a prosecution initiated. Wayte moved to dismiss the charges against him. He claimed that he was targeted by the Department of Justice for exercising his First Amendment rights.]

In our criminal justice system, the Government retains "broad discretion" as to whom to prosecute. * * * "[S]o long as the prosecutor has probable cause to believe that the accused committed an offense defined by statute, the decision whether or not to prosecute, and what charge to file or bring before a grand jury, generally rests entirely in his discretion." This broad discretion rests largely on the recognition that the decision to prosecute is particularly ill-suited to judicial review. Such factors as the strength of the case, the prosecution's general deterrence value, the Government's enforcement priorities, and the case's relationship to the Government's overall enforcement plan are not readily susceptible to the kind of analysis the courts are competent to undertake. Judicial supervision in this area, moreover, entails systemic costs of particular concern. Examining the basis of a prosecution delays the criminal proceeding, threatens to chill law enforcement by subjecting the prosecutor's motives and decision-making to outside inquiry, and may undermine prosecutorial effectiveness by revealing the Government's enforcement policy. All these are substantial concerns that make the courts properly hesitant to examine the decision whether to prosecute.

As we have noted in a slightly different context, however, although prosecutorial discretion is broad, it is not " 'unfettered.' Selectivity in the enforcement of criminal laws is * * * subject to contitutional contraints." In particular, the decision to prosecute may not be " 'deliberately based upon an unjustifiable standard such as race, religion, or other arbitrary classification,' " * * * including the exercise of protected statutory and constitutional right. [f] * * * It is appropriate to judge selective prosecution claims according to ordinary equal protection standards. * * * Under our prior cases, these standards require petitioner to show both that the passive enforcement system had a discriminatory effect and that it was motivated by a discriminatory purpose. * * * All petitioner has shown here is that those eventually prosecuted, along with many not prosecuted, reported themselves as having violated the law. He has not shown that the enforcement policy selected nonregistrants for prosecution on the basis of their speech. Inded, he could not have done so given the way the "beg" policy was carried out. The Government did not prosecute those who reported themselves but later registered. Nor did it prosecute those who protested registration but did not report themselves or were not reported by others. In fact, the Government did not even investigate those who wrote letters to Selective Service criticizing registration unless their letters stated affirmatively that they had refused to comply with the law. * * * The Government, on the other hand, did prosecute people who reported themselves or were reported by others but who did not publicly protest. These facts demonstrate that the Government treated all reported nonregistrants similarly. It did not subject vocal nonregistrants to any special burden. Indeed, those prosecuted in effect selected themselves for prosecution by refusing to register after being reported and warned by the Government.

Even if the passive policy had a discriminatory effect, petitioner has not shown that the Government intended such a result. The evidence he presented demonstrated only that the Government was aware that the passive enforcement policy would result in prosecution of vocal objectors and that they would probably make selective prosecution claims. As we have noted, however: " 'Discriminatory purpose' ... implies more than ... intent as awareness of consequences. It implies that the decisonmaker ... selected or reaffirmed a particular course of action at least in part 'because of,' not merely 'in spite of,' its adverse effects upon an identifiable group." * * * In the present case, petitioner has not shown that the Government prosecuted him *because of* his protest activities. Absent such a showing, his claim of selective prosecution fails.

* * *

We conclude that the Government's passive enforcement system together with its "beg" policy violated neither the First nor Fifth Amendment. Accordingly, we affirm the judgement of the Court of Appeals.

It is so ordered.

court becomes in the decision. Generally, the decision not to prosecute before the formal charge (information or indictment) is filed is left to the prosecutor without judicial intervention. However, a small number of states require judicial approval of *nolle prosequi* decisions.

Once the formal charge has been filed, judicial approval of dismissal is the rule rather than the exception. This is true in the federal system, which also requires leave of court to dismiss complaints.[2]

Second, decisions to prosecute which are motivated by improper criteria may violate equal protection. The Fourteenth Amendment prohibits each state from taking actions that "deny to any person within its jurisdiction the equal protection of the laws." Although the Fifth Amendment does not contain this language, the Supreme Court has interpreted the Fifth Amendment's due process clause as requiring equal protection of the laws. A claim that it is unfair to prosecute a person because other known violators are not prosecuted will not be successful, unless it can be shown that the accused has been singled out for an improper reason.

Generally, three elements must be shown to establish improper, discriminatory prosecution: first, that other people similarly situated were not prosecuted; second that the prosecutor intentionally singled out the defendant; third, that the selection was based upon an arbitrary classification. As the Supreme Court stated in *Oyler v. Boles*,[3] for there to be an equal protection violation it must be shown that "the selection was *deliberately* based upon an unjustified standard." What is an unjustified standard? Prosecutions based upon race, religion, and gender are examples. A prosecution intended to punish an individual for exercising a constitutional right is also improper.

To determine whether a classification is proper, equal protection analysis must be employed. Most decisions are tested under the rational relationship test. That is, if the decision to prosecute is rationally related to a legitimate governmental objective, it is valid. If a decision is based upon race, religion, or in retaliation for a person's exercise of a right, the decision is tested under the strict scrutiny test and is invalid unless it can be shown to further a compelling governmental interest. Finally, a few classifications, such as those based upon gender, are tested under a standard less demanding than strict scrutiny but more demanding than the rational relationship test. Such laws must bear a substantial relationship to a legitimate governmental interest. In reality, claims of selective enforcement are rarely successful.

Ethics

All attorneys are bound by ethical rules. Two sets of rules are used in the United States: the Model Code of Professional Responsibility and the Model Rules of Professional Conduct. The two are similar and every state has adopted some form of these rules. Ethical violations may result in discipline by the bar, an offended court, or both. Common sanctions include private and public reprimands, suspension, and disbarment. Under court rules and rules of procedure, other sanctions, such as monetary penalties, may be assessed. Also, all courts possess the authority to punish for contempt.

Prosecutors have special ethical responsibilities. You have already learned that the mission of the prosecutor is to achieve justice. The Model Code of Professional Responsibility states that the "responsibility of a public prosecutor differs from that of the usual advocate; his duty is to seek justice, not merely to convict."[4]

Prosecutors have an ethical obligation to be sure that a prosecution is warranted and to seek dismissal immediately upon discovering that one is not. Prosecutors are not to trump up charges to increase their power during plea negotiations. Prosecutors are only to request a fair sentence from a court. Of course, prosecutors may not use perjured or falsified evidence to obtain a conviction. In addition, you will learn later in this text that prosecutors have a constitutional duty to disclose exculpatory evidence.[5] Evidence that mitigates the degree of an offense or reduces a sentence must also be disclosed.[6] Further, prosecutors are not to avoid pursuing evidence because it may damage the government's case or assist the defendant.[7] Through discovery rules, prosecutors have a duty to disclose other evidence prior to or during trial. In short, prosecutors have an obligation to deal with defendants fairly.

On the other side, prosecutors have an obligation to pursue a prosecution when the facts of the case demand it. At trial, unless a prosecutor becomes convinced that the accused is innocent, the prosecutor is to zealously pursue a conviction.

§ 2.4 Judges

Judges are not executive branch officials, as are prosecutors and law enforcement officers. Judges are part of the judiciary, a separate and independent branch of government. Generally, the judiciary is responsible for the resolution of disputes and the administration of justice. In regard to criminal law, judges are responsible for issuing warrants, supervising pretrial activity, presiding over hearings and trial, deciding guilt or innocence in some cases, and passing sentence on those convicted.

Having a fair and impartial party make these determinations is an important feature of the U.S. criminal justice system, and is mandated by the Constitution in many instances, as you will learn in the following chapters. A judge has the obligation to remain unbiased, fair, and impartial in all cases before the bar.

Ethics

Like attorneys, judges are subject to a code of ethics. Most states have enacted the Code of Judicial Conduct. Judges are to be fair and impartial.[8] In criminal cases, judges must be sensitive to defendants' rights and be careful to not imply to a jury that a defendant is guilty.

§ 2.5 Defense Attorneys

Because of the complexity of the legal system and the advantage of having an advocate, competent legal counsel has become an important feature of the American system of criminal justice. The Sixth Amendment to the Constitution provides that all persons have a right to be represented by counsel in criminal cases. Today, indigent defendants have a right to counsel in all cases that may result in incarceration.

Ethics

Defense attorneys have high, and sometimes morally challenging, ethical responsibilities. Unlike the prosecutor, whose duty is to see that justice is achieved, the defense attorney must zealously represent the accused, within the bounds of the law,[9] regardless of innocence or guilt.

This obligation is the cause of some public disrespect for the legal profession. Attorneys are perceived as hired guns, not as advocates of civil liberties. Defense lawyers are frequently asked how they can defend people they know are guilty. There are two responses to this inquiry. First, defense attorneys often do not know whether their clients are in fact guilty, as this question is rarely asked. Second, defense attorneys are not defending the actions that the defendant is accused of committing; rather, defense attorneys are defending the rights of the accused, specifically, the right to have the government prove its case beyond a reasonable doubt using lawfully obtained evidence. By defending the rights of one person against governmental oppression, the rights of all the people are defended.

This approach, which is a vital part of the United States criminal justice system, is often misunderstood by the public. The defense attorney who fulfills this constitutional and ethical mission is often the source of public animosity and ridicule.

Communications between attorneys and clients are confidential and privileged. Attorneys are generally prohibited from disclosing those communications.[10] In the *Belge* case, an attorney was indicted for not revealing a client's privileged communication and was the subject of considerable public disdain. The indictment was dismissed in the interests of justice, namely, preservation of the attorney-client privilege. However, nothing could be done by the court to restore the attorney's good reputation and standing in his community.

Belge turned on the fact that the crimes had already occurred and the defendant posed no threat. An attorney is allowed, but not required, to report a client's intention to commit a crime.[11] Therefore, if a client informs his counsel that he intends to kill a witness if he is released on bond, the attorney may disclose this information without breaching any ethical obligations.

Attorneys are generally obligated to represent criminal defendants when appointed by a court or upon request by a bar association. However, an attorney may be excused for compelling reasons. In no event is belief in a defendant's guilt or disgust with the alleged acts compelling.[12]

An interesting ethical dilemma is presented when a defense attorney knows (or has a strong belief) that either the client or one of the defense witnesses has given or intends to give false testimony. On the one hand, the attorney is an officer of the court and thus prohibited from defrauding the court. On the other hand, the defense attorney has an obligation to the client. There is a split in the jurisdictions concerning how this situation is to be handled. There are three possibilities. First, the most preferable, the defense attorney dissuades the client from committing perjury. Second, the attorney moves to withdraw from the case, keeping

PEOPLE
v.
BELGE
372 N.Y.S.2d 798 (1975)

In the summer of 1973 Robert F. Garrow, Jr. stood charged in Hamilton County with the crime of murder. The defendant was assigned two attorneys, Frank H. Armani and Francis R. Belge. A defense of insanity had been interposed by counsel for Mr. Garrow. During the course of the discussions between Garrow and his two counsel, three other murders were admitted by Garrow, one being in Onondaga County. On or about September of 1973 Mr. Belge conducted his own investigation based upon what his client had told him and with the assistance of a friend the location of the body of Alicia Hauck was found in Oakwood Cemetery in Syracuse. Mr. Belge personally inspected the body and was satisfied, presumably, that this was Alicia Hauck that his client had told him he murdered.

This discovery was not disclosed to the authorities, but became public during the trial of Mr. Garrow in June of 1974, when, to affirmatively establish the defense of insanity, these three other murders were brought before the jury by the defense in the Hamilton County trial. Public indignation reached the fever pitch; statements were made by the District Attorney of Onondaga County relative to the situation and he caused the Grand Jury of Onondaga County, then sitting, to conduct a thorough investigation. As a result of this investigation Frank Armani was No Billed by the Grand Jury, but [an i]ndictment ... was returned against Francis R. Belge, Esq., accusing him of having violated [the public health law], which, in essence, requires that a decent burial be accorded the dead, and ... requires anyone knowing of the death of a person without medical attendance, to report the same to the proper authorities. Defense counsel moved for dismissal of the Indictment on the grounds that a confidential, privileged communication existed between him and Mr. Garrow, which should excuse the attorney from making full disclosure to the authorities. The National Association of Criminal Defense Lawyers, as Amicus Curiae ... succinctly stated the issue in the following language:

> "If this indictment stands, the attorney-client privilege will be effectively destroyed. No defendant will be able to freely discuss the facts of his case with his attorney. No attorney will be able to listen to those facts without being faced with the Hobson's choice of violating the law or violating his professional code of Ethics."

Initially in England the practice of law was not recognized as a profession and certainly some people are skeptics today. However, the practice of learned and capable men appearing before the Court on behalf of a friend or an acquaintance became more and more demanding. Consequently, the King granted a privilege to certain of these men to engage in such practice. There had to be rules governing their duties. These came to be known as "Canons." The King has, in this country, been substituted by a democracy, but the "Canons" are with us today, having been honed and refined over the years to meet the changes of time. Most are constantly being studied and revamped by the American Bar Association and by the bar associations of the various states. While they are, for the most part, general by definition, they can be brought to bear in a particular situation. Among those is the [rule that] confidential communications between an attorney and his client are privileged from disclosure ... as a rule of necessity in the administration of justice ... .

The effectiveness of counsel is only as great as the confidentiality of its client-attorney relationship. If the lawyer cannot get all the facts about the case, he can only give his client half of a defense. ...

When the facts of the other homicides became public, as result of the defendant's testimony to substantiate his claim of insanity, "Members of the public were shocked at the apparent callousness of these lawyers with the public interest and with simple decency." A hue and cry went up from the press and other news media suggesting that the attorneys should be found guilty of such crimes as obstruction of justice or becoming an accomplice after the fact. From a layman's standpoint, this certainly was a logical conclusion. However, the constitution of the United States of America attempts to preserve the dignity of the individual and to do that guarantees him the services of an attorney who will bring to the bar and to the bench every conceivable protection from the inroads of the state against such rights as are vested in the constitution for one accused of a crime. Among those substantial constitutional rights is that a defendant does not have to incriminate himself. His attorneys were bound to uphold that concept and maintain what has been called a sacred trust of confidentiality.

The following language of the brief of the Amicus Curiae further points up the statements just made: "The client's Fifth Amendment rights cannot be violated by his attorney. ... Because the discovery of the body of Alicia Hauck would have presented 'a significant link in the chain of evidence tending to establish his guilt' ... Garrow was constitutionally exempt from any statutory requirement to disclose the location of the body. And Attorney Belge, as Garrow's attorney, was not only equally exempt, but under a positive stricture precluding such disclosure. Garrow, although constitutionally privileged against a requirement to compulsory disclosure, was free to make such a revelation if he chose to do so. Attorney Belge was affirmatively required to withhold disclosure. The criminal defendant's self-incrimination rights become completely nugatory if compulsory disclosure can be exacted through his attorney." ...

It is the decision of this Court that Francis R. Belge conducted himself as an officer of the Court with all the zeal at his command to protect the constitutional rights of his client. Both on the grounds of a privileged communication and the interests of justice the Indictment is dismissed. [The decision was affirmed on appeal. *See* 376 N.Y.S.2d 771 (1975) and 390 N.Y.S.2d 867 (1976).]

the reason secret. Third, the attorney discloses the client's intention to commit perjury to the court. The law in each jurisdiction must be examined to determine which of these options is permitted or preferred.

Defense attorneys are sometimes asked to represent co-defendants. This can create a conflict of interest for a defense attorney if the defendants have conflicting or antagonistic defenses. Because of the inherent dangers of representing co-defendants, many defense attorneys refuse joint representation. It is a violation of a defendant's Sixth Amendment right to the assistance of effective counsel to have a lawyer with divided loyalties.

Finally, trial counsel for criminal defendants have an obligation to continue on appeal unless new counsel is retained or the court has authorized withdrawal. This is different from civil cases, where there is no general obligation to continue after trial.

§ 2.6 Legal Assistants

Legal assistants are employed by both prosecutors and defense attorneys, with the latter being more common.[13] In the defense context, legal assistants may be asked to perform several tasks, including conducting initial interviews, conducting legal research, preparing drafts of motions and other documents, maintaining and organizing files, acting as a contact with incarcerated clients, assisting in preparing the defendant and other witnesses for trial, and preparing the defendant for the presentence investigation interview. Some paralegals are called upon to conduct investigations.

As employees of attorneys, legal assistants must also follow ethical guidelines and responsibilities. Although no state has yet established mandatory certification of legal assistants, and therefore there is no enforceable set of ethics rules beyond what is required by law, the National Association of Legal Assistants (NALA) has promulgated a Code of Ethics.

First, legal assistants may not engage in the practice of law.[14] This includes rendering legal advice, establishing an attorney-client relationship, setting fees, and appearing in court on behalf of a client. Although some administrative agencies permit legal assistants to represent clients at hearings, this is never so in criminal law. The unauthorized practice of law is both criminal and unethical. Further, legal assistants are to act prudently in determining the extent to which a client may be assisted without the presence of a lawyer.[15] Finally, it is imperative that the attorney directly supervise the legal assistant's work in criminal law.[16]

Second, all employees of an attorney are bound by the confidentiality rule.[17] All communications made by a client to a legal assistant fall within the scope of the attorney-client privilege and may not be disclosed by the legal assistant.

Third, legal assistants must be careful not to suborn perjury when preparing the client and witnesses for trial. Instructing a witness in effective techniques, including dress and personal appearance, and methods of responding to inquiries (e.g., answer directly, honestly, and as succinctly as possible; look at the jury during your response) is proper. Suggesting, urging, encouraging, or directing a witness to lie or mislead a court is suborning perjury.

Fourth, legal assistants are also bound by the American Bar Association's Model Rules of Professional Conduct and Model Code of Professional Responsibility.[18]

§ 2.7 Victims

Recall that the victim of crimes is the government. That is why criminal prosecutions are brought in the name of the government. However, most crimes have another victim, the victim-in-fact. This is the person assaulted, battered, raped, or robbed. Victims affect criminal adjudications in a number of ways.

First, law enforcement officers may decline to make an arrest or conduct an investigation if the victim is disinterested in having the matter pursued. Second, the prosecutor may file a *nolle prosequi*, if there has been an arrest, or otherwise refuse to proceed with a prosecution if that is the victim's desire. Third, if the matter proceeds to trial, the victim may be required to testify at both pretrial hearings and trial. A victim may choose to attend even if his or her testimony is not required. Fourth, the victim may participate in the sentencing portion of the trial. As you will learn, statements concerning how a victim and a victim's family have been affected may be considered by judge and jury when passing sentence. Restitution is also made a condition of some sentences.

Victims' rights have received considerable attention since the mid-1980s. Victims' rights organizations have strenuously—and successfully—lobbied to introduce both state constitutional amendments and legislation concerning victims' rights. For example, the Arizona Constitution was amended to include a "Victims' Bill of Rights." Through that amendment and its enabling legislation, crime victims are allowed to participate in the initial appearance, be heard on conditions of release, be present at all court proceedings, confer with the prosecutor concerning disposition of the case, refuse a defense interview or other discovery request, provide an impact statement for sentencing, receive restitution and other damages, receive notice of probation modifications of the perpetrator, and receive notice of parole or death of the perpetrator.[19]

Rape shield legislation is another form of victims' rights laws. Rape shield laws exclude from trial evidence of a rape victim's sexual history (except evidence of sexual history with the accused) and reputation in the community. These laws were enacted to protect the rape victim from embarrassing, harassing, and intimidating inquiries.

In most jurisdictions, victims' rights are a matter of statutory, not constitutional, law. Change came quickly in this area. In 1982, only four states had victims' bills of rights. That number increased to forty-four by 1987. In 1982, only eight states allowed the use of **victim impact statements** at sentencing. By 1987, the number of states permitting victim impact evidence to be considered by sentencing judges and juries increased to thirty-nine. Only one state provided that a crime victim had a right to confer with the prosecutor concerning important prosecutorial decisions in 1982. That number increased to twenty-eight

TERMS

victim impact statement At the time of sentencing, a statement made to the court concerning the effect the crime has had on the victim or on the victim's family.

by 1987. Restitution was mandated by the law of eight states in 1982; twenty-nine states required the imposition of restitution in 1987.[20]

In addition to laws providing for victim participation in court proceedings, laws have been enacted for the protection of both victims and witnesses. These laws provide for the relocation of a witness or victim whose cooperation with an investigation or prosecution endangers his or her life. The federal law is well known. It provides for relocation of the victim or witness and his or her immediate family at taxpayer expense. Further, the United States provides the family with a new identity.[21]

Victims are likely to have civil remedies against perpetrators under traditional civil law theories. Intentional tort actions for assault, battery, invasion of privacy, and conversion are examples.

Finally, *victim assistance organizations* are available in many jurisdictions. Some are independent, not-for-profit, corporations and others are governmental entities. These organizations provide information, counseling, and other assistance to victims. Also, most states have enacted *victim compensation programs*. In many instances restitution proves inadequate, such as when the perpetrator is indigent. In these instances, a victim can request compensation from a state victim compensation fund. These programs reimburse victims for medical expenses and, sometimes, loss of income. Generally, they do not compensate victims for property losses.

§ 2.8 Witnesses

Witnesses come in two forms: experts and those who have personal knowledge concerning a case. Experts are used in criminal trials in a variety of circumstances. As examples, prosecutors use forensic science experts to provide and support fingerprint, blood, DNA, and similar scientific evidence; both defendants and prosecutors use mental health professionals (i.e., psychiatrists and psychologists) when the sanity of the defendant (and thus his or her ability to stand trial) or the defendant's insanity at the time of commission of the crime are at issue.

The second type of witness is the person who possesses personal knowledge concerning a crime, such as an eyewitness. These witnesses can be critical to either a defense or prosecution case. Witnesses may be ordered to appear for trial through the use of a **subpoena**. If it appears

TERMS

subpoena A command in the form of written process requiring a witness to come to court to testify; short for subpoena ad testificandum.

that a witness will not be available for trial (for instance, the witness is an illegal alien who is about to be deported), federal law provides that deposition testimony may be admitted at trial. The witness may be subpoenaed to appear at the deposition. If a witness refuses to appear for deposition, or for another reason is not likely to appear, federal law permits the party seeking the witness's appearance to move the trial court to have the witness arrested. Once arrested, the witness is entitled to the same rights that criminal defendants enjoy, including the right to be released on bail.[22] The witness is to be released once his or her deposition is taken, provided that the deposition will be admissible at trial over evidentiary and confrontation clause claims. If it is not, continued detention, subject to federal rules governing release of arrestees, is allowed.[23]

A judge may attempt to protect witnesses, like crime victims, from pretrial contact with a defendant by ordering the defendant to avoid contact as a condition of pretrial release.[24]

At trial, witnesses are commonly "separated" and ordered not to discuss the case or their testimony among themselves. At common law, witnesses are immune from slander suits, but may be prosecuted for perjury. When necessary, such as when possible self-incrimination issues arise, witnesses may have counsel present in the courtroom for consultation.

§ 2.9 Liability of Governments and Their Officials

Government officials, including law enforcement officers, prosecutors, and judges, are not above the law. Violation of an individual's rights by an official, even if during the performance of official duties, may lead to civil and criminal liability.[25] It is not in society's best interest, however, to create an environment where officials are threatened with civil or criminal liability for every incorrect decision and action, especially if taken in good faith and after thoughtful consideration of alternatives and repercussions. In such a world, civil authorities would be afraid to act and government would be paralyzed. Therefore, the laws governing liability of government officials are designed to provide remedies only for acts that are outrageous, malicious, shocking, or in clear violation of established rights.

States have laws that may provide remedies to the victims of improper governmental conduct. A police officer who commits an unjustified assault, battery, or false imprisonment may be liable under traditional tort and criminal law theories. These and other actions may lead to civil and criminal liability under state civil rights laws. In addition, violations of federally secured rights by state or federal officers can result in both civil and criminal prosecutions under federal civil rights statutes.[26] It was under these laws that several Los Angeles, California, police officers were prosecuted for violating the civil rights of Rodney King in 1993. Similarly, a prosecutor who violates a person's civil rights may be liable under federal law,[27] or a similar state law, or under a state tort theory. In fewer instances, judges may also be liable for their actions.

The civil liability of officials is limited by immunity doctrines. Immunities developed at common law, and the United States Supreme Court has determined that Congress did not intend to abolish these immunities when it enacted the civil rights acts.[28] Therefore, governmental officials may assert immunity as a defense if sued under the federal civil rights statutes.

There is a judicial immunity. Any action that is judicial in nature is shielded by *absolute immunity*. Because it is absolute, a government official is free from both suit and liability when performing judicial functions. Issuing orders (including warrants) and presiding over hearings are examples of judicial acts.

Most judicial acts are performed by judges, but not all. Prosecutors perform quasi-judicial acts and are shielded with absolute immunity for the performance of these acts. Appearing in court (including ex parte warrant application hearings) and complying with court orders are considered quasi-judicial acts. Similarly, police officers are shielded with absolute immunity when enforcing court orders (including warrants) and when testifying in court.

In other situations, another form of immunity may apply. A person entitled to *qualified immunity* is free from liability, but not necessarily free from suit. That means that the process of establishing nonliability may involve a greater commitment of time, energy, and money by a defendant. Under absolute immunity, issues of malice, intent, or the nature of the right alleged to be violated are immaterial, because the defendant is immune regardless. In contrast, whether an official acted with malice or whether the alleged right violated was clearly established at law are material in the qualified immunity case. Under some laws, an official is liable only if malice is shown, or, as required by federal law, a plaintiff can prove that a clearly established right was violated.

So, under federal law, although prosecutors are absolutely immune from civil liability for quasi-judicial acts, such as appearing in court and filing charges, they enjoy only a qualified immunity when performing other acts, such as rendering legal advice to law enforcement officers.[29] Similarly, judges are protected by qualified immunity when performing nonjudicial, but work-related, functions, such as making personnel decisions.[30] Police officers are shielded by qualified immunity when conducting investigations, making warrantless searches or seizures, and engaging in administrative and personnel matters (see Figure 2-1).

Finally, the government itself may be sued in some circumstances. A serious obstacle, which must be overcome to establish governmental

§ 1983 ACTIONS AND IMMUNITY: FUNCTIONS AND IMMUNITY		
Position	***Entitled to absolute immunity when performing the following:***	***Entitled to qualified immunity when performing the following:***
Judges	Judicial acts, such as conducting hearings and trials, issuing orders and warrants, and making statements during judicial or administrative proceedings	Administrative acts Personnel actions
Prosecutors	Quasi-judicial acts, such as appearing in court and complying with court orders	Investigations Counseling law enforcement officers Administrative acts Personnel actions
Law enforcement officers	Enforcing court orders Testifying in court	Investigations Making warrantless searches and arrests Administrative acts Personnel actions
Witnesses	Testifying in court and administrative tribunals	
Legislators and administrative officials responsible for promulgating regulations	Statements and writings resulting from legislative sessions or committee meetings and smaller administrative actions Voting Promulgating a rule	Administrative acts Personnel actions
Public defenders	No immunity	No immunity

FIGURE 2-1 Summary of Absolute and Qualified Immunities

liability, is **sovereign immunity**. The doctrine of sovereign immunity holds that the government is immune from lawsuits. Therefore, governments must consent to be sued. This is true of both state and federal governments. Most states have abolished sovereign immunity to some degree, some by statute, and a few by judicial decision.

The federal government has consented to be sued under several laws. One is the Federal Tort Claims Act (FTCA).[31] Through this statute the United States has waived immunity from suit for a number of torts. In 1974, the statute was amended to permit suits based upon assault, battery, false imprisonment, false arrest, abuse of process, or malicious prosecution committed by federal law enforcement officers.

States may not be sued directly under federal civil rights statutes, nor may the federal government. However, local forms of government may be sued under federal civil rights laws if the acts alleged to have violated the plaintiff's civil rights were committed pursuant to an ordinance, regulation, policy, or decision of the locality.[32]

TERMS

sovereign immunity The principle that the government—specifically, the United States or any state of the United States—is immune from suit except when it consents to be sued.

Review Questions

1. What is the constitutional mission of a prosecutor?
2. What is the policy behind requiring defense attorneys to zealously represent guilty persons?
3. What is the attorney-client privilege?
4. Legal assistants and other nonlawyers are prohibited from practicing law. What acts constitute the practice of law?
5. Are legal assistants who are employed in law offices obligated to maintain client confidences?
6. What are victims' bills of rights? Name three rights typically included in such a law.
7. According to the Police Code of Conduct promulgated by the International Association of Chiefs of Police, when may force be used?

Review Problems

1. Create a set of facts under which co-defendants could not be represented by the same attorney. Explain why separate counsel is necessary under your scenario.
2. Do you believe that a defense attorney should be required to zealously represent a client who has admitted guilt to the lawyer? What if the result is the release of a violent criminal (i.e., acquittal or dismissal of charges)? Can you suggest an alternative method?
3. Do you believe that police officers should arrest every violator they encounter, discover, or are made aware of? Support your answer. What factors should an officer consider when making the decision whether to arrest or otherwise pursue a prosecution?
4. In some nations, prosecutors are required to file a criminal charge if sufficient evidence exists. Should this form of compulsory prosecution replace the U.S. model of prosecutorial discretion? Explain your answer.
5. In some nations, individual victims are permitted to file a criminal charge against the person(s) who committed the alleged act(s). In these nations, the victim may prosecute the case or a public prosecutor may prosecute on the victim's behalf. Should such a method be employed in the United States? Explain your answer.

Notes

1 *Census of State and Local Law Enforcement Agencies, 1992* (Bureau of Justice Statistics 1993).

2 Fed. R. Crim. P. 48.

3 368 U.S. 448 (1962).

4 Ethical Consideration (EC) 7-13.

5 *Id. See also Brady v. Maryland,* 373 U.S. 83 (1963).

6 Model Code of Professional Responsibility, Disciplinary Rule (DR) 7-103 reads: "[a] public prosecutor or other government lawyer in criminal litigation shall make timely disclosure to counsel for the defendant, or to the defendant if he has no counsel, of the existence of evidence, known to the prosecutor or other government lawyer, that tends to negate the guilt of the accused, mitigate the degree of the offense, or reduce the punishment."

7 EC 7-13.

8 Code of Judicial Conduct, Canon 3.

9 EC 7-1; DR 7-101.

10 DR 4-101.

11 Model Code of Professional Responsibility, DR 4-101(c)(3); Model Rules of Professional Conduct 1.6(b)(1).

12 EC 2-29.

13 Approximately 13 percent of all paralegals in the United States work in criminal law. *See* Angela Schneeman, *Paralegals in American Law* (Lawyers Cooperative/Delmar Publishers 1994).

14 NALA Code of Ethics, Canons 1, 3, 4, and 6.

15 *Id.*, Canon 5.

16 *Id.*, Canon 2.

17 *Id.*, Canon 7.

18 *Id.*, Canon 12.

19 Christopher Johns, "Criminal Justice in America—Part One, The Costs of Victims' Rights," 29 *Arizona Attorney* 27 (Oct. 1992).

20 Don Siegelman & Courtney Tarver, "National Association of Attorneys General," 1 EISCL 163 (WL 1988).

21 Victim and Witness Protection Act, 18 U.S.C. § 224.

22 18 U.S.C. § 3144.

23 *See Aguilar-Ayala v. Ruiz,* 973 F.2d 411 (5th Cir. 1992); *United States v. Allie,* 978 F.2d 1401 (5th Cir. 1992).

24 18 U.S.C. § 3142.

25 For a more thorough discussion of governmental liability, including the liability of government officials, *see* Daniel Hall, *Administrative Law* (Lawyers Cooperative/Delmar Publishers 1994).

26 *See* 42 U.S.C. § 1983; 18 U.S.C. § 241 *et seq.*

27 *See* 42 U.S.C. § 1983.

28 *See Burns v. Reed,* 111 S. Ct. 1934 (1991); *Pierson v. Ray,* 386 U.S. 547 (1967).

29 *See* Daniel Hall, *Administrative Law* § 10.4 (Lawyers Cooperative/Delmar Publishers 1994) for a discussion of prosecutorial immunity.

30 *Id.*

31 28 U.S.C. §§ 1291, 1346, 1402, 1504, 2110, 2401–2402, 2411–2412, 2671–2678, and 2680.

32 *Monell v. Department of Social Services*, 436 U.S. 658 (1978). *See also* Daniel Hall, *Administrative Law* § 10.4 (Lawyers Cooperative/Delmar Publishers 1994).

CHAPTER 3

OVERVIEW OF CONSTITUTIONAL RIGHTS AND LIBERTIES

CHAPTER OUTLINE

> *The layman's constitutional view is that what he likes is constitutional and that which he doesn't like is unconstitutional.*
>
> ***Hugo L. Black, Associate Justice***
> ***United States Supreme Court***

§ 3.1 History of the Constitution

In 1781, the colonies of what is now the United States adopted their first constitution, the Articles of Confederation and Perpetual Union. A weak and ineffective national government and jealousy and conflicts among the states made it apparent that the union was not going to exist perpetually. Thus, in 1787, twelve of the thirteen colonies (Rhode Island refused to send a delegate) sent delegates to Philadelphia to "revise" the Articles of Confederation. Fearing that the nation could not survive under the Articles, even if revised, the delegates drafted a new Constitution. The decision was controversial, so much so that the delegates voted to keep their activities secret until completed.

The new constitution strengthened the national government. It could now, among other things, raise and maintain armies, establish national banks, and regulate interstate and international commerce. Even though the delegates intended to strengthen the federal government, they also significantly limited its power. The framers knew the risks of centralizing power—they had all experienced the oppression of British rule. They believed strongly in local governance and individual liberties. Accordingly, the national government's authority was limited to those powers enumerated in the Constitution. It was the states that possessed general jurisdiction, that is, general authority to regulate for the health and welfare of citizens. Even more, however, the framers intended for all forms of government to be limited by rights held by the people, the sovereign power of the United States.

The delegates completed their work in three months and sent the document to the states for ratification. The first state to ratify was Delaware, in 1787. The ninth state to ratify was New Hampshire, which did so in 1788. Rhode Island, which had refused to send a delegate to the Constitutional Convention, was the last state to ratify; it finally did so on May 29, 1790.

§ 3.2 Constitutional Rights and Liberties

The United States Constitution became effective when New Hampshire ratified it in 1788. The first ten amendments to the Constitution, the Bill of Rights, were added in 1791. The framers added the Bill of Rights to assure that federal governmental authority would remain limited—remember that the framers feared centralized authority.

Why did the framers not include the Bill of Rights in the original constitution if they were so suspicious of government? Because they believed they were creating a limited government, one that would not have the power to commit unreasonable searches, subject a person to cruel punishments, and the like. Alexander Hamilton saw no need to include a bill of rights, because the government lacked the authority to encroach upon an individual's liberty: "Why declare that things shall not be done, which there is no power to do?"

Hamilton did not foresee the significant changes that would come to the United States. Industrialization, a huge growth in population, and specialization of functions have led to increased interdependence of people. Today, few persons live so remotely that their activities do not affect others, and few individuals supply their own food, clothes, and other necessities. American culture today involves continuous and frequent contact with other people. As human contact increases, so do conflicts and, accordingly, rules to regulate conduct. We look to our government to establish and enforce most of these rules. To protect ourselves from an overzealous government, which we have entrusted with an ever-increasing amount of authority, we need the Bill of Rights.

At the time of the Constitutional Convention, however, Hamilton's view prevailed. The delegates decided not to include a bill of rights in the original document. They simply did not believe the government had the authority to legislate in the areas a bill of rights would cover. After the convention voted ten to none to exclude it, Eldridge Gerry moved that at least the freedom of the press should be included. For the same reason—that is, the delegates did not believe the government had the authority to regulate the press—this motion was also defeated. Thus, there was no bill of rights in the original Constitution.

The absence of a bill of rights was troubling to the nation. A few states, such as New York and Virginia, attached to their resolutions of approval of the Constitution proposals to amend the new Constitution to add a bill of rights. In total, over 200 amendments to the Constitution dealing with individual rights were discussed in the state ratifying conventions.[1] It was a popular idea; only three years after the Constitution was ratified, the Bill of Rights was ratified.

The Bill of Rights was enacted as a limitation upon the authority of the federal government. The states were not bound by the Bill of Rights until the adoption of the Fourteenth Amendment in 1868. Recall from the earlier discussion of incorporation that only two rights bearing on criminal cases have not been incorporated by the Supreme Court: grand jury indictment and the right to a reasonable bail. (The author predicts that the former is not likely to be incorporated soon, but suspects that the latter is.)

Although many rights can be found in the Bill of Rights, others were secured by the original Constitution or were added after the Bill of Rights. The original document included these protections:

1. *Habeas corpus.* Article I, § 9, provides for writs of **habeas corpus.** Also known as the "Great Writ of Liberty," *habeas corpus* translates from the Latin as "you have the body." Developed at common law, this writ is used to determine the lawfulness of detention.
2. *Bills of attainder.* Article I, § 9, clause 3, and § 10, clause 1, prohibit Congress and the states from passing **bills of attainder**. A *bill of attainder* is a judgment of conviction for a crime issued by a legislature. This function is reserved to the judiciary in the United States.
3. *Ex post facto laws.* Article I, § 9, clause 3, prohibits Congress from enacting **ex post facto laws.** A law that declares an act previously committed to be unlawful is *ex post facto.* This clause, as well as the due process clauses of the Fifth and Fourteenth Amendments, prohibits the states and federal government from enacting ex post facto laws.
4. *Treason.* Article III, § 3, provides that no person shall be convicted of **treason** except upon the testimony of two witnesses to the same act or upon a confession in open court.

TERMS

habeas corpus [Latin for] "you have the body." A writ whose purpose is to obtain immediate relief from illegal imprisonment by having the "body" (that is, the prisoner) delivered from custody and brought before the court. A writ of habeas corpus is a means for attacking the constitutionality of the statute under which, or the proceedings in which, the original conviction was obtained. There are numerous writs of habeas corpus, each applicable in different procedural circumstances. The full name of the ordinary writ of habeas corpus is *habeas corpus ad subjiciendum.*

bill of attainder A legislative act that inflicts capital punishment upon named persons without a judicial trial. Congress and the state legislatures are prohibited from issuing bills of attainder by the Constitution.

ex post facto law A law making a person criminally liable for an act that was not criminal at the time it was committed. The Constitution prohibits both Congress and the states from enacting such laws.

treason The act of transferring one's allegiance from one's own country to the enemy, and giving the enemy aid and comfort.

What follows is a brief introduction to the rights found in the Bill of Rights and subsequent amendments. You will learn more about most of these in subsequent chapters.

First Amendment

> Congress shall make no law respecting an establishment of religion, or prohibiting the free exercise thereof; or abridging the freedom of speech, or of the press; or the right of the people peaceably to assemble, and to petition the Government for a redress of grievances.

The First Amendment contains several rights that are central to American legal identity. First, there are two religious protections: the "establishment clause" and the "exercise clause." Because of the establishment clause, government may not establish an official national religion. Further, Congress is forbidden to favor any one religion or church over others. The exercise clause secures the rights of all individuals to worship any religion. Religious beliefs and thought are absolutely secure. However, religious conduct may be regulated in some circumstances. A government that seeks to regulate religious conduct must show that it has a compelling interest in so doing. Otherwise, the regulation is invalid. For example, the use of controlled substances (e.g., use of peyote by Native Americans) may be regulated even when that use is a legitimate and traditional part of a religion's practices.[2] In contrast, the right of adherents of Santería (a population exceeding 50,000 in southern Florida) to engage in animal sacrifice was held to override animal rights laws to the contrary.[3]

The framers believed that a "free market of ideas" was vital to the success of a democracy. Two clauses in the First Amendment were designed to facilitate the free exchange of ideas: the free speech and free press clauses.

The Supreme Court has interpreted *speech* to include all forms of "expression." Accordingly, speaking, writing, and expressive conduct are included within the ambit of the First Amendment. Expressive conduct includes the wearing of clothes and buttons, the displaying of flags, and the posting of signs.

Although protected to a great degree, the freedom of speech is not absolute. Over the years a large body of law has developed defining the right. Generally, commercial expression is subject to greater regulation than is political expression. Also, speech is protected to a greater extent than is expressive conduct. As is always true when a government attempts to regulate a constitutionally protected right, the government must have a compelling interest that outweighs the citizen's interest in exercising the right, if the regulation is to be valid. The Supreme Court has said that speech that creates a "clear and present danger" may be regulated.

The free press clause also protects the rights of individuals to express themselves. Censorship, which was used by the British to suppress dissent, is generally forbidden in the United States. Rather, persons injured by false publications must seek postpublication remedies, such as tort suits for defamation of character or public disclosure of private facts. Public officials may prevail in defamation suits only if the publisher possessed malice or acted with reckless disregard for the truth.

A few other limitations to the free speech and press clauses are worth mentioning. Obscenity and child pornography may be regulated. Also, because airwaves are considered public domain, television and radio broadcasts may be restricted to a greater extent than other forms of expression.

Finally, the First Amendment also guarantees citizens the right to peaceably assemble and petition their government. The right to petition government has not been the subject of much litigation and it is nearly absolute. People may assemble for any lawful purpose, with few restrictions; state and local fire laws are an example. Also, although the assembly and free speech clauses both protect the right to demonstrate, reasonable governmental regulation of demonstrations is permitted. Thus, a content-neutral law requiring a permit to demonstrate on public property is valid.

Even though the First Amendment refers only to Congress, through the process of **incorporation** this amendment, and most of the Bill of Rights, applies to the states as well.

Second Amendment

> A well regulated Militia, being necessary to the security of a free State, the right of the people to keep and bear Arms, shall not be infringed.

The precise meaning of the Second Amendment has not been determined. As to the right to bear arms, laws requiring waiting periods before final sales of guns, mandating registration of firearms, and prohibiting concealed weapons have all been upheld. This amendment applies to both the federal and state governments.

TERMS

incorporation The act of combining one thing with another.

Third Amendment

> No Soldier shall, in time of peace be quartered in any house, without the consent of the Owner, nor in time of war, but in a manner to be prescribed by law.

This provision was included in the Bill of Rights in reaction to a British practice of requiring families to house and feed soldiers without consent or compensation. The language of this provision makes it clear that it applies to both federal military and state militias.

Fourth Amendment

> The right of the people to be secure in their persons, houses, papers, and effects, against unreasonable searches and seizures, shall not be violated, and no Warrants shall issue, but upon probable cause, supported by Oath or affirmation, and particularly describing the place to be searched, and the persons or things to be seized.

The Fourth Amendment is one of the most critical to criminal procedure. It establishes the foundation rules that law enforcement officers must follow when conducting searches, seizures, and arrests. It applies to the states via the Fourteenth Amendment.

The Fourth Amendment has been interpreted as having two parts, the "reasonableness" requirement and the "warrants" requirement. As you will learn in later chapters, all searches, seizures, and arrests must be reasonable, but not all searches, seizures, and arrests have to occur under the authority of a warrant. You will discover much more about the Fourth Amendment in the following chapters.

Fifth Amendment

> No person shall be held to answer for a capital, or otherwise infamous crime, unless on a presentment or indictment of a Grand Jury, except in cases arising in the land or naval forces, or in the Militia, when in actual service in time of War or public danger; nor shall any person be subject for the same offence to be twice put in jeopardy of life or limb; nor shall he be compelled in any criminal case to be witness against himself, nor shall be deprived of life, liberty, or property, without due process of law; nor shall private property be taken for public use, without just compensation.

This amendment requires the federal government to indict, rather than charge through information, defendants charged with serious (*capital* or *infamous*) crimes. An **indictment** is a formal charge issued by a grand jury. An **information** is a formal charge filed by a prosecutor. A **grand jury** is a body of citizens that meets in secret and determines whether charges should be filed. This provision of the Fifth Amendment does not apply against the states. Therefore, a state may charge all defendants, regardless of the nature of their alleged crimes, by information. Many states, however, have their own constitutional or statutory grand jury rules.

The Fifth Amendment also contains the double jeopardy clause, which forbids both the federal and state governments from trying a person twice for the same crime or punishing a person twice for the same crime. Exceptions exist. For example, a defendant may be retried following a hung jury. Also, the rule only proscribes retrial by the same sovereign. Accordingly, two states, or the federal government and a state, may both try and punish the same individual for the same act.

Compelled self-incrimination is also prohibited by the Fifth Amendment. As a result, a defendant may remain silent forever—from the beginning of a police investigation through trial, sentencing, and appeal. The famous *Miranda v. Arizona* case,[4] wherein the Supreme Court announced a set of rules governing custodial interrogations by police, was founded upon the privilege against self-incrimination. A prosecutor is not even permitted to call a defendant to testify, for fear that a jury will be prejudiced in favor of conviction by hearing a defendant assert the right to be free from self-incrimination. Of course, the

TERMS

indictment 1. A charge made in writing by a grand jury, based upon evidence presented to it, accusing a person of having committed a criminal act, generally a felony. It is the function of the prosecution to bring a case before the grand jury. If the grand jury indicts the defendant, a trial follows. 2. The formal, written accusation itself brought before the grand jury by the prosecutor.

information 1. An accusation of the commission of a crime, sworn to by a district attorney or other prosecutor, on the basis of which a criminal defendant is brought to trial for a misdemeanor and, in some states, for a felony. 2. In some jurisdictions, which prosecute felonies only on the basis of indictment by a grand jury, an affidavit alleging probable cause to bind the defendant over to await action by the grand jury.

grand jury A body whose number varies with the jurisdiction, never less than 6 nor more than 23, whose duty it is to determine whether probable cause exists to return indictments against persons accused of committing crimes. The right to indictment by grand jury is guaranteed by the Fifth Amendment.

privilege may be waived. In the following chapters, you will learn of many more instances in which the privilege against self-incrimination is implicated.

This amendment also requires the government to provide "due process" any time it deprives a person of life, liberty, or property. *Due process* simply means "fair"; that is, the government must treat citizens fairly when life, liberty, or property is at stake. Due process has two forms, substantive and procedural. Laws may be substantively unfair (for example, laws declaring a person's status to be criminal are violative of due process). Thus, a person may be punished for drunk driving or public intoxication, but the same person cannot be punished for being an alcoholic.

Due process also requires the government to use a fair procedure. This usually requires the government to give notice of impending action and a fair hearing. In the criminal context, due process is more demanding than in the civil or administrative contexts.

The Fourteenth Amendment extended due process requirements to the states. Note that there is no mention of equal protection of the laws in the Fifth Amendment, but there is in the Fourteenth. The Supreme Court has interpreted the Fifth Amendment as including an equal protection requirement. Therefore, both the states and the federal government are bound by substantive due process, procedural due process, and equal protection requirements.

Sixth Amendment

> In all criminal prosecutions, the accused shall enjoy the right to a speedy and public trial, by an impartial jury of the State and district wherein the crime shall have been committed, which district shall have been previously ascertained by law, and to be informed of the nature and cause of the accusation; to be confronted with the witnesses against him; to have compulsory process for obtaining witnesses in his favor, and to have the Assistance of Counsel for his defence.

All defendants, whether in federal or state court, have the right to a speedy and public trial. The Supreme Court has not specifically defined *speedy,* but intentional delays or inexcusable neglect by the government in bringing a defendant to trial can lead to dismissal of charges. Most states have laws setting time periods within which a defendant must be tried. The period is shorter if a defendant is incarcerated pending trial. The "public" right is held by both the defendant and the public. Accordingly, trials are not automatically closed at a defendant's request. Citizens and the media may demand to be present under this and the First Amendment. Only in rare circumstances are portions of trials closed to the public.

Defendants have a right, under the Sixth Amendment, to be informed of the charges against them. This is also required by due process. At trial, defendants have the right to be present and confront their accusers, and also have the right to use the power of the court to compel witnesses to appear. The confrontation right is not absolute. For example, in some circumstances prosecutors are allowed to introduce videotaped depositions of witnesses who are unavailable for trial (e.g., a witness who has died). There is currently a controversy, and great differences of opinion among judges, concerning the use of remote television testimony. Some jurisdictions are permitting child abuse victims to testify via closed-circuit television from outside the courtroom to avoid the trauma of encountering the alleged perpetrator. The Supreme Court has not yet determined whether this violates a defendant's Sixth Amendment right to confrontation.

Finally, the Sixth Amendment provides that criminal defendants have a right to the assistance of counsel. Initially, this was interpreted as meaning only that a defendant had a right to have hired counsel. Today, the amendment assures indigent defendants the right to appointed counsel in any case in which imprisonment or another significant penalty may be imposed following conviction. Even more, a defendant may have his or her conviction overturned if he or she did not enjoy the "effective assistance of counsel." Counsel is ineffective if the competence of the attorney was substandard and that inability potentially affected the outcome of the case.

Seventh Amendment

> In Suits at common law, where the value in controversy shall exceed twenty dollars, the right of trial by jury shall be preserved, and no fact tried by a jury, shall be otherwise re-examined in any Court of the United States, than according to the rules of the common law.

This amendment does not apply to criminal proceedings. It secures the right to a jury in most federal civil trials. This amendment has not been incorporated. Therefore, the federal Constitution does not require juries in state civil trials.

Eighth Amendment

> Excessive bail shall not be required, nor excessive fines imposed, nor cruel and unusual punishments inflicted.

Bail is a payment of money or other assets in exchange for pretrial release. Defendants who become fugitive forfeit their bail. The objective of bail is to dissuade defendants from fleeing and to offset the costs associated with recovering fugitives. Bail is not a right. Some defendants may be held pending trial without bail, such as those who are likely to flee and those who pose a danger to witnesses. If bail is set, however, it must not be excessive.

Cruel and unusual punishments are prohibited. Certain punishments are **per se** cruel and thus are forbidden altogether, such as starving a person to death. Other punishments may not be per se cruel, but may be excessive or out of proportion to the crime committed. Life imprisonment, for example, is appropriate for rape but not for a parking ticket. It is unclear whether the fines clause applies to the states. The cruel and unusual punishment clause does apply against the states.

Ninth Amendment

> The enumeration in the Constitution, of certain rights, shall not be construed to deny or disparage others retained by the people.

Some of the framers who opposed including the Bill of Rights feared that its inclusion would be interpreted as limiting the rights of the people to those specifically enumerated in that Bill. To remedy this, the framers included the Ninth Amendment. Even though it clearly states that the people possess rights not found in the Constitution, the Ninth Amendment has never been used by the Supreme Court as the sole source of any right. It has been cited in support of other rights that are not expressed in the Constitution, such as the right to privacy.

Tenth Amendment

> The powers not delegated to the United States by Constitution, nor prohibited by it to the States, are reserved to the States respectively, or to the people.

TERMS

bail 1. The customary means of securing the release from custody of a person charged with a criminal offense, by assuring his or her appearance in court and compelling him or her to remain within the jurisdiction. 2. The security given for a defendant's appearance in court in the form of cash, real property, or a bail bond.

per se [Latin for] by itself; in and of itself.

Fearing that the federal government would become too powerful, the framers included the Tenth Amendment. It makes clear that the federal government has only limited powers. All powers not specifically assigned to the federal government belong to the states or to the people.

In recent years, the Supreme Court has interpreted the Tenth Amendment as a "truism." Said another way, it states the obvious, but is not an independent source of state powers. The states only have the remaining powers. So, as federal jurisdiction expands, state jurisdiction shrinks. This is what has occurred during the past 100 years. The federal government has used its delegated powers, especially over interstate commerce and civil rights, to increase its authority over the states and individuals. Like the Ninth Amendment, the Tenth has never been used to declare a new individual right.

Other Amendments

Important rights are also found in amendments subsequent to the Bill of Rights.

Amendment XIII

Section 1 Neither slavery nor involuntary servitude, except as punishment for crime whereof the party shall have been duly convicted, shall exist within the United States, or any place subject to their jurisdiction.

Section 2 Congress shall have power to enforce this article by appropriate legislation

Amendment XIV [in relevant part]

No State shall make or enforce any law which shall abridge the privileges or immunities of citizens of the United States; nor shall any State deprive any person of life, liberty, or property, without due process of law; nor deny to any person within its jurisdiction the equal protection of the laws.

Amendment XV

Section 1 The right of citizens of the United States to vote shall not be denied or abridged by the United States or by any State on account of race, color, or previous condition of servitude.

Section 2 The Congress shall have power to enforce this article by appropriate legislation.

The Thirteenth, Fourteenth, and Fifteenth Amendments are known as the *Civil War Amendments*. The Thirteenth outlaws slavery and the Fifteenth extends the vote to all people, regardless of color or previous condition of servitude.

The Fourteenth Amendment is important because it contains the due process and equal protection clauses that apply to the states. You will learn in Chapter 4 that it is the Fourteenth Amendment's due process clause that is used to guarantee rights to defendants in state criminal proceedings. The equal protection clause prohibits certain forms of discrimination by the government. In most instances, discrimination based upon race, religion, or gender is impermissible. There are exceptions, however. So-called **statutory rape** laws may punish men who victimize girls more severely than women who victimize boys because the government has a legitimate interest in preventing pregnancy in such circumstances.

Only the rights that are important in the criminal context have been introduced in this discussion. You will learn more about these and other rights in the following chapters. You may want to refer to this section or to the Constitution (reproduced in the Appendix) during discussions of constitutional rights.

TERMS

statutory rape Sexual intercourse with a female under the age of consent, with or without her consent.

Review Questions

1. What is the name of the first constitution of the United States?
2. In what year was the current United States constitution ratified?
3. In what year was the Bill of Rights ratified?
4. What amendment to the Constitution requires that searches and seizures be reasonable?
5. What amendment to the Constitution establishes a privilege against self-incrimination?
6. What amendment to the Constitution prohibits cruel and unusual punishments?
7. What does *habeas corpus* translate to, and what is its purpose?
8. What is an ex post facto law? Are such laws legal?
9. What amendment guarantees the right to speech, press, and religion?
10. Why did the framers design such a complex structure of government (i.e., the federal form and the tripartite separation of powers)?

Review Problems

1. In your opinion, why are courts reluctant to declare new rights under the Ninth Amendment?
2. Is there a right you would include in the Constitution that is not there? Is there one you believe should not have been included that is there? Explain your answers.

Notes

1 *The Bill of Rights and Beyond, The Fourth Amendment,* Bicentennial Calendar (Commission on the Bicentennial of the Constitution, 1991).

2 *Department of Human Resources v. Smith,* 494 U.S. 872 (1990).

3 *Church of Lukumi Babalu Aye, Inc. v. Hialeah,* 113 S. Ct. 2217 (1993).

4 384 U.S. 436 (1966).

CHAPTER 4

FEDERAL AND STATE CONSTITUTIONALISM

CHAPTER OUTLINE

> *State problems should involve state solutions.*
>
> ***Ronald Reagan***
> ***United States President***

§ 4.1 Introduction

Criminal justice is a policy subject that belongs largely to the states. Nearly 95 percent of all criminal prosecutions occur in state courts. Not only do the states conduct most of the prosecutions, but each state is also free, with few limitations, to design its criminal justice system in any manner it chooses. This was especially true in the early years of the United States. For the most part, the national government did not involve itself in state criminal law for 150 years.

This began to change in the 1950s, and today the United States plays a major role in defining the rights of criminal defendants in state prosecutions, as well as federal. The source of federal involvement is the United States Constitution, and two developments account for its increased role in state criminal law. First, the reach of the Constitution has been extended to the states through what is known as *incorporation*. Second, the rights found in the Bill of Rights have been significantly expanded.

§ 4.2 Incorporation

Prior to the adoption of the Fourteenth Amendment, the Bill of Rights guarantees were interpreted by the Supreme Court as restricting the power of the national government only. That meant that fundamental rights, such as the right to counsel and the right to be free from unreasonable searches and seizures, were guaranteed to a defendant only when prosecuted in federal court. If a state did not have a constitutional or statutory provision granting the right, the defendant was not entitled to its protection when prosecuted in state court.

In 1868 the Fourteenth Amendment to the United States Constitution was adopted. One objective of the Fourteenth Amendment is to protect certain civil liberties from state action. Section One of that amendment reads:

> All persons born or naturalized in the United States, and subject to the jurisdiction thereof, are citizens of the United States and of the State wherein they reside. No State shall make or enforce any law which shall abridge the privileges or immunities of citizens of the United States; nor shall any State deprive any person of life, liberty, or property, without due process of law; nor deny to any person within its jurisdiction the equal protection of the laws.

The language of the Fourteenth Amendment is similar to that found in the Fifth Amendment, insofar as they both contain a due process clause. It is through the due process and equal protection clauses that the powers of the states are limited. However, what is meant by *due process* has been the subject of great debate among jurists.

Note that the language of the Fourteenth Amendment does not include any of the specific guarantees found in the Bill of Rights, except that it requires the states to afford due process whenever depriving a person of life, liberty, or property. Thus, one of the most important issues raised in the context of the Fourteenth Amendment is whether it includes the rights found in the Bill of Rights, such as the rights to counsel, to freedom of the press, to freedom of speech, to freedom from self-incrimination, to freedom from unreasonable searches and seizures, and to freedom from cruel and unusual punishments. Several theories have developed in answer to this question.

At one extreme is the *independent content approach.* Under this theory, the Fourteenth Amendment's due process clause does not include any right found in the Bill of Rights, that is, due process does not overlap with the Bill of Rights. Rather, due process has an independent content and none of the rights secured in the Bill of Rights apply against the states. The Supreme Court has never adopted this position.

At the other extreme is *total incorporation.* Proponents of total incorporation, who included Supreme Court Associate Justice Black, argue that the entire Bill of Rights is incorporated by the Fourteenth Amendment and that all the rights contained therein may be asserted by defendants in both state and federal courts. The incorporation occurs automatically, as the proponents of this position believe that the drafters of the Fourteenth Amendment intended to incorporate the entire Bill of Rights. Under this approach, however, the due process clause was limited to recognizing rights contained in the Bill of Rights. Another group of jurists have been labeled *"total incorporation plus,"* because they contend that the due process clause not only incorporates the Bill of Rights, but also secures additional independent rights. Neither of these positions has been adopted by the Supreme Court.

Another position, which was held by the Supreme Court until the 1960s, is known as *fundamental fairness.* Those rights that are "fundamental" and "essential to an ordered liberty" are incorporated through this approach. The fundamental fairness doctrine held that no relationship existed between the Bill of Rights and those deemed fundamental, although the rights recognized under the fundamental fairness doctrine may parallel rights recognized by the Bill of Rights.

The Supreme Court rejected the fundamental fairness doctrine in the 1960s and replaced it with the *selective incorporation doctrine* (see Figure 4-1). Similar to the fundamental fairness doctrine, a right is incorporated under this doctrine if it is both fundamental and essential to the concept of ordered liberty. Like the fundamental fairness approach, independent rights are also recognized under selective incorporation analysis.

However, the two approaches differ in two major respects. First, under the fundamental fairness approach, cases were analyzed case-by-case. That is, it was possible to have essentially the same facts with different outcomes under the fundamental fairness doctrine. Critics charged that the approach was too subjective. Under the selective incorporation method, blanket rules are established to act as precedent for all similar cases in the future. In addition, the entire body of precedent interpreting a federal amendment becomes applicable to the states as a result of an amendments incorporation.

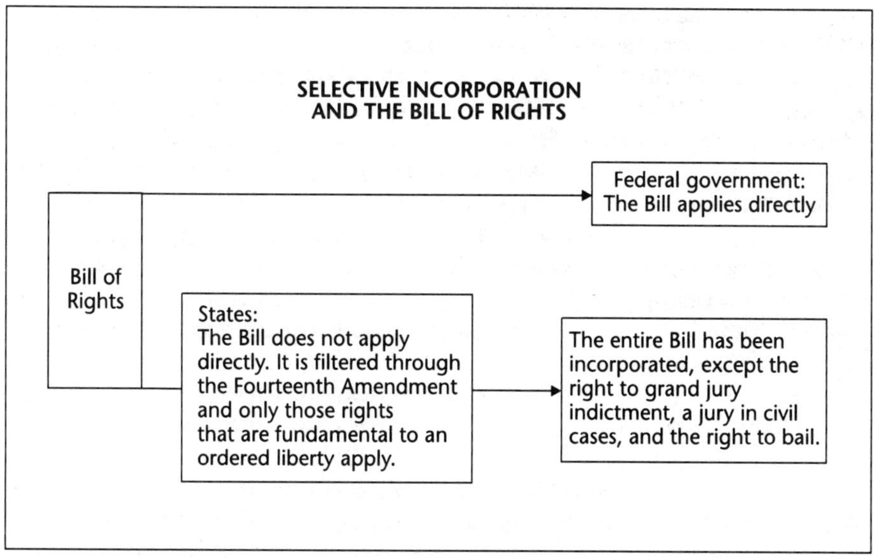

FIGURE 4-1 Selective Incorporation and the Bill of Rights

Second, selective incorporation gives special attention to the rights contained in the Bill of Rights. A right secured by the Bill of Rights is more likely to be protected by the Fourteenth Amendment's due process clause than others. Selective incorporation continues to be the approach of the Supreme Court today.

Nearly the entire Bill of Rights has been incorporated under the selective incorporation doctrine. The right to grand jury indictment has not been incorporated,[1] nor has the right to a jury trial in civil cases. Once incorporated, a right applies against the states to the extent and in the same manner as it does against the United States. Also, several independent due process rights have been declared. You will learn many of these in the following chapters.

§ 4.3 Expansion of Rights

Another major development in the area of constitutional criminal procedure has been the expansion of many rights. The language of the Constitution is concise. It refers to "unreasonable searches and seizures," "due process," "equal protection," "speedy and public trial," and so on. No further definition or explanation of the meaning of these provisions is provided. The process of determining the meaning of such phrases is known as *constitutional interpretation.* It is possible to make each right ineffective by reading it narrowly. The opposite is also true.

During the 1960s, many rights found in the Bill of Rights were expanded by court decisions. *Expansion* refers to extending a right beyond its most narrow reading. The effect of expansive interpretation is to increase defendants' rights. An example of an expansive interpretation is the *Miranda v. Arizona* decision, 384 U.S. 436 (1966). Although the language of the Fifth Amendment does not explicitly state that a defendant must be advised of the right to remain silent, to have the assistance of counsel, and so forth, the Court now requires that such admonishments be given because of an expanded interpretation of the Fifth Amendment.

Another example of expanded individual rights is the right to privacy. No explicit constitutional language provides for a right to privacy. However, the Supreme Court has found a right to privacy to be implicit in the Constitution. The Court has held that the right to privacy protects a woman's right to abortion, in some circumstances,[2] and a couple's right to use contraceptives,[3] amongst many others. Many more expansions will be discussed later.

§ 4.4 Exclusionary Rule

Another important constitutional development was the creation of the **exclusionary rule**. The rule is simple: Evidence that is obtained by an unconstitutional search or seizure is inadmissible at trial.

The rule was first announced by the Supreme Court in 1914.[4] However, at that time the rule had not been incorporated, and therefore the exclusionary rule did not apply to state court proceedings. This changed in 1961 when the Supreme Court declared that evidence obtained in violation of the Constitution could not be used in state or federal criminal proceedings. The case was *Mapp v. Ohio*.

The exclusionary rule has been the subject of intense debate. There is no explicit textual language establishing the rule in the Constitution. For that reason, many contend that the Supreme Court exceeded its authority by creating the rule; that it is the responsibility of the legislative branch to make such laws.

On the other side is the argument that without the exclusionary rule, the Bill of Rights is ineffective. Why have constitutional standards if there is no method to enforce them? For example, why require that the officers in the *Mapp* case have a search warrant, yet permit them to conduct a warrantless search and use the evidence obtained against the defendant? These questions go to the purpose of the exclusionary rule: it discourages law enforcement personnel from engaging in unconstitutional conduct.

The exclusionary rule works to prevent the admission into evidence of any item, confession, or other thing that was obtained by law enforcement officers in an unconstitutional manner. The evidence must have been obtained by the police in an unlawful manner. However, if a private citizen working on his or her own obtains evidence illegally and then turns it over to the police, it may be admitted.[5] People hired or authorized to assist the police are considered agents of the government, and therefore the exclusionary rule applies to their actions.

The exclusionary rule does not apply to pretrial matters. A defendant may not challenge a grand jury indictment because the grand jury considered illegally obtained evidence. The defendant's remedy is at trial. In addition, a defendant may not refuse to answer questions

TERMS

exclusionary rule The rule of constitutional law that evidence secured by the police by means of an unreasonable search and seizure, in violation of the Fourth Amendment, cannot be used as evidence in a criminal prosecution.

before a grand jury concerning illegally obtained evidence. In most cases, but not all, evidence obtained illegally may be used at sentencing.

Another important exception to the exclusionary rule allows the government to use illegally seized evidence to rebut statements made by a defendant.[6] The government may not use the evidence if the defendant does not "open the door."

Most exclusionary rule issues are resolved prior to trial by way of a motion to suppress. In some instances the motion may be made at the moment the prosecutor attempts to introduce such evidence at trial. This is known as a *contemporaneous objection*. The administration of the exclusionary rule is discussed in § 4.5.

MAPP
v.
OHIO
367 U.S. 643 (1961)

Appellant stands convicted of knowingly having had in her possession and under her control certain lewd and lascivious books, pictures, and photographs in violation [of Ohio law]. ...

On May 23, 1957, three Cleveland police officers arrived at appellant's residence in that city pursuant to information that "a person [was] hiding out in the home, who was wanted for questioning in connection with a recent bombing." ...

Upon their arrival at that house, the officers knocked on the door and demanded entrance but appellant, after telephoning her attorney, refused to admit them without a search warrant. They advised their headquarters of the situation and undertook a surveillance of the house.

The officers again sought entrance some three hours later when four or more additional officers arrived on the scene. When Miss Mapp did not come to the door immediately, at least one of the several doors to the house was forcibly opened and the policemen gained admittance. Meanwhile Miss Mapp's attorney arrived, but the officers, having secured their own entry, and continuing in their defiance of the law, would permit him neither to see Miss Mapp nor to enter the house. It appears that Miss Mapp was halfway down the stairs from the upper floor to the front door when the officers, in this highhanded manner, broke into the hall. She demanded to see the search warrant. A paper, claimed to be a warrant, was held up by one of the officers. She grabbed the "warrant" and placed it in her bosom. A struggle ensued in which the officers recovered the piece of paper and as a result of which they handcuffed appellant because she had been "belligerent" in resisting their official rescue of the "warrant" from her person. Running roughshod over appellant, a policeman "grabbed" her, "twisted [her] hand," and she "yelled [and] pleaded with him" because "it was hurting." Appellant, in handcuffs, was then forcibly taken upstairs to her bedroom where the officers searched a dresser, a chest of drawers, a closet and some suitcases. They also looked into a photo album and through personal papers belonging to the appellant. The search spread ... . The obscene materials for possession of which she was ultimately convicted were discovered in the course of that widespread search.

At the trial no search warrant was produced by the prosecution, nor was the failure to produce one explained or accounted for. At best, "There is, in the record, considerable doubt as to whether there ever was any warrant for the search."...

We hold that all evidence obtained by searches and seizures in violation of the Constitution is, by that same authority, inadmissible in a state court.

Since the Fourth Amendment's right of privacy has been declared enforceable against the States through the Due Process Clause of the Fourteenth, it is enforceable against them by the same sanction of exclusion as it used against the Federal Government. ...

Moreover, our holding that the exclusionary rule is an essential part of both the Fourth and Fourteenth Amendments is not only the logical dictate of prior cases, but it also makes very good sense. There is no war between the Constitution and common sense. Presently, a federal prosecutor may make no use of evidence illegally seized, but a State's attorney across the street may, although he supposedly is operating under the enforceable prohibitions of the same Amendment. Thus the State, by admitting evidence unlawfully seized, serves to encourage disobedience to the Federal Constitution which it is bound to uphold.

SIDEBAR

The Exclusionary Rule in Practice

Few topics in criminal procedure are as controversial and divisive as the exclusionary rule. Clearly the public perception of the rule is that it is a device that frees the guilty, allowing murderers, rapists, and other miscreants to continue their carnage because of technicalities. Whether constraining the government to constitutional procedures is merely technical is for each individual to decide.

In spite of its reputation, the exclusionary rule is not responsible for opening the door for countless criminals. In fact, less than 0.02 percent of all felony arrests in the United States are not prosecuted because of exclusionary rule problems. Davies, "A Hard Look At What We Know (And Still Need To Learn) About The 'Costs' of The Exclusionary Rule," 1983 *A.B.F. Research J.* 611, 635, cited in *Commonwealth v. Edmunds,* 526 Pa. 374 (1991). The total number of cases not prosecuted and unsuccessfully prosecuted that are attributable to the exclusionary rule is estimated at between 0.6 percent and 2.35 percent. *Id.*

In another study of federal cases, searches and seizures were conducted in 30 percent of the prosecutions, and 11 percent of all defendants filed motions to suppress on Fourth Amendment grounds. Motions to suppress were only granted in 1.3 percent of the total number of cases, and half of the defendants who were successful in having evidence suppressed were convicted. In cases not prosecuted, exclusionary rule problems were the cause in only 0.4 percent. Report of the Comptroller General, *Impact of the Exclusionary Rule on Federal Criminal Prosecutions* (1979).

Exclusionary Rule and Exceptions

The Rule: Evidence obtained by the government in an unconstitutional or otherwise illegal manner is inadmissible at criminal trial, unless one of the exceptions applies. The rule is not specifically expressed in the Constitution, but has been held to be implicitly part of the Fourth, Fifth, Sixth, and Fourteenth Amendments.

Exceptions and Limitations:

1. Pretrial hearings, including grand jury review
2. Sentencing
3. Independent source
4. Inevitable discovery
5. Rebuttal evidence
6. Evidence obtained by private source
7. Standing

§ 4.5 Fruit of the Poisonous Tree

The exclusionary rule applies to *primary evidence,* that is, evidence that is the direct result of an illegal search or seizure. It is possible that such primary evidence may lead the police to other evidence. Suppose that police officers beat a confession out of a bank robber. In that confession the defendant tells the police where he has hidden the stolen money. The confession is the primary evidence and is inadmissible under the exclusionary rule. The money (after it is retrieved by the police) is secondary, or "derivative," evidence. Such evidence is known as **fruit of the poisonous tree** and is also inadmissible. Generally, evidence that is "tainted" by the prior illegal conduct is inadmissible. The rule does not make all evidence later obtained by law enforcement inadmissible. In some instances, evidence may be admissible because the connection between the illegally seized evidence and the subsequently obtained evidence is marginal, or as the Supreme Court has stated it, "the causal connection ... may have become so attenuated as to dissipate the taint."[7]

Another situation in which such evidence may be admitted is when an independent source exists. An independent source must be an unconnected and legal method of obtaining evidence. Consider the preceding bank robbery example. If a co-conspirator in the robbery also told the police where the money is, it is admissible regardless of the illegal confession, so long as the co-conspirator's admission was lawfully obtained.

TERMS

fruit of the poisonous tree doctrine The constitutional law doctrine that evidence, including derivative evidence, obtained as the result of an illegal search is inadmissible.

Finally, evidence that would inevitably have been discovered by law enforcement may be admitted. This doctrine is similar to the **independent source** doctrine. However, police must actually obtain evidence from an untainted, lawful source to invoke the independent source doctrine. The **inevitable discovery doctrine** holds that evidence that is the fruit of an illegal search, seizure, or arrest may be admitted if it is probable that the evidence would have been obtained lawfully at a later date.

§ 4.6 Standing

A defendant must have **standing** before he or she may successfully have evidence suppressed. There are two aspects to standing. First, the person challenging the evidence must have an adversarial interest in the proceeding. Basically, only defendants in criminal cases may challenge evidence as seized in violation of the Fourth Amendment. A defendant's mother may not intervene in the criminal case and attempt to have evidence suppressed because her Fourth Amendment rights were violated by an illegal search and seizure—even if the claim is true. A mother lacks standing to make the claim.

The second aspect concerns the defendant's interest in the area searched or thing seized. A defendant must have a reasonable expectation of privacy to a place or thing before he or she can have it excluded at trial. To say it another way, the defendant's constitutional rights must have been violated before evidence will be suppressed.

TERMS

independent source rule Although evidence gained as the result of government misconduct cannot be used in a criminal prosecution, the facts obtained by such conduct are admissible if the government gained knowledge of these facts from an independent source.

inevitable discovery rule The fruit of the poisonous tree doctrine does not bar the introduction into evidence of facts obtained by a search that violates the Fourth Amendment, or a confession secured in violation of the Sixth Amendment, if the facts would have been discovered whether or not the illegal conduct occurred.

standing The position of a person with respect to his or her capacity to act in particular circumstances.

standing to sue The legal capacity to bring and to maintain a lawsuit. A person is without standing to sue unless some interest of his or hers has been adversely affected or unless he or she has been injured by the defendant. The term "standing to sue" is often shortened simply to "standing."

Therefore, the defendant may not assert his mother's right to be free from illegal searches and seizures. The *Rakas* case turned on questions of standing.

RAKAS
v.
ILLINOIS
439 U.S. 128 (1978)

Mr. Justice Rehnquist delivered the opinion of the Court. ...

A police officer on a routine patrol received a radio call notifying him of a robbery of a clothing store in Bourbonnais, Ill., and describing the getaway car. Shortly thereafter, the office spotted an automobile which he thought might be the getaway car. After following the car for some time and after the arrival of assistance, he and several other officers stopped the vehicle. The occupants of the automobile, petitioners and two female companions, were ordered out of the car and, after the occupants had left the car, two officers searched the interior of the vehicle. They discovered a box of rifle shells in the glove compartment, which had been locked, and a sawed-off rifle under the front passenger seat. ... After discovering the rifle and the shells, the officers took petitioners to the station and placed them under arrest.

Before trial petitioners moved to suppress the rifle and shells seized from the car on the ground that the search violated the Fourth and Fourteenth Amendments. They conceded that they did not own the automobile and were simply passengers; the owner of the car had been the driver of the vehicle at the time of the search. Nor did they assert that they owned the rifle or the shells seized. ... The trial court [held] that petitioners lacked standing and denied the motion to suppress the evidence. ...

Petitioners first urge us to relax or broaden the rule of standing enunciated in Jones v. United States, 362 U.S. 257 (1960), so that any criminal defendant at whom a search was "directed" would have standing to contest the legality of that search and object to the admission at trial of evidence obtained as a result of the search. Alternatively, petitioners argue that they have standing to object to the search under *Jones* because they were "legitimately on [the] premises" at the time of the search. ...

We decline to extend the rule of standing in Fourth Amendment cases in the manner suggested by petitioners. As we stated in Alderman v. United States, 394 U.S. 165, 174 (1969), "Fourth Amendment rights are personal rights which like some other constitutional rights, may not be vicariously asserted." ... A person who is aggrieved by an illegal search and seizure only through the introduction of damaging evidence secured by a search of third person's premises or property has not had any of his Fourth Amendment rights infringed. And since the exclusionary rule is an attempt to effectuate the guarantees of the Fourth Amendment, ... it is proper to permit only defendants whose Fourth Amendment rights have been violated to benefit from the rule's protections. ... There is no reason to think that a party whose rights have been infringed will not, if evidence is used against him, have ample motivation to move to suppress it. ... Even if such a person is not a defendant in the action, he may be able to recover damages for the violation of his Fourth Amendment rights, see Monroe v. Pape, 365 U.S. 167 (1961), or seek redress under state law of invasion of privacy or trespass. ...

Conferring standing to raise vicarious Fourth Amendment claims would necessarily mean a more widespread invocation of the exclusionary rule during criminal trials. ... Each time the exclusionary rule is applied it exacts a substantial social cost for the vindication of fourth Amendment rights. Relevant and reliable evidence is kept from the trier of fact and the search for the truth at trial is deflected. ...

Here petitioners, who were passengers occupying a car which they neither owned nor leased, seek to analogize their position to that of the defendant in Jones v. United States. In *Jones,* petitioner was present at the time of the search of an apartment which was owned by a friend. ...

We do not question the conclusion in *Jones* that the defendant in that case suffered a violation of his personal Fourth Amendment rights if the search in question was unlawful. Nonetheless, we believe that the phrase "legitimately on premises" coined in *Jones* creates too broad a gauge for measurement of Fourth Amendment rights. For example, applied literally, this statement would permit a casual visitor who has never seen, or been permitted to visit, the basement of another's house to object to a search of the basement if the visitor happened to be in the kitchen of the house at the time of the search. ...

We think that *Jones* on its facts merely stands for the unremarkable proposition that a person can have a legally sufficient interest in a place other than his own home so that the Fourth Amendment protects him from unreasonable governmental intrusion into that place. ...

In defining the scope of that interest, we adhere to the view expressed in *Jones* and echoed in later cases that arcane distinctions developed in property and tort law between guests, licensees, invitees, and the like, ought not to control.

Katz v. United States, 389 U.S. 347 (1967), provides guidance in defining the scope of the interest protected by the Fourth Amendment. ... *Katz* held that capacity to claim the protection of the Fourth Amendment depends ... upon whether the person who claims the protection of the Amendment has a legitimate expectation of privacy in the invaded place. ... Viewed in this manner, the holding in *Jones* can best be explained by the fact that Jones had a legitimate expectation of privacy in the premises he was using and therefore could claim the protection of the Fourth Amendment with respect to a governmental invasion of those premises, even though his "interest" in those premises might not have been a recognized property interest at common law. ...

Our Brother White in dissent expresses the view that by rejecting the phrase "legitimately on [the] premises" as the appropriate measure of Fourth Amendment rights, we are abandoning a thoroughly workable, "bright line" test in favor of a less certain analysis of whether the facts of a particular case give rise to a legitimate expectation of privacy. ... If "legitimately on premises" were the successful litmus test of Fourth Amendment rights that he assumes it is, his approach would have at least the merit of easy application, whatever it lacked in fidelity to the history and purposes of the Fourth Amendment. But a reading of lower court cases ... reveals that this expression is not a shorthand summary for a bright-line rule which somehow encapsulates the "core" of the Fourth Amendment's protections.

The dissent itself shows that the facile consistency it is striving for is illusory. The dissenters concede that "there comes a point when use of an area is shared with so many that one simply cannot reasonably expect seclusion." ... But surely the "point" referred to is not one demarcating a line which is black on one side and white on another; it is inevitably a point which separates one shade of gray from another. We are likewise told by the dissent that a person "legitimately on *private* premises ... , though his privacy is *not absolute,* is entitled to expect that he is sharing it only with those persons [allowed there] and that governmental officials will intrude only with *consent* or by complying with the Fourth Amendment." ... (emphasis added). This single sentence describing the contours of the supposedly easily applied rule virtually abounds with unanswered questions: What are "private" premises? Indeed, what are the "premises?" It may be easy to describe the "premises" when one is confronted with a 1-room apartment, but what of the case of a 10-room house, or of a house with an attached garage that is searched? Also, if one's privacy is not absolute, how is it bounded? If he risks governmental intrusion "with consent," who may give that consent? ...

In abandoning "legitimately on premises" for the doctrine that we announce today, we are not forsaking a time-tested and workable rule, which has produced consistent results when applied, solely for the sake of fidelity to the values underlying the Fourth Amendment. Rather, we are rejecting blind adherence to a phrase which at most has superficial clarity and which conceals underneath that thin veneer all of the problems of line drawing which must be faced in any conscientious effort to apply the Fourth Amendment. Where the factual premises for a rule are so generally prevalent that little would be lost and much would be gained by abandoning case-by-case analysis, we have not hesitated to do so. See United States v. Robinson, 414 U.S. 218, 235 (1973). But the phrase "legitimately on premises" has not been shown to be an easily applicable measure of Fourth Amendment rights so much as it has proved to be simply a label placed by the courts on results which have not been subjected to careful analysis. We would not wish to be understood as saying that legitimate presence on the premises is irrelevant to one's expectation of privacy, but it cannot be deemed controlling.

Judged by the foregoing analysis, petitioners' claims must fail. They asserted neither a property nor a possessory interest in the automobile, nor an interest in the property seized. And as we have previously indicated, the fact that they were "legitimately on [the] premises" in the sense that they were in the car with the permission of its owner is not determinative of whether they had a legitimate expectation of privacy in the particular areas of the automobile searched. ...

The Illinois courts were therefore correct in concluding that it was unnecessary to decide whether the search of the car might have violated the rights secured to someone else by the Fourth and Fourteenth Amendments to the United States Constitution. Since it did not violate any rights of these petitioners, their judgment of conviction is

Affirmed.

§ 4.7 Conflicting Rights

In *Simmons v. United States,*[8] the Supreme Court held that a defendant may testify at a suppression hearing without waiving the right not to testify at trial and that any testimony given at a suppression hearing by a defendant may not be used against him or her at trial.

Simmons eliminated the quandary many defendants had: should they give incriminating evidence during a suppression hearing in hopes of having the evidence excluded? Of course, if the suppression claim was unsuccessful, then a defendant faced the incriminating testimony at trial. This put many defendants in a position of having to choose one right or another: the right to be free from self-incrimination versus the right to have illegally seized evidence excluded from trial. The Supreme Court held that defendants should be free from such dilemmas.

§ 4.8 Supreme Court Influence

During the 1960s and early 1970s, many jurists predicted that the Supreme Court would become so involved with criminal procedure that it would, in effect, write its own "constitutional criminal procedure code." This has not proven to be true; however, many areas of criminal procedure are greatly influenced by Supreme Court decisions. It is common to refer to the expansion of individual rights and the extension of those rights to the states as the *constitutionalization* of criminal procedure.

In recent years, though, there appears to be a trend away from expansive interpretation. This is in large part because the composition of the Supreme Court is more conservative than it was during the 1960s. Some believe that the trend of increasing individual rights was hindering law enforcement and welcome regression. Those who believe strongly in the rights of the individual proclaim that it is better to free ten guilty persons than to imprison one innocent person. In any event, it is probable that the Supreme Court's policy of favoring expansive interpretation of individual rights is likely to cease.

§ 4.9 State Constitutions and the "New Federalism"

Each state has its own constitution. Most states' bills of rights are identical in language to the national Constitution's Bill of Rights. There are exceptions, however. For example, Florida's Bill of Rights protects "expression," whereas the national Constitution protects "speech." As you will learn later, however, the term *speech* has been interpreted as meaning "expression." Also, the Florida Constitution expressly protects the right to privacy and the national Constitution does not. Rather, a national right to privacy has only recently been declared by the Supreme Court and is somewhat controversial because of the absence of express language establishing that right in the Constitution.

Until recently, state constitutions have not played an important role in defining civil liberties. This is because both state and federal courts have looked almost exclusively to the national Constitution to answer questions concerning civil liberties. It is also due to the tendency of state courts to interpret state constitutional rights as identical to those secured by the national Constitution.

Increasingly, this is not the case. During the past two decades, commentators, judges, and attorneys have exhibited a renewed interest in state constitutional law. The resurgence in state constitutional law is known as the "New Federalism." State constitutions can be an independent source of civil liberties. Of course, a state constitution cannot be used to limit or encroach on a federally secured right, but it can be used to extend the scope of a right.

In several instances, state courts have determined that their state constitutions protect criminal defendants to a greater extent than does the national Constitution. The Supreme Court of Pennsylvania strongly asserted that its state's constitution has its own meaning separate and independent from the federal Constitution. In a 1991 case, that Court stated:

> [T]he decisions of the [U.S. Supreme] Court are not, and should not be, dispositive of questions regarding rights guaranteed by counterpart provisions of State Law. Accordingly, such decisions are not mechanically applicable to state law issues, and state court judges and members of the bar seriously err if they so treat them. Rather, state court judges, and also practitioners, do well to scrutinize constitutional decisions by federal courts, for only if they are found to be logically persuasive and well-reasoned, paying due regard to precedent and the policies underlying specific constitutional guarantees, may they properly claim persuasive weight as guide posts when interpreting counterpart state guarantees.[9]

The California courts have taken a similar approach. Even if a provision's interpretation parallels national law, the courts favor citing state law over federal law.

Whether a state court depends on state or federal law in defining a right determines what court has the final word on the subject. If a right is founded upon federal law, the Supreme Court of the United States is the final arbiter. If a right is founded upon state law, the highest court of the state is the final arbiter, again assuming that no federal right is encroached upon by the state decision. This problem normally arises when one person's exercise of a right affects another person's rights. For example, if a state court were to find that a fetus has a right to life in every instance, the decision would be void as violative of the federally secured right to privacy held by the mothers to elect abortions in some circumstances.

If a state court relies upon federal law when defining a right, the possibility of reversal by a federal court, usually the Supreme Court, exists. This is what occurred in California concerning the use of peyote, a drug made from cactus, by Native Americans. The Supreme Court of California decided in 1965 that the use of peyote by Native Americans during religious ceremonies was protected by the U.S. Constitution's

First Amendment free exercise of religion clause.[10] That decision was not disturbed until 1990, when the Supreme Court of the United States decided that the regulation of peyote as a drug was a reasonable burden upon the First Amendment[11] and therefore reversed the 1965 California decision. Although the defendant asserted both the federal and state free exercise guarantees, the California Supreme Court relied entirely upon federal law in making its decision. Whether that court will later find the activity protected by the California constitution remains to be seen.

Today, state courts are looking to state law with increasing frequency to define civil rights. Even when state courts rely on federal law, it is common to cite state law as well, thereby providing an alternative basis for upholding a decision.

The *Leon* case, issued by the Supreme Court of the United States, recognized a good-faith exception to the exclusionary rule; the *Edmunds* decision, by the Supreme Court of Pennsylvania, expressly rejects the good-faith exception in state prosecutions.

UNITED STATES
v.
LEON
468 U.S. 897 (1984)

[Facially valid warrants were issued by a state judge. The searches conducted under the warrants produced narcotics and other evidence of narcotics violations.]

The respondents ... filed motions to suppress the evidence seized pursuant to the warrant. The District Court held an evidentiary hearing and, while recognizing that the case was a close one, ... granted the motions to suppress in part. It concluded that the affidavit was insufficient to establish probable cause. ... In response to a request from the Government, the court made clear that Officer Rombach had acted in good faith. ... [This decision was affirmed on appeal before the court of appeals.]

The Government's petition for certiorari expressly declined to seek review of the lower courts' determinations that the search warrant was unsupported by probable cause and presented only the question "[w]hether the Fourth Amendment exclusionary rule should be modified so as not to bar the admission of evidence seized in reasonable, good-faith reliance on a search warrant that is subsequently held to be defective." ...

[T]he exclusionary rule is designed to deter police misconduct rather than to punish the errors of judges and magistrates. ...

If exclusion of evidence obtained pursuant to a subsequently invalidated warrant is to have any deterrent effect, therefore, it must alter the behavior of the individual law enforcement officers or the policies of their departments. One could argue that applying the exclusionary rule in cases where the police failed to demonstrate probable cause in the warrant application deters future inadequate presentations or "magistrate shopping" and thus promotes the ends of the Fourth Amendment. Suppressing evidence obtained pursuant to a technically defective warrant supported by probable cause also might encourage officers to scrutinize more closely the form of the warrant and to point out suspected judicial errors. We find such arguments speculative and conclude that suppression of evidence obtained pursuant to a warrant should be ordered only on a case-by-case basis and only in those unusual cases in which exclusion will further the purposes of the exclusionary rule.

We conclude that the marginal or nonexistent benefits produced by suppressing evidence obtained in objectively reasonable reliance on a subsequently invalidated search warrant cannot justify the substantial costs of exclusion. We do not suggest, however, that exclusion is always inappropriate in cases where an officer has obtained a warrant and abided by its terms. ... [A]n officer's reliance on the magistrate's probable-cause determination and on the technical sufficiency of the warrant he issues must be objectively reasonable ... and it is clear that in some circumstances the officer will have no reasonable grounds for believing that the warrant was properly issued.

As another example, several states have not followed the Supreme Court's lead in allowing statements made in violation of *Miranda* to be used by the prosecution in impeachment of a defendant.[12] These are but a few of the many instances in which a right has received greater protection under state law than under federal law.[13]

COMMONWEALTH
v.
EDMUNDS
526 Pa. 374 (1991)

[Defendant who was convicted in the Court of Common Pleas, Criminal Division, of possession of marijuana and related offenses, appealed. The Superior Court affirmed the conviction.]

The issue presented to this court is whether Pennsylvania should adopt the "good faith" exception to the exclusionary rule as articulated by the United States Supreme Court in the case of *United States v. Leon,* 468 U.S. 897, 104 S. Ct. 3405, 82 L. Ed. 2d 677 (1984). We conclude that a "good faith" exception to the exclusionary rule would frustrate the guarantees embodied in Article I, Section 8, of the Pennsylvania Constitution. Accordingly, the decision of the Supreme Court is reversed. ...

The trial court held that the search warrant failed to establish probable cause that the marijuana would be at the location to be searched on the date it was issued. The trial court found that the warrant failed to set forth with specificity the date upon which the anonymous informants observed the marijuana. ... However, the trial court went on to deny the defendant's motion to suppress the marijuana. Applying the rationale of *Leon,* the trial court looked beyond the four corners of the affidavit, in order to establish that the officers executing the warrant acted in "good faith" in relying upon the warrant to conduct the search. ...

We must now determine whether the good-faith exception to the exclusionary rule is properly part of the jurisprudence of this Commonwealth, by virtue of Article 1, Section 8 of the Pennsylvania Constitution. In concluding that it is not, we set forth a methodology to be followed in analyzing future state constitutional issues which arise under our own Constitution. ...

This Court has long emphasized that, in interpreting a provision of the Pennsylvania Constitution, we are not bound by the decisions of the United States Supreme Court which interpret similar (yet distinct) federal constitutional provisions. ... [T]he federal constitution establishes certain minimum levels which are "equally applicable to the [analogous] state constitutional provision." ... However, each state has the power to provide broader standards, and go beyond the minimum floor which is established by the federal Constitution. ...

Here in Pennsylvania, we have stated with increasing frequency that it is both important and necessary that we undertake an independent analysis of the Pennsylvania Constitution, each time a provision of that fundamental document is implicated. ...

The recent focus on the "New Federalism" has emphasized the importance of state constitutions with respect to individual rights and criminal procedure. As such, we find it important to set forth certain factors to be briefed and analyzed by litigants in each case hereafter implicating a provision of the Pennsylvania constitution. The decision of the United States Supreme Court in *Michigan v. Long,* 463 U.S. 1032, 103 S. Ct. 3469, 77 L. Ed 2d 1201 (1983), now requires us to make a "plain statement" of the adequate and independent state grounds upon which we rely, in order to avoid any doubt that we have rested our decision squarely on Pennsylvania jurisprudence. Accordingly, as a general rule it is important that litigants brief and analyze at least the following four factors:

1. text of the Pennsylvania constitutional provision;
2. history of the provision, including Pennsylvania case-law;
3. related case-law from other states;
4. policy considerations, including unique issues of state and local concern, and applicability within modern Pennsylvania jurisprudence.

Depending on the particular issue presented, an examination of related federal precedent may be useful as part of the state constitutional analysis, not as binding authority, but as one form of guidance. ... Utilizing the above four factors, and having reviewed *Leon,* we conclude that a "good faith" exception to the exclusionary rule would frustrate the guarantees embodied in Article I, Section 8 of our Commonwealth's Constitution. ...

The United States Supreme Court in *Leon* made clear that, in its view, the sole purpose for the exclusionary rule under the 4th Amendment [to the Constitution of the United States] was to deter police misconduct. ... The *Leon* majority also made clear that, under the Federal Constitution, the exclusionary rule operated as "a judicially created remedy designed to safeguard Fourth Amendment rights generally through its deterrent effect, rather than a personal constitutional right of the party aggrieved." ...

[T]he exclusionary rule in Pennsylvania has consistently served to bolster the twin aims of Article I, Section 8, to wit, the safeguarding of privacy and the fundamental requirement that warrants shall only be issued upon probable cause. ...

The linch-pin that has been developed to determine whether it is appropriate to issue a search warrant is the test of probable cause. ... It is designed to protect us from unwarranted and even vindictive incursions upon our privacy. It insulates from dictatorial and tyrannical rule by the state, and preserves the concept of democracy that assures the freedom of citizens. This concept is second to none in its importance in deliniating the dignity of the individual living in a free society. ...

Whether the United States Supreme Court has determined that the exclusionary rule does not advance the 4th Amendment purpose of deterring police conduct is irrelevant. Indeed, we disagree with the Court's suggestion in *Leon* that we in Pennsylvania have been employing the exclusionary rule all these years to deter police corruption. We flatly reject this notion. ... What is significant, however, is that our Constitution has historically been interpreted to incorporate a strong right to privacy, and an equally strong adherence to the requirement of probable cause under Article I, Section 8. Citizens in this Commonwealth possess such rights, even where a police officer in "good faith" carrying out his or her duties inadvertently invades the privacy or circumvents the strictures of probable cause. To adopt a "good faith" exception to the exclusionary rule, we believe, would virtually emasculate those clear safeguards which have been carefully developed under the Pennsylvania Constitution over the past 200 years.

Review Questions

1. What is selective incorporation? Total incorporation? Which reflects current law?
2. Name three rights that have been incorporated and one that has not.
3. What is the exclusionary rule?
4. Give an example of when evidence would be fruit of the poisonous tree.
5. Name three exceptions to the fruit of the poisonous tree doctrine.
6. What is the "New Federalism" in the context of constitutional law?

Review Problems

1. The Constitution of the United States significantly affects all criminal law. Why is that so when more than 95 percent of all prosecutions occur in state courts?
2. Do you believe that evidence that has been obtained by law enforcement in an unconstitutional manner should be inadmissible at trial? Explain your position.
3. England does not employ the exclusionary rule. Rather, police officers are subject to civil liability for illegal searches. Is this a satisfactory remedy that should be employed in the United States? Can you think of alternative remedies?

Notes

1 *Hurtado v. California,* 110 U.S. 516 (1884).

2 *Roe v. Wade,* 410 U.S. 113 (1973).

3 *Griswold v. Connecticut,* 381 U.S. 479 (1965).

4 The rule, as it applied in federal courts, was announced in *Weeks v. United States,* 232 U.S. 383 (1914). However, it appears that the rule was applied in at least one case prior to that date. *See* LaFave & Israel, *Criminal Procedure* 78 (Hornbook Series; West 1985).

5 *Burdeau v. McDowell,* 256 U.S. 465 (1921).

6 *Walder v. United States,* 347 U.S. 62 (1954); *United States v. Havens,* 446 U.S. 620 (1980).

7 *Nardone v. United States,* 308 U.S. 338 (1939).

8 390 U.S. 377 (1968).

9 *Commonwealth v. Ludwig,* 527 Pa. 472, 478 (1991).

10 *People v. Woody,* 61 Cal. 2d 716, 394 P.2d 813 (1965).

11 *Department of Human Resources v. Smith,* 494 U.S. 872 (1990).

12 *See People v. Disbrow,* 16 Cal. 3d 101, 545 P.2d 272 (1976) (California law); *State v. Santiago,* 53 Haw. 254, 492 P.2d 657 (1971) (Hawaii law); *Commonwealth v. Triplett,* 462 Pa. 244, 341 A.2d 62 (1975) (Pennsylvania law).

13 *See* Joseph Cook, *Constitutional Rights of the Accused* 2d ed. § 1:8, n.16 (Lawyers Cooperative 1989) for a more thorough list.

CHAPTER 5

SEARCHES AND SEIZURES

CHAPTER OUTLINE

It must always be remembered that what the Constitution forbids is not all searches and seizures, but unreasonable searches and seizures.

Potter Stewart, Associate Justice
United States Supreme Court

§ 5.1 The Fourth Amendment

Searches, seizures, and arrests are vital aspects of law enforcement. Because they involve significant invasions of individual liberties, limits on their use can be found in the constitutions, statutes, and other laws of the states and federal government.

The most important limitation is the Fourth Amendment of the United States Constitution, which reads:

> The right of the people to be secure in their persons, papers and effects, against unreasonable searches and seizures, shall not be violated, and no warrants shall issue but upon probable cause, supported by oath or affirmation, and particularly describing the place to be searched and the persons or things to be seized.

All searches and seizures must satisfy the Fourth Amendment's reasonableness requirement. Some searches and seizures must be supported by probable cause, but can be warrantless; other searches and seizures can occur only if supported by probable cause and upon a warrant. In still other instances, of lesser intrusions, the Fourth Amendment applies, but reasonable suspicion will support an intrusion. In this chapter you will learn when each of these standards applies.

Two remedies are available to the defendant whose Fourth Amendment rights have been violated by the government. First, in a criminal prosecution he or she may invoke the exclusionary rule. Second, he or she may have a civil action against the offending officer under a civil rights statute, under constitutional tort theory,[1] or under traditional tort theory.

Note that the protections in the Bill of Rights apply only against the government. Evidence obtained by a private citizen, acting on his or her own, is not subject to the exclusionary rule. So, if Ira's neighbor illegally enters and searches his house, discovers evidence of a crime, and turns that evidence over to law enforcement, it may be used at trial. Of course, the result would be different if the neighbor was working under the direction of a government official. See Figure 5-1.

The concepts of "reasonable expectation of privacy" and "probable cause" are important throughout the law of searches, seizures, and arrests. Accordingly, they are examined first.

FIGURE 5-1 Fourth Amendment Analysis

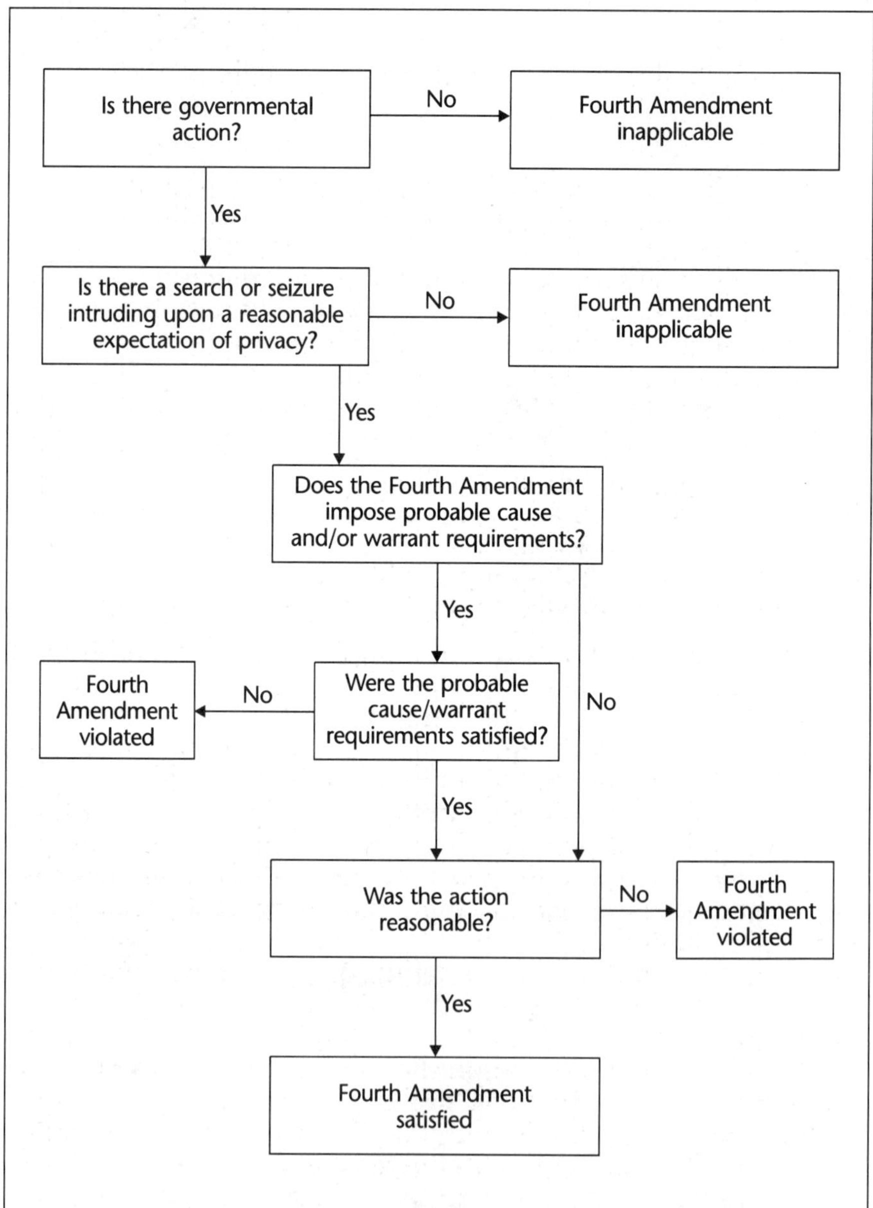

§ 5.2 Privacy

Until 1967, the Fourth Amendment had been interpreted to protect "areas." For a violation of the Fourth Amendment to occur, law enforcement officers had to physically trespass upon the property of the defendant. This standard was changed in *Katz v. United States.*

The *Katz* "reasonable expectation of privacy" test continues to be the method of determining whether a search or seizure has occurred. Consistent with *Katz,* the Supreme Court has defined a search as "when an expectation of privacy that society is prepared to consider reasonable is infringed." In the same opinion the Court defined a *seizure* as a "meaningful interference with an individual's possessory interest" in property.[2]

If there is no invasion of a reasonable expectation of privacy, there is no search. For example, a police officer's observations made from a public place, such as a sidewalk, are not searches, even if they are of the inside of a house through a window. Observing the exterior of an automobile, including a license plate, is not a search, nor is a dog sniff of an item or person.

Similarly, a momentary touching of an item or person is not always a "meaningful interference" with an interest in property (although it may be a search).

§ 5.3 Probable Cause

Probable Cause Defined

The Fourth Amendment requires the existence of **probable cause** before warrants are to be issued. When a warrant is first obtained, the probable cause determination is made by a judge. In cases where a police officer acts without a warrant, the officer makes that determination. In both cases, as you will see, probable cause is required.

TERMS

probable cause A reasonable amount of suspicion, supported by circumstances sufficiently strong to justify a prudent and cautious person's belief that certain alleged facts are probably true. A judge may not issue a search warrant unless he or she is shown probable cause to believe there is evidence of crime on the premises. A police officer may not make an arrest without a warrant unless he or she has reasonable cause, based upon reliable information, to believe a crime has been or is being committed.

KATZ
v.
UNITED STATES
389 U.S. 347 (1967)

The petitioner was convicted in the District Court for the Southern District of California under an eight-count indictment charging him with transmitting wagering information by telephone from Los Angeles to Miami and Boston, in violation of a federal statute. At trial the Government was permitted, over the petitioner's objection, to introduce evidence of the petitioner's end of telephone conversations, overheard by FBI agents who had attached an electronic listening and recording device to the outside of the public telephone booth from which he had placed his calls. In affirming his conviction, the Court of Appeals rejected the contention that the recordings had been obtained in violation of the Fourth Amendment, because "[t]here was no physical entrance into the area occupied by [the petitioner]." We granted certiorari in order to consider the constitutional questions thus presented.

The petitioner has phrased those questions as follows:

A. Whether a public telephone booth is a constitutionally protected area so that evidence obtained by attaching an electronic listening recording device to the top of such booth is obtained in violation of the right to privacy of the user of the booth.
B. Whether physical penetration of a constitutionally protected area is necessary before a search and seizure can be said to be violative of the Fourth Amendment to the United States Constitution.

We decline to adopt this formulation of the issues. In the first place, the correct solution of Fourth Amendment problems is not necessarily promoted by incantation of the phrase "constitutionally protected area." Secondly, the Fourth Amendment cannot be translated into a general constitutional "right to privacy." That Amendment protects individual privacy against certain kinds of governmental intrusion, but its protections go further, and often have nothing to do with privacy at all. Other provisions of the Constitution protect personal privacy from other forms of governmental invasion. But the protection of a person's *general* right to privacy—his right to be left alone by other people—is, like the protection of property and of his very life, left largely to the law of the individual States.

Because of the misleading way the issues have been formulated, the parties have attached great significance to the characterization of the telephone booth from which the petitioner placed his calls. The petitioner has strenuously argued that the booth was a "constitutionally protected area." The Government has maintained with equal vigor that it was not. But this effort to decide whether or not a given "area," viewed in the abstract, is "constitutionally protected" deflects attention from the problem presented by this case. For the Fourth Amendment protects people, not places. What a person knowingly exposes to the public, even in his own home or office, is not a subject of Fourth Amendment protection. ... But what he seeks to preserve as private, even in an area accessible to the public, may be constitutionally protected. ...

The Government stresses the fact that the telephone booth from which the petitioner made his calls was constructed partly of glass, so that he was as visible after he entered it as he would have been if he had remained outside. But what he sought to exclude when he entered the booth was not the intruding eye—it was the uninvited ear. He did not shed his right to do so simply because he made his calls from a place where he might be seen. No less than an individual in a business office, in a friend's apartment, or in a taxicab, a person in a telephone booth may rely upon the protection of the Fourth Amendment. One who occupies it, shuts the door behind him, and pays the toll that permits him to place a call is surely entitled to assume that the words he utters into the mouthpiece will not be broadcast to the world. To read the Constitution more narrowly is to ignore the vital role that the public telephone has come to play in private communication.

The Government contends, however, that the activities of its agents in this case should not be tested by Fourth Amendment requirements, for the surveillance technique they employed involved no physical penetration of the telephone booth from which the petitioner placed his calls. It is true that the absence of such penetration was at one time thought to foreclose further Fourth Amendment inquiry ... for that Amendment was thought to limit only searches and seizures of tangible property ... we have since departed from the narrow view on which that decision rested. Indeed, we have expressly held that the Fourth Amendment governs not only the seizure of tangible items, but extends as well to the recording of oral statements, overheard without any "technical trespass under ... local property law." *Silverman v. United States*, 365 U.S. 505, 511. Once this much is acknowledged, and once it is recognized that the Fourth Amendment protects people—and not simply "areas"—against unreasonable searches and seizures, it becomes clear that the reach of that Amendment cannot turn upon the presence or absence of a physical intrusion into any given enclosure.

We conclude that the underpinnings of [prior decisions] have been so eroded by our subsequent decisions that the "trespass" doctrine there enunciated can no longer be regarded as controlling. ...

[The Court then held that the warrantless search was conducted in violation of the Fourth Amendment.]

Probable cause is a phrase describing the minimum amount of evidence necessary before a search, seizure, or arrest is proper. There is no one universal definition of probable cause. In fact, the definition of probable cause differs depending on the context. In all situations, it is more than mere suspicion and less than the standard required to prove a defendant guilty at trial (beyond a reasonable doubt). As the Supreme Court has expressed, probable cause is present when the trustworthy facts within the officer's knowledge are sufficient in themselves to justify a "person of reasonable caution" in the belief that seizable property would be found or that the person to be arrested committed the crime in question.[3]

Sources Used to Establish Probable Cause

When making the probable cause determination, an officer may rely on his or her own observations, hearsay evidence, and statements of witnesses, victims, and other law enforcement officers. The fact that evidence will be inadmissible at trial does not exclude it from the probable cause determination.

However, innuendo or conjecture that is not supported by facts may not be considered. Although the evidence does not have to rise to the level of being admissible at trial, it must have some credibility.

It is common for the police to depend on information from informants to obtain a search warrant. An *informant* is a person who has knowledge concerning a crime because of his or her involvement in crime. The reliability of such information (and whether it should be the basis of a warrant) is hotly debated.

In *Aguilar v. Texas*,[4] the Supreme Court established a two-prong test for the use of such information (usually hearsay) when making a warrant determination. First, the affidavit had to contain information about the basis for the informant's information. This permitted the issuing judge to determine whether the informant's allegations were well founded. Second, the officer had to provide the judge with reasons for believing that the informant was reliable. This could be done, for example, by showing that the informant had been truthful in the past.

In *Illinois v. Gates*,[5] the Court reversed position and adopted a "totality of the circumstances" test, thereby overruling *Aguilar.* However, the Court did not abandon the two prongs of *Aguilar.* Although the two prongs are no longer determinative, they continue to be important factors when examining the totality of the circumstances. The Court stated that:

> The task of the issuing magistrate is simply to make a practical, common-sense decision whether, given all the circumstances set forth in the affidavit before him, including the "veracity" and the "basis of knowledge" of persons supplying hearsay information, there is a fair probability that contraband or evidence of a crime will be found in a particular place.[6]

This test does not require that the officer name the informant in the application for the warrant. All that is required is that the magistrate be given enough information to make his or her own determination concerning the credibility and reliability of the informant.

Probable cause may be established by an animal as well as a human. Dogs can be trained to discover bombs, drugs, and people. At the borders, dogs are used to sniff vehicles for the presence of illegal aliens. At airports, dogs are used to detect explosives. Many police departments depend upon dogs to detect drugs and track fugitives.

The Supreme Court has stated that the act of having a dog sniff a person or thing is not a search.[7] The question then becomes whether a dog's indication (a dog alert) that contraband is present is probable cause to issue a warrant or to pursue a warrantless search or seizure. That is the issue the Tenth Circuit Court of Appeals addressed in the *Ludwig* case.

The Tenth Circuit's ruling is the generally accepted rule. An alert by a properly trained dog furnishes probable cause. However, if the police are aware that a particular dog commonly errs, its alerts may not establish probable cause.

UNITED STATES
v.
LUDWIG
10 F.3d 1523
(10th Cir. 1993)

[The trial court granted a motion to suppress evidence, finding that a warrantless search of a car trunk, based upon probable cause established by a dog alert indicating that drugs were present in the vehicle, was violative of the Fourth Amendment.]

The United States appeals the denial of its motion to reconsider the district court's suppression order. The government argues that the challenged dog sniff of Keith Ludwig's car was not a search under the Fourth Amendment, and that no warrant was required to search the car after the dog alerted. We agree and reverse.

At about 11:15 P.M. on December 12, 1992, Joel Nickels, a Border Patrol agent at the permanent checkpoint near Truth or Consequences, New Mexico, walked a trained narcotics dog through the parking lot of the nearby Super 8 Motel to see if the dog would find any contraband. ... Less than a week earlier the motel manager had given the Border Patrol permission to walk dogs through the motel parking lot for this purpose. ...

As Nickles and the dog were walking through the lot, the dog pulled Nickles over to Keith Ludwig's Chevrolet Impala and alerted to the trunk, indicating that illegal drugs were in the trunk. ... Around half an hour later Border Patrol agents began surveillance of the car, which continued through the night until Ludwig first approached his car the next morning at 10:00 A.M.

Agent Phillip Sanchez, who had been surveilling the car, approached Ludwig five minutes later and identified himself. Ludwig acknowledged that the car was his, but denied the agent's request to inspect the car and look in the trunk. Sanchez then directed Nickles to have the dog sniff the car again, and the dog again alerted to the trunk. When Ludwig refused to open the trunk, Sanchez took the keys from the ignition, opened the trunk, and found several large bags of marijuana. Ludwig was indicted for possession with intent to distribute less than fifty kilograms of marijuana ... .

Ludwig also suggests that the dog sniffs of his car were unreasonable searches because the agents had no reason to suspect that there were drugs in his car. ...

Regardless of whether Ludwig subjectively expected that the drugs in his trunk would be smelled, society does not recognize that expectation as legitimate. ...

Ludwig suggests that dog sniffs are not as reliable as courts often assume, and therefore, the dog alert does not give the agents probable cause to open and search Ludwig's trunk. ...

Probable cause means that "there is a fair probability that contraband or evidence of a crime will be found in a particular place." ... Although Ludwig cites several cases of mistaken dog alerts, a dog alert usually is at least as reliable as many other sources of probable cause and is certainly reliable enough to create a "fair probability" that there is contraband.

Good Faith Reliance on a Warrant

Judges can differ in opinion. Judges can make mistakes. What happens if a judge finds that probable cause exists and accordingly issues a warrant, only to have the probable cause finding reversed later? Should any evidence discovered during the search be excluded?

The Supreme Court has answered this question in the negative. The Court found, in *United States v. Leon,*[8] that the exclusionary rule does not apply to evidence seized by a police officer, acting in good faith reliance on the warrant, while executing a facially valid warrant. The Court stated:

> We conclude that the marginal or nonexistent benefits produced by suppressing evidence obtained in objectively reasonable reliance on a subsequently invalidated search warrant cannot justify the substantial costs of exclusion. We do not suggest, however, that exclusion is always inappropriate in cases where an officer has obtained a warrant and abided by its terms. ... [A]n officer's reliance on the magistrate's probable-cause determination and on the technical sufficiency of the warrant he issues must be objectively reasonable ... and it is clear that in some circumstances the officer will have no reasonable grounds for believing that the warrant was properly issued.

The Court found that exclusion of evidence when an officer is relying on a judicially issued warrant would not advance the objective of the exclusionary rule; it would not deter future police misconduct.

For *Leon* to apply, an officer's reliance must be in good faith. An officer who misleads a judge in order to obtain a warrant is not acting in good faith. Further, the warrant must be facially valid. If a reasonable officer should know that a warrant is facially defective, then any evidence obtained under it must be excluded. Examples of facially invalid warrants include: unsigned warrants, warrants that contain an inadequate description of the place or thing to be searched or seized, failure of the magistrate to require the supporting affidavit to be under oath, and such a lack of evidence that an officer could not in reasonable, good faith believe that probable cause exists. An officer may, however, rely on a warrant that contains mere technical and typographical errors, unless the errors are so fundamental that they render some element of the warrant (e.g., description) defective.

Leon is only applicable to searches and seizures that occur pursuant to warrants. An officer's good faith, but mistaken, belief that probable cause exists to conduct a warrantless search or to make a warrantless seizure does not justify the admission of evidence obtained as a result thereof. As discussed previously in this text, several state courts have refused to follow the *Leon* holding when interpreting their state constitutions.

The *Leon* reasoning has been extended to situations in which police officers act in good faith reliance upon a statute,[9] or upon a court clerk's office record incorrectly indicating the existence of a warrant. The same standards apply as in *Leon,* that is, the statute or record relied upon must be facially valid.

§ 5.4 Searches and Seizures: The Warrant Requirement

Depending upon the circumstances, a search may be conducted with or without a warrant. The Supreme Court has expressed that there is a strong preference for the use of warrants, when possible, over warrantless actions.[10] The warrant preference serves an important purpose: it protects citizens from overzealous law enforcement practices.

> The presence of a search warrant serves a high function. Absent some grave emergency, the Fourth Amendment has interposed a magistrate between the citizen and police. This was done not to shield criminals nor to make the home a safe haven for illegal activities. It was done so that an objective mind might weigh the need to invade the privacy in order to enforce the law. The right of privacy was deemed too precious to entrust to the discretion of those whose job is the detection of crime and the arrest of criminals.[11]

Accordingly, a search conducted pursuant to a valid search warrant is per se reasonable. Warrantless searches are permitted only in special circumstances, and it is the responsibility of the government to prove that the facts of the case fit into one of the exceptions to the warrant requirement.

To give this preference some "teeth," the Supreme Court, in *Aguilar v. Texas,*[12] announced that "when a search is based upon a magistrate's, rather than a police officer's determination of probable cause," reviewing courts are to accept lesser competent evidence than if the officer made the determination personally, so long as there was a "substantial basis" for the magistrate's decision. To say it another way, less evidence is required to sustain a search if a warrant was obtained prior to the search.

"Reviewing courts" are referred to because the determination that probable cause exists by a magistrate when issuing a warrant is not final. A defendant may later attack any evidence seized pursuant to a warrant through a motion to suppress. As stated, determinations by a magistrate are less likely to be overturned than those made by police officers.

In *United States v. Leon,*[13] the Supreme Court created an exception to the rule that evidence must be suppressed if seized pursuant to an invalid warrant. In *Leon,* it held that evidence seized by an officer who executes a search warrant with a good faith belief that the warrant is valid will not be excluded, even though the warrant is later determined invalid. If a warrant is facially invalid, then any fruits of a search thereof must be excluded, because an officer cannot in good faith believe that such a warrant is valid. Of course, if an officer uses false information to convince the magistrate that probable cause exists, the good faith exception does not apply. The same is true if an officer knows that the magistrate issuing the warrant is not neutral and detached.

Requirements for Obtaining a Warrant

The Fourth Amendment enumerates the requirements that must be met before a warrant can be issued. It is the responsibility of the law enforcement officer requesting the warrant to establish these elements to the judge making the warrant determination. The form application for search warrant used in the federal courts appears in Figure 5-2.

First, the evidence presented must establish probable cause to believe that within the area to be searched the items sought will be found. Second, there must be probable cause to believe that the items sought are connected to criminal activity.

Third, the area to be searched and any item to be seized must be described with particularity. The amount of specificity required varies from case to case. A warrant that authorizes a police officer to search a particular home for "unauthorized contraband" clearly violates the Fourth Amendment, whereas a warrant authorizing a search of the same home for a "nine-inch knife with an ivory handle" is valid, provided the warrant is valid in all other respects (probable cause, etc.).

Warrants for the seizure of items that are illegal in themselves do not have to be as particular as others. For example, a warrant to search for a book must be more specific than one for drugs. The description "book" is clearly insufficient, whereas a warrant to search for "cocaine" probably is sufficient.

As to location, a street address is normally sufficient. If there is no street address, the warrant should describe the location, owner, color, and architectural style of the property. Of course, any additional information that aids in describing property should be included. If the building to be searched is an apartment building or similar multi-unit structure, the specific subunit to be searched must be stated in the warrant.

Fourth, the facts that are alleged to establish probable cause must be "supported by Oath or affirmation." In the typical case, this means that the government will produce one or more affidavits to prove that a warrant is justified. Note that the sample application for a search warrant (Figure 5-2; see also Figure 5-3) provides space for a supporting affidavit.

Finally, the warrant must be issued by a neutral and detached magistrate. Although judges are most commonly given the authority to issue warrants, a state may grant this authority to others. However, the Supreme Court has stated that the person authorized must be neutral and detached and be capable of determining whether probable cause exists.

AO 106 (Rev. 5/85) Affidavit for Search Warrant

United States District Court

_______________ DISTRICT OF _______________

In the Matter of the Search of
(Name, address or brief description of person or property to be searched)

APPLICATION AND AFFIDAVIT FOR SEARCH WARRANT

CASE NUMBER:

I _______________ being duly sworn depose and say:

I am a(n) _______________ and have reason to believe
Official Title

that ☐ on the person of or ☐ on the premises known as (name, description and/or location)

in the _______________ District of _______________
there is now concealed a certain person or property, namely (describe the person or property)

which is (give alleged grounds for search and seizure under Rule 41(b) of the Federal Rules of Criminal Procedure)

in violation of Title _______ United States Code, Section(s) _______________
The facts to support the issuance of a Search Warrant are as follows:

Continued on the attached sheet and made a part hereof. ☐ Yes ☐ No

____
Signature of Affiant

Sworn to before me, and subscribed in my presence

_______________ at _______________
Date City and State

_______________ _______________
Name and Title of Judicial Officer Signature of Judicial Officer

FIGURE 5-2 Application and Affidavit for Search Warrant

Thus, a state law permitting a state's attorney general, who had investigated the crime and would later be responsible for its prosecution, to issue a warrant, was invalid.[14] In another case, a court clerk was found sufficiently detached, neutral, and capable to issue a warrant, because the clerk worked for a court and was under the supervision of a judge.[15]

FIGURE 5-3
Search Warrant upon Oral Testimony

AO 93A (Rev. 5/85) Search Warrant Upon Oral Testimony

United States District Court

_______________ DISTRICT OF _______________

In the Matter of the Search of
(Name, address or brief description of person or property to be searched)

SEARCH WARRANT UPON ORAL TESTIMONY

CASE NUMBER:

TO: _______________ and any Authorized Officer of the United States

Sworn oral testimony has been communicated to me by _______________
Affiant

that ☐ on the person of or ☐ on the premises known as (name, description and/or location)

in the _______________ District of _______________ there is now concealed a certain person or property, namely (describe the person or property)

I am satisfied that the circumstances are such as to make it reasonable to dispense with a written affidavit and that there is probable cause to believe that the property or person so described is concealed on the person or premises above described and that grounds for application for issuance of the search warrant exist as communicated orally to me in a sworn statement which has been recorded electronically, stenographically, or in longhand and upon the return of the warrant, will be transcribed, certified as accurate and attached hereto.

YOU ARE HEREBY COMMANDED to search on or before _______________
Date

the person or place named above for the person or property specified, serving this warrant and making the search (in the daytime — 6:00 AM to 10:00 PM) (at anytime in the day or night as I find reasonable cause has been established) and if the person or property be found there to seize same, leaving a copy of this warrant and receipt for the person or property taken, and prepare a written inventory of the person or property seized and promptly return this warrant to _______________
U.S. Judge or Magistrate
as required by law.

_______________ at _______________
Date and Time Issued — City and State

_______________ _______________
Name and Title of Judicial Officer — Signature of Judicial Officer

I certify that on _______________ at _______________,
Date — Time

_______________ orally authorized the
U.S. Judge or Magistrate

issuance and execution of a search warrant conforming to all the foregoing terms.

_______________ _______________ _______________
Name of affiant — Signature of affiant — Exact time warrant executed

Scope of Warrants

Warrants may be issued to search and seize any item that constitutes evidence of a crime, is the fruit of a crime, is contraband, or is used to commit a crime.[16] A warrant may be issued to search or seize any place or property, whether belonging to a suspected criminal or an innocent third party.

AO 93A (Rev. 5/85) Search Warrant Upon Oral Testimony

RETURN

DATE WARRANT RECEIVED	DATE AND TIME WARRANT EXECUTED	COPY OF WARRANT AND RECEIPT FOR ITEMS LEFT WITH

INVENTORY MADE IN THE PRESENCE OF

INVENTORY OF PERSON OR PROPERTY TAKEN PURSUANT TO THE WARRANT

CERTIFICATION

I swear that this inventory is a true and detailed account of the person or property taken by me on the warrant.

Subscribed, sworn to, and returned before me this date.

U.S. Judge or Magistrate Date

FIGURE 5-3
(continued)

The particularity requirement acts to limit the breadth of a search. If an officer searches beyond the scope of a warrant, the exclusionary rule will make the fruits from the forbidden area inadmissible at trial.

In some circumstances the particularity requirement is heightened. For example, because of the importance of protecting the press from government intrusion, warrants to search newsrooms or similar areas must be drafted with "particular exactitude."[17] The same is true if a search will probe into confidential information, such as client records of attorneys and physicians.

As a general proposition, a warrant to search premises does not authorize the police to search the occupants of the premises.[18] Of course, a search may be conducted if an independent basis exists justifying the action. Generally, the occupants of an area to be searched may be detained until the search is complete. However, occupants cannot be detained for an "unduly prolonged" period of time.[19] Once the evidence sought is found or the threat of loss or destruction of evidence by an occupant has passed, he or she should be released.

Executing the Warrant

The warrant may direct a particular officer or an entire unit of police officers to conduct the search. The language of the warrant itself contains the duties of the officers executing the warrant, as well as their limitations.

As a general proposition, warrants are to be executed during the day. This is because a nighttime search is considered to be more intrusive than a daytime search[20] and because the probability of resistance is greater at night.

To conduct a nighttime search, a specific request for a warrant authorizing such must be made. To receive a warrant permitting a nighttime search, an officer must present the magistrate with facts evidencing the necessity for a nighttime search, usually including proof that a daytime search will not be successful. An anticipated nighttime delivery of illegal goods justifies a nighttime warrant, as does a concern that evidence of a crime will be destroyed in the night.

Most states have statutes requiring that warrants be executed within a specific amount of time after issuance. Warrants issued under federal law must be executed within ten days of issuance.[21]

In all cases, the search must be conducted when there is probable cause. If an officer fails to execute a warrant before probable cause has dissipated, then any resulting search is violative of the Fourth Amendment, and the fruits thereof are subject to the exclusionary rule. This is true even if the search is conducted within the period of time set by law.

At the premises of a search, the police must announce their purpose and provide the warrant to the owner or occupant for review. This is true whether entry is gained through the use of force or not. However, to prevent the destruction of evidence or injury to the officers, judges may issue "no-knock" warrants if the facts indicate that one or the other is likely to occur. The decision to issue a no-knock warrant must be based on the evidence. In one case, a blanket rule permitting no-knock warrants to be issued in all drug cases was held violative of the Fourth Amendment's reasonableness requirement.[22] The *Wilson* case also dealt with this issue.

WILSON
v.
ARKANSAS
_____ U.S. _____ (1995)

JUSTICE THOMAS delivered the opinion of the Court.

At the time of the framing, the common law of search and seizure recognized a law enforcement officer's authority to break open the doors of a dwelling, but generally indicated that he first ought to announce his presence and authority. In this case, we hold that this common-law "knock and announce" principle forms a part of the reasonableness inquiry under the Fourth Amendment. ...

During November and December 1992, petitioner Sharlene Wilson made a series of narcotics sales to an informant acting at the direction of the Arkansas State Police. In late November, the informant purchased marijuana and methamphetamine at the home that petitioner shared with Bryson Jacobs. On December 30, the informant telephoned petitioner at her home and arranged to meet her at a local store to buy some marijuana. According to testimony presented below, petitioner produced a semiautomatic pistol at this meeting and waved it in the informant's face, threatening to kill her if she turned out to be working for the police. Petitioner then sold the informant a bag of marijuana.

The next day, police officers applied for and obtained warrants to search petitioner's home and to arrest both petitioner and Jacobs. Affidavits filed in support of the warrants set forth the details of the narcotics transactions and stated that Jacobs had previously been convicted of arson and firebombing. The search was conducted later that afternoon. Police officers found the main door to petitioner's home open. While opening an unlocked screen door and entering the residence, they identified themselves as police officers and stated that they had a warrant. Once inside the home, the officers seized marijuana, methamphetamine, valium, narcotics paraphernalia, a gun, and ammunition. They also found petitioner in the bathroom, flushing marijuana down the toilet. Petitioner and Jacobs were arrested and charged with delivery of marijuana, delivery of methamphetamine, possession of drug paraphernalia, and possession of marijuana.

Before trial, petitioner filed a motion to suppress the evidence seized during the search. Petitioner asserted that the search was invalid on various grounds, including that the officers had failed to "knock and announce" before entering her home. The trial court summarily denied the suppression motion. After a jury trial, petitioner was convicted of all charges and sentenced to 32 years in prison.

The Arkansas Supreme Court affirmed petitioner's conviction on appeal. ... The court noted that "the officers entered the home *while they were identifying themselves,*" but it rejected petitioner's argument that "the Fourth Amendment requires officers to knock and announce prior to entering the residence." ... Finding "no authority for [petitioner's] theory that the knock and announce principle is required by the Fourth Amendment," the court concluded that neither Arkansas law nor the Fourth Amendment required suppression of the evidence. ...

We granted certiorari to resolve the conflict among the lower courts as to whether the common-law knock-and-announce principle forms a part of the Fourth Amendment reasonableness inquiry. ... We hold that it does, and accordingly reverse and remand. ...

The Fourth Amendment to the Constitution protects "[t]he right of the people to be secure in their persons, houses, papers, and effects, against unreasonable searches and seizures." In evaluating the scope of this right, we have looked to the traditional protections against unreasonable searches and seizures afforded by the common law at the time of the framing. ... "Although the underlying command of the Fourth Amendment is always that searches and seizures be reasonable," our effort to give content to this term may be guided by the meaning ascribed to it by the Framers of the Amendment. An examination of the common law of search and seizure leaves no doubt that the reasonableness of a search of a dwelling may depend in part on whether law enforcement officers announced their presence and authority prior to entering.

Although the common law generally protected a man's house as "his castle of defense and asylum," common-law courts long have held that "when the King is party, the sheriff (if the doors be not open) may break the party's house, either to arrest him or to do other execution of the K[ing]'s process, if otherwise he cannot enter." To this rule, however, common-law courts appended an important qualification:

> "But before he breaks it, he ought to signify the cause of his coming, and to make request to open doors ... , for the law without a default in the owner abhors the destruction or breaking of any house (which is for the habitation and safety of man) by which great damage and inconvenience might ensue to the party, when no default is in him; for perhaps he did not know of the process, of which, if he had notice, it is to be presumed that he would obey it. ... "

See also *Case of Richard Curtis,* Fost. 135, 137, 168 Eng. Rep. 67, 68 (Crown 1757) ("[N]o precise form of words is required in a case of this kind. It is sufficient that the party hath notice, that the officer cometh not as a mere trespasser, but claiming to act under a proper authority ... "); *Lee v. Gansell,* Lofft 374, 381–382, 98 Eng. Rep, 700, 705 (K.B. 1774) ("[A]s to the outer door, the law is now clearly taken" that it is privileged; but the door may be broken "when the due notification and demand has been made and refused").

The common-law knock-and-announce principle was woven quickly into the fabric of early American law. Most of the States that ratified the Fourth Amendment had enacted constitutional provisions or statutes generally incorporating English common law ... and a few States had enacted statutes specifically embracing the common-law view that the breaking of the door of a dwelling was permitted once admittance was refused. ... Early American courts similarly embraced the common-law knock-and-announce principle. ...

Our own cases have acknowledged that the common-law principle of announcement is "embedded in Anglo-American law," but we have never squarely held that this principle is an element of the reasonableness inquiry under the Fourth Amendment. We now so hold. Given the longstanding common-law endorsement of the practice of announcement, we have little doubt that the Framers of the Fourth Amendment thought that the method of an officer's entry into a dwelling was among the factors to be considered in assessing the reasonableness of a search or seizure. Contrary to the decision below, we hold that in some circumstances an officer's unannounced entry into a home might be unreasonable under the Fourth Amendment.

That is not to say, of course, that every entry must be preceded by an announcement. The Fourth Amendment's flexible requirement of reasonableness should not be read to mandate a rigid rule of announcement that ignores countervailing law enforcement interests.

We need not attempt a comprehensive catalog of the relevant countervailing factors here. For now, we leave to the lower courts the task of determining the circumstances under which an unannounced entry is reasonable under the Fourth Amendment. We simply hold that although a search or seizure of a dwelling might be constitutionally defective if police officers enter without prior announcement, law enforcement interests may also establish the reasonableness of an unannounced entry. ...

Respondent contends that the judgment below should be affirmed because the unannounced entry in this case was justified for two reasons. First, respondent argues that police officers reasonably believed that a prior announcement would have placed them in peril, given their knowledge that petitioner had threatened a government informant with a semiautomatic weapon and that Mr. Jacobs had previously been convicted of arson and firebombing. Second, respondent suggests that prior announcement would have produced an unreasonable risk that petitioner would destroy easily disposable narcotics evidence.

These considerations may well provide the necessary justification for the unannounced entry in this case. Because the Arkansas Supreme Court did not address their sufficiency, however, we remand to allow the state courts to make any necessary findings of fact and to make the determination of reasonableness in the first instance. The judgment of the Arkansas Supreme Court is reversed, and the case is remanded for further proceedings not inconsistent with this opinion.

It is so ordered.

After a search is completed, the officers are required to inventory items seized. Federal rules require that the owner of the property be given a receipt for the goods taken.[23] Property unlawfully taken must be returned to the owner, unless it is unlawful in itself, such as drugs.

§ 5.5 Exceptions to the Search Warrant Requirement

Although the general rule is that a warrant must be obtained before a search may be undertaken, there are many exceptions. The exceptions to the warrant requirement are sometimes referred to as *exigent circumstances.*

Consent Searches

A voluntary **consent** to a search obviates the warrant requirement. A person may consent to a search of his or her person or property. The

TERMS

consent Agreement; approval; acquiescence; being of one mind. Consent necessarily involves two or more persons because, without at least two persons, there cannot be a unity of opinion or the possibility of thinking alike.

scope of the search is limited by the person consenting. Absent special circumstances, a consent to search may be terminated at any time by the person giving consent.

A person's consent must be voluntary. All of the circumstances surrounding the consent are examined to determine whether the consent was voluntary. There is no requirement that police officers inform a person that he or she may refuse to consent.[24]

Of course, a defendant who is threatened or coerced into consenting has not voluntarily consented. It is not coercion for persons to be told that if they do not consent, a warrant will be obtained authorizing the desired search. It is coercion for officers to tell persons that if they do not consent to a search, a warrant will be obtained and the officers will ransack their home.[25]

Consent is invalid if it is obtained by a mistaken belief that the officer had a legal right to conduct the search. For example, if Officer Frisk tells Patty Patdown that he has a warrant, or that the law does not require that he have one, and she acquiesces, the search is invalid if he had no warrant or legal right to conduct the search.

The same is true when officers use fraud or deceit to obtain consent. For example, in one case a defendant was arrested and interrogated. He gave no incriminating information during the questioning. The following day the officers went to the home of the defendant and told his wife that he had confessed to the crime and had sent the police to seize the contraband. Based upon these statements, the defendant's wife consented to a search by the officers. The state court found that this tactic led to an involuntary consent and that the evidence seized was inadmissible at trial.[26]

The facts of that case raise another issue: third-party consent. This arises often in cases where many people share a single dwelling or room, such as families, fraternities, and dormitories. In *United States v. Matlock*,[27] the Supreme Court found that a third party may consent as long as the parties share access, control, and use of the property. If co-inhabitants section off a dwelling, with each tenant having exclusive control over a specific area, then only the tenant using an area may consent. If closets, desks, or similar areas are reserved for one person's private use, only that person may consent.

Having a property interest in property does not give one a right to consent to a search of the property. The Supreme Court has said that neither landlords nor hotel managers may consent to the search of their tenants' rooms.[28] They may have a property interest, but the privacy interest rests with the tenants.

Plain View

Another exception to the warrant requirement is the **plain view doctrine.** Under this rule, a warrantless seizure of evidence by an officer who is lawfully in a position to see the evidence is valid.

A large body of cases discusses the plain view doctrine. From those cases it can be gleaned that for a seizure to be lawful under the doctrine, the following must be shown: (1) The officer must lawfully be in an area (2) from which the object to be seized is in plain view (3) and the officer does in fact see the item (4) there is probable cause to believe the object is connected to a crime, and (5) the officer has a right to access the object itself.

First, the officer must be in a place where he or she has a right to be. An officer, as is true of anyone, has a right to be in public places. Thus, evidence seen in a public park, on the street, or in a business open to the public may be seized without a warrant.

Evidence located on private property is different. As a general rule, the police have no right to enter private property to seize evidence which was in plain view from a public area. In such cases the officer is expected to obtain a warrant; the officer's observation provides the requisite probable cause. However, if an exception applies, such as preventing the destruction of the evidence, the officer may immediately seize the evidence.

If an officer is on private property for a lawful reason, then the officer may seize evidence in plain view without first obtaining a warrant. There are many reasons why an officer may be in a position to see evidence. Many of these were discussed in *Coolidge.* An officer who has to enter a home to execute an arrest warrant is not expected to overlook illegal objects in plain sight. The same is true if the officer is executing a search warrant, is in hot pursuit, is responding to an emergency, or is conducting a stop and frisk.

An officer who sees evidence because he or she has gone beyond the scope of the law enforcement right violates the Fourth Amendment, and the plain view doctrine will not support a seizure. For example, if an officer has a warrant to search a defendant's garage, any evidence

TERMS

plain view doctrine An exception to the search warrant requirement of the Fourth Amendment, which allows warrantless seizure of evidence observed in "plain view" by an officer from a place where he or she had a legal right to be.

obtained, even if in plain view, from the defendant's home may not be used at trial.

Second, the evidence seized must be in plain sight or plain view. Only the senses of sight and touch may be used to establish plain view. Use of the sense of touch is discussed later. Of course, whether an item is in plain sight depends on the scope of the officer's authority. An officer who has a search warrant authorizing the search of a closet for a gun may seize cocaine lying on the floor of the closet. The same is not true if the warrant did not authorize a search of the closet. In any case, the item must be plainly visible from a place where the officer has a right to be.

If an officer moves something with the intent of gaining a better vantage of the item, it is not in plain view. In one case, the movement of a stereo to record its serial number was considered an illegal search, because the officers were on the premises for another reason. The Court noted in that case that merely observing the stereo, which was in plain view, was legal. If the serial number had been visible without moving the stereo, then recording its number would not have been violative of the Fourth Amendment. But moving the stereo constituted a "new invasion" of the defendant's rights.[29]

Officers may use mechanical or electrical aids in seeing evidence, so long as they are in a place they have a right to be and they are not conducting a search (encroaching on someone's right to privacy). Flashlights and binoculars are examples of such aids.

Third, the officer must see the item. In *Coolidge,* the Court stated that:

> [T]he discovery of evidence in plain view must be inadvertent. The rationale of the exception to the warrant requirement, as just stated, is that a plain-view seizure will not turn an initially valid (and therefore limited) search into a "general" one, while the inconvenience of procuring a warrant to cover an inadvertent discovery is great. But where the discovery is anticipated, where the police know in advance that location of the evidence and intend to seize it, the situation is altogether different. The requirement of a warrant imposes no inconvenience whatever.[30]

In most cases, the discovery will be inadvertent. However, in *Horton v. California,*[31] the Supreme Court rejected inadvertence as a requirement of plain view, although it recognized that, in most instances, a discovery will be inadvertent. In *Horton,* an officer sought a search warrant for both the proceeds of a robbery and the weapons used during the robbery. The warrant was issued, but only for the proceeds. During the search, the officer discovered the weapon, as expected, in plain view. The Court held that even though expected, the gun was properly seized.

Fourth, the officer must have probable cause to believe that the object is subject to seizure, or, as the Court stated in *Horton,* the incriminating character of the object must be immediately apparent. *Contraband*

COOLIDGE
v.
NEW HAMPSHIRE
403 U.S. 443 (1971)

It is well established that under certain circumstances the police may seize evidence in plain view without a warrant. But it is important to keep in mind that, in the vast majority of cases, *any* evidence seized by the police will be in plain view, at least at the moment of seizure. The problem with the "plain view" doctrine has been to identify the circumstances in which plain view has legal significance rather than being simply the normal concomitant of any search, legal or illegal.

An example of the applicability of the "plain view" doctrine is the situation in which the police have a warrant to search a given area for specified objects, and in the course of the search come across some other article of incriminating character. ... Where the initial intrusion that brings the police within plain view of such an article is supported, not by a warrant, but by one of the recognized exceptions to the warrant requirement, the seizure is also legitimate. Thus, the police may inadvertently come across evidence while in "hot pursuit" of a fleeing suspect. ... And an object that comes into view during a search incident to arrest that is appropriately limited in scope under existing law may be seized without a warrant. ... Finally, the "plain view" doctrine has been applied where a police officer is not searching for evidence against the accused, but nonetheless inadvertently comes across incriminating evidence. ...

What the "plain view" cases have in common is that the police officer in each of them had a prior justification for an intrusion in the course of which he came inadvertently across a piece of evidence incriminating the accused. ... Of course, the extension of the original justification is legitimate only where it is immediately apparent to the police that they have evidence before them; the "plain view" doctrine may not be used to extend a general exploratory search from one object to another until something incriminating at last emerges.

(an item which is illegal itself, such as drugs) can be seized, as can property used to commit crimes, which has been used in a crime, or which has been stolen.

Fifth, the officer must be located such that he or she had a legal right to access the object. If not, the officer must obtain a warrant.

Stop and Frisk

On October 31, 1963, a Cleveland, Ohio, police detective observed three men standing on a street corner. Suspicious of the men, the detective positioned himself to watch their behavior. After some time the officer concluded that the men were "casing a job, a stick-up."

The officer approached the men, identified himself, and asked them to identify themselves. After the men "mumbled something," the officer grabbed one of the men and conducted a frisk, or a *patdown,* of the man's clothing. The officer felt a pistol in the man's coat pocket. He removed the gun from his coat and then "patted down" the other two men. Another gun was discovered during those frisks.

The officer testified that he conducted the frisks because he believed the men were carrying weapons. The first man frisked was defendant Terry. At trial he was convicted of carrying a concealed weapon and was subsequently sentenced to one to three years in prison. His appeal made it to the United States Supreme Court.

In *Terry v. Ohio,*[32] the Supreme Court was confronted with these issues: Did the officer's behavior amount to a search or seizure under the Fourth Amendment? If so, was the search or seizure by the officer reasonable?

The Court decided that defendant Terry had been seized under the Fourth Amendment. "It must be recognized that whenever a police officer accosts an individual and restrains his freedom to walk away, he has 'seized' that person." As to the frisk, the Court stated that "it is nothing less than sheer torture of the English language to suggest that a careful exploration of the outer surfaces of a person's clothing all over his or her body in an attempt to find weapons is not a search."

With these statements, the Court made it clear that the police practice of stopping and frisking people is one governed by the Fourth Amendment. However, the Court then concluded that an exception to the probable cause requirement was justified because the intrusion upon a person's privacy is limited in a stop and frisk, as opposed to an arrest and full search.

Officers are not given carte blanche to stop and frisk. Although probable cause is not required, officers must have a "reasonable suspicion" that the person to be stopped has committed, is committing, or is about to commit a crime. The officer's suspicion must be supported by "specific and articulable facts which, taken together with rational inferences from those facts, reasonably warrant that intrusion."[33] An officer's intuition alone is not enough suspicion to support a *Terry* seizure. (See Figure 5-4.)

Not all contacts between an officer and a citizen amount to a seizure. In *United States v. Mendenhall,*[34] it was stated that a seizure occurs anytime a reasonable person believes that he or she is not free to leave. There need not be an attempt to leave. A person may feel restrained by physical contact from a police officer, tone of voice, threatening language, or the threatening presence of many officers.

Mere questioning of a citizen by a police officer does not rise to the level of a detention. However, if the interrogation becomes accusatory or its duration lengthy, the Fourth Amendment may come into play. A Texas statute that required an individual to comply with a police officer's order to identify himself, even though there was no basis to believe criminal activity was afoot, was held unconstitutional by the Supreme Court in 1979.[35] The Court held that the Fourth Amendment

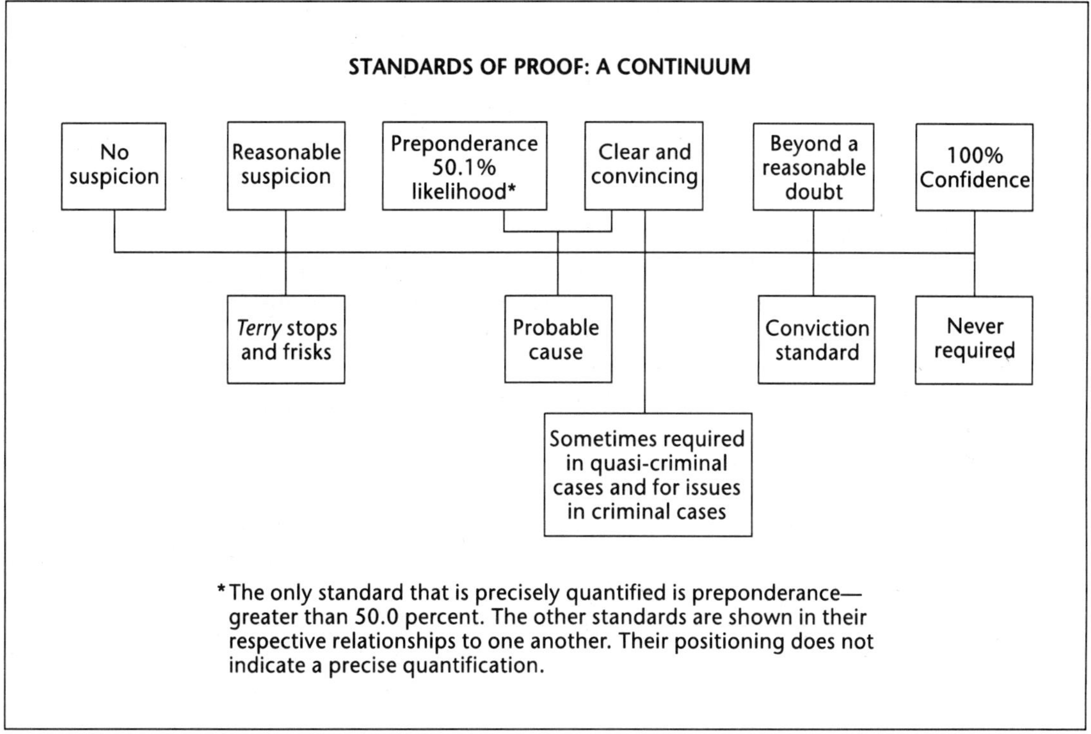

FIGURE 5-4 Standards of Proof: A Continuum

prohibits the police from temporarily detaining a person and demanding identification without at least a reasonable suspicion to believe the individual has committed, or is engaged in committing, a crime.

A motorist may be temporarily detained under *Terry*. Also, the Supreme Court has said that once a person is lawfully pulled over, he or she may be ordered out of the vehicle, even though there is no reason to believe that the driver is a threat. See later in this chapter for a more thorough discussion of automobiles and the Fourth Amendment.

In addition to requiring reasonable suspicion, the *Terry* Court also stated that stops are to "last no longer than is necessary," and the investigative methods employed during the stop should be the "least intrusive means reasonably available to verify or dispell the officer's suspicion in a short period of time." If an officer detains a person longer than necessary, the investigatory detention turns into a full seizure (arrest), and the probable cause requirement of the Fourth Amendment commences.

Florida v. Royer[36] provides an example of the distinction between an investigatory detention and an arrest. The defendant, a suspected drug dealer, was questioned in a public area of an airport. After a few minutes he was taken forty feet to a small police office, where he consented to a search of his luggage. The Court concluded that the search was the product of an illegal arrest, as less intrusive methods of investigation were available. As alternatives, the Court mentioned that the officers could have used narcotics dogs to inspect the luggage or could have immediately requested consent to search the defendant's luggage. The act of requiring the defendant to accompany the officers to a small room forty feet away transformed the detention from a *Terry* stop to an arrest, which was violative of the Fourth Amendment because it was not supported by probable cause.

The fact that there has been a lawful stop does not itself justify a frisk. The purpose behind permitting investigatory stops is the advancement of crime detection and prevention. Frisks, on the other hand, are permitted to protect officers and others from the person stopped.

To conduct a frisk, an officer must have a reasonable belief that the person is armed and dangerous. Again, the officer must be able to point to facts to support this conclusion. An officer may draw on his or her experience as a police officer in making the decision. Again, however, intuition (suspicion not supported by any facts) alone is not adequate.

Full searches require probable cause. A *Terry* frisk requires less, and, accordingly, the permitted intrusion is less. The search must be limited to the outer clothing. A search of interior clothing or pockets is improper.

If the defendant is in an automobile, the officer may search those areas within the person's immediate control.[37] Once any lawful stop of a vehicle is made, the driver may be ordered out of the vehicle. However, to frisk an occupant of a vehicle, the *Terry* standard must be met.

If during a patdown an officer feels an item that may be a weapon, then the officer may reach into the clothing of the citizen to seize the item. Any item seized, whether a weapon, contraband, or other item associated with a crime, may be used as evidence.

If the officer does not feel an item that may be a weapon, the search can go no further. If the officer feels evidence of another crime, the intrusion may continue under the "plain feel" doctrine.

Plain Feel

You have learned both the plain view doctrine and the *Terry* exception to the warrant and probable cause requirements of the Fourth Amendment. The plain feel doctrine is the product of their joining. That is, what happens when an officer who is conducting a *Terry* patdown discovers, through the sense of touch, not a weapon, but contraband? May this information be used to establish probable cause allowing a more intrusive search? This question was answered in the *Dickerson* case.

If an officer discovers contraband through the sense of touch, during a *Terry* frisk, probable cause exists to search further. If contraband is recovered, it is admissible at trial. The rules set out in *Terry* apply. First, stops must be supported by reasonable suspicion. Second, patdowns may be conducted only when an officer possesses a reasonable suspicion based on specific and articulable facts that the suspect may be armed and dangerous. Third, the patdown must be limited. Exploration of the clothing beyond what is necessary to determine dangerousness is not permitted, unless probable cause to believe that there is contraband is created through the officer's sense of touch.

MINNESOTA v. DICKERSON 113 S. Ct. 2130 (1993)

On the evening of November 9, 1989, two Minneapolis police officers were patrolling an area on the city's north side in a marked squad car. At about 8:15 P.M., one of the officers observed respondent leaving a 12-unit apartment building on Morgan Avenue North. The officer, having previously responded to complaints of drug sales in the building's hallways and having executed several search warrants on the premises, considered the building to be a notorious "crack house." According to testimony credited by the trail court, respondent began walking toward the police but, upon spotting the squad car and making eye contact with one of the officers, abruptly halted and began walking in the opposite direction. His suspicion aroused, this officer watched as respondent turned and entered an alley on the other side of the apartment building. Based upon respondent's seemingly evasive actions and the fact that he had just left a building known for cocaine traffic, the officers decided to stop respondent and investigate further.

The officers pulled their squad car into the alley and ordered respondent to stop and submit to a patdown search. The search revealed no weapons, but the officer conducting the search did take an interest in a small lump in respondent's nylon jacket. The officer later testified: "As I pat-searched the front of his body, I felt a lump, a small lump, in the front pocket. I examined it with my fingers and it slid and it felt to be a lump of crack cocaine in cellophane." The officer then reached into respondent's pocket and retrieved a small plastic bag containing one fifth of one gram of crack cocaine. Respondent was arrested and charged in Hennepin County District Court with possession of a controlled substance.

Before trial, respondent moved to suppress the cocaine. The trial court first concluded that the officers were justified under *Terry v. Ohio* ... in stopping respondent ... . The court further found that the officers were justified in frisking respondent to ensure that he was not carrying a weapon. Finally, analogizing to the "plain-view" doctrine ... the trial court ruled that the officers' seizure of the cocaine did not violate the Fourth Amendment ... . [The Minnesota Court of Appeals and Supreme Court reversed, rejecting the trial court's "plain feel" theory. In addition, the Supreme Court held that the search itself went beyond the frisk authorized by *Terry*.]

Most state and federal courts have recognized a so-called "plain feel" or "plain touch" corollary to the plain-view doctrine. ... Some state courts, however, like the Minnesota court in this case, have rejected such a corollary. ...

We have already held that police officers, at least under certain circumstances, may seize contraband detected during the lawful execution of a *Terry* search. In *Michigan v. Long,* for example, police approached a man who had driven his car into a ditch and who appeared to be under the influence of some intoxicant. As the man moved to reenter the car from the roadside, police spotted a knife on the floorboard. The officers stopped the man, subjected him to a patdown search, and then inspected the interior of the vehicle for other weapons. During the search of the passenger compartment, the police discovered an open pouch containing marijuana and seized it. This Court upheld the validity of the search and seizure under *Terry.* The Court held first that, in the context of a roadside encounter, where police have reasonable suspicion based on specific and articulable facts to believe that a driver may be armed and dangerous, they may conduct a protective search for weapons not only of the driver's person but also of the passenger compartment of the automobile. ... "If, while conducting a legitimate *Terry* search of the interior of the automobile, the officer should, as here, discover contraband other than weapons, he clearly cannot be required to ignore the contraband, and the Fourth Amendment does not require its suppression in such circumstances." ...

We think this doctrine has an obvious application by analogy to cases in which an officer discovers contraband through sense of touch during an otherwise lawful search. The rationale of the plain view doctrine is that if contraband is left in open view and is observed by a police officer from a lawful vantage point, there has been no invasion of a legitimate expectation of privacy and thus no "search" within the meaning of the Fourth Amendment—or at least no search independent of the initial intrusion that gave the officers their vantage point. ... The warrantless seizure of contraband that presents itself in this manner is deemed justified by the realization that resort to a neutral magistrate under such circumstances would often be impracticable and would do little to promote the objectives of the Fourth Amendment. ... The same can be said of tactile discoveries of contraband. If a police officer lawfully pats down a suspect's outer clothing and feels an object whose contour or mass makes its identity immediately apparent, there has been no invasion of the suspect's privacy beyond that already authorized by the officer's search for weapons; if the object is contraband, its warrantless seizure would be justified by the same practical considerations that inhere in the plain view context. ...

The Minnesota Supreme Court rejected an analogy to the plain-view doctrine on two grounds: first, its belief that "the sense of touch is inherently less immediate and less reliable than the sense of sight," and second, that "the sense of touch is far more intrusive into the personal privacy that is at the core of the Fourth Amendment." We have a somewhat different view. First, *Terry* itself demonstrates that the sense of touch is capable of revealing the nature of an object with sufficient reliability to support a seizure. The very premise of *Terry,* after all, is that officers will be able to detect the presence of weapons through the sense of touch ... . The court's second concern—that touch is more intrusive into privacy than is sight—is inapposite in light of the fact that the intrusion the court fears has already been authorized by the lawful search for weapons. ...

It remains to apply these principles to the facts of this case. ... Thus, the dispositive question before this Court is whether the officer who conducted the search was acting within the lawful bounds marked by *Terry* at the time he gained probable cause to believe the lump in respondent's jacket was contraband. ...

Under the State Supreme Court's interpretation of the record before it, it is clear that the court was correct in holding that the police officer in this case overstepped the bounds of the "strictly circumscribed" search for weapons allowed under *Terry.* [In *Terry*], as here, "an officer who is executing a valid search for one item seizes a different item," [and] this Court rightly "has been sensitive to the danger ... that officers will enlarge a specific authorization, furnished by a warrant or an exigency, into the equivalent of a general warrant to rummage and seize at will." ...

Although the officer was lawfully in a position to feel the lump in respondent's jacket, because *Terry* entitled him to place his hands upon respondent's jacket, the court below determined that the incriminating character of the object was not immediately apparent to him. Rather, the officer determined that the item was contraband only after conducting a further search, one not authorized by *Terry* or by another exception to the warrant requirement. Because this further search of respondent's pocket was constitutionally invalid, the seizure of the cocaine that followed is likewise unconstitutional.

For these reasons, the judgment of the Minnesota Supreme Court is affirmed.

Search Incident to Arrest

Two search issues arise during and immediately following an arrest. First, may officers search the arrestee's person without first obtaining a warrant? Second, may officers search the arrestee's home, apartment, or other structure where the defendant is arrested?

The issue of searching the defendant's person was addressed in *United States v. Robinson,*[38] in which the Court held that, after a lawful arrest, the defendant's person may be fully searched without first obtaining a warrant. The Court held that to require officers to obtain a warrant would needlessly endanger their lives and would increase the possibility of evidence being destroyed by the defendant. Search incident to arrest includes a search of the defendant's clothing. There is no probable cause requirement for a search incident to arrest.

The second issue concerns searching the area where the defendant is arrested. The premier case in this area is *Chimel v. California*, which significantly changed the law.

Before *Chimel* was decided, officers had the authority to search a much greater area as incident to arrest. The "within the defendant's immediate control" test continues to be the governing law. As with any other lawful search and seizure, any evidence obtained may be used to prosecute the defendant.

A related concept, the protective sweep, was given constitutional recognition in *Maryland v. Buie.*[39] A *protective sweep* is a brief and limited warrantless search of an arrestee's home, which is permitted if the defendant is arrested therein. The purpose of the protective sweep is to check the house for other persons who may pose a danger to the arresting officers. See later in this chapter for an extended discussion of searches incident to arrest and protective sweeps.

Finally, "when a policeman has made a lawful custodial arrest of the occupant of an automobile, he may, as a contemporaneous incident of that arrest, search the passenger compartment of that automobile," including the contents of any containers found in that area.[40]

CHIMEL
v.
CALIFORNIA
395 U.S. 752 (1969)

This case raises basic questions concerning the permissible scope under the Fourth Amendment of a search incident to a lawful arrest.

The relevant facts are essentially undisputed. Late in the afternoon of September 13, 1965, three police officers arrived at the Santa Ana, California, home of the petitioner with a warrant authorizing his arrest for the burglary of a coin shop. The officers knocked on the door, identified themselves to the petitioner's wife, and asked if they might come inside. She ushered them into the house, where they waited 10 to 15 minutes until the petitioner returned home from work. When the petitioner entered the house, one of the officers handed him the arrest warrant and asked for permission to "look around." The petitioner objected, but was advised that "on the basis of the lawful arrest," the officers would nonetheless conduct the search. No search warrant had been issued.

Accompanied by the petitioner's wife, the officers then looked through the entire three-bedroom house, including the attic, the garage, and a small workshop. In some rooms the search was relatively cursory. In the master bedroom and sewing room, however, the officers directed the petitioner's wife to open drawers and "to physically remove contents of the drawers from side to side so that [they] might view items that would have come from [the] burglary." After completing the search, they seized numerous items—primarily coins, but also several medals, tokens, and a few other objects. The entire search took between 45 minutes and an hour. ...

When an arrest is made, it is reasonable for the arresting officer to search the person arrested in order to remove any weapons that the latter might seek to use in order to resist arrest or effect his escape. Otherwise, the officer's safety might well be endangered, and the arrest itself frustrated. In addition, it is entirely reasonable for the arresting officer to search for and seize any evidence on the arrestee's person in order to prevent its concealment or destruction. And the area into which an arrestee might reach in order to grab a weapon or evidentiary items must, of course, be governed by a like rule. A gun on a table or in a drawer in front of one who is arrested can be as dangerous to the arresting officer as one concealed in the clothing of the person arrested. There is ample justification, therefore, for a search of the arrestee's person and the area "within his immediate control"—construing that phrase to mean the area from within which he might gain possession of a weapon or destructible evidence.

There is no comparable justification, however, for routinely searching any room other than that in which an arrest occurs—or, for that matter, for searching through all the desk drawers or other closed or concealed areas in the room itself. Such searches, in the absense of well-recognized exceptions, may be made only under the authority of a search warrant. ...

Application of sound Fourth Amendment principles to the facts of this case produces a clear result. ... The scope of the search was ... "unreasonable" under the Fourth and Fourteenth Amendments, and the petitioner's conviction cannot stand.

Reversed.

Preservation of Evidence

In some instances evidence may be destroyed before a warrant can be obtained. In such cases an officer may make a warrantless search and seizure.

Although the typical case involves the destruction of evidence, the preservation-of-evidence theory also has been applied to evanescent evidence (evidence that may vanish on its own). For example, in one case a defendant, who was arrested for drunk driving, was subjected to a warrantless blood alcohol test. The Court concluded that the warrantless test was reasonable under the Fourth Amendment.

> The officer in the present case, however, might reasonably have believed that he was confronted with an emergency, in which the delay necessary to obtain a warrant, under the circumstances, threatened "the destruction of evidence."... We are told that the percentage of alcohol in the blood begins to diminish shortly after drinking stops, as the body functions to eliminate it from the system. Particularly in a case such as this, where time had to be taken to bring the accused to the hospital and to investigate the scene of the accident, there was no time to seek out a magistrate and secure a warrant. Given these special facts, we conclude that the attempt to secure evidence of blood-alcohol content in this case was an appropriate incident to petitioner's arrest.[41]

So, any evidence that may be destroyed, intentionally or not, before a warrant can be obtained, can be the foundation of a warrantless search and seizure under the preservation-of-evidence exception to the Fourth Amendment's warrant requirement.

Emergency Searches and Hot Pursuit

One of the many responsibilities of being a police officer is to respond to emergencies and to assist those in danger. Police officers are permitted to enter areas protected by the Fourth Amendment without a warrant if there is an emergency.

An officer may respond to cries for help from within a home or may enter a building that is on fire to assist firefighters. The possibilities are endless. Provided the officer has a genuine and reasonable belief that there is an emergency, the entry does not violate the Fourth Amendment. Of course, once inside, any evidence in plain view may be seized.

It has been argued that the government has such a great interest, especially in murder cases, in having immediate access to crime scenes that the Fourth Amendment warrant requirement should be dispensed with. The Supreme Court rejected that position in *Mincey v. Arizona,*[42] in which a warrantless four-day search of an apartment where a police officer was murdered was held violative of the Fourth Amendment.

Police officers may make warrantless entries into buildings if an exigency exists, such as to assist a person in danger, to prevent the loss or destruction of evidence, or to arrest a person while in hot pursuit. Once inside, if officers discover that a crime has been committed, they may remedy any immediate problems, secure the premises, and then obtain a warrant before proceeding further, provided that no exigent circumstances justify a continued presence and search.

Similar to the emergency exception is the hot pursuit exception. An officer who is chasing a suspect does not have to end the pursuit at the door of a home or business. The normally unlawful entry into the structure is permitted to catch the defendant. Again, once inside, the plain view exception applies.

Open Fields

The open fields doctrine is not, technically, an exception to the search warrant requirement. That is because, to be an exception to the Fourth Amendment warrant requirement, the Fourth Amendment must apply to the conduct of the officers. The Supreme Court has held that the "open fields" around one's home are not protected by the Fourth Amendment, so officers are free to intrude upon such areas without first obtaining a warrant. In addition, officers will not be liable for trespass if they make such an intrusion while performing a lawful duty.[43]

The reason that open fields are not protected is because of the language of the Fourth Amendment itself: "The right of the people to be secure in their persons, houses, papers, and effects ... ." The Supreme Court has found that this extends the Fourth Amendment's protection only to a person's home and the curtilage of that home.

Curtilage is the area directly around one's home. It is treated as part of the home, as the Court has recognized that a person's privacy interest does not end at the front door of the home. Determining whether an area is curtilage, and protected, or an open field, and unprotected, can be troublesome. In *United States v. Dunn,*[44] the high Court held that a barn located sixty yards from a house was not within the curtilage, even though a fence enclosed the barn. In that opinion, the Court stated four factors that should be considered when making an open fields determination. Those are:

1. The proximity of the area claimed to be curtilage from the home.
2. Whether the area enclosed is enclosed with the home.
3. The nature of the use of the area.
4. The attempts of the residents to keep the area private.

The proximity of the area in question to the home, the fact that it is enclosed by fencing, that it is commonly used by the residents, and that the residents have taken measures to assure privacy in the area, all increase the probability that the area will be determined to be curtilage.

The issue is whether the residents have a reasonable expectation of privacy in the area.

The advent of aerial surveillance has made it possible for law enforcement officers to see what were once remote areas. The question in the Fourth Amendment context is: Do people have a reasonable expectation of privacy in areas observable from aircraft?

One federal district court outlined five factors to be considered when examining the validity of aerial surveillance:

1. The height of the aircraft.
2. The size of the objects viewed.
3. The nature of the use of the area.
4. The number of flights over the area.
5. The frequency and duration of the aerial surveillance.[45]

Structures, even though in an open field, may be protected if it appears that one took measures to assure privacy.[46] However, the fact that an area is curtilage does not mean that a warrantless aerial observation is unreasonable. In a 1986 case, the Supreme Court upheld an aerial observation of a backyard that was surrounded by a fence and not visible from the street.[47]

Finally, although the Fourth Amendment speaks of "houses," its protection extends to businesses and other structures as well. However, it is likely that the expectation of privacy will be less in a business than in a dwelling.

Border Searches and Profiles

Unlike ordinary searches, searches at the borders of the United States do not require probable cause. In fact, no suspicion is required whatsoever. This rule applies to searches of both luggage and persons.[48] However, these searches must comply with the reasonableness requirement of the Fourth Amendment.[49]

For a strip search to be conducted, a customs official must have a "real suspicion" that illegality is afoot. As for more invasive searches, such as cavity searches, more suspicion is required. A customs official must be aware of a "clear indication" of illegality before such searches are conducted. Further, these searches must be conducted in a private and medically safe environment. A *clear indication* is less than probable cause, but more than either the *Terry* reasonable suspicion or the border strip-search "real suspicion" standards.

The border search exception to the Fourth Amendment actually extends beyond the border. For example, first arrival ports in the United

States of international flights are treated as borders for purposes of the Fourth Amendment. Roadblock-style checkpoints miles from a border intended to discover illegal aliens have been approved,[50] but the authority to search is more limited than at the border. Officers may not search the occupants of the vehicles stopped at these checkpoints without probable cause.[51] Random stops of vehicles away from the border must be supported by reasonable suspicion, because they are treated as *Terry* detentions.

Customs officials commonly use profiles to determine who to detain and search. A *profile* is an established set of criteria that are believed to indicate a probability that a person is involved in illegal activity. For example, a person who makes frequent trips between the United States and Colombia (a nation noted for its drug production and exportation), carries little or no luggage, who has paid for airline tickets with cash, whose visits to Colombia are for short periods of time (e.g., 48 hours), and who behaves nervously at the customs desk, would meet a drug courier profile. Similar profiles have been used to stop motorists in Florida suspected of transporting and trafficking drugs.

Two issues are raised by profiles: first, whether a profile may be used to establish a reasonable suspicion, thereby permitting a *Terry* stop; and second, whether profiles justify searches.

As to the first question, the answer is yes. However, a profile must be reasonable. Courts examine the totality of the circumstances when examining the validity of a profile. Although no one factor in a profile may justify a temporary detention, the whole picture may. Although race may be a factor in the decision, the Supreme Court held in *United States v. Brignoni-Ponce*[52] that race alone does not establish reasonable suspicion, even if the detention occurs near the Mexican border and the occupants appear to be of Mexican ancestry. The Court enumerated factors that may be taken into account:

1. The characteristics of the area, including the proximity to the border, the usual patterns of traffic on the road, and experience with alien traffic
2. Information concerning recent illegal border crossings in the area
3. The driver's behavior, such as erratic driving and obvious attempts to evade officers
4. The type of vehicle, such as a station wagon with large compartments, which are frequently used for transporting concealed aliens
5. Whether the vehicle appears heavily loaded or has an extraordinary number of occupants
6. Whether passengers are attempting to hide
7. The characteristics of persons living in Mexico, including mode of dress and hair styles

8. Other meaningful factors in light of the officers' experiences in detecting illegal aliens.

This list is not exclusive, and profiles vary depending upon the situation. Nevertheless, the *Brignoni-Ponce* decision provided a basis upon which law enforcement agencies can create profiles and courts can adjudge the validity of those profiles.

This leads to the second question: May profiles be used to justify searches? Recall that at borders, no suspicion is necessary to conduct general searches of persons and things. However, to conduct body searches a "real suspicion" must exist, and to conduct more invasive searches there must be a "clear indication" of some illegality. Although a profile may satisfy the real suspicion test, it does not, acting alone, justify more invasive searches.

Outside the border areas, profiles may be used to conduct *Terry* stops, but no more. To conduct a frisk of the persons detained, a reasonable belief as to dangerousness must exist. Probable cause is required if a full search of a person, vehicle, or other things is conducted.

Finally, although profiles may be used to support detentions, they may not be used at trial to establish guilt.[53]

Motor Vehicles and Roadblocks

Privacy in automobiles is protected by the Fourth Amendment. However, the Supreme Court has not extended full Fourth Amendment protection to the occupants of automobiles. The Court's rationale for decreased protection is twofold. First, because of the mobile nature of automobiles, evidence can disappear quickly. Second, automobiles are used on the public roads where they and their occupants are visible to the public; thus, an occupant of an automobile has a lesser expectation of privacy than does the occupant of a home.

Of course, a motorist may be stopped if an officer has probable cause. In addition, a *Terry* stop may be made if there is reasonable suspicion. As discussed earlier, *Terry* stops must be limited in duration and reasonable in method, and a frisk of the occupant is permissible only if the officer possesses a reasonable belief that the individual may have a weapon.

Where the Fourth Amendment's mandates have been reduced is in the context of the warrant requirement. In *Carroll v. United States,*[54] it was announced that a warrantless search of a vehicle stopped on a public road is reasonable, provided the officer has probable cause to believe that an object subject to seizure will be found in the vehicle. The existence of probable cause is the key to the search. This authority has been extended to permit the search to continue after the vehicle is impounded.[55]

The sticky question in this area is the scope of the search. Generally, an officer is given the scope that a magistrate would have if a warrant were sought. Thus, if an officer has probable cause to believe that a shotgun used in a crime will be found in a car, a search of the glove box is improper. The opposite would be true if the item sought was a piece of jewelry, such as a ring.

Officers may also search closed items found in the vehicle, provided probable cause exists to believe an item sought may be contained therein.[56] The same rules apply as previously discussed. Rifling through a suitcase found in a car in search of a stolen painting that is larger than the suitcase is unreasonable and violative of the Fourth Amendment. Once the sought-after item is found, the search must cease.

An automobile may be searched incident to the arrest of its driver, but that search is also limited. If a motorist is arrested and removed from a vehicle, but there is no independent probable cause to search the vehicle, items contained therein may not be opened.[57] This is true even if the vehicle is impounded and an inventory is performed. The inventory should note the luggage found, but no effort to discover its contents should be made.

May the occupants of a vehicle be searched incident to a proper search of the vehicle? The answer is no[58]—but if an officer has probable cause to believe that one of the occupants has hidden the item sought on his or her person, a search of that occupant is permissible.

Fourth Amendment issues also arise in the context of roadblocks, which are used by law enforcement officers in two situations. First, they assist in the apprehension of a particular suspect. Second, serving the regulatory function of protecting the public from unsafe drivers, officers may stop vehicles to determine if the car satisfies the state's safety requirements, whether the driver is properly licensed, and whether the vehicle is properly registered. In regard to the former, reasonable suspicion is required before a stop can be made. As to the latter, temporary regulatory detentions are permitted so long as they are both objectively random and reasonable. That is, the police must use an objective system in deciding what automobiles will be stopped. Every car, or every tenth car, or some similar method is permissible.

The Supreme Court has also upheld roadblocks intended to discover drunk drivers. *Michigan State Police v. Sitz*[59] upheld a highway sobriety checkpoint program where 126 vehicles passed through the checkpoint, the average delay for each vehicle was 25 seconds, and 2 intoxicated drivers were arrested. The Court found that the stops were seizures under the Fourth Amendment, but that they were reasonable. In support of this conclusion, the Court stressed that the stops were of limited duration; that drunk drivers are a serious problem in the nation, and accordingly Michigan had a compelling interest in performing the sobriety checks; that all stops were governed by objective guidelines; that the guidelines required all vehicles to be stopped, thereby preventing arbitrary decisions by individual officers; that all officers were fully uniformed, thereby lessening motorists' concerns; and finally, that data support the conclusion that sobriety checkpoints are effective in apprehending drunk drivers.

Although systematic roadblocks are proper, discretionary spot checks are not. In the *Prouse* case, the Supreme Court held that arbitrary stops of automobiles by law enforcement officers violate the Fourth Amendment.

Finally, note that profiles are used by some law enforcement agencies to establish a reasonable suspicion to stop motorists. For example, drug courier profiles are used in Florida and illegal alien profiles are used by the Border Patrol. See earlier in this chapter for a more thorough discussion of the use of profiles.

DELAWARE
v.
PROUSE
440 U.S. 648 (1979)

At 7:20 P.M. on November 30, 1976, a New Castle County ... patrolman in a police cruiser stopped the automobile occupied by respondent. The patrolman smelled marihuana smoke as he was walking toward the stopped vehicle, and he seized marihuana in plain view on the car floor. Respondent was subsequently indicted for illegal possession of a controlled substance. At a hearing on respondent's motion to suppress the marihuana seized as a result of the stop, the patrolman testified that prior to stopping the vehicle he had observed neither traffic or equipment violations nor any suspicious activity, and that he made the stop only in order to check the driver's license and registration. The patrolman was not acting pursuant to any standards, guidelines, or procedures pertaining to document spot checks, promulgated by either his department or the State Attorney General. Characterizing the stop as "routine," the patrolman explained, "I saw the car in the area and wasn't answering any complaints, so I decided to pull them off." The trial court granted the motion to suppress, finding the stop and detention to have been wholly capricious and therefore violative of the Fourth Amendment. ...

The Delaware Supreme Court affirmed. ...

But the State of Delaware urges ... these stops are reasonable under the Fourth Amendment because the State's interest in the practice as a means of promoting public safety upon its roads more than outweighs the intrusion entailed. Although the record discloses no statistics concerning the extent of the problem of highway safety, in Delaware or in the Nation as a whole, we are aware of danger to life and property posed by vehicular traffic and the difficulties that even a cautious and experienced driver may encounter. We agree that the States have a vital interest in ensuring that only those qualified to do so are permitted to operate motor vehicles, that these vehicles are fit for safe operation, and hence that licensing, registration, and vehicle inspection requirements are being observed. ...

The question remains, however, whether in the service of these important ends the discretionary spot check is a sufficiently productive mechanism to justify the intrusion upon Fourth Amendment interests which stops entail. On the record before us, that question must be answered in the negative. Given the alternative mechanisms available, both those in use and those that might be adopted, we are unconvinced that the incremental contribution to highway safety of the random spot check justifies the practice under the Fourth Amendment.

The foremost method of enforcing traffic and vehicle safety regulations, it must be recalled, is acting upon observed violations. Vehicle stops for traffic violations occur countless times each day; and on these occasions, licenses and registration papers are subject to inspection and drivers without them will be ascertained. Furthermore, drivers without licenses are presumably the less safe drivers whose propensities may well exhibit themselves. ...

Much the same can be said about the safety aspects of automobiles as distinguished from drivers. Many violations of minimum vehicle-safety requirements are observable, and something can be done about them by the observing officer, directly and immediately. Furthermore, in Delaware, as elsewhere, vehicles must carry and display current license plates, which themselves evidence that the vehicle is properly registered; and, under Delaware law, to qualify for annual registration a vehicle must pass the annual safety inspection and be properly insured. ...

The marginal contribution to roadway safety possibly resulting from a system of spot checks cannot justify subjecting every occupant of every vehicle on the roads to a seizure—limited in magnitude compared to other intrusions but nonetheless constitutionally cognizable—at the unbridled discretion of law enforcement officials. To insist neither upon an appropriate factual basis for suspicion directed at a particular automobile nor upon some other substantial and objective standard or rule to govern the exercise of discretion "would invite intrusions upon constitutionally guaranteed rights based on nothing more substantial than inarticuable hunches ... . This kind of standardless and unconstrained discretion is the evil the Court has discerned when in previous cases it has insisted that the discretion of the official in the field be circumscribed, at least to some extent. ...

Accordingly, we hold that except in those situations in which there is at least articulable and reasonable suspicion that a motorist is unlicensed or that an automobile is not registered, or that either the vehicle or an occupant is otherwise subject to seizure for violation of law, stopping an automobile and detaining the driver in order to check his driver's license and the registration of the automobile are unreasonable under the Fourth Amendment. This holding does not preclude the State of Delaware or other States from developing methods for spot checks that involve less intrusions or that do not involve unconstrained exercise of discretion. Questioning of all oncoming traffic at roadblock-type stops is one possible alternative. We hold only that persons in automobiles on public roadways may not for that reason alone have their travel and privacy interfered with at the unbridled discretion of police officers. The judgment below is affirmed.

Inventory Searches

Police officers may impound vehicles whenever the driver or owner is arrested. *Impoundment* means towing the vehicle to a garage or parking lot for storage.

Although the decision to impound a vehicle is generally left to the discretion of the police officer, an officer may not refuse a less intrusive manner of caring for the vehicle. For example, if a husband and wife are riding together, and the husband is arrested for drunk driving, the wife is to be permitted to drive the vehicle home, provided she is capable.

Once impounded, an inventory search may be conducted. The purpose of an inventory search is to protect the owner of the vehicle from vandalism, protect the safety of the officers and others, and to protect the police department from claims of theft.

Because inventory searches are not conducted with an intent to discover evidence, there is no requirement of probable cause. If the facts of a case show that the police impounded a vehicle for the purpose of searching it, the search is improper.

Inventory searches are limited in scope. Although it is reasonable to search unlocked glove compartments and trunks, it is unreasonable under the Fourth Amendment if they are locked. A search of a vehicle's seats, floor area, and dashboard are routine. The Supreme Court has also stated that closed items found in impounded vehicles are subject to inventory searches.[60]

To avoid arbitrary inventory searches, police departments are expected, if not required, to establish an inventory search policy and procedure. All items discovered during an inventory search are to be recorded.

Prisoners

The Fourth Amendment is not fully applicable in prisons, for three reasons. First, security concerns outweigh privacy concerns. Second, loss of privacy is considered by our society to be an attribute of confinement and punishment. Third, inmates generally do not have reasonable expectations of privacy.

Hence, the Fourth Amendment is not implicated in the search of an inmate's cell, as there is no reasonable expectation of privacy in that area. The Supreme Court stated:

> A prison "shares none of the attributes of privacy of a home, an automobile, an office, or a hotel room." ... We strike the balance in favor of institutional security, which we have noted is "central to all other correctional goals." ... A right of privacy in traditional Fourth Amendment terms is fundamentally incompatible with the close and continual surveillance of inmates and their cells required to ensure institutional security and internal order. We are satisfied that society would insist that the prisoner's expectation of privacy always yield to what must be considered the paramount interest in institutional security. We believe that it is accepted by our society that "[l]oss of freedom of choice and privacy are inherent incidents of confinement."[61]

Although the Fourth Amendment does not apply to searches of inmates' cells, it does apply to searches of their persons. However, the probable cause and warrant requirements are dispensed with in the prison context. Rather, they are tested by the Fourth Amendment's reasonableness provision. Prisoners may be searched without any particular suspicion if the search is part of a routine system. Analogous to roadblocks, if the custodians search every prisoner, or every other prisoner, or use some other system, no suspicion is required. Prisoners may also be searched without suspicion if they have recently come into contact with visitors. In *Bell v. Wolfish*,[62] the Supreme Court held that strip searches of prisoners, conducted after they have contact with visitors or upon their return to the institution from outside, are permissible even without individualized suspicion. Otherwise, individual searches of inmates are allowed only when an officer has a reasonable suspicion that the inmate possesses contraband.

Although searches of inmates' cells are not included within the grasp of the Fourth Amendment, repeated searches intended to harass an inmate may be violative of the Eighth Amendment's prohibition of cruel and unusual punishment, as may searches of an inmate's person.

Review Questions

1. In what way did *Katz v. United States* change Fourth Amendment law?
2. What are the basic requirements for obtaining a search warrant?
3. Stacey is a suspect in an embezzlement investigation. The police believe that she has hidden evidence in her neighbor's house, without the neighbor's consent. The neighbor will not consent to a search. Can the police obtain a search warrant for the nonsuspect's home?
4. What is the plain view doctrine?
5. What is curtilage? Open fields? Why are the concepts important in criminal law?
6. May police stop vehicles at a systematic roadblock without suspicion that drivers are violating the law?
7. What level of suspicion is required before customs and border officers may search luggage at an United States border?
8. What level of suspicion is required before customs and border officers may conduct strip searches of persons at United States borders?
9. Does an alert by a trained police dog to an item establish probable cause for search of the item?
10. May prison officials search an inmate's person without cause? The inmate's cell?

Review Problems

1. Tommy Transmitter planned to burglarize a local audio/video dealer. On the night he intended to commit the burglary, Tommy was observed standing in an alley behind the shop by a police officer. It was 11:50 P.M., June, and Tommy was wearing a pair of jeans, tennis shoes, and a shirt.

   After five minutes, the officer approached Tommy and asked him "what he was doing in the alley at such a late hour." Tommy responded that he lived only a few blocks away, was suffering from insomnia, and had decided to take a walk. He produced identification that confirmed that he lived a short distance from the store. The officer then grabbed Tommy, swung him around, pushed him against the wall of the store, and "frisked him." After feeling a hard object in his back pocket, the officer reached in and discovered a small 3″×3″ container full of locksmith tools. He then arrested Tommy for possession of burglary tools and conducted a search incident to arrest. During that search he discovered a diagram of the audio/video store hidden in Tommy's pants.

   Tommy was subsequently charged with attempted burglary and possession of burglary tools. He has filed a motion to suppress the tools and diagram, as well as a motion to dismiss. Should the motions be granted? Discuss.

2–5. Assume that officers have a valid search warrant for the defendant's apartment. The warrant specifies that the officers may search for stolen stereos. May the officers do the following?

2. Search the defendant's desk drawers in his study?
3. Search the defendant's closets in his bedroom?
4. Search the defendant's body?
5. Seize a transparent bag of cocaine found lying on the defendant's dining room table?
6. Do you agree with Justice Brennan that the protective sweep goes beyond the *Terry v. Ohio* decision? Explain your position.
7. In *United States v. Leon,* the Supreme Court created a "good faith" exception to the probable cause requirement of the Fourth Amendment. Under *Leon,* evidence seized in good faith pursuant to a search warrant is admissible at trial, even though it is later determined that probable cause was lacking. Should this exception be extended to warrantless searches when an officer has a good faith belief that probable cause exists?

Notes

1 *Bivens v. Six Unknown Named Agents,* 403 U.S. 388 (1971).

2 *United States v. Jacobsen,* 466 U.S. 109, 113 (1984).

3 *Carroll v. United States,* 267 U.S. 132 (1934).

4 378 U.S. 108 (1964).

5 462 U.S. 213 (1983).

6 *Gates,* 462 U.S. at 233.

7 *United States v. Place,* 462 U.S. 696 (1983). A dog sniff of a person or thing, assuming no more intrusion, is not a search under the Fourth Amendment because no reasonable expectation of privacy has been violated.

8 468 U.S. 897 (1984).

9 *See Michigan v. DeFillippo,* 443 U.S. 31 (1979); *Illinois v. Krull,* 480 U.S. 340 (1987); *Arizona v. Evans,* ____ U.S. ____ (1995).

10 *Beck v. Ohio,* 379 U.S. 89 (1964).

11 *McDonald v. United States,* 335 U.S. 451, 455–56 (1948).

12 378 U.S. 108, 111 (1964).

13 468 U.S. 897 (1984).

14 *Coolidge v. New Hampshire,* 403 U.S. 443 (1971).

15 *Shadwick v. Tampa,* 407 U.S. 345 (1972).

16 Fed. R. Crim. P. 41(b).

17 *Zurcher v. Stanford Daily,* 436 U.S. 547 (1978).

18 *Ybarra v. Illinois,* 444 U.S. 85 (1979).

19 *Michigan v. Summers,* 452 U.S. 692 (1981).

20 *Jones v. United States,* 357 U.S. 493 (1958).

21 Fed. R. Crim. P. 41(c)(1).

22 *United States v. Moore,* 956 F.2d 843 (8th Cir. 1992).

23 Fed. R. Crim. P. 41(d).

24 *Schneckloth v. Bustamonte,* 412 U.S. 218 (1973).

25 *United States v. Kampbell,* 574 F.2d 962 (8th Cir. 1978).

26 *Commonwealth v. Wright,* 190 A.2d 709 (Pa. 1963).

27 415 U.S. 164 (1974).

28 For a discussion of landlord-tenant situations, *see Stoner v. California,* 376 U.S. 483 (1964).

29 *Arizona v. Hicks,* 480 U.S. 321 (1987).

30 403 U.S. at 470–71.

31 496 U.S. 128 (1990).

32 392 U.S. 1 (1968).

33 *Terry,* 392 U.S. at 21.

34 446 U.S. 544 (1980).

35 *Brown v. Texas,* 443 U.S. 47 (1979).

36 460 U.S. 491 (1983).

37 *Michigan v. Long,* 463 U.S. 1032 (1983).

38 414 U.S. 260 (1973).

39 494 U.S. 325 (1990).

40 *New York v. Belton,* 453 U.S. 454 (1981).

41 *Schmerber v. California,* 384 U.S. 757, 770–71 (1966).

42 437 U.S. 385 (1978).

43 *Oliver v. United States,* 466 U.S. 170 (1984).

44 480 U.S. 294 (1987).

45 *United States v. Bassford,* 601 F. Supp. 1324, 1330 (D. Mass. 1985).

46 *United States v. Broadhurst,* 612 F. Supp. 777 (C.D. Cal. 1985).

47 *California v. Ciraolo,* 476 U.S. 207 (1986).

48 *United States v. Ramsey,* 431 U.S. 606 (1977).

49 *See* Torcia, *Wharton's Criminal Evidence* §§ 733 (13th ed., Lawyers Cooperative Publishing Co., 1986 Supp.).

50 *United States v. Martinez-Fuerte,* 428 U.S. 543 (1976).

51 *United States v. Ortiz,* 422 U.S. 891 (1975).

52 422 U.S. 873 (1975).

53 *See United States v. Hernandez-Cuartas,* 717 F.2d 552 (11th Cir. 1983).

54 267 U.S. 132 (1925).

55 *Chambers v. Mahoney,* 399 U.S. 42 (1970).

56 *United States v. Ross,* 456 U.S. 798 (1982).

57 *Arkansas v. Sanders,* 442 U.S. 753 (1979).

58 *United States v. DiRe,* 332 U.S. 581 (1948).

59 496 U.S. 444 (1990).

60 *Colorado v. Bertine,* 479 U.S. 367 (1986).

61 *Hudson v. Palmer,* 468 U.S. 517 (1984).

62 441 U.S. 520 (1979).

CHAPTER 6

ARREST

CHAPTER OUTLINE

> *The police must obey the law while enforcing the law.*
>
> ***Earl Warren***
> ***United States Supreme Court Justice***

§ 6.1 Introduction

One of the most serious interferences with a person's liberty is to be physically seized by a government. Equally, arrest plays an important role in effective law enforcement.

Because of the significant impact arrest has on a person's life, the right to arrest is limited by the Fourth Amendment.

§ 6.2 Defining Arrest

Generally, an **arrest** is a deprivation of freedom by a legal authority. As you have already learned, seizures by the police take two primary forms. First, at the lower end of the spectrum is the *Terry v. Ohio* seizure. Such seizures occur whenever a person reasonably believes that he or she is not free to leave. In addition, the seizure must be as brief as possible and be of limited intrusion to the person detained.

Any seizure that goes beyond the *Terry* standard is an arrest. A *Terry* investigatory detention may be transformed into an arrest if the person is detained for an unreasonable length of time or the police use intrusive investigatory tactics. Whether an officer intends to arrest is not dispositive, nor is an announcement to the citizen that he or she is or is not under arrest. The totality of the facts will determine whether the intrusion amounts to an arrest under the Fourth Amendment.

The requirements for a *Terry* stop were discussed in Chapter 5. The following is a discussion of the Fourth Amendment requirements for arrest.

TERMS

arrest Detention of a person on a criminal charge.

§ 6.3 The Warrant Preference

Searches must be conducted pursuant to a valid warrant (see Figure 6-1), unless an exception to the warrant requirement can be shown. Arrests are quite different. Rather than a requirement for a warrant,

FIGURE 6-1
Warrant for Arrest

AO 442 (Rev. 5/85) Warrant for Arrest

United States District Court

_____ DISTRICT OF _____

UNITED STATES OF AMERICA
V.

WARRANT FOR ARREST

CASE NUMBER:

To: The United States Marshal
and any Authorized United States Officer

YOU ARE HEREBY COMMANDED to arrest _____
Name

and bring him or her forthwith to the nearest magistrate to answer a(n)

☐ Indictment ☐ Information ☐ Complaint ☐ Order of court ☐ Violation Notice ☐ Probation Violation Petition

charging him or her with (brief description of offense)

in violation of Title _____ United States Code, Section(s) _____

_____
Name of Issuing Officer

_____
Title of Issuing Officer

_____
Signature of Issuing Officer

_____
Date and Location

_____
(By) Deputy Clerk

Bail fixed at $ _____ by _____
Name of Judicial Officer

RETURN		
This warrant was received and executed with the arrest of the above-named defendant at _____		
DATE RECEIVED	NAME AND TITLE OF ARRESTING OFFICER	SIGNATURE OF ARRESTING OFFICER
DATE OF ARREST		

in most instances, there is simply a preference for one. The "informed and deliberate determinations of magistrates empowered to issue warrants ... are to be preferred over the hurried action of officers."[1] As is the case with warrantless searches, probable cause determinations by magistrates will be supported on appeal with less evidence than those made by police officers.

AO 442 (Rev. 5/85) Warrant for Arrest

THE FOLLOWING IS FURNISHED FOR INFORMATION ONLY:

DEFENDANT'S NAME: ______

ALIAS: ______

LAST KNOWN RESIDENCE: ______

LAST KNOWN EMPLOYMENT: ______

PLACE OF BIRTH: ______

DATE OF BIRTH: ______

SOCIAL SECURITY NUMBER: ______

HEIGHT: ______ WEIGHT: ______

SEX: ______ RACE: ______

HAIR: ______ EYES: ______

SCARS, TATTOOS, OTHER DISTINGUISHING MARKS: ______

FBI NUMBER: ______

COMPLETE DESCRIPTION OF AUTO: ______

INVESTIGATIVE AGENCY AND ADDRESS: ______

FIGURE 6-1
(continued)

Notwithstanding the preference, most arrests are made without first obtaining a warrant. The authority to make warrantless arrests has a long history. Under the common law, a law officer could arrest whenever he had reasonable grounds to believe that a defendant committed a felony. Misdemeanants who breached the peace could be arrested without warrant if the crime was committed in the presence of an officer.

United States v. Watson[2] was the case in which the Supreme Court recognized that warrantless arrests in public places, based upon probable cause, did not violate the Fourth Amendment. There is no constitutional requirement that an officer obtain a warrant to effect an arrest in a public place—even if the officer has adequate time to get the warrant prior to making the arrest. However, the Fourth Amendment does require that probable cause exist before an arrest can be made.

For a warrantless arrest in a public place to be upheld, it must be shown that the officer who made the arrest: (1) had probable cause to believe that a crime was committed and (2) that the person arrested committed that crime. As with searches and seizures, probable cause can be established in a number of ways: statements from victims and witnesses; personal knowledge and observations of the officer; reliable hearsay; and informant tips.

Most, if not all, states permit officers to arrest without a warrant if there is probable cause to believe that the suspect committed a felony. States vary in their treatment of misdemeanors, but most only permit warrantless arrest for a misdemeanor committed in an officer's presence. Some states have a broader rule that permits the arrest of a misdemeanant, even if the crime was not committed in the presence of an officer, provided there is both probable cause and an exigent circumstance.

An officer's determination of probable cause may later be attacked by the defendant. If the officer was wrong, then the defendant may be successful in obtaining his or her freedom or suppressing any evidence which is the fruit of the illegal arrest.

When an officer does seek an arrest warrant, the requirements previously discussed concerning search warrants apply. That is, the warrant must be issued by a neutral and detached magistrate upon a finding of probable cause, supported by oath or affirmation.

§ 6.4 Arrests in Protected Areas

So far the discussion of arrests has been confined to arrests made in public. If the arrest is to be made in an area protected by the Fourth Amendment, such as a person's home, a warrant must be obtained, unless an exception exists.

In *Payton v. New York,*[3] it was held that a valid arrest warrant implicitly carries with it a limited right to enter the suspect's home to effect the arrest, provided there is reason to believe the suspect is within. Under *Payton,* the search must be limited to areas where the suspect may be hiding. Because the entry is lawful, any evidence discovered in plain view may be seized.

Arrest warrants do not authorize entry into the private property of third persons. In the absence of consent or exigent circumstances, a search warrant must be obtained before a search of a third person's home or property may be conducted.[4]

The warrant requirement is obviated if the occupant gives consent to the search. Exigent circumstances, such as hot pursuit, also justify warrantless entries into homes to effect an arrest.

§ 6.5 Search Incident to Arrest and the Protective Sweep

As you learned in Chapter 5, an officer may search an arrestee fully as incident to arrest. In addition, the area within the arrestee's immediate control may also be searched. The scope of a search incident to arrest, however, is limited to areas where a weapon might be obtained by the person arrested. Clearly, a search of any room other than the one where a defendant is being held is not supported by the doctrine of search incident to arrest.

The search-incident-to-arrest doctrine does not consider the possibility that other potentially dangerous persons may be present, but out of sight, when an arrest is made. Must police take the risk that no other dangerous persons are on the premises when making a lawful arrest? This question was answered by the Supreme Court in *Maryland v. Buie.*

It is important to note that the protective sweep may not be automatically conducted by the police, unlike a search incident to arrest. An officer must have a reasonable belief, supported by specific and articulable facts, that a dangerous person may be hiding in the home, before a protective sweep may be conducted. There need not be a belief of dangerousness to conduct a search incident to arrest.

A protective sweep must be limited to searching those areas where a person might be hiding. How far this will be permitted to go remains to be seen. Justice Brennan, dissenting in *Buie,* made this statement:

> Police officers searching for potential ambushers might enter every room including basements and attics, open up closets, lockers, chests, wardrobes, and cars; and peer under beds and behind furniture. The officers will view letters, documents and personal effects that are on

tables or desks or are visible inside open drawers; books, records, tapes, and pictures on shelves; and clothing, medicines, toiletries and other paraphernalia not carefully stored in dresser drawers or bathroom cupboards. While perhaps not a "full-blown" or "top-to-bottom" search ... a protective sweep is much closer to it than to a "limited patdown for weapons" or a "frisk" [as authorized by *Terry v. Ohio*].

MARYLAND
v.
BUIE
494 U.S. 325 (1990)

A "protective sweep" is a quick and limited search of a premises, incident to an arrest and conducted to protect the safey of police officers or others. It is narrowly confined to a cursory visual inspection of those places in which a person might be hiding. In this case we must decide what level of justification is required by the Fourth and Fourteenth Amendments before police officers, while effecting the arrest of a suspect in his home pursuant to an arrest warrant, may conduct a warrantless protective sweep of all or part of the premises. ...

On February 3, 1986, two men committed an armed robbery of a Godfather's Pizza restaurant in Prince George's County, Maryland. One of the robbers was wearing a red running suit. The same day, Prince George's County police obtained arrest warrants for respondent Jerome Edward Buie and his suspected accomplice in the robbery, Lloyd Allen. Buie's house was placed under police surveillance.

On February 5, the police executed the arrest warrant for Buie. They first had a police department secretary telephone Buie's house to verify that he was home. The secretary spoke to a female first, then to Buie himself. Six or seven officers proceeded to Buie's house. Once inside, the officers fanned out through the first and second floors. Corporal James Rozar announced that he would "freeze" the basement so that no one could come up and surprise the officers. With his service revolver drawn, Rozar twice shouted into the basement, ordering anyone down there to come out. When a voice asked who was calling, Rozar announced three times: "this is the police, show me your hands." Eventually, a pair of hands appeared around the bottom of the stairwell and Buie emerged from the basement. He was arrested, searched, and handcuffed by Rozar. Thereafter, Detective Joseph Frolich entered the basement "in case there was someone else" down there. ... He noticed a red running suit lying in plain view on a stack of clothing and seized it.

The trial court denied Buie's motion to suppress the running suit, stating in part: "The man comes out from a basement, the police don't know how many other people are down there."...

It goes without saying that the Fourth Amendment bars only unreasonable searches and seizures. ... Our cases show that in determining reasonableness, we have balanced the intrusion on the individual's Fourth Amendment interests against its promotion of legitimate governmental interests. ... Under this test, a search of the house or office is generally not reasonable without a warrant issued on probable cause. There are other contexts, however, where the public interest is such that neither a warrant nor probable cause is required. ...

The *Terry* case is most instructive for present purposes. There we held that an on-the-street "frisk" for weapons must be tested by the Fourth Amendment's general proscription against unreasonable searches because such a frisk involves "an entire rubric of police conduct—necessarily swift action predicated upon the on-the-spot observations of the officer on the beat—which historically has not been, and as a practical matter could not be, subjected to the warrant procedure."...

The ingredients to apply the balance struck in *Terry* and *Long* are present in this case. Possessing an arrest warrant and probable cause to believe Buie was in his home, the officers were entitled to enter and to search anywhere in the house in which Buie might be found. Once he was found, however, the search for him was over, and there was no longer that particular justification for entering any rooms that had not yet been searched.

That Buie had an expectation of privacy in those remaining areas of his house, however, does not mean such rooms were immune from entry. In *Terry* and *Long* we were concerned with the immediate interest of the police officers in taking steps to assure themselves that the persons with whom they were dealing were not armed with or able to gain immediate control of a weapon that could unexpectedly and fatally be used against them. In the instant case, there is an analogous interest of the officers in taking steps to assure themselves that the house in which the suspect is being or has just been arrested is not harboring other persons who are dangerous and who could unexpectedly launch an attack. The risk of danger in the context of an arrest in the home is as great as, if not greater than, it is in the on-the-street or roadside investigatory encounter. ...

We should emphasize that such a protective sweep, aimed at protecting the arresting officers, if justified by the circumstances, is nevertheless not a full search of the premises, but may extend only to a cursory inspection of those spaces where a person may be found. The sweep lasts no longer than is necessary to dispel the reasonable suspicion of danger and in any event no longer than it takes to complete the arrest and depart from the premises.

... The Fourth Amendment permits a properly limited protective sweep in conjunction with an in-home arrest when the searching officer possesses a reasonable belief based on specific and articulable facts that the area to be swept harbors an individual posing a danger to those on the arrest scene.

§ 6.6 Executing Arrest Warrants

Arrest warrants may be executed at the officer's discretion, whether day or night. However, common sense dictates that warrants be served at a reasonable hour, unless an exigency exists.

In *Ker v. California*,[5] an unannounced entry into a person's home was found to be violative of the Fourth Amendment. Therefore, the general rule is that officers must knock and announce their reason for being there. A number of exceptions to this rule have been recognized, including:

1. When the safety of the police or others will be endangered by the announcement.
2. When the announcement will allow those inside to destroy evidence or escape.
3. When the occupants know the purpose of the officers.

The Court has said that the knock-and-announce requirement applies whether or not the police gain entry by force. It is not important whether the police gain entry through using a key, opening an unlocked door, smashing a window, or breaking a door down. Police may obtain no-knock warrants in exceptional circumstances.

§ 6.7 Good Faith Reliance on Warrant or Court Records

You learned in Chapter 5 that evidence seized during execution of a facially valid warrant that is later determined to be invalid may be used at trial. What happens when an officer makes an arrest pursuant to an incorrect court record indicating an outstanding warrant? Should evidence seized as a result be admitted? The Supreme Court answered that question in *Arizona v. Evans.*

§ 6.8 Illegal Arrests

Does the exclusionary rule apply to people as it does to things? That is, should a defendant be excluded from trial because he or she has been arrested unlawfully? Generally, the Supreme Court has answered no.[6] Therefore, the fact that a defendant is kidnapped has no bearing on whether the criminal proceeding will continue.

There may be an exception to this rule. If the conduct of the government is outrageous, shocking, and a gross invasion of a defendant's constitutional rights, he or she may be set free. This is known as a *Toscanino* claim, named after the defendant in that case.

Later, the Second Circuit Court of Appeals reiterated that the *Toscanino* reasoning only applies to situations in which the government's conduct is both shocking and outrageous, as was true of the allegations in *Toscanino.*[7] Be aware that not all courts have followed the Second Circuit's lead. Rather than deal with the thorny legal issue, most courts factually distinguish their cases from *Toscanino.* The Supreme Court has not yet addressed the issue.

Even though a defendant's person may not be excluded because of an illegal arrest, the evidence obtained pursuant to that arrest may be. For example, if there is a causal connection between an illegal arrest and a subsequent confession, then the statement must be excluded.[8] Or, if evidence is obtained through a search incident to an illegal arrest, it must also be suppressed. In short, any evidence obtained as a result of an illegal arrest must be excluded, unless an independent basis for its discovery can be shown by the government.

ARIZONA
v.
EVANS
___ U.S. ___ (1995)

CHIEF JUSTICE REHNQUIST delivered the opinion of the Court.

This case presents the question whether evidence seized in violation of the Fourth Amendment by an officer who acted in reliance on a police record indicating the existence of an outstanding arrest warrant—a record that is later determined to be erroneous—must be suppressed by virtue of the exclusionary rule regardless of the source of the error. The Supreme Court of Arizona held that the exclusionary rule required suppression of evidence even if the erroneous information resulted from an error committed by an employee of the office of the Clerk of Court. We disagree.

In January 1991, Phoenix police officer Bryan Sargent observed respondent Evans driving the wrong way on a one-way street in front of the police station. The officer stopped respondent and asked to see his driver's license. After respondent told him that his license had been suspended, the officer entered respondent's name into a computer data terminal located in his patrol car. The computer inquiry confirmed that respondent's license had been suspended and also indicated that there was an outstanding misdemeanor warrant for his arrest. Based upon the outstanding warrant, Officer Sargent placed respondent under arrest. While being handcuffed, respondent dropped a hand-rolled cigarette that the officers determined smelled of marijuana. Officers proceeded to search his car and discovered a bag of marijuana under the passenger's seat.

The State charged respondent with possession of marijuana. When the police notified the Justice Court that they had arrested him, the Justice Court discovered that the arrest warrant previously had been quashed and so advised the police. Respondent argued that because his arrest was based on a warrant that had been quashed 17 days prior to his arrest, the marijuana seized incident to the arrest should be suppressed as the fruit of an unlawful arrest. Respondent also argued that "[t]he 'good faith' exception to the exclusionary rule [was] inapplicable ... [to] the invalid arrest."

At the suppression hearing, the Chief Clerk of the Justice Court testified that a Justice of the Peace had issued the arrest warrant on December 13, 1990, because respondent had failed to appear to answer for several traffic violations. On December 19, 1990, respondent appeared before a pro tem Justice of the Peace who entered a notation in respondent's file to "quash warrant."

The Chief Clerk also testified regarding the standard court procedure for quashing a warrant. Under that procedure a justice court clerk calls and informs the warrant section of the Sheriff's Office when a warrant has been quashed. The Sheriff's Office then removes the warrant from its computer records. After calling the Sheriff's Office, the clerk makes a note in the individual's file indicating the clerk who made the phone call and the person at the Sheriff's Office to whom the clerk spoke. The Chief Clerk testified that there was no indication in respondent's file that a clerk had called and notified the Sheriff's Office that his arrest warrant had been quashed. A records clerk from the Sheriff's Office also testified that the Sheriff's Office had no record of a telephone call informing it that respondent's arrest warrant had been quashed.

At the close of testimony, respondent argued that the evidence obtained as a result of the arrest should be suppressed because "the purposes of the exclusionary rule would be served here by making the clerks for the court, or the clerk for the Sheriff's office, whoever is responsible for this mistake, to be more careful about making sure that warrants are removed from the records." The trial court granted the motion to suppress because it concluded that the State had been at fault for failing to quash the warrant. Presumably because it could find no "distinction between State action, whether it happens to be the police department or not," the trial court made no factual finding as to whether the Justice Court or Sheriff's Office was responsible for the continued presence of the quashed warrant in the police records.

A divided panel of the Arizona Court of Appeals reversed because it "believe[d] that the exclusionary rule [was] not intended to deter justice court employees or Sheriff's Office employees who are not directly associated with the arresting officers or the arresting officers' police department." Therefore, it concluded, "the purpose of the exclusionary rule would not be served by excluding the evidence obtained in this case."

The Arizona Supreme Court reversed. The court rejected the "distinction drawn by the court of appeals ... between clerical errors committed by law enforcement personnel and similar mistakes by court employees." The court predicted that application of the exclusionary rule would "hopefully serve to improve the efficiency of those who keep records in our criminal justice system." Finally, the Court concluded that "[e]ven assuming that deterrence is the principal reason for application of the exclusionary rule, we disagree with the court of appeals that such a purpose would not be served where carelessness by a court clerk results in an unlawful arrest."

We granted certiorari to determine whether the exclusionary rule requires suppression of evidence seized incident to an arrest resulting from an inaccurate computer record, regardless of whether police personnel or court personnel were responsible for the record's continued presence in the police computer. We now reverse.

The Fourth Amendment states that "[t]he right of the people to be secure in their persons, houses, papers, and effects, against unreasonable searches and seizures, shall not be violated, and no Warrants shall issue, but upon probable cause, supported by Oath or affirmation, and particularly describing the place to be searched, and the persons or things to be seized." We have recognized, however, that the Fourth Amendment contains no provision expressly precluding the use of evidence obtained in violation of its commands. "The wrong condemned by the [Fourth] Amendment is 'fully accomplished' by the unlawful search or seizure itself."

"The question whether the exclusionary rule's remedy is appropriate in a particular context has long been regarded as an issue separate from the question whether the Fourth Amendment rights of the party seeking to invoke the rule were violated by police conduct." The exclusionary rule operates as a judicially created remedy designed to safeguard against future violations of Fourth Amendment rights through the rule's general deterrent effect. As with any remedial device, the rule's application has been restricted to those instances where its remedial objectives are thought most efficaciously served. Where "the exclusionary rule does not result in appreciable deterrence, then, clearly, its use ... is unwarranted."

In *Leon,* we applied these principles to the context of a police search in which the officers had acted in objectively reasonable reliance on a search warrant, issued by a neutral and detached Magistrate, that later was determined to be invalid. On the basis of three factors, we determined that there was no sound reason to apply the exclusionary rule as a means of deterring misconduct on the part of judicial officers who are responsible for issuing warrants. First, we noted that the exclusionary rule was historically designed " 'to deter police misconduct rather than to punish the errors of judges and magistrates.' " Second, there was " 'no evidence suggesting that judges and magistrates are inclined to ignore or subvert the Fourth Amendment or that lawlessness among these actors requires the application of the extreme sanction of exclusion.' " Third, and of greatest importance, there was no basis for believing that exclusion of evidence seized pursuant to a warrant would have a significant deterrent effect on the issuing judge or magistrate.

The *Leon* Court then examined whether application of the exclusionary rule could be expected to alter the behavior of the law enforcement officers. We concluded:

> "[W]here the officer's conduct is objectively reasonable, 'excluding the evidence will not further the ends of the exclusionary rule in any

appreciable way; for it is painfully apparent that ... the officer is acting as a reasonable officer would and should act in similar circumstances. Excluding the evidence can in no way affect his future conduct unless it is to make him less willing to do his duty.' "

Applying the reasoning of *Leon* to the facts of this case, we conclude that the decision of the Arizona Supreme Court must be reversed. The Arizona Supreme Court determined that it could not "support the distinction drawn ... between clerical errors committed by law enforcement personnel and similar mistakes by court employees," and that "even assuming ... that responsibility for the error rested with the justice court, it does not follow that the exclusionary rule should be inapplicable to these facts."

This holding is contrary to the reasoning of *Leon.* If court employees were responsible for the erroneous computer record, the exclusion of evidence at trial would not sufficiently deter future errors so as to warrant such a severe sanction. First, as we noted in *Leon,* the exclusionary rule was historically designed as a means of deterring police misconduct, not mistakes by court employees. Second, respondent offers no evidence that court employees are inclined to ignore or subvert the Fourth Amendment or that lawlessness among these actors requires application of the extreme sanction of exclusion. To the contrary, the Chief Clerk of the Justice Court testified at the suppression hearing that this type of error occurred once every three or four years.

Finally, and most important, there is no basis for believing that application of the exclusionary rule in these circumstances will have a significant effect on court employees responsible for informing the police that a warrant has been quashed. Because court clerks are not adjuncts to the law enforcement team engaged in the often competitive enterprise of ferreting out crime, they have no stake in the outcome of particular criminal prosecutions. The threat of exclusion of evidence could not be expected to deter such individuals from failing to inform police officials that a warrant had been quashed.

If it were indeed a court clerk who was responsible for the erroneous entry on the police computer, application of the exclusionary rule also could not be expected to alter the behavior of the arresting officer. As the trial court in this case stated: "I think the police officer [was] bound to arrest. I think he would [have been] derelict in his duty if he failed to arrest." (" 'Excluding the evidence can in no way affect [the officer's] future conduct unless it is to make him less willing to do his duty.' ") The Chief Clerk of the Justice Court testified that this type of error occurred "on[c]e every three or four years." In fact, once the court clerks discovered the error, they immediately corrected it, and then proceeded to search their files to make sure that no similar mistakes had occurred. There is no indication that the arresting officer was not acting objectively reasonably when he relied upon the police computer record. Application of the Leon framework supports a categorical exception to the exclusionary rule for clerical errors of court employees.

The judgment of the Supreme Court of Arizona is therefore reversed, and the case is remanded to that court for proceedings not inconsistent with this opinion.

It is so ordered.

§ 6.9 Fourth Amendment Problems

Search and seizure problems can be complex. This area of the law is highly fact-sensitive. It is also an area where one must be careful and precise in analysis. Often search and seizure issues will be numerous in a single case, with all of the issues interrelated and interdependent.

UNITED STATES
v.
TOSCANINO
500 F.2d 267 (2d Cir. 1974)

Francisco Toscanino appeals from a narcotics conviction entered against him in the Eastern District of New York. ...

Toscanino does not question the sufficiency of the evidence or claim any error with respect to the conduct of the trial itself. His principal argument ... is that the entire proceedings in the district court against him were void because his presence within the territorial jurisdiction of the court had been illegally obtained. ... He offered to prove the following:

"On or about January 6, 1973 Francisco Toscanino was lured from his home in Montevideo, Uruguay by a telephone call. This call has been placed by or at the direction of Hugo Campos Hermedia. Hermedia was at that time and still is a member of the police in Montevideo, Uruguay. ...

"The telephone call ruse succeeded in bringing Toscanino and his wife, seven months pregnant at the time, to an area near a deserted bowling alley in the City of Montevideo. Upon their arrival there Hermedia together with six associates abducted Toscanino. This was accomplished in full view of Toscanino's terrified wife by knocking him unconscious with a gun. ...

"At no time had there been any formal or informal request on the part of the United States or the government of Uruguay for the extradiction of Francisco Toscanino nor was there any legal basis to justify this rank criminal enterprise. ...

"Later that same day Toscanino was brought to Brasilia. ... For seventeen days Toscanino was incessantly tortured and interrogated. Throughout this entire period the United States government and the United States Attorney for the Eastern District of New York ... did in fact receive reports as to its progress. ... [Toscanino's] captors denied him sleep and all forms of nourishment for days at a time. Nourishment was provided intravenously in a manner precisely equal to an amount necessary to keep him alive. Reminiscent of the horror stories told by our military men who returned from Korea and China, Toscanino was forced to walk up and down a hallway for seven or eight hours at a time. When he could no longer stand he was kicked and beaten but all in a manner contrived to punish without scarring. When he could not answer, his fingers were pinched with metal pliers. Alcohol was flushed into his eyes and nose and other fluids ... were forced up his anal passage. Incredibly, these agents of the United States government attached electrodes to Toscanino's earlobes, toes, and genitals. Jarring jolts of electricity were shot throughout his body, rendering him unconscious for indeterminate periods of time but again leaving no physical scars. ...

[Toscanino was eventually drugged and brought to the United States to stand trial.]

Since *Frisbie,* the Supreme Court in what one distinguished legal luminary describes as a "constitutional revolution," ... has expanded the interpretation of "due process." No longer is it limited to the guarantee of "fair" procedure at trial. In an effort to deter police misconduct, the term has been extended to bar the government from realizing directly the fruits of its own deliberate and unnecessary lawlessness in bringing the accused to trial. ...

Accordingly, we view due process as now requiring a court to divest itself of jurisdiction over the person of a defendant where it has been acquired as the result of the government's deliberate, unnecessary and unreasonable invasion of the accused's constitutional rights.

In many instances, the validity of a search or seizure will depend on the validity of an earlier search or seizure. Therefore, if the government fails at an earlier stage, it is probable it may fail again later. For example, the police arrest Barry Burglar and conduct a search incident to arrest. During that search they discover burglar's tools and other evidence of the alleged burglary. If it is determined that the arrest was invalid, then the fruits of the search incident to arrest must be suppressed. If the evidence discovered from the search led to other evidence, it may also be excluded.

Often officers obtain evidence in stages—each stage increasing the governmental interest in crime prevention, and concurrently increasing the officer's suspicion—thereby permitting a greater invasion of a person's privacy.

Even though search and seizure laws can be complex, do not forget to use common sense when analyzing Fourth Amendment issues. The exceptions to the search warrant requirement are not surprising; common sense tells a person that an officer may continue to pursue a fleeing murderer into the suspect's home without first obtaining a warrant. Similarly, it is not shocking that illegally obtained evidence may not be used to convict a defendant. Figure 6-2 summarizes these principles.

Two very strong policies battle in Fourth Amendment issues: crime detection and prevention versus the citizens' right to be free from intrusive governmental behavior. Consider these concerns when contemplating Fourth Amendment problems.

SUMMARY OF WARRANT RULES AND EXCEPTIONS

SEARCHES

RULE: Pursuant to the Fourth and Fourteenth Amendments, in both federal and state cases, a warrant to search must be obtained, unless one of the following exceptions is established.

EXCEPTIONS and LIMITATIONS:

1. Consent
2. *Terry* frisks
3. Plain view
4. Plain feel
5. Incident to arrest
6. Preservation of evidence
7. Emergencies and hot pursuit
8. Borders
9. Motor vehicles
10. Vehicle inventories
11. Prisoners
12. Protective sweeps
13. Open fields

ARRESTS

RULE: The Fourth and Fourteenth Amendments govern arrests by both federal and state officials. Arrests in public areas may be warrantless. Arrests made in the home or other property of the defendant must be supported by either an arrest warrant or a search warrant for the defendant's person. Arrests in the homes or other property of third parties must be supported by a search warrant authorizing the search for the defendant at the particular property.

FIGURE 6-2 Summary of Warrant Rules and Exceptions

Review Questions

1. Distinguish a stop from an arrest; a frisk from a search.
2. A police officer is approached by a man on the street who tells the officer that he was just robbed. The man points out the robber, who is standing in a park just across the street. Must the officer obtain a warrant to make the arrest?
3. A police officer is approached by a man on the street who tells the officer that he was just robbed. Although he did not see where the robber fled, he knew the assailant's name and address, as the two men "grew up together." The officer and the victim went to the police station and completed an incident report. After a telephone call to one of suspect's neighbors they learned that he was at home. Must the officer obtain a warrant to make the arrest?
4. Same facts as in question 3, except that the victim points to a fleeing suspect. The officer chases the suspect to a house, where the officer sees the suspect enter with the use of a key. Must the officer end the chase and obtain a warrant?
5. What is a protective sweep?
6. Theodore, a police officer, possesses an arrest warrant for Shirley. He personally observes Shirley enter her friend's house. Does the arrest warrant authorize Theodore to enter the friend's home to arrest Shirley over the friend's objection?
7. Must officers knock and announce themselves before forcibly entering property to execute a warrant? Explain your answer.
8. Does the exclusionary rule apply to unlawfully seized persons?

Review Problems

1. Do you believe that the exclusionary rule is required under the Fourth Amendment? Can you think of any alternatives to the rule?
2. May Yun had failed to appear at a court hearing for a speeding ticket. The court issued a bench warrant for her arrest. She discovered this, went to the court and paid the fine, and was assured by the clerk of the court that the warrant would be withdrawn. However, the clerk failed to withdraw the warrant, and May was later arrested after being pulled over for speeding. Following policy, May was searched incident to arrest and the officer discovered cocaine on her person during that search. May was charged with

possession of a controlled substance. She moved to suppress the cocaine, claiming that the search was illegal because there was no valid warrant for her arrest. Should she prevail? Discuss your answer.

Notes

1 *Aguilar v. Texas,* 378 U.S. 108, 110–11 (1964).

2 423 U.S. 411 (1976).

3 445 U.S. 573 (1980).

4 *Stealgald v. United States,* 451 U.S. 204 (1981).

5 374 U.S. 23 (1963).

6 *Frisbie v. Collins,* 342 U.S. 519 (1952).

7 *United States ex rel. Lujan v. Gengler,* 510 F.2d 62 (2d Cir.), *cert. denied,* 421 U.S. 1001 (1975).

8 *Taylor v. Alabama,* 457 U.S. 687 (1982).

ARREST
seize a person
Prefered
probable cause
Third party consent
Public v protected areas.
Knock & announce
Reasonable tim

Search
Look for property
Requires except.
Probable cause
Specific area
Day light

CHAPTER 7

INTERROGATIONS, CONFESSIONS, AND ELECTRONIC SURVEILLANCE

CHAPTER OUTLINE

> *You want to make a guy comfortable enough to confess to murder.*
>
> ***Bill Clark***
> ***Brooklyn, New York, detective***

§ 7.1 Interrogations, Confessions, and Admissions

Questioning by police officers is a commonly used law enforcement tool. An **interrogation** occurs whenever officers question a person they suspect has committed a crime. A **confession** is a statement made by a person claiming that he or she has committed a crime. If a person asserts certain facts to be true, which are inculpatory, but do not amount to a confession, he or she has made an **admission**.

As a matter of evidence law, admissions or confessions are admissible, even though hearsay, as statements against interest.[1] However, the use of interrogations, confessions, and admissions to prove guilt is controversial. The United States Supreme Court has recognized that admissions are highly suspect when relied upon alone to obtain a confession. The Court stated, in *Escobedo v. Illinois,*[2] that a "system of criminal law enforcement which comes to depend on the 'confession' will, in the long run, be less reliable and more subject to abuses than a system which depends on extrinsic evidence independently" obtained through other law enforcement practices.

At common law, confessions and admissions could be used freely, as long as they were made voluntarily. The early basis for excluding involuntary confessions was the due process clauses of the Fifth and Fourteenth Amendments.[3] Eventually, federal defendants could seek to have

TERMS

interrogation 1. The questioning of a criminal suspect by the police. 2. The questioning of any person.

confession A voluntary admission by a person that he or she has committed a crime.

admission A statement of a party to an action which is inconsistent with his or her claim or position in the lawsuit and which therefore constitutes proof against him or her.

confessions suppressed if they were not taken before a magistrate promptly after arrest. This was known as the McNabb-Mallory rule.

Today, interrogations, confessions, and admissions are governed by these rules, as well as two broader rights: the Fifth Amendment right to be free from self-incrimination and the Sixth Amendment right to counsel.

§ 7.2 *Miranda*

Contrary to popular belief, the famous *Miranda v. Arizona* case is not a Sixth Amendment right to counsel case; rather, the right to counsel theory is founded upon the Fifth Amendment right to be free from self-incrimination.

Custodial Interrogation

Not all questioning by law enforcement officers must be preceded by the *Miranda* warnings. A defendant must be "in custody" and "interrogated" by police before *Miranda* has effect. This is known as the "custodial interrogation" requirement.

The Court used the phrase "taken into custody or otherwise deprived of his freedom of action in any significant way" to define the custody element of *Miranda.* Although a statement by a police officer to a suspect that the suspect is not under arrest is not dispositive, it may be considered. Of course, a person is in custody if an officer announces that an arrest is being made or that the person is not free to leave. The Court made it clear that the in-custody element may be satisfied anywhere—it is not required that the defendant be at the police station to be in custody.

All of the surrounding facts must be considered in making the custody determination. The location of the interrogation is very important. There is a greater chance of finding a person in custody if the questioning took place in a police station or prosecutor's office rather than the suspect's home or in public. The presence of other persons during the interrogation decreases the odds of the suspect being in custody. The Court found the fact that the suspects in *Miranda* were "cut off from the outside world" troubling. The length and intensity of the questioning are also relevant. A brief encounter between a citizen and a police officer is generally not a custodial situation.

In addition to being in custody, a defendant must be subjected to an interrogation before *Miranda* applies. Clearly, interrogation includes

MIRANDA v. ARIZONA 384 U.S. 436 (1966)

The cases before us raise questions that go to the roots of our concepts of American criminal jurisprudence: the restraints society must observe consistent with the Federal Constitution in prosecuting individuals for crime. More specifically, we deal with the admissibility of statements obtained from an individual who is subjected to custodial police interrogation and the necessity for procedures which assure that the individual is accorded his privilege under the Fifth Amendment to the Constitution not to be compelled to incriminate himself. ...

Our holding will be spelled out with some specificity in the pages which follow but briefly stated it is this: the prosecution may not use statements, whether exculpatory or inculpatory, stemming from custodial interrogation of the defendant unless it demonstrates the use of procedural safeguards effective to secure the privilege against self-incrimination. By custodial interrogation, we mean questioning initiated by law-inforcement officers after a person has been taken into custody or otherwise deprived of his freedom of action in any significant way. As for the procedural safeguards to be employed, unless other fully effective means are devised to inform accused persons of their right of silence and to assure a continuous opportunity to exercise it, the following measures are required. Prior to any questioning, the person must be warned that he has a right to remain silent, that any statement he does make may be used as evidence against him, and that he has a right to the presence of an attorney, either retained or appointed. The defendant may waive effectuation of these rights, provided the waiver is made voluntarily, knowingly, and intelligently. If, however, he indicates in any manner and at any stage of the process that he wishes to consult with an attorney before speaking there can be no questioning. Likewise, if the individual is alone and indicates in any manner that he does not wish to be interrogated, the police may not question him. The mere fact that he may have answered some questions or volunteered some statements on his own does not deprive him of the right to refrain from answering any further inquiries until he has consulted with an attorney and thereafter consents to be questioned.

The constitutional issue we decide in each of these cases is the admissibility of statements obtained from a defendant questioned while in custody or otherwise deprived of his freedom of action in any significant way. In each, the defendant was questioned by police officers, detectives, or a prosecuting attorney in a room in which he was cut off from the outside world. In none of these cases was the defendant given a full and effective warning of his rights at the outset of the interrogation process. In all of the cases, the questioning elicited oral admissions, and in three of them, signed statements as well which were admitted at their trials. They all thus share salient features—incommunicado interrogation of individuals in a police-dominated atmosphere, resulting in self-incriminating statements without full warnings of constitutional rights.

An understanding of the nature and setting of this in-custody interrogation is essential to our decisions today. The difficulty in depicting what transpires at such interrogations stems from the fact that in this country they have largely taken place incommunicado. From extensive factual studies undertaken in the early 1930s ... it is clear that police violence and the "third degree" flourished at that time. In a series of cases decided by the Court long after those studies, the police resulted to physical brutality—beating, hanging, whipping—and to sustained and protracted questioning incommunicado in order to extort confessions. ...

Again we stress that the modern practice of in-custody interrogation is psychologically rather than physically oriented. As we have stated before " ... this court has recognized that coercion can be mental as well as physical, and that the blood of the accused is not the only hallmark of an unconstitutional inquisition." ...

The circumstances surrounding in-custody interrogation can operate very quickly to overbear the will of one merely made aware of his privilege [against self-incrimination] by his interrogators. Therefore, the right to have counsel present at the interrogation is indispensable to the protection of the Fifth Amendment privilege under the system we delineate today. Our aim is to assure that the individual's right to choose between silence and speech remains unfettered throughout the interrogation process. A once-stated warning, delivered by those who will conduct the interrogation, cannot itself suffice to that end among those who most require knowledge of their rights. A mere warning given by the interrogators is not alone sufficient to accomplish that end. Prosecutors themselves claim that the admonishment of the right to remain silent without more "will benefit only the recidivist and the professional." Even preliminary advice given to the accused by his own attorney can be swiftly overcome by the secret interrogation process. ... Thus, the need for counsel to protect the Fifth Amendment privilege comprehends not merely a right to consult with counsel prior to questioning, but also to have counsel present during any questioning if the defendant so desires.

The presence of counsel at the interrogation may serve several significant subsidiary functions as well. If the accused decides to talk to his interrogators, the assistance of counsel can mitigate the dangers of trustworthiness. With a lawyer present the likelihood that the police will practice coercion is reduced, and if coercion is nevertheless exercised the lawyer can testify to it in court. The presence of a lawyer can also help to guarantee that the accused gives a fully accurate statement to the police and that the statement is rightly reported to the prosecution.

questioning by law enforcement officers, but this is not all. In *Rhode Island v. Innis*,[4] the Supreme Court held that any "functional equivalent" to express questioning is also interrogation. That is, all actions or words by police officers that can reasonably be expected to elicit an incriminating response are interrogation.

The nature of the information elicited is not relevant; the *Miranda* court stated that the decision applies to both inculpatory and exculpatory statements. Accordingly, *Miranda* is effective whether a defendant confesses or simply makes an admission.

Exceptions to *Miranda*

Not every communication between a police officer and a suspect amounts to an interrogation under *Miranda*. First, volunteered statements are not the product of interrogation. The *Miranda* decision explicitly states that officers are under no duty to interrupt a volunteered confession in order to read a confessor his or her *Miranda* rights.

Second, routine questions that are purely informational normally do not lead to incriminating responses and need not be preceded by a reading of the *Miranda* warnings. Questions about one's name, age, address, and employment are not treated as interrogation.

Third, questions made by officers in the interest of public safety need not be preceded by a *Miranda* warning. In one case, a woman told two police officers that she had just been raped by a man carrying a gun and that the rapist had gone into a nearby grocery. The officers went to the store and arrested the man. However, he did not have the gun on his person. One of the police officers asked the arrestee where the gun was, and the arrestee responded by indicating the location where the gun was hidden in the store. The Supreme Court decided that, despite the fact that the question was interrogation and the defendant had not been mirandized, the evidence could be used at trial. The Court recognized that in such situations, when there is a danger to the officers or the public, officers must be permitted to extinguish the public threat. Thus, the relatively rigid *Miranda* rules are relaxed when there is a public safety exigency that was the impetus of a brief and limited interrogation designed to meet that exigency.[5]

Fourth, related to the public safety exception is spontaneous questioning by police. If a question is asked spontaneously, such as in response to an emergency, there is no interrogation. For example, if an officer were to return to a room where he has placed two arrestees to find one dead, it would not be an interrogation if the officer were to excitedly utter, "Who killed this man?"

Fifth, the *Miranda* warnings do not have to be given by undercover officers because there is no custody, no "police-dominated atmosphere."[6] However, once criminal charges have been filed, undercover officers may not be used to extract information from a defendant.[7]

Sixth, the Supreme Court has determined that *Miranda* warnings do not have to be recited during routine traffic stops, even though an interrogation occurs. The Court concluded that although traffic stops are seizures for Fourth Amendment purposes, they are not custodial for Fifth Amendment purposes. The "noncoercive aspect of ordinary traffic stops prompts us to hold that persons temporarily detained pursuant to such stops are not 'in custody' for the purposes of *Miranda*."[8]

Multiple Interrogations and Reinterrogation

Miranda clearly states that once a defendant invokes the right to remain silent, whether before or during questioning, the interrogation must stop. The same is true once a defendant states that he or she wants counsel present; the interrogation must cease until the defendant's attorney is available. If the defendant's attorney is not available, the police are to respect the defendant's right to remain silent and not question him or her until the attorney arrives.

Under very limited circumstances, police officers may reattempt to interrogate a defendant who has invoked the right to remain silent.

Although multiple attempts to interrogate an arrestee about the same crime are not permitted, it has been determined that a second interrogation about a separate and unrelated crime may be valid.[9]

Miranda clearly stated that once an accused has invoked the right to counsel, the police are prohibited from interrogating him or her until he or she has conferred with counsel. *Miranda* did not answer this question: may police reinterrogate a defendant without counsel present once the defendant has consulted with a lawyer? The answer is found in *Minnick v. Mississippi*. *Minnick* makes it clear that once an accused has asserted a right to counsel, all police-initiated interrogations must occur with defense counsel present.

MINNICK
v.
MISSISSIPPI
498 U.S. 146 (1990)

To protect the privilege against self-incrimination guaranteed by the Fifth Amendment, we have held that the police must terminate interrogation of an accused in custody if the accused requests the assistance of counsel. *Miranda v. Arizona,* 384 U.S. 436, 474 (1966). We reinforced the protections of *Miranda* in *Edwards v. Arizona,* 451 U.S. 477, 484–485 (1981), which held that once the accused requests counsel, officials may not reinitiate questioning "until counsel has been made available" to him. The issue in the case before us is whether *Edwards* protection ceases once the suspect has consulted with an attorney.

Petitioner Robert Minnick and fellow prisoner James Dyess escaped from a county jail in Mississippi and, a day later, broke into a mobile home in search of weapons. In the course of the burglary they were interrupted by the arrival of the trailer's owner, Ellis Thomas, accompanied by Lamar Lafferty and Lafferty's infant son. Dyess and Minnick used the stolen weapons to kill Thomas and the senior Lafferty. Minnick's story is that Dyess murdered one victim and then forced Minnick to shoot the other. Before the escapees could get away, two young women arrived at the mobile home. They were held at gunpoint, then bound by hand and foot. Dyess and Minnick fled in Thomas' truck, abandoning the vehicle in New Orleans. The fugitives continued to Mexico, where they fought, and Minnick then proceeded alone to California. Minnick was arrested in Lemon Grove, California, on a Mississippi warrant, some four months after the murders.

The confession at issue here resulted from the last interrogation of Minnick while he was held in the San Diego jail, but we first recount the events which preceded it. Minnick was arrested on Friday, August 22, 1986. Petitioner testified that he was mistreated by local police during and after the arrest. The day following the arrest, Saturday, two FBI agents came to the jail to interview him. Petitioner testified that he refused to go to the interview, but was told he would "have to go down or else" … . The FBI report indicates that the agents read petitioner his *Miranda* warnings, and that he acknowledged he understood his rights. He refused to sign a rights waiver form, however, and said he would not answer "very many" questions. Minnick told the agents about the jail break and the flight, and described how Dyess threatened and beat him. Early in the interview, he sobbed "[i]t was my life or theirs," but otherwise he hesitated to tell what happened at the trailer. The agents reminded him he did not have to answer questions without a lawyer present.

According to the report, "Minnick stated 'Come back Monday when I have a lawyer,' and stated that he would make a more complete statement then with his lawyer present." ...

After the FBI interview, an appointed attorney met with petitioner. Petitioner spoke with the lawyer on two or three occasions, though it is not clear from the record whether all of these conferences were in person.

On Monday, August 25, Deputy Sheriff J.C. Denham of Clarke County, Mississippi, came to the San Diego jail to question Minnick. Minnick testified that his jailers again told him he would "have to talk" to Denham and that he "could not refuse." ... Denham advised petitioner of his rights, and petitioner again declined to sign a rights waiver form. Petitioner told Denham about the escape and then proceeded to describe the events at the mobile home. ...

Minnick was tried for murder in Mississippi. He moved to suppress all statements given to the FBI or other police officers, including Denham. The trial court denied the motion with respect to petitioner's statements to Denham, but suppressed his other statements. Petitioner was convicted on two counts of capital murder and sentenced to death.

On appeal, petitioner argued that the confession to Denham was taken in violation of his rights to counsel under the Fifth and Sixth Amendments. The Mississippi Supreme Court rejected the claims. ...

The Mississippi Supreme Court relied on our statement in *Edwards* that an accused who invokes his right to counsel "is not subject to further interrogation by the authorities until counsel has been made available to him ... ." 451 U.S., at 484–485. We do not interpret this language to mean, as the Mississippi court thought, that the protection of *Edwards* terminates once counsel has consulted with the suspect. In context, the requirement that counsel be "made available" to the accused refers to more than an opportunity to consult with an attorney outside the interrogation room.

In *Edwards,* we focused on *Miranda's* instruction that when the accused invokes his right to counsel, the "interrogation must cease until an attorney is *present* during custodial interrogation." 451 U.S., at 482 (emphasis added). In the sentence preceding the language quoted by the Mississippi Supreme Court, we referred to the "right to have counsel *present* during custodial interrogation." ...

In our view, a fair reading of Edwards and subsequent cases demonstrates that we have interpreted the rule to bar police-initiated interrogation unless the accused has counsel with him at the time of questioning. Whatever the ambiguities of our earlier cases on this point, we now hold that when counsel is requested, interrogation must cease, and officials may not reinitiate interrogation without counsel present, whether or not the accused has consulted with his attorney.

The Warnings

Before a person in custody may be interrogated, the required warning must be recited to the arrestee. Specific language need not be used, as long as the defendant is fully and effectively apprised of each right.

The Supreme Court stated, in *Miranda,* that the following rights and information must be conveyed to the defendant:

1. The right to remain silent.
2. Any statements made may be used against the defendant to gain a conviction.

3. The right to consult with a lawyer and to have a lawyer present during questioning.
4. For the indigent, a lawyer will be provided without cost.

The warnings are to be read to all persons in custody who are to be interrogated. The law does not presume that any person, including an attorney, knows these rights. The warnings should be presented in a timely manner and read at such a speed that the arrestee can gain a full understanding of their import.

Many law enforcement agencies have made it a policy to record (video/audio or audio only) the giving of the warnings and any waiver of rights to eliminate any question concerning whether the warnings were given and whether coercion was used to gain a waiver.

Waiver

A defendant may waive the right to have the assistance of counsel and/or to remain silent. The waiver must be made voluntarily and knowingly. In *Miranda,* the Supreme Court said that the "heavy burden" of proving that a defendant made a knowing and voluntary waiver rests with the prosecution; courts are to presume no waiver.

In determining whether there has been a waiver, the totality of the circumstances is considered. The actions of the police, as well as the defendant's age, intelligence, and experience, are all relevant to this inquiry.

An express waiver, preferably written, is best for the prosecution. However, a defendant's waiver does not have to be express to be valid. In *North Carolina v. Butler,*[10] the Court held that "in at least some cases waiver can be clearly inferred from the actions and words of the person interrogated." However, silence on the part of a defendant never amounts to a waiver. So, if a defendant refuses to state, or otherwise indicate, that he or she understands a right and wishes to waive it, the police should not conduct an interrogation.

Violating *Miranda*

Any statement obtained in violation of *Miranda* is inadmissible at trial to prove guilt. Further, any other evidence that is the fruit of such a statement must also be excluded from trial. The defendant ordinarily raises the issue prior to trial through a motion to suppress.

Although statements that are illegally obtained may not be admitted to prove a defendant's guilt, the Supreme Court has said that statements that violate *Miranda* may be admitted, under certain circumstances, to impeach the defendant.[11]

Sixth Amendment

Miranda has effect as soon as a person is in custody and is subject to interrogation. This can occur long before or directly prior to the filing of a formal charge. Once the adversary judicial proceeding has begun, the source of protection changes from the Fifth Amendment (*Miranda*) to the Sixth Amendment.

In *Michigan v. Jackson,*[12] the Supreme Court held that the Sixth Amendment provides the same protections as *Miranda, Edwards,* and similar cases. The Court reasoned that interrogations by the government of a defendant after criminal charges have been filed are a critical stage at which counsel is necessary to protect the defendant's rights.

Voluntariness Requirement

As was true at common law, all confessions must be made voluntarily. This is required by the due process clauses of the Fifth and Fourteenth Amendments. The totality of the circumstances must be examined when making the voluntariness determination.

Police officers do not have to physically coerce a confession for it to be involuntary. Mental or emotional coercion by law enforcement also violates a defendant's due process rights.

Involuntary confessions are to be excluded at trial. For years, the admission of a coerced confession resulted in an automatic reversal of conviction. This was changed in *Arizona v. Fulminante,*[13] in which the United States Supreme Court decided that a conviction is not to be automatically reversed because a coerced confession was admitted at trial. Rather, the Court held that if the prosecution can show beyond a reasonable doubt that the trial court error was harmless, the conviction is to be affirmed. That is, if there was sufficient other evidence to sustain the conviction, then it stands.

§ 7.3 Electronic Surveillance

Many forms of electronic surveillance are used by law enforcement agencies. Wiretaps and highly sensitive microphones are examples. When the Supreme Court first addressed the issue of wiretapping, it concluded that there was no Fourth Amendment protection because there was no trespass into a constitutionally protected area. This changed when the Court issued the *Katz* decision, which advanced the idea that the Fourth Amendment protects people, not places. Now, if a person has a justifiable expectation of privacy, the Fourth Amendment applies.

Despite the constitutional aspect of using such devices, this area of law is highly regulated by a federal statute: Title III of the Omnibus Crime Control Act and Safe Streets Act of 1968.

Title III of the Omnibus Crime Control Act

Title III of the Omnibus Crime Control Act and Safe Streets Act of 1968[14] is a federal statute that regulates the use of electronic surveillance. It is also known as the Federal Wiretap Act.

The act prohibits wiretapping, bugging, or other electronic surveillance of a conversation when the parties to that conversation possess a reasonable expectation of privacy. Violation of the act may result in civil and criminal penalties. Evidence obtained in violation of the act is excluded at trial.

The statute permits states to enact their own electronic surveillance laws; however, those laws cannot provide less protection of individual rights than the federal statute. A state may, however, provide greater protection of individual rights through its surveillance law than does the federal statute.

Court-Ordered Surveillance

Law enforcement officers may not intercept telephone conversations or other electronic messages without first obtaining court approval. The act permits court approval only for certain crimes. Espionage, treason, murder, kidnapping, robbery, extortion, drug crimes, and bribery of public officials are included in that list.

To obtain a court order for the interception of electronic communications, an officer must present an application supported by oath or affirmation to a court. The requirements for obtaining such a court order are similar to those for obtaining a warrant. The application must contain the following:[15]

1. The identity of the official applying for the order and the official authorizing the application
2. Evidence establishing probable cause to believe that the person whose communication is to be intercepted has committed, is committing, or is about to commit one of the named crimes
3. Evidence establishing probable cause to believe that the communication to be intercepted concerns the crime
4. A statement that other normal investigative procedures have been tried and failed, or that no other procedure is available
5. The time period during which the interception will occur

6. A full description of the location where the interception will take place
7. A statement reflecting all prior attempts to obtain a similar order for any of the same places or persons.

If the judge grants the application, the order must specify the person whose communication is to be intercepted, the location of the interception, the nature of the communication to be intercepted, the crime involved, and the duration of the interception. In all cases, the surveillance is to cease once the desired information has been seized (recorded). After the interception has ended, the recording is to be given to the judge who issued the order, for safekeeping.

Execution of Title III Orders

The statute provides that all communications intercepted shall, if possible, be recorded. The method of recording is to protect against editing and other alterations. The purpose of this requirement is obvious: to preserve the integrity of the evidence.

The statute also requires that all interceptions of irrelevant information be minimized. Said another way, if an officer intercepting a conversation knows that it is unrelated to the investigation, the interception is to cease. The minimization requirement is no more than a codification of the Fourth Amendment's reasonableness requirement.

Of course, determining whether an interception is related to the offense under investigation is not always easy, and courts tend to defer to the judgment of the intercepting officer in close cases. The following factors are considered by a reviewing court when a claim is made that interceptions were not properly minimized:

1. The percentage of calls that were related to the investigation. The lower the percentage, the greater the likelihood that the government did not properly minimize its interceptions.
2. The number of calls that were one-time only.
3. The length of the calls intercepted. The shorter the calls, the less opportunity the government had to determine whether the interception was proper.
4. The nature of the calls. The more ambiguous the call, the greater the government's interest in prolonging its interception.[16]

Other factors may also be important to the inquiry. For example, if a known co-conspirator makes frequent calls, interception of all the calls is probably valid, even though the majority of conversations does not concern the conspiracy. Each case must be examined on its own facts to determine whether Title III or the Fourth Amendment has been violated.

Implicit in court orders under this statute is the authority to enter premises to install listening devices. Courts have held that it would be nonsensical to give an officer the authority to conduct surveillance, but not to enter the premises of the defendant to install the necessary device. The court order does not have to specifically give this authority; it is implicit in the order itself. Of course, where an officer may go depends on the facts of each case.

The statute authorizes judges to order third parties, such as telephone company personnel, to assist law enforcement officers in executing an electronic surveillance order. Third parties must be compensated for their assistance.

Exceptions to Title III

In a number of situations, a court order is not required to intercept an electronic communication. Eight exceptions are discussed here.

First, be aware that the act tracks the privacy aspect of the *Katz* decision; that is, only communications for which a person has a reasonable expectation of privacy are protected. Because Title III does not expand the privacy protection aspect of the Fourth Amendment, decisions concerning whether a person has a reasonable expectation of privacy under the Fourth Amendment are applicable to Title III.

One party to a communication has no reasonable expectation that the other party will not record the conversation or permit others to listen. Therefore, no court order has to be obtained for a law enforcement officer to listen in on an extension (or later listen to a recording), as long as one party to the conversation consents. The Federal Wiretap Act has a provision reflecting this position.

It has also been held that a person has no reasonable expectation of privacy when using a cordless telephone. Because cordless phones use radio waves, which are broadcast in all directions and are subject to being received by countless people, courts have reasoned that a person cannot have a reasonable expectation of privacy when using one.[17] However, whenever one party is using a cordless phone and the other a traditional line phone, it is likely, unless the second party knows that the other is using a cordless phone, that the second party has a reasonable expectation of privacy.

Critics of this position charge that whenever a person places a call to a particular person, whether on a cordless phone or a traditional phone, it is reasonable to expect the conversation to be private. Another view contends that such hair-splitting is confusing to the average person. As Professor Lawrence Tribe of Harvard University School of Law noted, it may be true that the professional criminal knows that he has no reasonable expectation of privacy on a cordless phone, but the average citizen does not.

Second, any employee of a communications company who intercepts an incriminating communication while engaged in ordinary duties (i.e., maintenance) may disclose such information to the authorities, and it may be used at trial.

Third, officers need not obtain a court order when engaged in certain national security investigations.

Fourth, in emergency situations, when an officer does not have time to obtain a court order, the interception may begin immediately, but an application must be made within forty-eight hours. If the judge determines that there was no emergency justifying a warrantless tap, then any evidence obtained must be suppressed.

Finally, electronic beepers and transmitters used to track a person or thing are governed by normal search and seizure law. Additionally, the Supreme Court has held that pen registers and similar devices that make a record of telephone numbers called do not implicate the Fourth Amendment because there is no search when they are used.[18]

Review Questions

1. List the rights included in the *Miranda* warnings. When must they be read to a defendant?
2. What happens if an officer fails to read a defendant his or her rights prior to obtaining a confession?
3. Is it a violation of the Federal Wiretap Law (Title III of the Omnibus Crime Control and Safe Streets Act) for Gary to allow law enforcement officers to listen to a telephone conversation between himself and Terry without Terry's knowledge? If so, what happens if Terry makes incriminating statements?
4. Why must law enforcement officers obtain a court order to intercept a telephone conversation using traditional line phones and not a conversation using a cordless phone?

Review Problems

1. While on patrol, officer Norman heard a scream from the backyard of a house. The officer proceeded to the back of the house where he observed

two people, a badly beaten victim and a young man (Tom) standing over her. Shocked by the sight of the victim, the officer exclaimed, "What happened here?" Tom responded, "I killed her and threw the baseball bat over the fence." Officer Norman restrained the young man, called for an ambulance, and retrieved the bat. While waiting for the ambulance to arrive, Officer Norman asked the young man what his motive was for injuring the woman. Tom explained his motive to the officer. The officer never mirandized Tom. A motion to suppress the statement, "I killed her and threw the baseball bat over the fence," as well as the statement explaining his motive, has been filed. Additionally, Tom claims that the bat should be excluded because it is a fruit of an illegal interrogation. What should be the outcome? Explain your answer.

2. An officer has made application for a court order approving electronic surveillance of Defendant. The order is granted, stating: "From June 1 to June 7, Officer X, having established probable cause, is granted the authority to intercept the wire communications of Defendant." The officer proceeded to enter Defendant's house, without a warrant, to install the listening device. Eventually, a recording is made of Defendant discussing his illegal activities with a friend. Defendant is arrested, charged, and has filed a motion to suppress the interception. Defendant asserts that the entry into his house was illegal. Discuss.
3. Why are the rules concerning the admissibility of confessions more stringent than for other forms of evidence?

Notes

1 Fed. R. Evid. 804(b)(5).

2 378 U.S. 478 (1964).

3 *Brown v. Mississippi*, 295 U.S. 278 (1936).

4 446 U.S. 291 (1980).

5 *New York v. Quarles*, 467 U.S. 649 (1984).

6 *Illinois v. Perkins*, 496 U.S. 292 (1990).

7 *Massiah v. United States*, 377 U.S. 201 (1964).

8 *Pennsylvania v. Bruder*, 488 U.S. 9 (1988).

9 *Michigan v. Mosley*, 423 U.S. 96 (1975).

10 441 U.S. 369 (1962).

11 *Oregon v. Haas*, 420 U.S. 714 (1975).

12 475 U.S. 625 (1986).

13 499 U.S. 279 (1991).

14 18 U.S.C. § 2510 *et seq.*

15 18 U.S.C. § 2518.

16 *Scott v. United States*, 436 U.S. 128 (1978).

17 *Tyler v. Berodt*, 877 F.2d 705 (8th Cir. 1989).

18 *Smith v. Maryland*, 442 U.S. 735 (1979).

CHAPTER 8

EYEWITNESS AND SCIENTIFIC IDENTIFICATIONS

> *[Polygraph tests] are 20th-century witchcraft.*
>
> ***Sam Ervin***
> ***United States Senator***

§ 8.1 Introduction

Law enforcement officers use a variety of techniques to identify a person as a criminal, such as eyewitness identifications, fingerprinting, blood tests, and, recently, deoxyribonucleic acid (DNA) tests. The use of any of these procedures raises certain constitutional issues, such as the right to be free from self-incrimination and the right to counsel.

There is also another concern: reliability. Eyewitness identification, though powerful, has a few inherent problems. First, each person will testify to his or her perception of an event, and people often perceive the same event differently. Second, not every person will use the same language to decribe what was witnessed. Third, a witness may simply have a faulty memory and unintentionally testify to an untruth. Fourth, for a variety of reasons, a witness may intentionally lie.

Scientific testing may also prove to be invalid or unreliable. How accurate is the test when performed properly? Was the test performed properly in this case? Is the evidence tested actually the defendant's? These types of questions are asked of expert witnesses who testify to the results of scientific testing. This discussion begins with eyewitness identification procedures.

§ 8.2 Lineups and One-Person Showups

A **lineup** is where the police exhibit a group of people, among whom is the suspect, to a witness or victim for identification as the

TERMS

lineup A police practice in which a number of individuals, including the criminal suspect, are displayed to the victim of the crime or other witnesses to determine if one of the individuals can be identified as the perpetrator of the offense.

criminal. A one-person **showup** is an exhibition of one person to a witness or victim for identification as the criminal.

In practice, police first conduct a lineup and, then if the suspect is identified, the witness is asked at trial to testify that he or she identified the perpetrator of the crime at the lineup. Therefore, if the initial identification is faulty, the subsequent in-court identification is also faulty. Even if the witness is asked to identify anew the perpetrator of the crime, such an identification is tainted by the witness's earlier identification. In the landmark case of *United States v. Wade,* the Supreme Court addressed the problems inherent in pretrial identification procedures.

The Right to Counsel

What *Wade* mandates is that counsel be provided at pretrial lineups and showups. For years it was unknown whether this meant all pretrial lineups and showups or just those after the Sixth Amendment attaches. *Kirby v. Illinois*[1] resolved this dispute by requiring counsel only after initiation of "adversary judicial proceedings—whether by way of formal charge, preliminary hearing, indictment, information, or arraignment."

The Fairness Right

In addition to having a right to counsel at postindictment lineups, an accused is entitled to a fair lineup, one that is not unnecessarily suggestive of guilt. In *Stoval v. Denno,*[2] the Supreme Court found that the due process clauses of the Fifth and Fourteenth Amendments prohibit identifications that are so unnecessarily suggestive that there is a real chance of misidentification. In addition to being impermissibly suggestive, an identification must be unreliable to be excluded.[3] When making the determination of whether an identification violates due process, a court is to examine the "totality of the circumstances" surrounding the identification. Examples of impermissibly suggestive were mentioned in the *Wade* opinion. For example, if a witness states that a white male committed a crime, it would be improper to exhibit four black men and one white man in a lineup.

One-person showups, obviously, are more suggestive of guilt than lineups. As such, they should be used with caution. Generally, a one-person showup should occur within a short period of time after the

TERMS

show-up A police practice by which a witness to a crime confronts the suspect. Like a lineup, its purpose is to make an identification; unlike a lineup, it involves only the suspect and the witness.

UNITED STATES
v.
WADE
338 U.S. 218 (1967)

The question here is whether courtroom identifications of an accused at trial are to be excluded from evidence because the accused was exhibited to the witness before trial at a post-indictment lineup conducted for identification purposes without notice to and in the absence of the accused's appointed counsel.

The federally insured bank in Eustace, Texas, was robbed on September 21, 1964. A man with a small strip of tape on each side of his face entered the bank, pointed a pistol at the female cashier and the vice president, the only persons in the bank at the time, and forced them to fill a pillowcase with the bank's money. The man then drove away with an accomplice who had been waiting in a stolen car outside the bank. On March 23, 1965, an indictment was returned against respondent, Wade, and two others for conspiring to rob the bank, and against Wade and accomplice for the robbery itself. Wade was arrested on April 2, and counsel was appointed to represent him on April 26. Fifteen days later an FBI agent, without notice to Wade's lawyer, arranged to have the two bank employees observe a lineup made up of Wade and five or six other prisoners and conducted in a courtroom of the local county courthouse. Each person in the line wore strips of tape such as allegedly worn by the robber and upon direction each said something like "put the money in the bag," the words allegedly uttered by the robber. Both bank employees identified Wade in the lineup as the bank robber.

At trial, the two employees, when asked on direct examination if the robber was in the courtroom, pointed to Wade. The prior lineup identification was then elicited from both employees on cross examination. ... But the confrontation compelled by the State between the accused and the victim or witnesses to a crime to elicit identification evidence is peculiarly riddled with innumerable dangers and variable factors which might seriously, even crucially, derogate from a fair trial. The vagaries of eyewitness identification are well-known; the annals of criminal law are rife with instances of mistaken identification. ... The identification of strangers is proverbially untrustworthy. ... A major factor contributing to the high incidence of miscarriage of justice from mistaken identification has been the degree of suggestion inherent in the manner in which the prosecution presents the suspect to witness for pretrial identification. A commentator has observed that "[t]he influence of improper suggestion upon identifying witnesses probably accounts for more miscarriages of justice than any other single factor—perhaps it is responsible for more such errors than all other factors combined." ... Suggestion can be created intentionally or unintentionally in many subtle ways. And the dangers for the suspect are particularly grave when the witness'[s] opportunity for observation was insubstantial, and thus his susceptibility to suggestion the greatest.

> Moreover, "[i]t is a matter of common experience that, once a witness has picked out the accused at the line-up, he is not likely to go back on his word later on, so that in practice the issue of identity may (in the absence of other relevant evidence) for all practical purposes be determined there and then, before the trial." ...

What facts have been disclosed in specific cases about the conduct of pretrial confrontations for identification illustrate both the potential for substantial prejudice to the accused at that stage and the need for its revelation at trial. A commentator provides some striking examples:

> In a Canadian case ... the defendant had been picked out of a line-up of six men, of which he was the only Oriental. In other cases, a black-haired suspect was placed among a group of light-haired persons, tall suspects have been made to stand with short non-suspects, and, in a case where the perpetrator of the crime was known to be a youth, a suspect under twenty was placed in a line-up with five other persons, all of whom were forty or over.

Similarly, state reports, in the course of describing prior identifications admitted as evidence of guilt, reveal numerous instances of suggestive procedures, for example, that all in the lineup but the suspect were known to the identifying witness, that the other participants in a lineup were grossly dissimilar in appearance to the suspect, that only the suspect was required to wear distinctive clothing which the culprit allegedly wore. ...

Since it appears that there is grave potential for prejudice, intentional or not, in the pretrial lineup, which may not be capable of reconstruction at trial, and since presence of counsel can often avert prejudice and assure a meaningful confrontation at trial, there can be little doubt that for Wade the post-indictment lineup was a critical stage of the prosecution at which [he] was [entitled to counsel]. ...

[The Court then concluded that in-court identifications must be excluded if they follow a lineup at which a defendant is not permitted counsel, unless the in-court identification has an independent origin.]

crime (minutes or hours). If there is time to organize a lineup, this is the preferable method of identification procedure.

Self-Incrimination

It is not violative of the Fifth Amendment's privilege against self-incrimination for a defendant to be compelled to appear in a lineup. The privilege against self-incrimination applies to "testimony" and not to physical acts, such as walking, gesturing, measuring, or speaking certain words for identification purposes.[4] If a defendant has changed in appearance, he or she may be made to shave, to don a wig or hairpiece, or wear a certain article of clothing.

The question under the Fifth Amendment is whether the act requested is "communicative." If so, then the defendant may not be compelled to engage in the act. If not, the opposite is true.

§ 8.3 Photographs

Police may show a witness photographs to obtain an identification. The due process test discussed earlier applies to the use of photos; that is, the event must not be impermissibly suggestive and unreliable. The showing of one picture is likely to be determined improper, absent an emergency. As is true of lineups, the people in the photos should be similar in appearance. Also, a "mug shot" (a picture taken by law enforcement agencies after arrest) of the accused should not be mixed with ordinary photos of nonsuspects. Nor should the photos be presented in such a manner that the defendant's picture stands out.

The Supreme Court has determined that there is no right to counsel at a photo identification session, either before initiation of the adversary judicial proceeding or thereafter.

§ 8.4 Scientific Identification Procedures

Law enforcement officials may use scientific methods of identification to prove that a defendant committed a crime. Fingerprinting, blood tests, genetic tests (deoxyribonucleic acid, or DNA, testing), voice tests, and handwriting samples are examples of such techniques.

Such tests are not critical stages of the criminal proceedings, and, accordingly, there is no right to counsel. There is also no right to refuse to cooperate with such testing on Fifth Amendment grounds, because the defendant is not being required to give testimony. However, if a test involves an invasion of privacy, then the Fourth Amendment requires probable cause before the procedure may be forced on an unwilling defendant.

Validity and Reliability

Scientific evidence must be reliable before it may be introduced at trial. In a landmark case, *Frye v. United States,*[5] it was held that scientific techniques must be generally accepted as valid and reliable by the scientific community to be admissible. *Frye* was the law from 1923 until 1993 when the Supreme Court issued *Daubert v. Merrell Dow Pharmaceuticals.*[6] *Daubert* changed the standard of admissibility from acceptance in the scientific community to scientific validity. Under this new standard, the trial judge is required to make a preliminary determination that the proffered evidence is valid before it may be presented to a jury. In making this decision, the trial judge is to consider the following factors:

1. Whether the evidence or theory has, or can be, tested
2. Whether it has been reviewed and tested by other scientists
3. Whether the method has been published and the quality of the publication(s) in which it is found
4. Whether its error rate and other potential defects are known
5. Whether standards and protocols for its use have been established
6. Whether its use is widely accepted in the relevant scientific community.

Techniques that are experimental and not highly reliable are not admissible. A few common scientific techniques are discussed here.

Note that the results of a specific test may be denied admission, even if the scientific basis of the testing is valid, if the test is administered incorrectly. Further, scientific testing also raises Fourth, Fifth, Sixth, and Fourteenth Amendment issues, some of which are discussed later.

Fingerprinting

A fingerprint consists of several identifiable characteristics, such as loops, arches, whorls, islands, and bifurcations. The arrangement, frequency, and design of these features are among the many characteristics used to distinguish prints from one another. Although it is common to state that every person has a unique set of prints, there is a possibility of duplication. However, the odds of that occurring has been estimated to be as low as one in 64 billion.[7]

Fingerprint identification is a highly accurate science and is universally accepted by federal and state courts. Federal and state law enforcement agencies, as well as international agencies, possess libraries of fingerprints. Through the use of computers, fingerprints lifted from crime scenes, weapons, and other objects can be matched to a particular individual's fingerprints in a matter of minutes. Lifted prints may be matched to a print already on file or to a print taken from a suspect.

The taking of fingerprints does not implicate the Fifth Amendment because the accused is not compelled to give testimony. Further, it is not a search to take a suspect's fingerprints. This being so, neither probable cause nor a warrant is required to take the suspect's prints. Courts have analogized fingerprints to physical characteristics such as hair and eye color. Because it is not an invasion of a reasonable expectation to privacy (search) for an officer to visually observe a defendant, courts have reasoned that it is not an invasion of privacy to observe and record a suspect's fingerprints.

Blood Testing

Blood testing is commonly employed and universally accepted by courts in the United States. Although the science of blood testing is generally beyond scrutiny, individual blood tests are not. Laboratories make mistakes, and both the defense and the prosecution may challenge a particular test.

Securing a suspect's blood is different from rolling a fingerprint. The process of withdrawing blood involves a bodily invasion and the possibility of pain and infection. Therefore, a person's expectation of privacy is higher when the government seeks blood rather than fingerprints. Whether the government possesses the authority to compel a suspect to undergo a blood test was the subject of *Schmerber v. California*.

Schmerber stands for the principle that the withdrawal of blood, as well as other body-intrusive procedures, constitutes a search under the Fourth Amendment. Probable cause is required, as is a warrant, unless exigent circumstances, such as those in *Schmerber*, justify bypassing the warrant requirement. In addition, such procedures must be conducted in a safe, discrete, medical environment.

There is a limit to the government's authority to intrude into the defendant's body. For example, in *Winston v. Lee*,[8] the Supreme Court employed the analysis outlined in *Schmerber* and concluded that a defendant accused of armed robbery could not be compelled to undergo surgery to remove a bullet in his chest. The Court held that the suspect's interest in his health and bodily privacy outweighed the government's interest in obtaining the evidence. Also important to the Court was the fact that the government had other evidence to prove the defendant's guilt. This lowered the government's interest in having the bullet removed. If the bullet had been critical to the government's case, the result might have been different.

SCHMERBER v. CALIFORNIA 384 U.S. 757 (1966)

Petitioner was convicted in Los Angeles Municipal Court of the criminal offense of driving an automobile while under the influence of intoxicating liquor. He had been arrested at a hospital while receiving treatment for injuries suffered in an accident involving the automobile that he was apparently driving. At the direction of a police officer, a blood sample was then withdrawn from petitioner's body by a physician at the hospital. The chemical analysis of this sample revealed a percent by weight of alcohol in his blood at the time of the offense which indicated intoxication, and the report of this analysis was admitted in evidence at trial. ...

The Privilege Against Self-Incrimination Claim

... We ... must now decide whether the withdrawal of the blood and admission in evidence of the analysis involved in this case violated petitioner's privilege. We hold that the privilege protects an accused only from being compelled to testify against himself, or otherwise provide the State with evidence of a testimonial or communicative nature, and that the withdrawal of blood and use of the analysis in question in this case did not involve compulsion to these ends. ...

The Search and Seizure Claim

The overriding function of the Fourth Amendment is to protect personal privacy and dignity against unwarranted intrusion by the State. ...

The values protected by the Fourth Amendment thus substantially overlap those the Fifth Amendment helps to protect. ...

Because we are dealing with intrusions into the human body rather than with state interferences with property relationships or private papers—"house, papers, and effect"—we write on a clean slate. ...

In this case, as will often be true when charges of driving under the influence of alcohol are pressed, these questions arise in the context of an arrest made by an officer without a warrant. Here, there was plainly probable cause for the officer to arrest petitioner and charge him with driving an automobile while under the influence of intoxicating liquor. The police officer who arrived at the scene shortly after the accident smelled liquor on petitioner's breath, and testified that petitioner's eyes were "bloodshot, watery, sort of a glassy appearance." The officer saw petitioner again at the hospital, within two hours of the accident. There he noticed similar symptoms of drunkenness. He thereupon informed petitioner "that he was under arrest and that he was entitled to the services of an attorney, and that he could remain silent, and that anything he told me would be used against him in evidence." ...

Although the facts which established probable cause to arrest in this case also suggested the required relevance and likely success of a test of petitioner's blood for alcohol, the question remains whether the arresting officer was permitted to draw these inferences himself, or was required instead to procure a warrant before proceeding with the test. Search warrants are ordinarily required for searches of dwellings, and, absent an emergency, no less could be required where intrusions of the human body are concerned. ... The importance of informed, detached and deliberate determinations of the issue whether or not to invade another's body in search of evidence of guilt is indisputable and great.

The officer in the present case, however, might reasonably have believed that he was confronted with an emergency, in which the delay necessary to obtain a warrant, under the circumstances, threatened "the destruction of evidence" ... . We are told that the percentage of alcohol in the blood begins to diminish shortly after drinking stops, as the body functions to eliminate it from the system. Particularly in a case such as this, where time had to be taken to bring the accused to a hospital and to investigate the scene of the accident, there was no time to seek out a magistrate and secure a warrant. ...

Finally, the records show that the test was performed in a reasonable manner. Petitioner's blood was taken by physician in a hospital environment according to accepted medical practices. We are thus not presented with the serious questions which would arise if a search involving use of a medical technique, even of the most rudimentary sort, were made by other than medical personnel or in other than a medical environment—for example, if it were administered by police in the privacy of the stationhouse. To tolerate searches under these conditions might be to invite an unjustified element of personal risk of infection and pain.

DNA Testing

Deoxyribonucleic acid (DNA) is a complex compound with two strands that spiral around one another, forming a double helix. Within the helix are molecules, called *nucleotide bases*, that connect the strands. There are four bases, identified by the letters A, T, G, and C. The A base of one strand attaches to the T base of its counterpart strand. In the same manner, the G base of one strand connects to the C base of the opposing strand. There are more than three billion base pairs in human DNA. However, only three million of these differ from person to person. The precise vertical ordering of these pairs determines a person's genetic code.

Through biological specimens, such as hair, blood, tissue, and semen, evidence from crime scenes can be compared with specimens from suspects. This testing is known as **DNA printing** or *genetic fingerprinting*. DNA printing compares the codes and determines if they are from the same individual. DNA testing is sophisticated, and if properly performed, nearly conclusively establishes identity. The possibility of a chance match, assuming perfect testing, has been estimated to be one in three trillion.[9]

DNA has proven to be an effective weapon for both prosecutors and defendants. In recent years, several convicted felons have used DNA testing to prove their innocence and secure their release. This has occurred, for example, in rape cases where blood and semen were used as prosecution evidence, but DNA testing was unavailable. After conviction, and from prison, these men used DNA testing to establish their innocence and set aside their verdicts.

DNA testing is not perfect. The testing method is sophisticated and errors can be made. For instance, methodology was hotly contested in the O.J. Simpson murder trial of 1995. Further, interpretations of test results differ. It is, therefore, imperative that a reliable laboratory be selected. Further, in some cases, the defense and prosecution may have independent DNA testing conducted. In spite of the possibility of error (false positive and false negative findings), courts have generally held that DNA evidence is sufficiently reliable for admission into evidence. The parties may, of course, challenge the accuracy of a particular DNA test.

Voice Tests

Compelling a suspect to speak for the purposes of audio identification is not violative of the Fifth Amendment's prohibition against compelled self-incrimination. This is because the purpose in compelling the statements is identification, not to secure testimony. Again, the voice is considered a physical characteristic that is readily observable to

TERMS

DNA fingerprinting A method for identifying the perpetrator of a crime by comparing tissue ... found at the scene of the crime with similar tissue from the defendant. It is also a method for establishing paternity. DNA (short for deoxyribonucleic acid) is a basic material in all living cells, which transmits the hereditary pattern. DNA evidence is admissible in some jurisdictions in criminal prosecutions and, in most jurisdictions, in paternity suits. Other terms for DNA fingerprinting are HLA testing and genetic marker testing.

the ordinary person; accordingly, it is not a search under the Fourth Amendment to compel a suspect to speak.

Voice is also at issue whenever a party intends to introduce audio records that purport to be a particular individual's, such as the defendant. For example, assume John is charged with murdering Henry. The police have in their possession a tape from John's telephone answering machine. The tape contains a threat to Henry's life that the government claims was made by John. To prove that John made the threat, the prosecutor plans to introduce voice spectrographic identification evidence.

This test involves a comparison of the recording and a voice sample provided by the defendant. It compares the complex sound waves of the two for similarity. The accuracy of voice spectrographics is questionable, and thus this type of evidence is not universally accepted by courts. In some jurisdictions, admissibility is prohibited, whereas in others the decision is left to the trial judge.

Polygraph Tests

Polygraph testing, also known as lie detection testing, measures a subject's physical responses, such as heartbeat, blood pressure, and perspiration, during questioning. This is not a new concept. The Chinese monitored the heartbeat of suspects as long as 4,000 years ago. If a suspect's heartbeat increased during a response, he was presumed to have lied.[10]

Until recently, courts have held that the results of polygraph evidence are too unreliable to be admitted at trial, unless the parties have stipulated to admission. Today, however, a few jurisdictions permit the introduction of polygraph evidence if it is determined reliable. That is, polygraph evidence is not automatically excluded, but may be if found to be unreliable in a specific case.

In addition to the issue of reliability, a Fifth Amendment self-incrimination issue surfaces when a prosecutor seeks an order requiring a defendant to undergo a polygraph examination. The Supreme Court has stated in dictum,[11] and the lower courts have similarly ruled directly, that lie detector tests involve communications and, accordingly, that the Fifth Amendment applies. Defendants may refuse to respond to questions when the answers may be incriminating, and *Miranda*-type warnings should be given before the test begins, assuming that custody exists. Further, a prosecutor may not refer to a defendant's refusal to submit to polygraph testing at trial.

§ 8.5 Chain of Custody

To assure that physical evidence discovered during an investigation remains unchanged and is not confused with evidence from other investigations, police must maintain the **chain of custody**. The officer who discovered the evidence must mark it, and all subsequent contacts with the evidence, such as by forensics officers, must be recorded. This creates a record known as the chain of custody. Chain-of-custody records must be kept from the time the evidence is seized until it is introduced at trial. Breaks in the chain of custody may result in exclusion of the evidence at trial.

In some instances, evidence may be admitted even though the chain of custody has been broken. If evidence is easily identified by a witness, such as its owner, then proving the chain of custody may not be necessary. This may also be true if an item is unique and can be precisely identified by its characteristics (e.g., serial and model numbers). Even in these cases, chain of custody is sometimes required, and the best practice is for the police to maintain a chain in every instance.

The burden of establishing the chain of custody rests with the party seeking admission. The standard of proof is characterized differently among the states, but usually amounts to a preponderance of the evidence. In some jurisdictions, proof of police policy, custom, and practice may be used to prove chain of custody.

§ 8.6 Exclusion of Improper Identifications

The consequences of not providing counsel during an identification procedure after the adversary judicial proceeding has begun were discussed in *Wade*. First, testimony about an illegal identification must be excluded at trial. Second, in-court identifications may be excluded if

TERMS

chain of custody The succession of people who had possession or control of an object, or of the places an object was stored or located, from one point in time to another. In many instances, a chain of custody must be established for physical evidence to be admissible at trial. A chain of custody is sometimes called a chain of possession.

tainted by the pretrial identification. However, if the government can show, by clear and convincing evidence, that an in-court identification has a source independent of the illegal pretrial identification, then it is to be allowed. The *Wade* Court said the following factors are to be considered when making the taint or no taint determination:

1. The prior opportunity to observe the criminal act
2. The difference between a witness's pre-lineup description and actual description of an accused
3. Whether the witness identified another person as the criminal before the lineup
4. Whether the witness identified the accused by photograph prior to the lineup
5. Whether the witness was unable to identify the accused on a previous occasion
6. The lapse of time between the crime and the identification.

In most cases, a court will find an independent source for an in-court identification and will allow a witness to identify the defendant during trial, while prohibiting mention of the pretrial identification.

The same rules apply to identifications that are impermissibly suggestive and unreliable. They must be excluded, as must the fruits thereof, unless an independent basis for an in-court identification can be shown.

Review Questions

1. Does a defendant have a right to counsel at a lineup? If so, what is the source of that right?
2. Does a defendant have a right to counsel at a photograph identification session? If so, what is the source of that right?
3. What is chain of custody?
4. Assume that a prosecutor wants a defendant to submit to genetic testing to compare the defendant's DNA with that of hair found on a victim. Does the defendant have a Fourth Amendment challenge? A Fifth?

Review Problems

1. Do you believe that it is self-incrimination to give blood, hair, and other such items that might prove one's guilt?
2. Describe a pretrial identification which you believe is unduly suggestive. Explain why it is too suggestive of guilt.

Notes

1 406 U.S. 682 (1972).

2 388 U.S. 293 (1967).

3 *Manson v. Braithwaite,* 432 U.S. 98 (1977).

4 *Schmerber v. California,* 384 U.S. 757 (1966).

5 293 F. 1013 (D.C. Cir. 1923).

6 113 S. Ct. 2786 (1993).

7 Braun, "Quantitative Analysis and the Law: Probability Theory as a Tool of Evidence in Criminal Trials," 1982 *Utah L. Rev.* 41, 57 n.82.

8 470 U.S. 753 (1985).

9 Dodd, "DNA Fingerprinting in Matters of Family and Crime," 26 *Med. Sci. L.* 5 (1986).

10 Morland, *An Outline of Scientific Criminology* 59–60 (2d ed. 1971).

11 *Schmerber v. California,* 384 U.S. 757, 764 (1966).

CHAPTER 9

THE PRETRIAL PROCESS: INITIATION THROUGH FORMAL CHARGE

CHAPTER OUTLINE

> *If the district attorney wanted, a grand jury would indict a ham sandwich.*
>
> ***Barry Slotnick***

§ 9.1 Introduction

The next two chapters outline the basic process a case goes through, from before arrest to after trial. As previously mentioned, the federal process is used for illustration; individual state procedures vary somewhat.

§ 9.2 Discovery and Investigation of Criminal Activity

The process begins when law enforcement officials learn of a crime that has been committed (or is to be committed). Police learn of criminal activity in two ways. They may discover it themselves, or a citizen may report such activity.

Once police are aware of criminal activity, the prearrest investigation begins. There are two objectives at this stage. First, police must determine whether a crime has been committed. Second, if a crime has been committed, police attempt to gather sufficient evidence to charge and convict the person believed to be guilty.

§ 9.3 Arrest

Once adequate evidence exists, an **arrest** is made in most cases. However, in some misdemeanor cases a defendant is asked to come to the police station, and an arrest is not made unless the defendant

TERMS

arrest Detention of a person on a criminal charge.

refuses. The arrest may be made without an arrest warrant in some situations. In others, an *ex parte* hearing may be held to determine if probable cause exists to believe that the person under investigation committed the crime. If so, the judge may issue an arrest warrant.

At the time of arrest, police ordinarily search the defendant. Once at the police station, the defendant is "booked." *Booking* consists of obtaining biographical information about the defendant (name, address, etc.), fingerprinting the defendant, and taking the defendant's photograph, commonly known as a "mug shot." The defendant is usually permitted to make a telephone call at this stage.

The defendant is then searched (sometimes deloused and showered) and held in jail until further arrangements are made. For minor offenses, the defendant may be able to post bail prior to appearing before a judge. In such cases, defendants are out of jail within hours. All others have to wait for a judge to set a bail amount at an initial appearance. During and after this stage, law enforcement investigation and gathering of evidence may continue.

§ 9.4 The Complaint

At this stage, a police officer, or in some instances a prosecutor, files a **complaint**, which acts as the charging instrument. (See Figure 9-1.) Fed. R. Crim. P. 3 states: "The complaint is a written statement of the essential facts constituting an offense charged. It shall be made upon oath before a magistrate." The complaint need not be written upon personal knowledge. That is, an officer may use hearsay and circumstantial evidence in a complaint. Affidavits from those who have personal knowledge, such as witnesses and victims, are often attached to the complaint.

When a warrant is sought to arrest a defendant, the complaint is often produced in support of the request for a warrant. This occurs at the *ex parte* hearing mentioned earlier. Federal law requires that a warrant be issued if probable cause is established by the complaint and its accompanying affidavits. Upon the request of the government, a summons (an order to appear) may be issued rather than an arrest warrant.[1] (See Figure 9-2.)

TERMS

complaint 1. The initial pleading in a civil action, in which the plaintiff alleges a cause of action and asks that the wrong done ... be remedied by the court. 2. A formal charge of a crime.

FIGURE 9-1 Criminal Complaint

AO 91 (Rev. 5/85) Criminal Complaint

United States District Court

______________ DISTRICT OF ______________

UNITED STATES OF AMERICA
V.

CRIMINAL COMPLAINT

CASE NUMBER:

(Name and Address of Defendant)

I, the undersigned complainant being duly sworn state the following is true and correct to the best of my knowledge and belief. On or about ______________ in ______________ county, in the ______________ District of ______________ defendant(s) did, (Track Statutory Language of Offense)

in violation of Title ______ United States Code, Section(s) ______________.

I further state that I am a(n) ______________ (Official Title) and that this complaint is based on the following facts:

Continued on the attached sheet and made a part hereof: ☐ Yes ☐ No

____
Signature of Complainant

Sworn to before me and subscribed in my presence,

______________ at ______________
Date / City and State

______________ ______________
Name & Title of Judicial Officer / Signature of Judicial Officer

FIGURE 9-2
Summons in a Criminal Case

AO 83 (Rev. 5/85) Summons in a Criminal Case

United States District Court

_______________ DISTRICT OF _______________

UNITED STATES OF AMERICA

SUMMONS IN A CRIMINAL CASE

CASE NUMBER:

(Name and Address of Defendant)

YOU ARE HEREBY SUMMONED to appear before the United States District Court at the place, date and time set forth below.

Place	Room
	Date and Time
Before:	

To answer a(n)
☐ Indictment ☐ Information ☐ Complaint ☐ Violation Notice ☐ Probation Violation Petition

Charging you with a violation of Title __________ United States Code, Section __________.

Brief description of offense:

_______________ Signature of Issuing Officer

_______________ Date

_______________ Name and Title of Issuing Officer

FIGURE 9-2
(continued)

AO 83 (Rev. 5/85) Summons in a Criminal Case

RETURN OF SERVICE

Service was made by me on:[1] ______ Date

Check one box below to indicate appropriate method of service

☐ Served personally upon the defendant at: ______________________

☐ Left summons at the defendant's dwelling house or usual place of abode with a person of suitable age and discretion then residing therein and mailed a copy of the summons to the defendant's last known address.
Name of person with whom the summons was left: ______________________

☐ Returned unexecuted: ______________________

I declare under penalty of perjury under the laws of the United States of America that the foregoing Information contained in the Return of Service is true and correct.

Returned on ______________________
Date

____
Name of United States Marshal

____
(by) Deputy United States Marshal

1) As to who may serve a summons see Rule 4 of the Federal Rules of Criminal Procedure

If the defendant was arrested without a warrant, the complaint serves as the charging document at the initial appearance or preliminary hearing.

For traffic violations and some lesser misdemeanors, the complaint acts as both a summons to appear in court and the charging document. In such cases, the defendant appears in court on only one occasion and the ticket is used in place of an information or indictment.

§ 9.5 Initial Appearance

After arrest, the defendant is taken "without unnecessary delay" before the nearest available federal magistrate.[2] In most cases this means that a defendant will be brought before the judge within twenty-four hours. However, if a defendant is arrested on a weekend, it may be the following Monday before the defendant has the initial appearance, unless a weekend session of court is held.

The first appearance is brief. If the arrest was executed under an arrest warrant, it is the duty of the presiding judge to make sure that the person arrested is the person named in the warrant. The defendant is also informed of various rights, such as the rights to remain silent and to have the assistance of counsel. If the defendant is indigent, the court will appoint counsel. The right to counsel is discussed more fully later. If the arrest was warrantless, an initial probable cause determination must occur.

In 1991, the United States Supreme Court examined the need for prompt probable cause determinations in warrantless arrest situations. In *County of Riverside v. McLaughlin*,[3] the Court held that persons arrested without a warrant must have a probable cause determination within forty-eight hours after arrest or quicker if reasonable. A defendant who asserts unreasonable delay, but was held less than forty-eight hours before a probable cause hearing was conducted, bears the burden of proving that the delay was unreasonable under the Fourth Amendment. If a defendant is held longer than forty-eight hours without a probable cause hearing, the burden of showing a bona fide emergency or other extraordinary circumstance falls on the government. The need for time to gather additional evidence, ill will, or the fact that the defendant was arrested on a weekend are not sufficient to delay the probable cause determination longer than forty-eight hours.

Finally, a preliminary hearing date is set, and if the defendant is in jail, the court determines whether he or she should be released prior to trial.

§ 9.6 Pretrial Release and Detention

In many cases, defendants are released prior to trial. A court may order many types of release, but the predominantly used methods are cash bail, surety bond, property bond, and personal recognizance.

Types of Release

The most obvious method of gaining release is to post **bail.** A defendant who has the resources may simply pay into the court the amount of the bail.

Whenever a third party, usually a professional bondsman, agrees to pay the bond for a defendant, a surety bond is created. The common practice is for the defendant to pay the surety 10 percent or more of the bond amount in exchange for the bondsman making the defendant's bail. The 10 percent is not refunded to the defendant after the case is concluded.

Some sureties require security (collateral) before a bond will be issued. Defendants may pledge cars, houses, or other property to obtain release. This is a property bond.

For many misdemeanors and a few felonies, a defendant may be released on personal recognizance. To gain such a release, a defendant need only promise to appear.

Regardless of the type of release, courts frequently impose conditions upon the defendant. Defendants who are arrested, caught intimidating witnesses, or interfering with the judicial process may be jailed until trial.

Eighth Amendment

The Eighth Amendment proscribes the imposition of "excessive bail." This provision may be applicable to the states through the Fourteenth Amendment. The purpose of imposing money bail is to assure the defendant's appearance at trial, not to inflict punishment. Bail set higher than necessary to accomplish this purpose is deemed excessive.[4] In practice, courts have significant discretion in setting bail and are rarely reversed.

TERMS

bail 1. The customary means of securing the release from custody of a person charged with a criminal offense, by assuring his or her appearance in court and compelling him or her to remain within the jurisdiction. 2. The security given for a defendant's appearance in court in the form of cash, real property, or a bail bond.

The Supreme Court has held that the mere fact that a defendant cannot pay the amount set by a court does not make it excessive. Additionally, the Court has stated that not all defendants have a right to bail. Defendants who are a danger to the community or are unlikely to appear for trial may be held without bail.

The exact meaning of the Eighth Amendment has not been spelled out by the Supreme Court. Whether pretrial detention laws, especially those that create a presumption of detention, are constitutional remains to be seen.

Detention

The federal government (and presumably most states, if not all) provides for detention of some defendants prior to trial.

Pretrial detention may not be used to punish a person. To do so violates a person's due process right to be free from punishment without a fair trial. However, a defendant may be detained if there is reason to believe that he or she will not appear for trial or if he or she poses a threat to others.

In the federal system, the defendant is entitled to an adversary hearing concerning pretrial detention, and the government must prove by clear and convincing evidence that the defendant is either dangerous or unlikely to appear for trial.[5] The adversary hearing must be held at the initial appearance, or upon the motion of the defendant or the government it may be continued.

Although the general rule is that the government bears the burden of proving that a defendant must be detained, there are exceptions. There are two classes of presumptions in the federal statute. One presumes that certain defendants will not appear for trial, and another presumes that certain defendants are a danger to the community. For example, defendants charged with crimes of violence who have a prior conviction for a crime of violence, which was committed while the defendant was released pending trial, are presumed to be dangerous to the community. It is also presumed that defendants charged with drug crimes that carry ten years or more imprisonment will flee. These presumptions also apply to many other defendants.[6] The presumption is rebuttable, and the defendant has the burden of disproving it. Some question the constitutionality of such presumptions, and it remains to be seen whether such statutes will be reversed or upheld.

Many states have statutes that require detention of persons charged with crimes punishable by life imprisonment or death, provided that the proof of guilt is great.

§ 9.7 Preliminary Hearing

The defendant's second appearance before a judge is the **preliminary hearing**. How this stage is handled by the states varies significantly. At the preliminary hearing, the court determines if probable cause to believe the accused committed the crime exists. If probable cause is found, the defendant is "bound over" to the next stage of the process. The next stage is either trial or review by grand jury. If probable cause is not established, the defendant is released.

If indictment by grand jury is required, the case is bound over to the grand jury. The grand jury is not bound by the judge's decision that probable cause exists; it makes an independent decision whether to charge the defendant. If grand jury review is not required, the defendant is bound over for trial.

The purpose of the preliminary hearing is to have an impartial third party review the facts to be sure that probable cause exists. There is no constitutional requirement for a preliminary hearing.[7] However, many states do provide for preliminary hearings.

It is common to permit prosecutors to bypass the preliminary hearing either by submitting the case to a grand jury or by directly filing an information. Defendants often waive the preliminary hearing. In some states, prosecutors may demand a preliminary hearing over the objection of the defendant.

The preliminary hearing can be quite lengthy compared to a defendant's initial appearance. The hearing is adversarial. Witnesses are called and the attorneys are allowed to make arguments. Rules of evidence are applied in modified form, so hearsay and illegally obtained evidence are often considered. Defendants have a right to counsel, and may also be allowed to cross-examine the prosecution witnesses and to present defense witnesses. The right to counsel is a matter of federal constitutional law. The other two rights are granted by state laws. The preliminary

TERMS

preliminary hearing A hearing to determine whether there is probable cause to formally accuse a person of a crime; that is, whether there is a reasonable basis for believing that a crime has been committed and for thinking the defendant committed it. If the judge concludes that the evidence is sufficient to hold the defendant for trial, and if the offense is a bailable offense, the court sets bail. If the judge concludes that the evidence is insufficient to bind the defendant over for trial, the defendant is discharged from custody.

hearing can be an important asset to both prosecution and defense, as it can serve as a source of discovery.

The preliminary hearing is different from the initial probable cause determination required by *County of Riverside v. McLaughlin.* The initial determination is constitutionally required, whereas the preliminary hearing is not. Further, although the same terminology is used (i.e., probable cause), less evidence is needed to satisfy the government's obligation at the initial determination than at the preliminary hearing. Probable cause at the initial hearing equates with the probable cause required to obtain a warrant, which is generally recognized as requiring less proof than probable cause at the later preliminary hearing. Also in contrast is the fact that the probable cause hearing required by *County of Riverside* will likely be one-sided. That is, only the government will present evidence. Some states, however, such as California, permit defendants to present evidence at preliminary hearings.

COUNTY OF RIVERSIDE
v.
McLAUGHLIN
500 U.S. 44 (1991)

JUSTICE O'CONNOR delivered the opinion of the Court.

In *Gerstein v. Pugh,* this Court held that the Fourth Amendment requires a prompt judicial determination of probable cause as a prerequisite to an extended pretrial detention following a warrantless arrest. This case requires us to define what is "prompt" under *Gerstein.*

This is a class action brought under 42 U.S.C. § 1983 challenging the manner in which the County of Riverside, California (County), provides probable cause determinations to persons arrested without a warrant. At issue is the County's policy of combining probable cause determinations with its arraignment procedures. Under County policy, ... arraignments must be conducted without unnecessary delay and, in any event, within two days of arrest. This two-day requirement excludes from computation weekends and holidays. Thus, an individual arrested without a warrant late in the week may in some cases be held for as long as five days before receiving a probable cause determination. Over the Thanksgiving holiday, a 7-day delay is possible.

* * *

In *Gerstein,* this Court held unconstitutional Florida procedures under which persons arrested without a warrant could remain in police custody for 30 days or more without a judicial determination of probable cause.

* * *

In so doing, we gave proper deference to the demands of federalism. We recognized that "state systems of criminal procedure vary widely" in the nature and number of pretrial procedures they provide, and we noted that there is no single "preferred" approach. ... Our purpose in *Gerstein* was to make clear that the Fourth Amendment requires every state to provide prompt determinations of probable cause, but that the Constitution does not impose on the States a rigid procedural framework. Rather, individual States may choose to comply in different ways.

Inherent in *Gerstein*'s invitation to the States to experiment and adapt was the recognition that the Fourth Amendment does not compel an immediate determination of probable cause upon completing the administrative steps incident to arrest. Plainly, if a probable cause hearing is constitutionally compelled the moment a suspect is finished being "booked," there is no room whatsoever for "flexibility and experimentation by the States." ... Incorporating probable cause determinations "into the procedure for setting bail or fixing other conditions of pretrial release"—which *Gerstein* explicity contemplated, ... —would be impossible. Waiting even a few hours so that a bail hearing or arraignment could take place at the same time as the probable cause determination would amount to a constitutional violation. Clearly, *Gerstein* is not that inflexible.

* * *

Given that *Gerstein* permits jurisdictions to incorporate probable cause determinations into other pretrial procedures, some delays are inevitable. For example, where, as in Riverside County, the probable cause determination is combined with arraignment, there will be delays caused by paperwork and logistical problems. Records will have to be reviewed, charging documents drafted, appearance of counsel arranged, and appropriate bail determined. On weekends, when the number of arrests is often higher and available resources tend to be limited, arraignments may get pushed back even further. In our view, the Fourth Amendment permits a reasonable postponement of a probable cause determination while the police cope with the everyday problems of processing suspects through an overly burdened criminal justice system.

But flexibility has its limits; *Gerstein* is not a blank check. A State has no legitimate interest in detaining for extended periods individuals who have been arrested without probable cause. The Court recognized in *Gerstein* that a person arrested without a warrant is entitled to a fair and reliable determination of probable cause and that this determination must be made promptly.

Unfortunately, as lower court decisions applying *Gerstein* have demonstrated, it is not enough to say that probable cause determinations must be "prompt." This vague standard simply has not provided sufficient guidance. Instead, it has led to a flurry of systemic challenges to city and county practices, putting federal judges in the role of making legislative judgments and overseeing local jailhouse operations. ... Our task in this case is to articulate more clearly the boundaries of what is permissible under the Fourth Amendment. Although we hesitate to announce that the Constitution compels a specific time limit, it is important to provide some degree of certainty so that States and counties may establish procedures with confidence that they fall within constitutional bounds. Taking into account the competing interests articulated in *Gerstein*, we believe that a jurisdiction that provides judicial determinations of probable cause within 48 hours of arrest will, as a general matter, comply with the promptness requirement of *Gerstein*. For this reason, such jurisdictions will be immune from systemic challenges.

This is not to say that the probable cause determination in a particular case passes constitutional muster simply because it is provided within 48 hours. Such a hearing may nonetheless violate *Gerstein* if the arrested individual can prove that his or her probable cause determination was delayed unreasonably. Examples of unreasonable delay are delays for the purpose of gathering additional evidence to justify the arrest, a delay motivated by ill will against the arrested individual, or delay for delay's sake. In evaluating whether the delay in a particular case is unreasonable, however, courts must allow a substantial degree of flexibility. Courts cannot ignore the often unavoidable delays in transporting arrested persons from one facility to another, handling late-night bookings where no magistrate is readily available, obtaining the presence of an arresting officer who may be busy processing other suspects or securing the premises of an arrest, and other practical realities.

Where an arrested individual does not receive a probable cause determination within 48 hours, the calculus changes. In such a case, the arrested individual does not bear the burden of proving an unreasonable delay. Rather, the burden shifts to the government to demonstrate the existence of a bona fide emergency or other extraordinary circumstance. The fact that in a particular case it may take longer than 48 hours to consolidate pretrial proceedings does not qualify as an extraordinary circumstance. Nor, for that matter, do intervening weekends. A jurisdiction that chooses to offer combined proceedings must do so as soon as is reasonably feasible, but in no event later than 48 hours after arrest.

... In advocating a 24-hour rule, the dissent would compel Riverside County—and countless others across the Nation—to speed up its criminal justice mechanisms substantially, presumably by allotting local tax dollars to hire additional police officers and magistrates. There may be times when the Constitution compels such direct interference with local control, but this is not one. As we have explained, *Gerstein* clearly contemplated a reasonable accommodation between legitimate competing concerns. We do no more than recognize that such accommodation can take place without running afoul of the Fourth Amendment.

Everyone agrees that the police should make every attempt to minimize the time a presumptively innocent individual spends in jail. One way to do so is to provide a judicial determination of probable cause immediately upon completing the administrative steps incident to arrest—*i.e.*, as soon as the suspect has been booked, photographed, and fingerprinted. As the dissent explains, several States, laudably, have adopted this approach. The Constitution does not compel so rigid a schedule, however. Under *Gerstein*, jurisdictions may choose to combine probable cause determinations with other pretrial proceedings, so long as they do so promptly. This necessarily means that only certain proceedings are candidates for combination. Only those proceedings that arise very early in the pretrial process—such as bail hearings and arraignments—may be chosen. Even then, every effort must be made to expedite the combined proceedings.

Fed. R. Crim. P. 5 requires that the date for "preliminary examination" be scheduled at the defendant's initial appearance. It shall be held within ten days of the initial appearance if the defendant is in custody and within twenty if the defendant has been released.

In federal courts and in many states, probable cause may be founded upon hearsay evidence.[8] Motions to suppress illegally seized evidence are made after the preliminary hearing, so such evidence may be considered at the preliminary examination stage. If a grand jury has issued an indictment, the preliminary hearing may be dispensed within the federal system[9]; many states have a similar rule.

§ 9.8 The Formal Charge

There are two formal charges: the **information** and the **indictment**. Informations are charges filed by prosecutors. Indictments are charges issued by grand juries. Once filed, an information or indictment replaces the complaint and becomes the formal charging instrument.

TERMS

information 1. An accusation of the commission of a crime, sworn to by a district attorney or other prosecutor, on the basis of which a criminal

Indictment and Grand Jury

Purpose of the Grand Jury

In early American history, **grand juries** were used to guard against unfair and arbitrary government prosecutions. The framers of the United States Constitution believed grand jury review so important that they stated in the Fifth Amendment: "[N]o person shall be held to answer for a capital, or otherwise infamous, crime, unless on a presentment or indictment of a Grand Jury."

Grand juries consist of twelve to twenty-three persons who are usually selected in the same method as petit juries (juries that determine guilt or innocence). Grand juries sit for longer periods of time and are called to hear cases as needed.

The primary objective of grand jury review is the same as the preliminary hearing: to determine whether there is probable cause to believe that a target of the investigation committed the alleged crime. The grand jury, therefore, was intended to protect individuals from unwarranted prosecutions. Because the grand jury proceedings are closed, individuals investigated but not charged are not subjected to the public humiliation and damage to reputation that often results from a more public investigation. The secondary objective of the grand jury has become its primary purpose, as defined by prosecutors: to facilitate investigation.

Procedures of the Grand Jury

First, grand juries are closed. The public, including the defendant, is not entitled to attend. Second, the prosecutor runs the show before the grand jury, and the defendant has no right to present evidence or to

TERMS

defendant is brought to trial for a misdemeanor and, in some states, for a felony. 2. In some jurisdictions, which prosecute felonies only on the basis of indictment by a grand jury, an affidavit alleging probable cause to bind the defendant over to await action by the grand jury.

indictment 1. A charge made in writing by a grand jury, based upon evidence presented to it, accusing a person of having committed a criminal act, generally a felony. It is the function of the prosecution to bring a case before the grand jury. If the grand jury indicts the defendant, a trial follows. 2. The formal, written accusation itself brought before the grand jury by the prosecutor.

grand jury A body whose number varies with the jurisdiction, never less than 6 nor more than 23, whose duty it is to determine whether probable cause exists to return indictments against persons accused of committing crimes. The right to indictment by grand jury is guaranteed by the Fifth Amendment.

make a statement. Third, the actions of grand juries are secret. Those who attend are not permitted to disclose what transpires. Defendants have no right to know what evidence is presented to a grand jury, unless it is exculpatory (tends to prove the defendant's innocence). Fourth, those who testify before the grand jury are not entitled to have counsel in the jury room.[10] In most states witnesses are permitted to leave the proceeding to confer with counsel waiting directly outside. Because statements made to a grand jury can be used later, the Fifth Amendment right to be free from self-incrimination is available to witnesses. Grand juries can overcome Fifth Amendment claims (refusals to testify) by granting witnesses immunity from prosecution. Also, witnesses may not refuse to testify because the inquiry is the result of illegally seized evidence. To permit refusal or exclusion would not further the objective of the exclusionary rule (to deter police misconduct) and would substantially interfere with the grand jury process.[11]

Grand juries possess the power to order people to appear, to subpoena documents (see Figure 9-3), to hold people in contempt, and to grant immunity in order to procure testimony. The grand jury can issue subpoenas for any information it determines it needs. Probable cause is not required; however, subpoenas that seek privileged information may be quashed in some cases. Although targets of grand jury investigations are not entitled to counsel in the grand jury room, they must be given the *Miranda* warnings and be permitted to consult with counsel outside the room. Some states permit counsel for a target to appear in the grand jury room.

As a general proposition, prosecutors control grand juries. For the most part, grand juries convene only when called by the prosecutor. The prosecutor decides what witnesses need to be called and who should be given immunity. Nearly all people targeted (the person the prosecutor believes guilty) by prosecutors are indicted. Many criticize the grand jury system for this reason: the government has too much control over the grand juries. The argument is reasonable when one considers the historical purpose of grand jury review.

The proponents of abolishing the grand jury system argue that not only have grand juries lost their independence, but they also now act to the benefit of prosecutors by allowing discovery of information that may have otherwise been unavailable.

The Indictment

After a grand jury has completed its investigation, a vote on whether to charge is taken. In the federal system, grand juries consist of sixteen to twenty-three people. At least twelve must vote for indictment.[12] In many cases indictments are sealed until the indicted defendant is arrested.

AO 110 (Rev. 5/85) Subpoena to Testify Before Grand Jury

United States District Court

______________ DISTRICT OF ______________

TO:

SUBPOENA TO TESTIFY BEFORE GRAND JURY

SUBPOENA FOR:
☐ PERSON ☐ DOCUMENT(S) OR OBJECT(S)

YOU ARE HEREBY COMMANDED to appear and testify before the Grand Jury of the United States District Court at the place, date, and time specified below.

PLACE	COURTROOM
	DATE AND TIME

YOU ARE ALSO COMMANDED to bring with you the following document(s) or object(s):*

☐ *Please see additional information on reverse*

This subpoena shall remain in effect until you are granted leave to depart by the court or by an officer acting on behalf of the court.

CLERK	DATE
(BY) DEPUTY CLERK	

This subpoena is issued on application of the United States of America	NAME, ADDRESS AND PHONE NUMBER OF ASSISTANT U.S. ATTORNEY

*If not applicable, enter "none"

FIGURE 9-3 Subpoena to Testify Before Grand Jury

The Constitution requires that all federal prosecutions for capital and infamous crimes be by indictment. However, if a defendant waives the right to grand jury review, he or she may be charged by information. The waiver of indictment form used in federal court is shown in Figure 9-4. Crimes punishable by one year or longer in prison are

FIGURE 9-3
(continued)

AO 110 (Rev. 5/85) Subpoena to Testify Before Grand Jury

RETURN OF SERVICE (1)		
RECEIVED BY SERVER	DATE	PLACE
SERVED	DATE	PLACE
SERVED ON (NAME)		
SERVED BY		TITLE

STATEMENT OF SERVICE FEES		
TRAVEL	SERVICES	TOTAL

DECLARATION OF SERVER(2)

I declare under penalty of perjury under the laws of the United States of America that the foregoing information contained in the Return of Service and Statement of Service Fees is true and correct.

Executed on ____________________ ____________________
Date *Signature of Server*

____
Address of Server

ADDITIONAL INFORMATION

(1) As to who may serve a subpoena and the manner of its service see Rule 17(d), Federal Rules of Criminal Procedure, or Rule 45(c), Federal Rules of Civil Procedure.
(2) "Fees and mileage need not be tendered to the witness upon service of a subpoena issued on behalf of the United States or an officer or agency thereof (Rule 45(c), Federal Rules of Civil Procedure; Rule 17(d), Federal Rules of Criminal Procedure) or on behalf of certain indigent parties and criminal defendants who are unable to pay such costs (28 USC 1825, Rule 17(b) Federal Rules of Criminal Procedure)".

"infamous."[13] A defendant may not waive indictment in federal capital cases. It is always proper to charge corporations by information, as imprisonment is not possible.

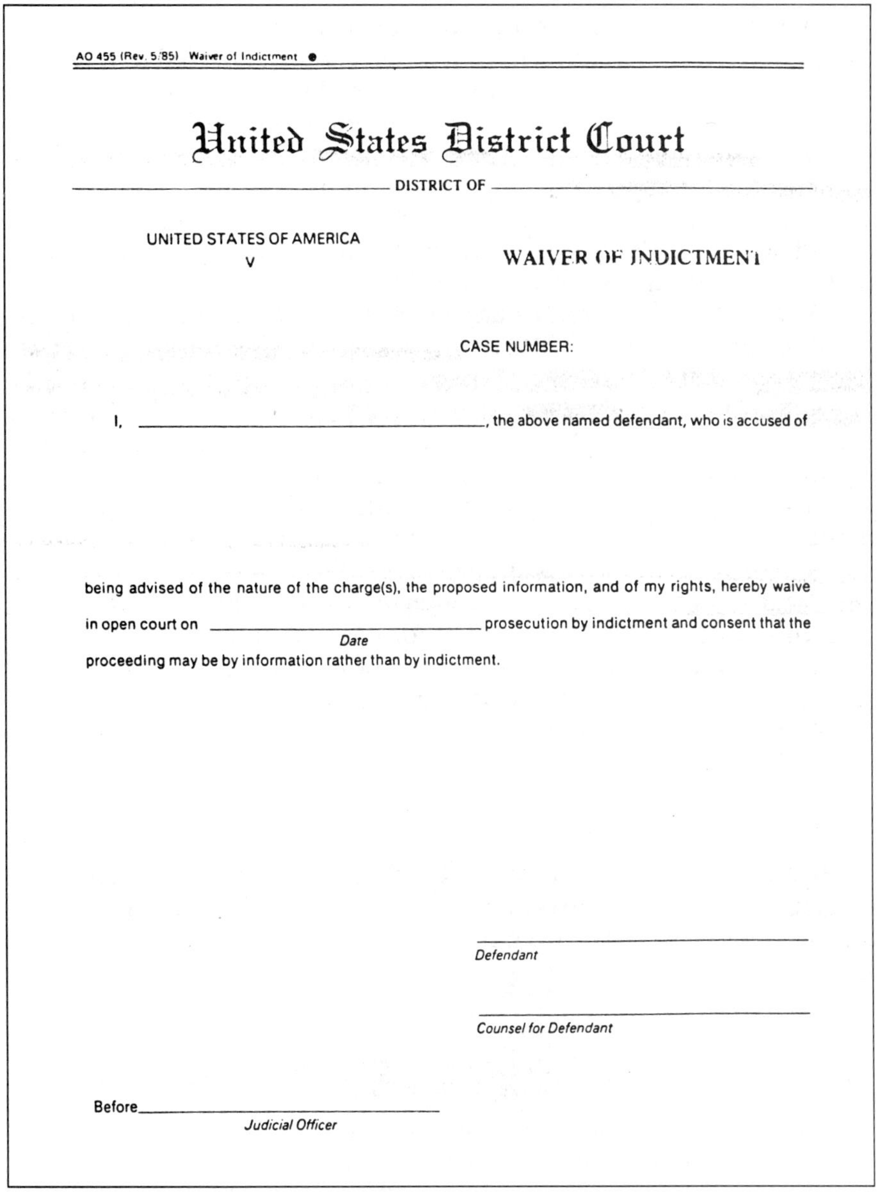

AO 455 (Rev. 5/85) Waiver of Indictment

United States District Court

_______________ DISTRICT OF _______________

UNITED STATES OF AMERICA
v

WAIVER OF INDICTMENT

CASE NUMBER:

I, ______________________, the above named defendant, who is accused of

being advised of the nature of the charge(s), the proposed information, and of my rights, hereby waive in open court on ______________ (Date) prosecution by indictment and consent that the proceeding may be by information rather than by indictment.

____
Defendant

____
Counsel for Defendant

Before______________________
Judicial Officer

FIGURE 9-4 Waiver of Indictment

The United States Supreme Court has ruled that grand jury review is not a fundamental right; therefore, the Fifth Amendment requirement for indictment is not applicable against the states. However, many states have grand juries and require that serious charges be brought by indictment.

Indictments must be written and state in "plain and concise" terms the essential facts constituting the offense charged.[14] Indictments are liberally read, and technical errors do not make them invalid. However, an indictment must contain all the essential elements of the crime charged. If an indictment charges more than one crime, each crime must be made a separate count.[15] Jurisdiction must be noted, and the law upon which the charge is made must be cited. The indictment filed against Ted Bundy is shown in Figure 9-5. It was upon this indictment that Ted Bundy was prosecuted, convicted, and executed.

If a defendant believes that an indictment is fatally deficient it may be attacked by a **motion** to **quash.** Indictments are not quashed because of technical errors. An example of a valid reason to quash is failure to allege an essential element of the crime charged. It is not violative of the Fifth Amendment's double jeopardy clause for a grand jury to issue a second indictment after the first has been quashed or dismissed.

In some jurisdictions, a prosecutor may refuse to prosecute, even though an indictment has been issued. In that situation, the prosecutor must assist the jury in preparing the document and must usually explain why a prosecution will not be maintained. In other instances, the prosecutor *must* pursue the case. The former situation represents federal law, that is, the decision on whether to prosecute falls within the purview of the federal prosecutor, who may properly refuse to sign an indictment and prosecute the case.[16]

Information

The second formal method of charging someone with a crime is by information. Informations are filed by prosecutors without grand jury review. The trend is away from indictments and toward charging by information.

TERMS

motion An application made to a court for the purpose of obtaining an order or rule directing something to be done in favor of the applicant. The types of motions available to litigants, as well as their form and the matters they appropriately address, are set forth in detail in the Federal Rules of Civil Procedure and the rules of civil procedure of the various states, as well as in the Federal Rules of Criminal Procedure and the various states' rules of criminal procedure. Motions may be written or oral, depending on the type of relief sought and on the court in which they are made.

quash To suppress; to set aside; to vacate; to abrogate. Thus, a motion to quash indictment is a motion that asks the court to suppress an indictment that is defective. Similarly, one may quash an information or quash a subpoena.

FIGURE 9-5
Ted Bundy Indictment

IN THE CIRCUIT COURT OF THE SECOND JUDICIAL CIRCUIT, IN AND FOR LEON COUNTY, FLORIDA.

CASE NO. 78-670

	)	INDICTMENT FOR:
THE STATE OF FLORIDA,		
	)	BURGLARY OF DWELLING
-vs-	)	MURDER IN THE FIRST DEGREE
	)	MURDER IN THE FIRST DEGREE
THEODORE ROBERT BUNDY,	)	ATTEMPTED MURDER IN THE FIRST DEGREE
	)	ATTEMPTED MURDER IN THE FIRST DEGREE
	)	BURGLARY OF DWELLING
Defendant,	)	ATTEMPTED MURDER IN THE FIRST DEGREE

IN THE NAME OF AND BY THE AUTHORITY OF THE STATE OF FLORIDA:

The Grand Jurors of the State of Florida, empaneled and sworn to inquire and true presentment made in and for the County of Leon, upon their oaths, do present that

THEODORE ROBERT BUNDY

on the 15th day of January, 1978, in Leon County, Florida, did then and there unlawfully enter or remain in a structure located at 661 West Jefferson Street, the dwelling of Karen Chandler and/or Kathy Kleiner, with the intent to commit the offense of Battery therein, and in the course of committing such burglary the said THEODORE ROBERT BUNDY did make an assault upon Karen Chandler and/or Kathy Kleiner, contrary to Section 810.02, Florida Statutes;

And Your Grand Jurors being present in said Court further gives the Court to be informed and understand that THEODORE ROBERT BUNDY on the 15th day of January, 1978, in Leon County, Florida, did then and there unlawfully kill a human being, to-wit: Margaret Bowman, by strangling and/or beating her, and said killing was perpetrated by said THEODORE ROBERT BUNDY from, or with a premeditated design or intent to effect the death of said Margaret Bowman, contrary to Section 782.04, Florida Statutes;

And Your Grand Jurors being present in said Court further gives the Court to be informed and understand that THEODORE ROBERT BUNDY on the 15th day of January, 1978, in Leon County, Florida, did then and there unlawfully kill a human being, to-wit: Lisa Levy, by strangling and/or beating her, and said killing was perpetrated by said THEODORE ROBERT BUNDY from, or with

FIGURE 9-5
(continued)

a premeditated design or intent to effect the death of said Lisa Levy, contrary to Section 782.04, Florida Statutes;

And Your Grand Jurors being present in said Court further gives the Court to be informed and understand that THEODORE ROBERT BUNDY on the 15th day of January, 1978, in Leon County, Florida, did then and there unlawfully attempt to kill a human being, to-wit: Karen Chandler, by beating her about the head and knowingly or intentionally causing great bodily harm, and said attempt was perpetrated by said THEODORE ROBERT BUNDY from, or with a premeditated design or intent to effect the death of said Karen Chandler, contrary to Sections 777.04 and 782.04, Florida Statutes;

And Your Grand Jurors being present in said Court further gives the Court to be informed and understand that THEODORE ROBERT BUNDY on the 15th day of January, 1978, in Leon County, Florida, did then and there unlawfully attempt to kill a human being, to-wit: Kathy Kleiner, by beating her about the head and knowingly or intentionally causing great bodily harm, and said attempt was perpetrated by said THEODORE ROBERT BUNDY from, or with a premeditated design or intent to effect the death of said Kathy Kleiner, contrary to Sections 777.04 and 782.04, Florida Statutes;

And Your Grand Jurors being present in said Court further gives the Court to be informed and understand that THEODORE ROBERT BUNDY on the 15th day of January, 1978, in Leon County, Florida, did then and there unlawfully enter or remain in a structure located at 431-A Dunwoody, the dwelling of Cheryl Thomas, with the intent to commit the offense of Battery therein, and in the course of committing such burglary the said THEODORE ROBERT BUNDY did make an assault upon Cheryl Thomas, contrary to Section 810.02, Florida Statutes;

And Your Grand Jurors being present in said Court further gives the court to be informed and understand that THEODORE ROBERT BUNDY on the 15th day of January, 1978, in Leon County, Florida, did then and there unlawfully attempt to kill a human being, to-wit: Cheryl Thomas, by beating her about the head and knowingly or intentionally causing great bodily harm, and said attempt was perpetrated by said THEODORE ROBERT BUNDY from, or with a premeditated design or intent to effect the death of said Cheryl Thomas, contrary to Sections 777.04 and 782.04, Florida Statutes; and

Contrary to the form of the Statute in such case made and provided and against the peace and dignity of the State of Florida.

Harry Morrison

AS STATE ATTORNEY, SECOND JUDICIAL CIRCUIT OF FLORIDA, IN AND FOR LEON COUNTY; PROSECUTING FOR SAID STATE.

If a defendant has been initially charged by complaint, the prosecutor must independently review the evidence and determine whether a prosecution is warranted. If not, a prosecutor may file a *nolle prosequi*. If so, the information is filed.

Informations serve the same function as indictments. Under the federal rules, informations must take the same form as indictments. They must be plain, concise, and in writing. All essential elements, as well as the statute relied upon by the government, must be included.[17] (See Figure 9-6.) As is true of indictments, informations must be filed with the appropriate court.

Defendants may seek to have defective informations quashed or dismissed. The rules regarding defectiveness are the same for informations as for indictments. Technical errors are not fatal.

Review Questions

1. For what two reasons may a defendant be detained prior to trial?
2. What is the difference between an indictment and an information?
3. What are the purposes of indictments and informations?
4. If a defendant needs more information than appears in the indictment to prepare a defense, what should be done?
5. Lance is charged with aggravated assault. His bail has been set at $200,000. This is far beyond his financial means and he challenges it as such. Is the bail amount constitutional?
6. The Supreme Court defined what is a "prompt" probable cause determination in *County of Riverside v. McLaughlin*. Briefly describe the holding in that case.
7. What is a pretrial release on personal recognizance?

Review Problems

1. What is the historical purpose of the grand jury? Many feel that grand juries should be abolished. Why?
2. Do you believe that indictment by grand jury should be incorporated? Explain your position.

STATE OF WISCONSIN | CIRCUIT COURT CRIMINAL DIVISION | MILWAUKEE COUNTY

STATE OF WISCONSIN, Plaintiff

vs.

Jeffrey L. Dahmer 05/21/60
924 N. 25th St.
Milwaukee, WI

Defendant.

FILED
SEP 10 1991
J. BARCZAK
CLERK OF COURTS

INFORMATION

CRIME(S):
See Charging Section Below
STATUTE(S) VIOLATED
See Charging Section Below
COMPLAINING WITNESS:
Donald Domagalski
CASE NUMBER:
F-912542

I, E. MICHAEL MC CANN, DISTRICT ATTORNEY FOR MILWAUKEE COUNTY, WISCONSIN, HEREBY INFORM THE COURT THAT THE ABOVE NAMED DEFENDANT IN THE COUNTY OF MILWAUKEE, STATE OF WISCONSIN,

COUNT 01: FIRST DEGREE MURDER

COUNT 12: FIRST DEGREE INTENTIONAL HOMICIDE

on or about June 30, 1991, at 924 North 25th Street, City and County of Milwaukee, did cause the death of another human being, Matt Turner a/k/a Donald Montrell, with intent to kill that person contrary to Wisconsin Statutes section 940.01(1).

Upon conviction of each count of First Degree Intentional Homicide and each count of First Degree Murder, Class A Felonies, the penalty is life imprisonment.

DATED 9/10/91

E. MICHAEL MC CANN
DISTRICT ATTORNEY

E. Michael McCann
District Attorney

Jeffrey L. Dahmer
9.10.91

Jeffrey L. Dahmer 9.10.91
x The statement on page 1 is accurate as it applies to this page (3)
Jeffrey L. Dahmer
9.10.91

FIGURE 9-6 Part of the criminal information in Dahmer serial murder case. (Only count 12 is shown; the other counts were similar.)

Notes

1 Fed. R. Crim. P. 4.

2 Fed. R. Crim. P. 5.

3 500 U.S. 44 (1991).

4 *Stack v. Boyle*, 342 U.S. 1 (1951).

5 18 U.S.C. § 3142(f).

6 18 U.S.C. § 3142(e), (f).

7 *Gerstein v. Pugh*, 420 U.S. 103 (1975).

8 Fed. R. Crim. P. 5.1; 18 U.S.C. § 3060.

9 18 U.S.C. § 3060(e).

10 *United States v. Mandujano*, 425 U.S. 564 (1976).

11 *United States v. Calandra*, 414 U.S. 338 (1974).

12 Fed. R. Crim. P. 6.

13 *Ex parte Wilson*, 114 U.S. 417 (1884). *See also* Fed. R. Crim. P. 7.

14 Fed. R. Crim. P. 7(c).

15 Fed. R. Crim. P. 8(a).

16 *See United States v. Cox*, 342 F.2d 167 (5th Cir.), *cert. denied*, 381 U.S. 935 (1965).

17 Fed. R. Crim. P. 7(c).

CHAPTER 10

PRETRIAL PROCESS: ARRAIGNMENT THROUGH TRIAL

CHAPTER OUTLINE

> *If criminals wanted to grind justice to a halt, they could do it by banding together and all pleading not guilty.*
>
> ***Dorothy Wright Wilson***
> ***Dean, University of Southern California Law Center***

§ 10.1 Arraignment

After the formal charge has been filed, the defendant is brought to the trial court for **arraignment.** This is the hearing at which the defendant is read the formal charge and is asked to enter a **plea.**

Defendants may plead guilty, not guilty, or *nolo contendere.* By pleading guilty a defendant admits all the charges contained in the charging document, unless a plea agreement has been reached with the government. A **plea agreement**, also known as a *plea bargain,* is the product of negotiations between the prosecutor and the defendant. It is common for the prosecution to dismiss one or more charges of a multicount charge, reduce a charge, or agree to recommend a particular sentence in exchange for a defendant's plea of guilty.

Plea bargaining is an important aspect of criminal procedure. More than 90 percent of all felony cases are disposed of by pleas of guilty. Although practice varies, in most jurisdictions judges do not become involved in plea negotiations. Most guilty pleas are the result of plea bargaining.

TERMS

arraignment The act of bringing an accused before a court to answer a criminal charge ... and calling upon him or her to enter a plea of guilty or not guilty.

plea In criminal cases, a response required by law of a person formally accused of crime, specifically, either a plea of guilty, a plea of nolo contendere, or a plea of not guilty.

plea bargain (plea agreement) An agreement between the prosecutor and a criminal defendant under which the accused agrees to plead guilty, usually to a lesser offense, in exchange for receiving a lighter sentence than he or she would likely have received had he or she been found guilty after trial on the original charge.

SIDEBAR

Plea Bargaining

Statistics vary, but it is widely accepted that approximately 90 percent of all felony cases are disposed of by pleas of guilty. The number is probably higher for misdemeanors. There is no question that plea bargaining greatly reduces the amount of time expended on trials. Warren Burger, past Chief Justice of the United States Supreme Court, estimated that judicial resources in the United States would have to be doubled if only 20 percent of all criminal cases went to trial. This conclusion was in large part a matter of simple math and has been criticized. In any event, plea bargaining is an important part of the criminal justice system. It is so important that the Supreme Court has stated that it "is not only an essential part of the process but a highly desirable part." *Santobello v. New York,* 404 U.S. 257, 261 (1971).

In *Boykin v. Alabama,* 395 U.S. 238 (1969), it was announced that all defendants who plead guilty do so voluntarily and knowingly, the latter meaning that the defendant understands the rights that are waived by entering a plea of guilty.

The plea negotiation involves the defendant and the prosecutor. Judges do not participate in plea negotiations. After a bargain is reached, it is presented to the trial court. The court may then accept the agreement and sentence the defendant accordingly. With good cause, the court may also reject the agreement. Some states permit defendants to withdraw their guilty pleas if the judge rejects the bargain. In others the judge has the discretion of allowing the defendant to withdraw the guilty plea or sentencing the defendant contrary to the bargain.

Sources: Burger, *The State of the Judiciary,* 56 A.B.A. J. 929 (1970); Note, *Is Plea Bargaining Inevitable?,* 97 Harv. L. Rev. 1037 (1984).

By pleading guilty, defendants waive a host of rights. The right to a jury trial and to be proven guilty beyond a reasonable doubt are two of the rights waived by a guilty plea. Because of the significance of such waivers, courts must be sure that guilty pleas are given knowingly and voluntarily. To be knowing, a defendant must understand his or her rights and that he or she is waiving them by making the plea. The plea must be free of coercion or duress to be voluntary.

The court must also find that a factual basis exists before a plea of guilty can be accepted. This means that there must be sufficient facts in the record to support the conclusion that the defendant committed the crime. A defendant has no right to plead guilty to a crime he or she did not commit. The factual basis may be established by the testimony of the investigating officer or by the defendant recounting what transpired. Once the plea is taken, the court will either impose sentence or set a future date for sentencing.

A court may accept a guilty plea or, with good cause, may reject it. In some instances the judge may accept the defendant's guilty plea, but reject the agreed-upon terms. In some such situations, the defendant is sometimes permitted to withdraw the plea; in others, the judge is free to sentence the defendant more or less severely than called for in the agreement. The judge must inform the defendant of this possibility before the defendant enters a guilty plea.

Defendants and academics have asserted that the plea bargaining system is violative of both the due process right and the jury trial right because it penalizes defendants who choose to exercise their right to a jury trial. After all, the inducement to defendants is that they will fare better if they plead guilty (waive the right to jury trial) than if they demand a jury trial. As true as this may be, the practical necessity of plea bargaining has lead the Supreme Court to determine that the process is legitimate.

Bordenkircher dealt with inducements presented by prosecutors on a case-by-case basis. Is a statutory inducement not to proceed to trial impermissible coercion? The answer is yes and no. A statute that punished defendants with death only upon a jury verdict and did not make that punishment a possibility for defendants who pled guilty was invalidated by the Supreme Court in *United States v. Jackson.*[1] However, the Court did not extend this reasoning to the lesser punishment of life imprisonment. In *Corbitt v. New Jersey,*[2] the defendant proceeded to trial and was convicted. The judge's sentencing range was limited to that of first-degree murder. The defendant was sentenced to the maximum amount, life imprisonment. If he had pled *nolo contendere,* the sentencing range would have been broader, and he could have been sentenced as a murderer of either the first or the second degree. The Court rejected his claim that this type of sentencing scheme was invalid under *Jackson.* The fact that *Jackson* involved the death penalty was significant to the Court, as was the fact that the sentence the defendant actually received (life imprisonment) was available if he pled *nolo contendere* or was convicted by jury verdict. The Court noted, however, that there is a limit to what a state can do to chill the right to a jury trial. This case was nevertheless not an example of unconstitutional coercion.

What occurs if one of the parties breaches the plea agreement? There are several remedies. First, if the prosecutor breaches after the defendant has entered a guilty plea, withdrawal of the plea is possible. Then, the parties may either proceed to trial or renegotiate. If withdrawal of the plea is unfair to the defendant (for example, if the defendant has already spent a considerable period of time incarcerated or has already provided the state with the information sought), then specific performance may be ordered by the court. If a defendant breaches, the prosecutor may seek rescission of the agreement and vacation of the guilty plea. The case may then be tried. It is not a violation of double jeopardy or due process to vacate a plea in such circumstances.[3]

Plea negotiations are critical stages of the process at which defendants have a right to counsel. Recall that defendants have a right to the

BORDENKIRCHER v. HAYES 434 U.S. 357 (1978)

The respondent, Paul Lewis Hayes, was indicted by a grand jury on a charge of uttering a forged instrument … . After arraignment, Hayes, his retained counsel, and the Commonwealth's Attorney met in the presence of the Clerk of the Court to discuss a possible plea agreement. During these conferences the prosecutor offered to recommend a sentence of five years in prison if Hayes would plead guilty to the indictment. He also said that if Hayes did not plead guilty and "save the court the inconvenience and necessity of a trial," he would return to the grand jury to seek an indictment under the Kentucky Habitual Criminal Act, which would subject Hayes to a mandatory sentence of life imprisonment by reason of two prior felony convictions. Hayes chose not to plead guilty, and the prosecutor did obtain an indictment charging him under the Habitual Criminal Act.

A jury found Hayes guilty on the principal charge of uttering a forged instrument [and of being a habitual offender]. As required by the habitual offender statute, he was sentenced to life … .

While the prosecutor did not actually obtain the recidivist indictment until after the plea conferences had ended, his intention to do so was clearly expressed at the outset of the plea negotiations. Hayes was thus fully informed of the true terms of the offer when he made his decision to plead not guilty.

To punish a person because he has done what the law plainly allows him to do is a due process violation of the most basic sort, and for an agent of the State to pursue a course of action whose objective is to penalize a person's reliance on his legal rights is "patently unconstitutional." But in the "give-and-take" of plea bargaining, there is no such element of punishment or retaliation so long as the accused is free to accept or reject the prosecution's offer.

Plea bargaining flows from "the mutuality of advantage" to defendants and prosecutors, each with his own reasons for wanting to avoid trial. …

While confronting a defendant with the risk of more severe punishment clearly may have a "discouraging effect on the defendant's assertion of his trial rights, the imposition of these difficult choices is an inevitable"—and permissible—"attribute of any legitimate system which tolerates and encourages the negotiation of pleas." It follows that, by tolerating and encouraging the negotiation of pleas, this Court has necessarily accepted as constitutionally legitimate the simple reality that the prosecutor's interest at the bargaining table is to persuade the defendant to forgo his right to plead not guilty.

There is no doubt that the breadth of discretion that our country's legal system vests in prosecuting attorneys carries with it the potential for both individual and institutional abuse. We hold only that the course of conduct engaged in by the prosecutor in this case, which no more than openly presented the defendant with the unpleasant alternatives of forgoing trial or facing charges on which he was plainly subject to prosecution, did not violate the Due Process Clause of the Fourteenth Amendment.

effective assistance of counsel. Thus, if an attorney harms a client through incompetence during plea negotiations, the defendant may have both Fifth and Sixth Amendment remedies.

Finally, note that most jurisdictions today permit conditional pleas. The plea is usually conditioned upon the outcome of a particular hearing.

For example, a defendant may plead guilty conditioned upon the outcome of appeal. If the defendant prevails on appeal (the appellate court determines that a piece of evidence should be excluded from the defendant's trial), the defendant is to be allowed to withdraw the guilty plea and proceed to trial.

If a defendant enters a not guilty plea, the court will set a trial date. In some instances, courts will set a pretrial schedule, which may include a pretrial conference date and a deadline for filing pretrial motions.

Finally, a plea of *nolo contendere* may be entered. *Nolo contendere* is a Latin phrase that translates to "I do not contest it." The defendant who pleads *nolo contendere* neither admits nor denies the charges and has no intent of defending himself or herself.

Nolo contendere is treated as a plea of guilty. That is, the government must establish that a factual basis exists to believe the defendant committed the offense, and the court accepting the plea must be sure that the plea is made voluntarily and knowingly. In most jurisdictions a defendant may plead *nolo contendere* only with the approval of the court. This is true in the courts of the United States.[4]

The advantage of a no contest plea over a guilty plea is that the no contest plea cannot be used in a later civil proceeding against the defendant, whereas a guilty plea may be used. If the case is not disposed of by a plea of guilty or *nolo contendere,* the parties begin preparing for trial.

§ 10.2 Discovery

Discovery refers to a process of exchanging information between the prosecution and defense. Discovery is not as broad in criminal cases as in civil.

The amount of discovery that should be allowed is heavily debated. Those favoring broad discovery contend that limited discovery leads to "trial by ambush," which is not in the best interests of justice. The purpose of a trial is to discover the truth and achieve justice, not to award the better game-player. Proponents of this position claim that

TERMS

discovery A means for providing a party, in advance of trial, with access to facts that are within the knowledge of the other side, to enable the party to better try his or her case. A motion to compel discovery is the procedural means for compelling the adverse party to reveal such facts or to produce documents, books, and other things within his or her possession or control.

unexpected evidence at trial is inefficient, costly, and unfair. It is inefficient because trials often have to be delayed to give one party time to prepare a response to the unexpected evidence. Such tactics lead to time problems for the parties as well as the trial court. They may also be unfair. It is possible that evidence that was once available may not be so at trial. If the party surprised at trial had known about the unexpected evidence, other contrary evidence could have been secured and a proper defense or response could have been prepared.

Finally, it appears unfair to subject defendants to the possibility of surprise when the government is insulated from certain surprises. For example, affirmative defenses must be specially pled. Intent to rely on alibi and insanity defenses must be provided to the government in most jurisdictions, often with strict enforcement of time requirements. The purpose of these rules is to prevent surprises to the government at trial. Those who support expanded discovery feel that it is unfair to place such requirements upon defendants but not upon the government.

Those opposed contend that expansive discovery increases the likelihood that defendants will manipulate the system. In particular, defendants might intimidate government witnesses. Additionally, opponents contend that it is easier for a defendant to skillfully plan his or her testimony, even if false, if a defendant knows the government's entire case. For example, if a defendant originally planned to assert an alibi but finds out through discovery that the government has a witness placing him at the location of the crime, he has been provided an opportunity to change his defense. Today, discovery in criminal proceedings is quite limited in many jurisdictions, including federal courts. A few states have enlarged what information may be obtained prior to trial.

What follows is an examination of the federal rules, as well as constitutional requirements for discovery.

Bill of Particulars

One method that defendants have to obtain information about the government's case is through a **bill of particulars.** The purpose of bills of particulars is to make general indictments and informations more specific. Fed. R. Crim. P. 7(f) allows district courts to order prosecutors to file a bill of particulars.

TERMS

bill of particulars In criminal prosecutions, a more detailed statement of the offense charged than the indictment or information provides. A criminal defendant is entitled to a bill of particulars, as part of the discovery process, if the nature and extent of the offense are not alleged with sufficient particularity to allow the preparation of an adequate defense.

Bills of particulars are not true discovery devices. If the charging instrument is sufficiently clear and detailed, the court will not grant a defense motion for particularization of the charge. A bill of particulars is intended to provide a defendant with details about the charges that are necessary for the preparation of a defense and to avoid prejudicial surprise at trial.[5] The test is not whether the indictment is sufficiently drawn; the question is whether the information is necessary to avoid prejudice to the defendant.

Statements of the Defendant

Fed. R. Crim. P. 16(a)(1)(A) states that upon request the government must allow the defendant to inspect, copy, or photograph all prior relevant written and recorded statements made by the defendant. This includes testimony that defendants give before grand juries—an exception to the rule of secrecy of grand jury proceedings.

Prosecutors are required to allow inspection of all statements made by the defendant which are in the possession of the prosecution or which may be discovered through due diligence. Hence, if a defendant makes a statement to an arresting officer, which is recorded or reduced to writing, the prosecutor must allow defense inspection even though the statement may be in the possession of the officer and not the prosecutor.

In addition to recorded statements and writings, the government is required to inform the defendant of "the substance of any oral statement that the government intends to offer in evidence." This means that statements made by a defendant that are summarized by the police (or other government agent), but not verbatim or signed by the defendant, are also discoverable. However, such evidence is discoverable only if the prosecution intends to use it at trial. This is not true of written and recorded statements of a defendant.

Criminal Record of the Defendant

Fed. R. Crim. P. 16 also requires prosecutors to furnish a copy of the defendant's criminal record to the defendant. This includes not only the records known to the prosecutor, but also those that can be discovered through due diligence.

Documents and Tangible Objects

Under Rule 16, defendants are also entitled to inspect and copy photographs, books, tangible objects, papers, buildings, and places that are in the possession of the government if:

1. The item is material to preparation of the defendant's defense, or
2. The item is going to be used by the government at trial, or
3. The item was obtained from, or belongs to, the defendant.

The situations in which this might apply are countless. For example, if the police take pictures of the scene of a crime, this provision allows the defendant to view and copy those pictures prior to trial. Or, if the police seize a building that was used to manufacture drugs, the defendant can invoke this rule to gain access to the premises.

This section of Rule 16 has a reciprocal provision. That is, defendants must allow the government to inspect and copy defense items. However, the rule is not as broad for government discovery. Defendants only have to permit inspection and copy of those items intended to be used at trial.

Scientific Reports and Tests

All scientific reports and tests in the possession of the government (or which can be discovered through due diligence) must be turned over to the defendant, if requested. This provision includes reports and conclusions of mental examinations of the defendant, autopsy reports, drug tests, fingerprint analysis, blood tests, DNA (genetic) tests, ballistic tests, and other related tests and examinations.

The defendant must accord the government reciprocity, if requested. For example, if a defendant undergoes an independent mental examination, the government is entitled to review the report of the evaluator prior to trial.

Statements of Witnesses/Jencks Act

In the federal system, defendants are not entitled to inspect or copy statements of prosecution witnesses prior to trial. However, a federal statute, commonly known as the Jencks Act,[6] permits a defendant to review a prior written or recorded statement after the witness has testified for the government. Reviewing such statements may prove important to show that a witness is inconsistent, biased, or has a bad memory.

This procedure often causes trial delay, as defendants usually request time between direct examination and cross-examination to review such statements. For this reason, some federal prosecutors provide such information prior to trial. The Jencks Act is a matter of federal statutory law and does not apply in state criminal prosecutions.

Depositions

A **deposition** is oral testimony given under oath, not in a court. In civil procedure, depositions are freely conducted. Upon notice to a party or subpoena to a witness, an attorney can call a person to testify prior to trial. This is not so in criminal practice.

Fed. R. Crim. P. 15 allows depositions only when "exceptional circumstances" exist. Expected absence of a witness at trial is an example of an exceptional circumstance. If such a circumstance is shown, the deposition may be ordered by the trial court, and the deposition may be used at trial. Of course, both the defendant and government have the opportunity to question the witness at the deposition.

Brady Doctrine

Although most discovery occurs under the authority of statutes and court rules, the Constitution also requires disclosure of information by the government in some situations. In *Brady v. Maryland,* the Supreme Court announced what is now referred to as the Brady doctrine.

Obviously, *Brady* applies to both state and federal prosecutions. Note that only exculpatory evidence must be provided. Evidence that tends to prove a defendant's innocence is exculpatory. *Brady* does stand for the proposition that prosecutors must reveal incriminating evidence to defendants.

In most situations, disclosure at trial will satisfy *Brady.* However, if disclosure at trial would prejudice a defendant, pretrial disclosure may be constitutionally required. As is sometimes the case with Jencks Act materials, prosecutors may provide such information prior to trial as a courtesy.

In a case related to *Brady,* the Supreme Court found that it is violative of due process for prosecutors to use perjured testimony or to deceive juries. This is true even if the perjury was unsolicited by the prosecuting attorney. As such, a prosecutor has a duty to correct any testimony of a witness that he or she knows is false.[7]

Although *Brady* and related cases are law in both state and federal prosecutions, the other discovery rules differ. Be sure to check local law to determine what your client has a right to discover.

TERMS

deposition 1. The transcript of a witness's testimony given under oath outside of the courtroom, usually in advance of the trial or hearing, under oral examination or in response to written interrogatories. 2. In a more general sense, an affidavit; a statement under oath.

BRADY
v.
MARYLAND
373 U.S. 83 (1962)

Petitioner and companion, Boblit, were found guilty of murder in the first degree and were sentenced to death. ... Their trials were separate, petitioner being tried first. At his trial Brady took the stand and admitted his participation in the crime, but he claimed that Boblit did the actual killing. And, in his summation to the jury, Brady's counsel conceded that Brady was guilty of murder in the first degree, asking only that the jury return that verdict "without capital punishment." Prior to the trial petitioner's counsel had requested the prosecution to allow him to examine Boblit's extrajudicial statements. Several of those statements were shown to him; but one dated July 9, 1958, in which Boblit admitted the actual homicide, was withheld by the prosecution and did not come to petitioner's notice until after he had been tried, convicted, and sentenced, and after his conviction had been affirmed.

Petitioner moved the trial court for a new trial based on the newly discovered evidence that had been suppressed by the prosecution. Petitioner's appeal from a denial of that motion was dismissed by the Court of Appeals without prejudice to relief under the Maryland Post Conviction Procedures Act. ... The petition for post-conviction relief was dismissed by the trial court; and on appeal the Court of Appeals held that suppression of the evidence by the prosecution denied petitioner due process of law and remanded the case for a retrial of the question of punishment, not the question of guilt. ...

We now hold that the suppression by the prosecution of evidence favorable to an accused upon request violates due process where the evidence is material either to guilt or to punishment, irrespective of the good faith or bad faith of the prosecution.

[This principle] is not punishment of society for misdeeds of a prosecutor but avoidance of an unfair trial to the accused. Society wins not only when the guilty are convicted but when criminal trials are fair; our system of the administration of justice suffers when any accused is treated unfairly. An inscription on the walls of the Department of Justice states the proposition candidly for the federal domain: "The United States wins its point whenever justice is done its citizens in the courts." A prosecution that withholds evidence on demand of an accused which, if made available, would tend to exculpate him or reduce the penalty helps shape a trial that bears heavily on the defendant. That casts the prosecutor in the role of an architect of a proceeding that does not comport with standards of justice.

Freedom of Information Laws

The federal government and most, if not all, states have statutes requiring the public disclosure of files, documents, and other information in the possession of the government.[8] The federal statute is known as the Freedom of Information Act (FOIA).[9]

There are nine exemptions to the federal FOIA. If a request for information falls into one of the nine exemptions, the government may withhold disclosure. Otherwise, disclosure is mandated. One of the exemptions provides that law enforcement records may be withheld if disclosure will:

1. Interfere with enforcement proceedings
2. Deprive a person of a fair trial or an impartial adjudication
3. Constitute an unwarranted invasion of personal privacy
4. Disclose the identity of a confidential source
5. Disclose investigative techniques and procedures
6. Endanger the life or physical safety of law enforcement personnel.

The FOIA is not a discovery device. It is a statute of general applicability and any person may request inspection or production of documents under its authority. The purpose of the FOIA, which is unrelated to litigation, is the promotion of democracy by having an informed citizenry; it keeps the governors accountable to the governed.

The fact that the FOIA was not specifically intended to be used for discovery in litigation does not foreclose that use. However, although the FOIA may be used to obtain information, it is not intended to displace or supplement the recognized forms of discovery.[10] Nor shall the process of obtaining information through the FOIA be cause for delaying a criminal proceeding. Therefore, requests for information under the FOIA are separate from a defendant's discovery requests in a criminal case.[11] Hence, defendants may seek information under the FOIA, but such requests are not part of the criminal discovery process, and criminal proceedings will not be delayed to wait for such requests to be answered or disputes over disclosure to be adjudicated.

The same principles apply to other disclosure laws. For example, the federal Privacy Act[12] provides that individuals have a right to discover the contents of files containing information about them. Again, requests for information under this law are aside from, not in addition to, criminal discovery rules.

§ 10.3 Affirmative Defenses

There is a special class of defenses known as **affirmative defenses.** Affirmative defenses go beyond a simple denial; they raise special or new issues, which, if proven, can result in an acquittal or lesser liability.

TERMS

affirmative defense A defense that amounts to more than simply a denial of the allegations in the plaintiff's complaint. It sets up new matter which, if proven, could result in a judgment against the plaintiff even if all the allegations of the complaint are true.

Defenses that raise the question of a defendant's mental state to commit a crime (e.g., insanity and intoxication), whether justification or excuse existed to commit the crime (e.g., self-defense), and alibi fall into the affirmative defenses class.

As a general rule, criminal defendants may sit passively during trial, as the prosecution bears the burden of proving the government's allegations. In all instances, **burden of proof** refers to two burdens, the burden of production and the burden of persuasion. Because it is not practical to require prosecutors to prove that every defendant was sane, was not intoxicated, or did not have justification to use force, the burdens for affirmative defenses are different than for other defenses. First, defendants have the duty of raising all affirmative defenses. At trial this means that defendants must produce some evidence to support the defense. This is known as the **burden of production**. Defendants do not have to convince the factfinder that the defense is valid. They are only required to bring forth enough evidence to establish the defense.

After defendants have met the burden of production, the **burden of persuasion** then must be met. There is a split among the states; some require the defendant to carry this burden, whereas others require it of the prosecution. If the defendant has the burden, then he or she must convince the factfinder that the defense is true. Defendants must prove this by a preponderance of evidence. In jurisdictions that require prosecutors to disprove an affirmative defense, there is again a split as to the standard of proof required. Some require proof by a preponderance and others require proof beyond a reasonable doubt.

Some of the defenses covered in this chapter are affirmative defenses. It is necessary to research local law to determine which procedure is followed in a particular jurisdiction and what defenses are considered affirmative defenses.

TERMS

burden of proof The duty of establishing the truth of a matter; the duty of proving a fact that is in dispute. In most instances the burden of proof, like the burden of going forward, shifts from one side to the other during the course of a trial as the case progresses and evidence is introduced by each side.

burden of going forward (production) The duty of a party, with respect to certain issues being tried, to produce evidence sufficient to justify a verdict before the other party is obligated to produce evidence to the contrary. This burden is also referred to as the *burden of evidence,* the *burden of proceeding,* and the *burden of producing evidence.* The burden of going forward may shift back and forth between the parties during the course of a trial.

burden of persuasion The ultimate burden of proof; the responsibility of convincing the jury, or, in a nonjury trial, the judge, of the truth.

§ 10.4 Motion Practice

In both civil and criminal practice, a motion is a request made to a court for it to do something. In most cases a party who files a motion is seeking an order from the court. Generally, when a person desires something from a court, a formal motion must be filed and copies sent to opposing counsel. On occasion, oral motions are made. This is most common during trials and hearings. Some of the most common motions are discussed here.

Motion to Dismiss/Quash

If a defendant believes that the indictment or information is fatally flawed, the appropriate remedy is a motion to dismiss. In some jurisdictions, this would be called a motion to quash. Examples of fatal flaws in the charging instrument are: the court lacks jurisdiction; the facts alleged do not amount to a crime; an essential element is not charged; or the defendant has a legal defense, such as double jeopardy.

If the form of the charging instrument is attacked, courts often permit prosecutors to amend the charge rather than dismissing it entirely. Dismissal of an indictment or information does not mean that the defendant cannot be recharged. A person is not in "jeopardy" under the Fifth Amendment until later in the proceeding.

Motion to Suppress

The motion to suppress evidence, also known as a *motion to exclude evidence,* is used by defendants to have unlawfully obtained evidence excluded from trial. Most suppression motions arise under the Constitution. For example, evidence obtained from an unreasonable search may be excluded pursuant to the Fourth Amendment and coerced confessions are excluded pursuant to the Fifth Amendment. In some cases, a statute may establish a right; when this is so, a suppression motion may be premised upon it.

There are actually two ways to challenge unlawful evidence: through a motion to suppress or by *contemporaneous objection* at trial. The federal government, and most states, require defendants to file motions to suppress evidence before trial.[13] For good cause, this rule is waived. So, a defendant who first learns of the existence of a piece of prosecution evidence at trial may contemporaneously object to its admission at trial.

Nevertheless, pretrial motions to suppress are sensible for several reasons. First, in jurisdictions that permit government interlocutory appeals, such motions provide a mechanism to correct trial court errors before jeopardy attaches. Second, they facilitate plea agreements. By knowing the admissibility of evidence before trial, the parties are better informed concerning the strengths of their cases and, accordingly, are more likely to reach an agreement. Third, such motions lessen the likelihood of a jury being exposed to prejudicial unlawful evidence. This reduces the possibility of mistrials.

Finally, trials are smoother when suppression issues are resolved in advance. When they are not, the trial must be interrupted, the jury excused, and a separate hearing conducted.

When the pretrial suppression method is used, a separate hearing on the motion is conducted before trial. A defendant may testify at a suppression hearing and that testimony may not be used at trial.[14] To allow a defendant's testimony from a suppression hearing to be used at trial would place the defendant in a position of choosing between the right to suppress illegally obtained evidence and the right to be free from self-incrimination. The best alternative is to allow the defendant to testify and to prohibit the later use of that testimony.

Failure to object to illegally obtained evidence is a waiver of the issue. Thus, if a defendant does not timely object at the trial level, the issue may not be raised on appeal. The definition of *timely* depends on whether the particular jurisdiction requires pretrial motions or permits contemporaneous objections at trial. In a few states that require pretrial motions, the defendant is required to renew the objection during trial. Failure to do either amounts to a waiver of objection.

Who bears the burden of proof at suppression hearings varies between jurisdictions and what it is the defendant seeks to have excluded. As to searches and seizures, the most common situation, the federal courts place the burden of proving the action unlawful on the defendant if a warrant was issued. If there was no warrant, the burden of proving the action to be lawful falls on the United States. The states vary, but many follow the federal method. However, if the government asserts that its search occurred with the defendant's consent, the government bears the burden or proving that the consent was knowing and voluntary. Similarly, the government bears the burden of proving that a confession was knowingly and voluntarily given. This is true of *Miranda* waivers as well.

Motion for Change of Venue

Venue means place for trial. In state criminal proceedings, venue usually lies in the county where the crime occurred. In federal proceedings, venue lies in the district where the crime occurred. Many federal crimes are interstate in character, and the charges may be filed in any district where the crime took place.

Fed. R. Crim. P. 21 permits transfer of a case from one district to another if "the defendant cannot obtain a fair and impartial trial" at the location where the case is pending. In addition, a district judge may transfer a case if it is most convenient for the defendant and witnesses.

Pretrial publicity of criminal matters may be cause to transfer a case (change venue in state proceedings). If a defendant receives considerable negative media coverage, it may be necessary to try the defendant in another location. (See Figure 10-1.)

Because of the First Amendment free press issue, judges are generally prohibited from excluding the press or public from hearings.[15] In some instances judges may order the attorneys involved in a case not to provide information to anyone not involved in the proceeding. (See § 11.1 for more information on publicity and a defendant's due process rights.)

UNITED STATES v. McVEIGH

Counsel for Defendant Timothy James McVeigh submit this brief which is being submitted simultaneously with Mr. McVeigh's Motion to Transfer this case to a federal district outside the State of Oklahoma.

Facts

1) At approximately, 9:00 A.M., on Wednesday, April 19, 1995, the Alfred P. Murrah Building federal office building, a nine storey structure in Oklahoma City, Oklahoma, was shattered by an explosion. A car bomb is alleged as the source of the explosion. The defendant, Timothy James McVeigh, is accused of planting the bomb;

2) Rescue efforts began moments after the explosion and have continued, virtually uninterrupted, for the past four days. The death toll has steadily increased. Hundreds of people are wounded. The shock and outrage experienced by the City of Oklahoma expanded to the State and the nation as news of the bombing has become an international event. Continuous press and broadcast coverage has resulted in a contemporaneous record of the tragic events;

3) The United States District Court for the Western District is located in a four storey structure directly across the street from the Murrah building. The courthouse sustained damage and people inside the courthouse were injured;

4) The office of the Federal Public Defender Organization for the Western District of Oklahoma is located on the fifth floor of the Old Post Office building. The Old Post Office Building is a nine storey structure which shares the city

FIGURE 10-1 Excerpts of McVeigh Brief on Motion for Change of Venue block with the United States Courthouse. The Old Post Office tenants include the bankruptcy court and court services related to the function of the United States District Court. The Old Post Office Building; including the office of Federal Public Defender, sustained damage in the explosion and the occupants were evacuated during the emergency;

5) A criminal complaint was filed Friday, April 21, 1995 charging Timothy McVeigh with violating Title 18, United States Code, 844(f). United States Magistrate Judge Ronald L. Howland authorized the filing of the complaint and issued the warrant for Mr. McVeigh. The complaint accuses Mr. McVeigh of causing the explosion which destroyed the A.P. Murrah Federal Building; damaged the Federal Courthouse and the Old Post Office, killed over a dozen children, scores of adults, injured hundreds and subjected the occupants of downtown Oklahoma City to unprecedented terror and carnage;

6) Mr. McVeigh appeared before United States Magistrate Judge Ronald L. Howland at approximately 8:45 P.M., Friday, April 21, 1995, for purposes of an initial appearance. Mr. McVeigh requested the appointment of counsel. Susan M. Otto, Federal Public Defender, was appointed by the court. Based on the allegations in the complaint, Miss Otto requested the appointment of cocounsel, citing Title 18, United States Code, 3005. Miss Otto submitted Mr. John W. Coyle III as an attorney qualified for appointment in a federal death penalty case. Magistrate Judge Howland granted the request and appointed Mr. Coyle;

7) A combined preliminary and detention hearing is scheduled for 2:00 P.M., Thursday, April 27, 1995.

Argument and Authorities

* * *

Rule 219(a), Federal Rule of Criminal Procedure, provides, in part:

> The court upon motion of the defendant shall transfer the proceeding as to that defendant to another district whether or not such district is specified in the defendant's motion if the court is satisfied that there exists in the district where the prosecution is pending so great a prejudice against the defendant that the defendant cannot obtain a fair and impartial trial at any place fixed by law for holding court in that district. ...

Mr. McVeigh is entitled to have the threshold probable cause determination decided by a Magistrate Judge who was not a percipient witness to the events and who is not personally acquainted with many of the law enforcement and citizen victims. Concomitantly, Mr. McVeigh is entitled to have his case presented to a grand jury composed of qualified citizens who are not living in the community or the State which has suffered the events. The Federal Rules of Criminal Procedure and case precedent support Mr. McVeigh's request.

* * *

In *Irvin v. Dowd,* 366 U,S. 717 (1961), the Supreme Court [held] that, in some cases, publicity may be so widespread that courts can presume actual prejudice. The news coverage thus far has, for the most part[,] consisted of factual accounts of the progress of the case. Nevertheless, prejudice must be presumed. The media reports have been so continuous and extensive, and the subject matter

FIGURE 10-1 *(continued)*

so deeply disturbing, that impairment of the grand jurors' judgment is inescapable.

* * *

When one reviews these factors, it is apparent this court should transfer the case at this time. The gravity and nature of the crime is unsurpassed. The extent of the pretrial publicity only days after the crime is unparalleled in Oklahoma history and rivals any other crime committed in the United States, except, perhaps, the assassination of President Kennedy.

* * *

[T]he California Supreme Court considered the effect of enormous publicity on the accused's right to a fair trial:

> The prisoner, whether guilty or not, is unquestionabl[y] entitled by the law of the land to have a fair and impartial trial. Unless this result be attained, one of the most important purposes for which government is organized and Courts of Justice established will have definitely failed. Cases sometimes occur, and this would appear to be one of them, in which the very enormity of the offense itself arouses the honest indignation of the community to such a degree as to make it apparent that a dispassionate investigation of the case cannot be had. Under such circumstances the law requires that the place of trial be changed. [citations omitted]

In short, "It would be judicial murder to affirm a judgment thus rendered, when the reason of the people of a whole country was so clouded with passion and prejudice as to prevent mercy and deny justice." (quoting *People v. Lee,* 53 Cal. 566, 571)

* * *

The coverage in the instant case is unparalleled. [T]he events have been reported matter by newspapers worldwide. Every television station in the Oklahoma City area has provided continuous coverage since the event, providing live links for national broadcast channels. The publicity has continued unabated through the President of the United States's attendance at a prayer service in Oklahoma City for the victims on Sunday, April 23, 1995. Applying the reasoning of the United States Supreme Court, as well as the highest state appellate courts, transfer of this case is the only appropriate relief.

Conclusion

Counsel for Timothy McVeigh request this Court enter an order directing the transfer of this case for all further proceedings at this time. The case should be transferred to a federal district outside the State of Oklahoma, but within the jurisdiction of the Tenth Circuit. [T]he magnitude of the issues presented in this case and the need to ensure its orderly management from this, the first critical stage of this capital case, will make this case difficult in any court. Every federal judicial officer in the Western District of Oklahoma had been affected by these events. Most of the judicial officers were witnesses to the event. Counsel submit the decision of to which district this case should be transferred should be referred to the Chief Judge of the Tenth Circuit Curt of Appeals.

Respectfully submitted, ...
UNITED STATES OF AMERICA, Plaintiff

FIGURE 10-1 *(continued)*

Motion for Severance

Fed. R. Crim. P. 8 permits two or more defendants to be charged in the same information or indictment if they were involved in the same crime. That rule also permits joinder of two offenses by the same person in one charging instrument, provided they are similar in character or arise out of the same set of facts.

In some situations, severance of the two defendants may be necessary to assure fair trials. For example, if two defendants have antagonistic defenses, severance must be granted. Defenses are *antagonistic* if the jury must disbelieve one by believing the other. For example, if Defendant A denies being at the scene of a crime, and Defendant B claims that they were both there, but also claims that A forced him to commit the crime, their defenses are antagonistic.

If a defendant is charged with two or more offenses, it may be necessary to sever them to have a fair trial. For example, if a defendant plans to testify concerning one charge and not the other, severance is necessary.

Motion in Limine

Prior to trial, both the defendant and the prosecution may file motions in limine. This is a request that the court order the other party not to mention or attempt to question a witness about some matter. A motion in limine is similar to a motion to suppress, except that it encompasses more than admission of illegally seized evidence.

For example, if one anticipates that the opposing counsel will attempt to question a witness about evidence that is inadmissible under the rules of evidence (e.g., hearsay), a motion in limine may be filed to avoid having to object at trial. This is important, as often a witness may blurt out the answer before an attorney has had an opportunity to object. In addition, knowing whether the judge will permit the admission of evidence prior to trial helps an attorney to plan the case.

Other Motions

A variety of other motions may be filed. If the prosecution fears that revealing information required under a discovery rule will endanger the case or a person's life, a motion for a protective order may be filed. In such cases the trial court reviews the evidence *in camera* and decides if it is necessary to keep it from the defendant. If so, the judge will enter a protective order so stating.

Motions for continuance of hearings and trial dates are common. In criminal cases, courts must be careful not to violate speedy trial requirements.

If two defendants have been charged jointly, one or both may file a motion for severance of trial. If defense counsel believes that the defendant is not competent to stand trial, a motion for mental examination may be filed.

§ 10.5 Pretrial Conference

Sometime prior to trial, the court will hold a pretrial conference. This may be weeks or only days before trial.

At this conference the court will address any remaining motions and discuss any problems the parties have. In addition, the judge will explain his or her method of trying a case, such as how the jury will be selected. The next stage is trial. Figure 10-2 graphically depicts the basic criminal process.

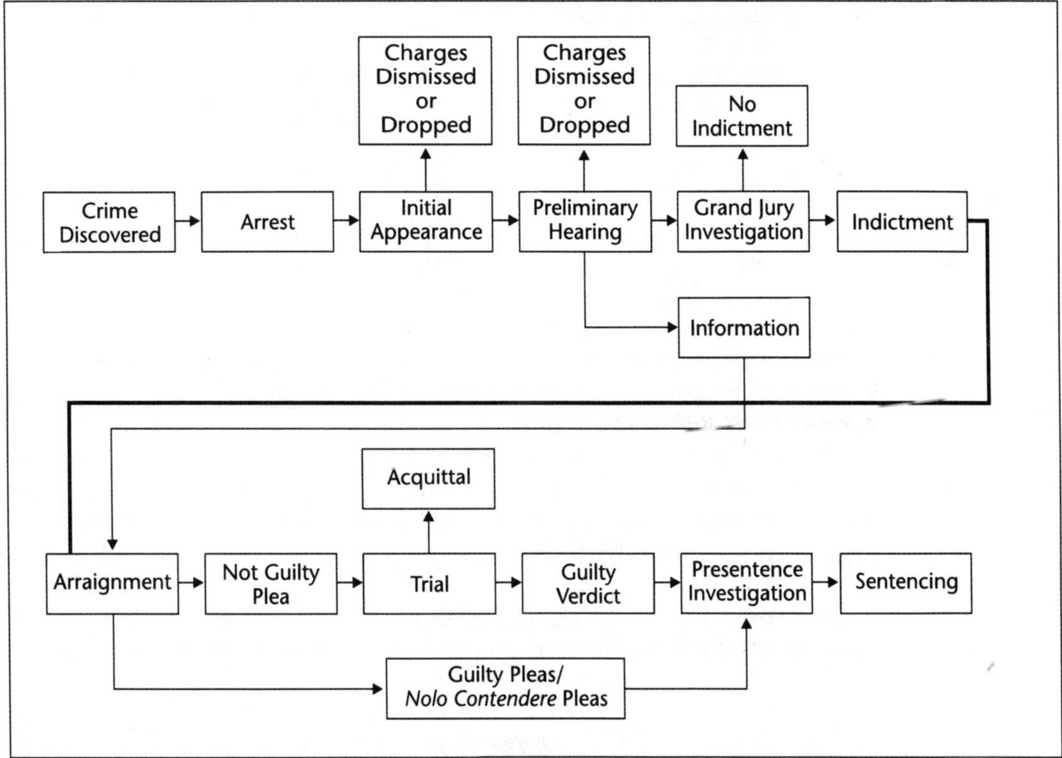

FIGURE 10-2 The Basic Criminal Process This charts the basic process of felony criminal cases from detection to sentencing. Misdemeanor cases normally progress through the system faster, as many stages are omitted. For example, misdemeanors are commonly prosecuted by information rather than indictment, and presentence reports are often not prepared in misdemeanor cases.

§ 10.6 Extradition and Detainers

If wanted persons are located outside the jurisdiction where they are, or will be, charged, **extradition** is one method of securing their presence in the charging jurisdiction. *Extradition* is the surrender of a person from one jurisdiction to another where the person has been charged or convicted of a crime.

Extradition usually occurs under the provisions of a treaty. Extradition includes transfers between states, as well as between nations. Extradition, especially international, is as much a political decision as a legal one.

Pursuant to the Uniform Interstate Criminal Extradition Act, which has been adopted by forty-seven states,[16] the request for extradition is made between governors. If a governor determines that the person sought should be delivered, an arrest warrant is issued by that governor.

Once seized, the arrestee is brought before a judge and may file a petition for writ of habeas corpus. During the proceedings, release on bail is permitted, unless the crime charged is one punishable by death or life imprisonment in the state where the crime was committed. If the person sought is under charge in the sending state, the governor may order his or her surrender immediately or may wait until the prosecution and punishment is completed in the first state.

Generally, the guilt or innocence of the accused may not be considered by the governor or courts during the proceedings; that issue is left to the requesting jurisdiction. It is the obligation of the governor and courts of the sending state to be sure that the correct person is seized and that proper procedures are followed.

Defendants may waive extradition. This waiver must be made in court, and defendants must be informed of their rights, including habeas corpus, for waivers to be valid.

The law permits arrests by police officers from outside a state in hot pursuit situations. If an arrest is made in hot pursuit, the officer is to bring the accused before a local court, which is to order the defendant held, or released on bail, until an extradition warrant is issued by the governor.

A **detainer** is a request (or order) for the continued custody of a prisoner. For example, suppose federal charges are pending against

TERMS

extradition The surrender by one nation or state to another of a person accused or convicted of an offense within the territory of the second.

detainer A writ for the continued detention of a prisoner.

a Utah prisoner. The United States would issue a detainer requesting that Utah hold the prisoner after his or her sentence is completed so that the United States may take custody. This situation does not raise jurisdictional issues, as federal authorities have nationwide jurisdiction. As to interstate detention, the detainer is used in conjunction with extradition.

Pursuant to the Interstate Agreement on Detainers, a state may request the temporary custody of a prisoner of another state in order to try the person. Once the trial is completed, the prisoner is returned, regardless of the outcome. If convicted, a detainer is issued for the prisoner and he or she is again returned after the sentence is completed in the sending state.

The Agreement also provides that prisoners are to be notified of any detainers against them. Further, if a state issues a detainer for a prisoner, that prisoner may request to be temporarily transferred to that state for final disposition of that case. A request for final disposition by a prisoner is deemed a waiver of extradition to and from the sending state. Also, it is deemed a waiver of extradition to the receiving state to serve any resulting sentence after the sentence in the sending state is completed.

The Supreme Court has held that the exclusionary rule does not exclude persons who have been illegally seized from trial. In *Frisbie v. Collins,*[17] the fact that Michigan police officers kidnapped a defendant from Illinois and returned him to Michigan, disregarding extradition laws, did not affect the court's jurisdiction to try the defendant. The same result was reached in a case in which international extradition laws were not followed.[18] Today, if the government's conduct in seizing a defendant were outrageous or shocking, there is a possibility that a court would bar prosecution.[19]

§ 10.7 Removal

Congress has provided that, in certain circumstances, criminal cases may be removed from state courts to federal courts. Removal is premised upon the principle that certain cases are more properly adjudicated in a federal, rather than state, court. The purpose of removal is to preserve the sovereignty of the federal government by assuring a fair trial to particular criminal defendants. Otherwise, the states could interfere with the functioning of the federal government by harassing federal officials through criminal proceedings.

28 U.S.C. § 1442 provides that a federal official sued in state court, whether the action is civil or criminal, may remove the case to the federal district court where the action is pending, if the suit concerns

the performance of his or her official duties. Similarly, 28 U.S.C. § 1442(a) provides for removal of cases, civil or criminal, filed against members of the United States armed forces for actions taken in the course of their duties. 28 U.S.C. § 1443 provides for removal of certain civil rights cases.

Removal of criminal cases is the same as for civil: the defendant must file a notice of, and petition for, removal.[20] Improperly removed actions are remanded to the state court from which they came.[21]

Review Questions

1. What advantage does a plea of *nolo contendere* have over a guilty plea?
2. Kevin has been charged with murder. He believes a weapon that the prosecutor plans on using at trial was unconstitutionally seized from his home. How can he raise this issue prior to trial?
3. Place the following in the proper order of occurrence: preliminary hearing; formal charge; initial appearance; arraignment; trial; and complaint.
4. What is the Brady doctrine?
5. When is removal from state to federal court allowed?
6. What is extradition?
7. Approximately what percentage of cases are disposed of by guilty pleas: 50%, 75%, or 90%?
8. A prosecutor believes that a defendant intends to use evidence that is prohibited by the rules of evidence. What motion may the prosecutor file in advance of trial to resolve the issue?

Review Problems

1. Discovery in civil cases is very broad. Fed. R. Civ. P. 26 permits discovery of anything "reasonably calculated to lead to the discovery of admissible evidence." Should discovery in criminal cases be broader? Explain your position.
2. A theory concerning the unconstitutionality of the plea bargaining system was discussed in this chapter. Explain the theory, the applicable law, and your opinion.

Notes

1 390 U.S. 570 (1968).

2 439 U.S. 212 (1978).

3 *Santobello v. New York,* 404 U.S. 257 (1971).

4 Fed. R. Crim. P. 11.

5 *United States v. Diecidue,* 603 F.2d 535 (5th Cir.), *cert. denied,* 445 U.S. 946 (1979).

6 18 U.S.C. § 3500.

7 *Mooney v. Holohan,* 294 U.S. 103 (1935).

8 *See* Daniel Hall, *Administrative Law* ch. 9 (Lawyers Co-operative/Delmar Publishing, 1994), for a more thorough discussion of the Freedom of Information Act.

9 5 U.S.C. § 552.

10 *John Doe Corp. v. John Doe Agency,* 493 U.S. 146 (1989).

11 *North v. Walsh,* 881 F.2d 1088 (D.C. Cir. 1989).

12 5 U.S.C. § 552(a).

13 Fed. R. Crim. P. 12(b).

14 *Simmons v. United States,* 390 U.S. 377 (1968).

15 *Richmond Newspapers, Inc. v. Virginia,* 448 U.S. 555 (1980).

16 Rhonda Wasserman, "The Subpoena Power: *Pennoyer's* Last Vestige," 74 *Minn. L. Rev.* 37 (1989).

17 342 U.S. 519 (1952).

18 *Ker v. Illinois,* 119 U.S. 436 (1886).

19 *See United States v. Toscanino,* 500 F.2d 267 (2d Cir. 1974).

20 28 U.S.C. § 1446.

21 28 U.S.C. § 1447.

CHAPTER 11

TRIAL

Your verdict will be "Guilty" or "Not Guilty."
Your job is not to find innocence.

Russell R. Leggett, Judge
Westchester County Court

§ 11.1 Trial Rights of Defendants

The Right to a Jury Trial

A trial is a method of determining guilt or innocence. In medieval England, trials by ordeal, combat, and compurgation were used.

To demonstrate how trials have changed, consider trial by ordeal. Trial by ordeal was considered trial by God; that is, God determined the person's guilt or innocence. There were two ordeals: by water and fire. Two water ordeals were used. In the first the accused was thrown into a body of water. If he sank he was adjudged innocent, and if he floated he was guilty. In the second water ordeal, the accused's arm was submerged in boiling water. The defendant had to survive this unhurt to be proven innocent. The fire ordeal was similar, the accused having to walk over fire or grasp hot irons.

Trial as we know it today finds its roots in the Magna Carta (1215), which guaranteed freemen trial by their peers. Unlike today, those juries comprised people who knew the facts of the case. The concept of trial by a jury of one's peers was of great importance to the colonists of the United States and made its way into the Constitution of the United States.

The Sixth Amendment to the United States Constitution reads, in part, "[i]n all criminal prosecutions, the accused shall enjoy the right to a speedy and public trial, by an impartial jury of the State and district wherein the crime shall have been committed." The Sixth Amendment is fully applicable against the states via the Fourteenth Amendment.

The Sixth Amendment has been interpreted to mean that defendants have a right to a jury trial for all offenses that may be punished with more than six months' imprisonment. Most crimes that have as their maximum punishment less than six months are **petty offenses**, and there is no right to trial by jury.[1]

Note that the term "most" is used. Some argue that when fines become large enough, one is entitled to a jury trial, regardless of the amount of time one could be sentenced to spend in jail. In addition, it is argued that crimes that are moral in nature and subject the defendant to ridicule and embarrassment justify trial by jury, even when the punishment is less than six months' imprisonment. The same question is raised concerning crimes that were indictable at common law. The Supreme Court has not answered these questions, and the lower courts that have addressed these issues are split.

The maximum penalty allowed determines if a crime is petty, not the actual sentence. For example, if a crime is punishable by from three months to one year in jail, the defendant is entitled to a jury, even if the trial judge routinely sentences those convicted to three months for the offense. Some crimes do not have a legislatively established punishment, such as contempt. In such cases the issue is whether the defendant is sentenced to more than six months in jail. If so, the defendant is entitled to a jury.

Although the right to a jury trial for nonpetty offenses nearly always attaches, there are a few exceptions. There is no right to a jury in military trials. In addition, those appearing in juvenile court (delinquency proceedings) are not entitled to a jury trial.[2] Of course, juveniles who are tried as adults are entitled to the same rights as adults, including the right to have a jury trial.

Juries sit as factfinders. A defendant may be entitled to have a jury decide guilt or innocence, but there is no right to have a jury decide other matters, such as the proper sentence or what law to apply. Some jurisdictions have juries impose sentence, or make a sentence recommendation to the trial court; however, this is not usually the practice and there is no federal constitutional reason for it.

The Supreme Court has held that there is no constitutional requirement for twelve jurors.[3] Nor does the Constitution require juror unanimity. There is a limit to how small a jury may be and how few jurors must concur in a verdict. In one case, the Supreme Court found a law unconstitutional that required trial by six jurors and permitted conviction with a vote of five to one.[4]

It is common for six-person juries to be used for misdemeanors. However, a unanimous verdict is constitutionally required for conviction. If

TERMS

petty offenses A minor criminal offense, usually tried before a justice of the peace or a magistrate.

a twelve-member jury is used, it is constitutional to permit conviction upon a concurrence of nine or more jurors.

Finally, a defendant cannot be penalized for choosing to proceed to trial rather than pleading guilty. In *United States v. Jackson,*[5] the Supreme Court found a statute that made the death penalty available for those who were tried and not for those who pled guilty violative of the Sixth Amendment.

A Fair and Impartial Jury

The right to a fair and impartial jury is guaranteed by the Sixth Amendment. A jury and jurors may be challenged at three levels: the entire array, specific jurors, and the final jury. First, a party may challenge the entire array of individuals who are called as prospective jurors. This occurs when the selection process violates either constitutional or legislative mandates. For example, a state procedure that eliminates blacks from being called to service is violative of the Fourteenth Amendment and is invalid.[6] Similarly, if state law requires prospective jurors' names to be selected from voter registration rolls and a court uses property tax rolls instead, the entire panel may be challenged. In short, an array must represent a fair cross section of the community. This does not mean that the array must actually represent a cross-section of the community (i.e., precise racial percentages); rather, it is only required that the array be selected from a fair cross-section of the community. A challenge is brought as a motion challenging the array, also known as a *motion to quash the venire.* It is not violative of the Sixth Amendment, however, for a state to decide to exempt members of certain occupations from service, such as doctors and lawyers.

At trial, individual jurors may be objected to by either the prosecution or the defense. Jurors who cannot be fair are eliminated by the court for cause. Each party is then given a certain number of peremptory strikes with which it may eliminate other jurors. A party may eliminate a prospective juror for any cause, except race, gender, or religion. Again, defendants are not entitled to a jury that has a certain composition; they are only entitled to a fair selection *process.* So long as the process is fair (the array is representative of the community and the prosecutor did not eliminate jurors for improper reasons), a defendant cannot object to the composition of the jury simply because there are no representatives of his or her racial or gender group serving.

Finally, the verdict of a properly empaneled jury may be challenged in some cases, such as when members of a jury have engaged in their own investigation of the case while in recess and when jurors have received bribes.

A Fair and Impartial Judge

In all cases, judges must be fair and impartial. Due process demands that a judge disqualify or "recuse" herself if this is not possible. Thus, if a judge has a financial interest in a case, recusal is required. If a judge is related to any of the parties, their attorneys, or any other person material to a case, recusal or disclosure to the parties is necessary.

Following this principle, laws that financially reward judicial officers for convictions are invalid. In *Tumey v. Ohio,*[7] for example, a law that empowered the mayor of a city to try minor offenses and also to receive the fees and costs assessed by him against violators was held to violate due process. In a later case, the reasoning of *Tumey* was extended to prohibit a mayor from sitting in judgment on traffic offenders when the fines assessed would benefit not the mayor personally, but the village for which he was a financial officer.[8]

In some instances, a judge's personal interest that demands recusal may be the product of the case itself. For example, in one case a defendant insulted the judge repeatedly during the defendant's trial. At the close of the trial, the judge found the defendant guilty of eleven counts of contempt and sentenced him to eleven to twenty-two years in jail. The Supreme Court reversed the decision. The Court noted that every judge has the authority to control courtroom proceedings; had the judge stopped the trial after each individual incident to cite and sentence the defendant, the decision would have been different. But, because the judge waited until the proceedings were completed, the issue was not one of courtroom decorum, but of trial for previously committed acts. This demanded a neutral judge, one who had no personal interest in the case.[9]

In no instance is a judge's personal philosophy or history of decision making adequate grounds for disqualification. For example, it is inadequate to assert that a judge disfavors big business or has a history of ruling unfavorably to minority criminal defendants.

Judges have a personal responsibility to recuse themselves when they have a conflict of interest or otherwise cannot be fair and impartial. A party may also seek to disqualify a judge. Some states permit parties to automatically disqualify judges; others require cause. In most instances, at the trial level, the disqualification decision is made by the trial judge who the party is seeking to disqualify. In most jurisdictions, a denial of a motion to disqualify is not a final order. As such, the party must await final judgment before appealing the issue. In a minority of jurisdictions, and in extreme cases probably all, interlocutory appeals are permitted.

The behavior of judges is critical in criminal cases. Judges are not to act in such a manner as to infer guilt. Generally, a trial judge is obliged to treat the attorneys fairly and similarly, as preferential treatment of a prosecutor may influence or prejudice a jury. Of course, the judge may admonish any person in the courtroom, including the defendant and attorneys, for disruptive or unprofessional behavior. If a judge's statements or actions rise to the level of prejudicing the jury and the defendant is convicted, the case will either be reversed or remanded for a new trial.

The Right to a Public Trial

The Sixth Amendment also guarantees the right to a public trial. This applies throughout the trial, from openings to return of the verdict, and also applies to many pretrial hearings, such as suppression hearings. The presence of the public is intended to keep prosecutions "honest." As the Supreme Court stated in *Estes v. Texas*[10]: "History has proven that secret tribunals were effective instruments of oppression."

The right to a public hearing does not mean that everyone who wishes to attend has to be permitted to be in the courtroom. The trial judge is responsible for maintaining order in the courtroom and may require the doors to be shut once all seats have been filled. Also, a disruptive citizen may be removed.

The defendant's right to a public trial is not absolute. Trial judges, acting with extreme caution, may order that a hearing be conducted in private. Facts that support excluding the public are rare. An example of when exclusion of the public may be justified is when an undercover law enforcement agent testifies and public exposure would put the officer's life in jeopardy.

If a court closes a hearing (or trial) without justification, the defendant is entitled to a new hearing, regardless of whether the defendant was actually harmed.

Generally, members of the press have no greater right to attend a hearing than do other members of the public. However, many judges provide special seating for reporters.

Publicity and the Right to a Fair Trial

The 1995 trial of O.J. Simpson stands as proof that the publicity attending a trial can be overwhelming. In the contemporary United States, the media has an insatiable appetite for sensational stories. Crime satisfies this urge, especially crimes that involve public figures or are particularly heinous. The First Amendment's free speech and press clauses secure the right of the public to attend criminal trials—but the Fifth and Fourteenth Amendments assure defendants due process. These two concepts clash when pretrial publicity creates public hysteria or otherwise colors the perspective of potential jurors, the prosecutors, or the judge.

This is particularly troubling when one considers the stakes. Criminal defendants are faced with loss of liberty and sometimes life. Whether by conviction of the innocent or acquittal of the guilty, the public loses when justice is not served. Trials are precise. The rules of evidence have been developed over hundreds of years. They are designed to sift out the unreliable and untrustworthy. Media reports, in contrast, are less concerned with accuracy. The nature of televised media in particular is not conducive to thorough investigation and thoughtful reflection. However, because of its reach and apparent reliability to the public, it significantly influences public opinion. Although prosecutors and judges may be improperly influenced by public opinion, the greatest problem lies with the influence pretrial publicity has on the jury system. Empanelling a fair and impartial jury in a community that has been immersed in media coverage of the crime to be tried can be problematic.

The landmark case in this area is *Sheppard v. Maxwell,*[11] 384 U.S. 333 (1966). In July 1954, Marilyn Sheppard was murdered. From the outset, her husband, Dr. Sam Sheppard, was suspected by authorities of committing the crime. In the months that followed, the murder investigation topped the news. Most of the media stories presumed Sheppard's guilt and advocated that he be prosecuted. Sheppard was tried and convicted. The Supreme Court, in its opinion, detailed the pervasive (and biased) nature of the pretrial publicity, as well as the trial judge's failure to control media in the courtroom. For example, the courtroom was packed with newsmen and their movements in and out of the courtroom were so disruptive that it was difficult to hear the proceedings, even though the courtroom had been equipped with a loudspeaker. Further, the judge allowed a media table to be set up near the jury box where the jurors could observe the members of the press staring at the defendant and taking notes. Much of the information against Sheppard that was detailed in newspapers and on television was not introduced at trial. Much of the information received by the media came from both prosecutors and Sheppard's counsel.

Coverage continued on a daily basis well into the trial. For example, television media conducted debates concerning the trial during the voir dire. Photos of the jurors were permitted and one station ran stories about the personal lives of the jurors. At home, jurors received telephone calls from people who wished to express their opinions about the case. In short, the Court stated that

> [w]e believe that the trial arrangements made by the judge with the news media caused Sheppard to be deprived of that judicial serenity and calm to which he was entitled. The fact is that bedlam reigned at

> the courthouse during the trial and newsmen took over practically the entire courtroom, hounding most of the participants in the trial, especially Sheppard.[12]

The Supreme Court determined that Sheppard had been deprived of due process. The Court established a legal standard that is to be applied in pretrial publicity cases. Actual prejudice, which would be difficult for a defendant to prove, need not be shown; rather, a defendant is only required to establish that pretrial publicity created a "reasonable likelihood of prejudice."

In its opinion, the Court discussed a trial judge's options in such cases. First, the judge can attempt to control pretrial publicity. Second, the judge can minimize the damage of pretrial publicity at trial. Finally, the judge has a responsibility to control the courtroom so that a defendant may enjoy an atmosphere of "judicial serenity and calm."

The judge's power to control pretrial publicity is limited by the First Amendment. Note, however, that the Sixth Amendment's public trial requirement is one held by a defendant, not the public. Accordingly, the Sixth Amendment is not a basis upon which a member of the public may demand that a hearing be opened. Nevertheless, the Supreme Court has determined that the First Amendment includes a public right to attend not only criminal trials, but also pretrial hearings in criminal cases. The Court has said that the right of the public, and in particular the media, to attend is important not only to disseminate information, but also to satisfy the larger objective of checking the government. However, the rule is not absolute. A trial judge may close a hearing if the government has a compelling reason that outweighs the First Amendment interest of openness. The interest of the government in protecting child victims of sex crimes justifies temporarily closing trials, on a case-by-case basis, when a victim testifies.[13]

So, in most instances, the trial judge will be prohibited from closing the hearing, though other measures may be taken to prevent prejudicial pretrial publicity. The Court asserted in *Sheppard* that a trial judge has the inherent authority to control the release of information by participants in the process, such as police, lawyers, and witnesses. Therefore, a court may order, under the threat of contempt, the participants not to disclose sensitive or inflammatory information to the press prior to trial. The American Bar Association's codes of conduct also proscribe pretrial statements to the press concerning a case.

Generally, prior restraint, or an order not to publish information, is violative of the First Amendment. Because of the nefarious history of prior restraint by the British, its use has been disfavored in American law. It may be permissible in extreme situations for a judge to bar the publication of certain sensitive and highly prejudicial information, although this is not definite.

At trial, the judge has an obligation to assure that pretrial publicity does not cause the defendant to be deprived of a fair trial. The judge has many remedies. First, a change of venue sometimes remedies the problem. The Court stated in *Sheppard* that trial judges should "continue the case until the threat abates, or transfer it to another county not so permeated with publicity." A change of venue is only remedial, however, whenever the new venue has been free of the pervasive press coverage that the initial venue has seen. In a time when Court TV, CNN, and other national media sources routinely run stories detailing local crime, this remedy is likely to be less frequently used.

If it appears that public interest and passions concerning a case will fade in a reasonable time, the judge may order a continuance of trial.

Once a forum and date are selected, the judge has an obligation to use the voir dire to eliminate prospective jurors who have been prejudiced by pretrial publicity. Exposure to pretrial publicity does not always warrant elimination; rather, the question is whether the prospective jurors can set aside what they have read or heard and be fair. If a party is unsuccessful in challenging a juror for cause, then the prospective juror may be eliminated by using a peremptory challenge.

Once the trial has begun, the possibility of contamination of the jury continues. To control this, judges usually admonish juries not to read or listen to media reports concerning the trial. They are also admonished not to discuss the case with any person, including each other, until deliberations. The most extreme action is sequestration of the jury during the trial. This was done in the O.J. Simpson trial.

Finally, the judge has an obligation to control the courtroom. First, although criminal trials are public, there is no constitutional right to take still photographs or videotapes of court proceedings. Regardless, most states permit cameras in the courtroom today and the federal courts are experimenting with their use. In fact, the government may televise a trial over a defendant's objection, so long as the defendant's due process rights are not violated in the process.[14] Even in states that permit cameras in the courtroom, a judge may suspend the rule if necessary to assure the defendant a fair trial.

The Right to Confrontation and Cross-Examination

The Sixth Amendment also contains a right to confront one's accusers. This means that a defendant has the right to cross-examine the witnesses of the prosecution. Each state drafts its own rules of evidence; however, it may not enact a rule of evidence that conflicts with a defendant's right to confrontation.

For example, a state procedure permiting government witnesses to refuse to identify themselves was found violative of the Sixth Amendment.[15]

The Supreme Court reasoned that the procedure was invalid because it did not permit the defendant to conduct his or her own investigation into the credibility of government witnesses.

Statutes allowing victims to testify remotely, such as by closed-circuit television, also raise confrontation issues. However, the Supreme Court has stated that the confrontation clause does not per se prohibit child witnesses in child abuse cases from testifying outside the defendant's physical presence by one-way closed-circuit television. Before such a procedure is used, however, the court must examine the facts of the case and determine that remote testimony is necessary.[16] Failure to make such a finding (e.g., the child fears the defendant) can lead to reversal.[17]

MARYLAND
v.
CRAIG
497 U.S. 836 (1990)

JUSTICE O'CONNOR delivered the opinion of the Court.

[In 1986 Craig was charged with committing sex crimes against a six-year-old girl who attended a child care center owned by Craig. The prosecution wanted to invoke a state statutory procedure permitting child victims to testify by closed circuit television. Under the Maryland statute, the trial judge could allow the procedure only if a courtroom appearance by the child would cause her serious emotional distress such that the child could not reasonably communicate. When this procedure is used, the child, judge, defense counsel, and prosecutor gather in a separate room and the testimony is displayed on a monitor in the courtroom to the defendant and jury. The witness cannot see the defendant. Following a hearing, at which expert witnesses testified that the victim would suffer serious emotional distress, the judge ordered that the procedure could be used. The defendant objected, was convicted, and raised the issue on appeal.]

This case requires us to decide whether the Confrontation Clause of the Sixth Amendment categorically prohibits a child witness in a child abuse case from testifying against a defendant at trial, outside the defendant's physical presence, by one-way closed circuit television.

* * *

We granted certiorari to resolve the important Confrontation Clause issues raised by this case.

* * *

We observed in *Coy v. Iowa* that "the Confrontation Clause guarantees the defendant a face-to-face meeting with witnesses appearing before the trier of fact." ... This interpretation derives not only from the literal text of the Clause, but also from our understanding of its historical roots. ...

We have never held, however, that the Confrontation Clause guarantees criminal defendants the absolute right to a face-to-face meeting with witnesses against them at trial. Indeed, in *Coy v. Iowa,* we expressly "le[ft] for another day ... the question whether any exceptions exist" to the "irreducible literal meaning of the Clause: 'a right to meet *face to face* all those who appear and give evidence at trial.'" ... The procedure challenged in *Coy* involved the placement of a screen that prevented two child witnesses in a child abuse case from seeing the defendant as they testified against him at trial. ... In holding that the use of this procedure violated the defendant's right to confront witnesses against him, we suggested that any exception to the right "would surely be allowed only when necessary to further an important public policy"—*i.e.,* only upon a showing of something more than the generalized, "legislatively imposed presumption of trauma" underlying the statute at issue in that case. ... We concluded that "[s]ince there ha[d] been no individualized findings that these particular witnesses needed special protection, the judgment [in the case before us] could not be sustained by any conceivable exception." ... Because the trial court in this case made individualized findings that each of the child witnesses needed special protection, this case requires us to decide the question reserved in *Coy.*

The central concern of the Confrontation Clause is to ensure the reliability of the evidence against a criminal defendant by subjecting it to rigorous testing in the context of an adversary proceeding before the trier of fact.

* * *

We have recognized, for example, that face-to-face confrontation enhances the accuracy of factfinding by reducing the risk that a witness will wrongfully implicate an innocent person. ... We have also noted the strong symbolic purpose served by requiring adverse witnesses at trial to testify in the accused's presence. ... Although face-to-face confrontation forms "the core of the values furthered by the Confrontation Clause," ... we have nevertheless recognized that it is not the sine qua non of the confrontation right. ... See *Delaware v. Fensterer,* 474 U.S. 15, 22 (1985) (per curiam) ("the Confrontation Clause is generally satisfied when the defense is given a full and fair opportunity to probe and expose [testimonial] infirmities [such as forgetfulness, confusion, or evasion] through cross-examination, thereby calling to the attention of the factfinder the reasons for giving scant weight to the witness' testimony"). ...

For this reason, we have never insisted on an actual face-to-face encounter at trial in *every* instance in which testimony is admitted against a defendant. Instead, we have repeatedly held that the Clause permits, where necessary, the admission of certain hearsay statements against a defendant despite the defendant's inability to confront the declarant at trial. ... In *Mattox [v. United States],* 156 U.S. 237, 244 (1895), for example, we held that the testimony of a Government witness at a former trial against the defendant, where the witness was fully cross-examined but had died after the first trial, was admissible in evidence against the defendant at his second trial.

* * *

[A] literal reading of the Confrontation Clause would "abrogate virtually every hearsay exception, a result long rejected as unintended and too extreme." ... Thus, in certain narrow circumstances, "competing interests, if 'closely examined,' may warrant dispensing with confrontation at trial." ... We have recently held, for example, that hearsay statements of nontestifying coconspirators may be admitted against a defendant despite the lack of any face-to-face encounter with the accused. ... Given our hearsay cases, the word "confront," as used in the Confrontation Clause, cannot simply mean face-to-face confrontation, for the Clause would then, contrary to our cases, prohibit the admission of any accusatory hearsay statement made by an absent declarant—a declarant who is undoubtedly as much a "witness against" a defendant as one who actually testifies at trial.

In sum, our precedents establish that "the Confrontation Clause reflects a preference for face-to-face confrontation at trial," ... a preference that "must occasionally give way to considerations of public policy and the necessities of the case."

* * *

[W]e hold that, if the State makes an adequate showing of necessity, the state interest in protecting child witnesses from the trauma of testifying in a child abuse case is sufficiently important to justify the use of a special procedure that permits a child witness in such cases to testify at trial against a defendant in the absence of face-to-face confrontation with the defendant.

The requisite finding of necessity must of course be a case-specific one: The trial court must hear evidence and determine whether use of the one-way closed circuit television procedure is necessary to protect the welfare of the particular child witness who seeks to testify. ...

The trial court must also find that the child witness would be traumatized, not by the courtroom generally, but by the presence of the defendant. ... Denial of face-to-face confrontation is not needed to further the state interest in protecting the child witness from trauma unless it is the presence of the defendant that causes the trauma. In other words, if the state interest were merely the interest in protecting child witnesses from courtroom trauma generally, denial of face-to-face confrontation would be unnecessary because the child could be permitted to testify in less intimidating surroundings, albeit with the defendant present. Finally, the trial court must find that the emotional distress suffered by the child witness in the presence of the defendant is more than *de minimis, i.e.,* more than "mere nervousness or excitement or some reluctance to testify" ... . We need not decide the minimum showing of emotional trauma required for use of the special procedure, however, because the Maryland statute, which requires a determination that the child witness will suffer "serious emotional distress such that the child cannot reasonably communicate," ... clearly suffices to meet constitutional standards. To be sure, face-to-face confrontation may be said to cause trauma for the very purpose of eliciting truth, ... but we think that the use of Maryland's special procedure, where necessary to further the important state interest in preventing trauma to child witnesses in child abuse cases, adequately ensures the accuracy of the testimony and preserves the adversary nature of the trial. ... Indeed, where face-to-face confrontation causes significant emotional distress in a child witness, there is evidence that such confrontation would in fact disserve the Confrontation Clause's truth-seeking goal. ...

In sum, we conclude that where necessary to protect a child witness from trauma that would be caused by testifying in the physical presence of the defendant, at least where such trauma would impair the child's ability to communicate, the Confrontation Clause does not prohibit use of a procedure that, despite the absence of face-to-face confrontation, ensures the reliability of the evidence by subjecting it to rigorous adversarial testing and thereby preserves the essence of effective confrontation. Because there is no dispute that the child witnesses in this case testified under oath, were subject to full cross-examination, and were able to be observed by the judge, jury, and defendant as they testified, we conclude that, to the extent that a proper finding of necessity has been made, the admission of such testimony would be consonant with the Confrontation Clause.

The confrontation clause does not give defendants carte blanche to probe any area on cross-examination. If a state can show a compelling reason, it may prohibit cross-examination of a subject. For example, rape shield laws prohibit defendants from inquiring into a rape victim's sexual background in most cases. Courts have affirmed such laws, finding that the protection of the rape victims from unwarranted personal attacks is a legitimate reason to limit defense cross-examination.

The confrontation clause also restricts the government's use of hearsay evidence. *Hearsay* is a statement made by a person out of court. The Federal Rules of Evidence prohibit hearsay, unless it falls into a recognized exception. For the prosecution to use hearsay, it must be shown that (1) the witness is unavailable at trial through no fault of the government and (2) the statement was made in a situation wherein it appears reliable.

The confrontation clause implicitly includes a right of a defendant to be at the trial. This right includes the entire trial, from selection of the jury to return of the verdict. It also includes many pretrial matters, such as suppression hearings. Of course, defendants have a right to be present at both sentencing and probation revocation hearings. Although the right to be present during one's trial is fundamental, it may be lost by disruptive behavior.

Compulsory Process

The Sixth Amendment extends the power of compulsory process for obtaining witnesses to defendants in criminal prosecutions. Thus, a defendant may issue subpoenas to witnesses commanding their attendance at either a hearing or a trial. If a witness fails to comply, the court must use whatever additional process (arrest) is provided for by law to secure the attendance of the witness. The defendant is entitled to the process that the prosecutor enjoys. Statutes enforcing this constitutional provision differ. Some require defendants to justify the use of process against individuals, others do not. In the federal system, the clerk of court provides defendants with signed, but otherwise blank, subpoenas. The defendant then may complete and serve the subpoena on any person. A person who objects to a subpoena may file a motion to quash with the issuing court.

State and federal evidentiary rules must be carefully crafted to avoid violating the compulsory process, confrontation, and due process clauses. The compulsory process clause not only protects a defendant's right to bring a witness to court, but also her right to have that witness take the stand and testify. Hence, an evidentiary law that forbids an accomplice from testifying on a defendant's behalf is arbitrary and violative of all three clauses.[18] Similarly, hearsay rules may be invalid if they prohibit a defendant from introducing otherwise trustworthy and credible evidence.[19]

The Presumption of Innocence: Burden and Standard of Proof

One of the most basic rights underlying the right to a fair trial is the presumption of innocence. All those accused must be proven guilty by the government. Criminal defendants have no duty to defend themselves and may remain silent throughout the trial. In fact, the government is prohibited from calling defendants to testify, and defendants cannot be made to decide whether they will testify at the start of the trial.[20] The fact that a defendant chooses not to testify may not be mentioned by the prosecutor to the jury. Defendants may testify in their own behalf. If so, they are subject to full cross-examination by the prosecutor.

The standard imposed upon the government in criminal cases is to prove guilt **beyond a reasonable doubt**. A doubt that would cause a reasonable or prudent person to question the guilt of the accused is a reasonable doubt. Although not precisely quantified, beyond a reasonable doubt is greater than the civil preponderance (51 percent likely) and less than absolute (100 percent confidence of guilt). The prosecution must prove every element of the charged crime beyond a reasonable doubt. The reasonable doubt standard is an important feature of the accusatorial system of the United States and is required by due process.[21] A juror must vote for acquittal if he or she harbors a reasonable doubt.

To further the presumption of innocence, judges must be careful not to behave in a manner that implies to a jury that a defendant is guilty.

The Supreme Court has stated that the presence of a defendant at a jury trial in prison clothing is prejudicial.[22] In the *Young* case, a federal appellate court reviewed the use of "prisoner docks" for a Sixth Amendment violation. A criminal defendant also has a right to be free from appearing before the jury in handcuffs or shackles.

This right to be free of restraint is not absolute. Judges have the authority to take whatever measures are necessary to assure safety in the courtroom and to advance the administration of justice. Accordingly, a defendant who is disorderly may be expelled from the trial. However, before exclusion is ordered the court should consider other alternatives. Defendants who are threatening may be restrained, and those who verbally interfere with the proceeding may be gagged.[23]

The Right to Speedy Trial

All criminal defendants have a right to a speedy trial. It is the Sixth Amendment, as extended by the Fourteenth Amendment to the states, that guarantees speedy trial. This right has a history dating back to at least the Magna Carta.

TERMS

beyond a reasonable doubt The degree of proof required to convict a person of a crime. A reasonable doubt is a fair doubt based upon reason and common sense, not an arbitrary or possible doubt. To convict a criminal defendant, a jury must be persuaded of his or her guilt to a level beyond "apparently" or "probably." Proof beyond a reasonable doubt is the highest level of proof the law requires.

YOUNG
v.
CALLAHAN
700 F.2d 32 (1st Cir. 1983)

[The Court included a footnote which stated that a *prisoner dock* is "a box approximately four feet square and four feet high. It is open at the top so that the defendant's head and shoulders can be seen when he or she is seated. The dock is placed typically at the center of the bar enclosure which separates the spectator's section from that portion of the courtroom reserved for trial principals. The dock is usually fifteen to twenty feet behind counsel table, and is sometimes on a raised platform."]

In January of 1979 appellant was tried in Massachusetts Superior Court on one count of assault and battery with a dangerous weapon and two counts of murder. The jury returned a guilty verdict on the assault and battery but was unable to reach a verdict on the two murder indictments. In a new trial in February of 1979, appellant was found guilty of second-degree murder on both counts. These convictions were affirmed by the Massachusetts Supreme Judicial Court. ...

Prior to appellant's second trial, counsel moved that he be allowed to sit at counsel table rather than in the prisoner's dock on the grounds that "forcing him to sit in the prisoner's dock would deprive him of his constitutional rights to a fair trial, to the presumption of innocence, to access to counsel, non-suggestive eyewitness identifications, and due process of law." That motion was accompanied by an affidavit from appellant's trial counsel averring, based on his own observations and those of corrections officers during appellant's two years of incarceration and on appellant's conduct at the first trial, that "allowing [appellant] to sit at counsel table will not present any hazards to the orderly judicial process or to the security of its personnel," and that the trial of the case would involve a substantial amount of testimony concerning acts and conduct of the appellant over a several-day period and would thus "require consultation with the defendant." ...

In once again evaluating for constitutional error the confinement of an accused to the prisoner's box, we reiterate ... that such confinement, like appearance in prison attire, is a "constant reminder of the accused's condition" which "may affect a juror's judgment," eroding the presumption of innocence which the accused is due. ...

The prisoner's dock, like other physical restraints, should thus be employed only when "the trial judge has found such restraint reasonably necessary to maintain order" and when cured by an instruction to the "jurors that such restraint is not to be considered in assessing the proof and determining guilt."

To date, the United States Supreme Court has not set a specific number of days within which trial must be conducted. Rather, the Court said, in *Barker v. Wingo,* that four factors must be considered when determining if a defendant has enjoyed a speedy trial. First, the length of the delay; second, the reason for the delay; third, whether the defendant has asserted the right to a speedy trial; fourth, how seriously the defendant was prejudiced.[24]

Time for speedy trial begins once the defendant is arrested or formally charged.[25] If a defendant is charged by sealed indictment, speedy trial does not start until the indictment has been opened.

Dismissal with prejudice is the remedy for violation of speedy trial. That is, the charge is dismissed and may not be refiled by the prosecutor.

All the states and the national government have enacted speedy trial acts. The Speedy Trial Act of 1974[26] is the federal statute. That act requires that individuals be formally charged within thirty days from the date of arrest and tried within seventy days of the date of the filing of the information or indictment or from the date the defendant had the initial appearance before the court that will try the case, whichever is later.

To avoid prejudice by having a trial before a defendant has had an opportunity to prepare a defense, the statute provides that trial shall not occur for thirty days, unless the defendant consents to an earlier date.

The statute specifies certain delays that are excluded from computing time for purpose of speedy trial. A few of the periods excluded by the Speedy Trial Act of 1974 are when the defendant is a fugitive; when trial is delayed because an issue is on appeal; when delays are caused by motions of the parties; and when delays result from mental examinations of the defendant.

The Speedy Trial Act of 1974 gives the trial court the discretion to decide whether violation of its provisions justifies a dismissal with or without prejudice. Factors that must be considered are the seriousness of the offense, the reason for delay, other facts of the case, and the impact of reprosecution on the administration of justice.[27]

Because the United States Supreme Court has not established specific time requirements for speedy trial, each state has its own time requirements. Of course, states must comply with the requirements of *Barker v. Wingo*. Most states have speedy trial provisions in their constitutions, which are similar, if not identical, to the Sixth Amendment. Other states set their speedy trial requirements out in statute or court rules. Time requirements differ, but trial within six months is common.

Statutes of Limitations

Many crimes must be prosecuted within a specified time after being committed. A **statute of limitation** sets the time limit. If prosecution is initiated after the applicable statute has expired, the defendant is entitled to a dismissal.

TERMS

statutes of limitations Federal and state statutes prescribing the maximum period of time during which various types of civil actions and criminal prosecutions can be brought after the occurrence of the injury or the offense.

Statutes vary in length, and serious crimes, such as murder, have no limitation. Generally, the higher the crime, the longer the statute. Statutes begin running when the crime occurs; however, statutes may be tolled in some situations. *Tolling* refers to stopping the clock. The time during which a defendant is a fugitive is commonly tolled. For example, assume that the limitation on felony assault is six years. If an assault was committed on June 1, 1991, normally, prosecution would have to be started by June 1, 1997. However, if the defendant was fugitive from June 1, 1991 to June 1, 1993, then the statute would be tolled, and the new date of limitation would be June 1, 1998.

At common law there were no limitations. Statutes of limitation are legislative creations. There is no constitutional basis for limiting the time in which to prosecute someone for criminal behavior. This being so, legislatures are free to alter or abolish statutes of limitation. If there is no limitation fixed, prosecution may occur any time after the crime.

Sometimes a prosecution for a serious crime may begin after the statute on a lesser included crime has expired. For example, battery is a lesser included crime of aggravated battery. Assume that aggravated battery has a six-year statute and battery three. In most jurisdictions, a prosecutor may not circumvent the three-year statute by charging aggravated battery and including the lesser battery offense in the information or indictment. After the time has run out on the lesser offense, but not on the more serious offense, the defendant is either convicted of the greater offense or acquitted, but can no longer be convicted on the lesser offense. However, at least one jurisdiction does not follow this rule.[28]

The Right to Counsel

The Sixth Amendment to the United States Constitution provides that "in all criminal prosecutions, the accused shall enjoy the right ... to have the Assistance of Counsel for his defense." The right to counsel is one of the most fundamental rights guaranteed to criminal defendants and is fully applicable to the states.

The right to the assistance of counsel is found not only in the Sixth Amendment, but also in the Fifth and Fourteenth Amendments. These alternative sources are discussed later in the particular contexts within which they apply.

Indigency

It has always been clear that criminal defendants are entitled to retain the attorney of their choice. It was not until 1923, though, that the

United States Supreme Court recognized a constitutional right to appointed counsel for indigent defendants, in *Powell v. Alabama*.[29]

In the *Powell* case (commonly known as the Scottsboro case), nine young black males were charged with the rape of two white girls. Within one week of arrest, the defendants were tried. Eight of the "Scottsboro boys" were convicted and sentenced to death. The defendants appealed, claiming that they should have been provided counsel. The Supreme Court agreed.

However, the right to appointed counsel in *Powell* was not founded upon the Sixth Amendment, but upon the Fourteenth. The Court reasoned that the absence of counsel deprived the defendants of a fair trial, and, accordingly, violated the defendants' due process rights. This decision was narrow: it applied only to capital cases in which the defendant was incapable of preparing an adequate defense and did not have the resources to hire an attorney.

The due process right to counsel was subsequently extended to all situations in which a defendant would not have a fair trial in the absence of defense counsel. Whether counsel was required depended on each particular case's "totality of facts." If denial of counsel was "shocking to the universal sense of justice," then the defendant's right to a fair trial, as guaranteed by the Fourteenth Amendment, was violated.[30] The Court refused to extend the right to counsel to all state criminal proceedings. Cases that involve complex legal issues or a defendant of low intelligence are the types of situation that required the appointment of counsel under the *Betts* due process standard.

In 1938 the Court decided *Johnson v. Zerbst,*[31] which held that the Sixth Amendment guarantees a right to counsel. The Sixth Amendment right to counsel was found to be broader than the right to counsel announced in *Powell,* as it applied to all criminal prosecutions. However, *Zerbst* did not apply to state proceedings. Eventually, the Sixth Amendment right to counsel was extended to all state felony proceedings, in *Gideon v. Wainwright.*

Subsequently, the right to counsel was again extended to encompass all criminal cases punished with a jail term. Whether the crime is labeled a misdemeanor or felony is not dispositive of the right to counsel issue.[32]

In some cases, it may be to the prosecution's advantage for a defendant to have counsel, even though a sentence of imprisonment is not available for a first conviction, but is for subsequent convictions. This is because a sentence may not be enhanced to include jail time based on a prior conviction where the defendant possessed a right to, but was denied, counsel.[33] For example, the penalty for first-offense drunk driving is not punished by a term in jail; however, subsequent violations are. If Jack is arrested and convicted without counsel for his first offense, he may not be sentenced to jail time for his second drunk driving conviction because he did not have counsel during his first trial.

GIDEON v. WAINWRIGHT 372 U.S. 335 (1963)

Petitioner was charged in Florida state court with having broken and entered a poolroom with intent to commit a misdemeanor. This offense is a felony under Florida law. Appearing in court without funds and without a lawyer, petitioner asked the court to appoint counsel for him, whereupon the following colloquy took place:

THE COURT: Mr. Gideon, I am sorry, but I cannot appoint Counsel to represent you in this case. Under the laws of the State of Florida, the only time the Court can appoint Counsel to represent a defendant is when that person is charged with a capital offense. I am sorry, but I will have to deny your request to appoint Counsel to defend you in this case.

THE DEFENDANT: The United States Supreme Court says I am entitled to be represented by Counsel.

Put to trial before a jury, Gideon conducted his defense about as well as could be expected from a layman. He made an opening statement to the jury, cross-examined the State's witnesses, presented witnesses in his own defense, declined to testify himself, and made a short argument "emphasizing his innocence to the charge contained in the Information filed in this case." The jury returned a verdict of guilty, and petitioner was sentenced to five years in the state prison. Since 1942, when *Betts v. Brady,* 316 U.S. 455, was decided by a divided Court, the problem of a defendant's federal constitutional right to counsel in a state court has been a continuing source of controversy and litigation in both state and federal courts. ... Since Gideon was proceeding in forma pauperis, we appointed counsel to represent him and requested both sides to discuss in their briefs and oral arguments the following: "Should this Court's holding in *Betts v. Brady* ... be reconsidered? ...

Governments, both state and federal, quite properly spend vast sums of money to establish machinery to try defendants accused of crime. Lawyers to prosecute are everywhere deemed essential to protect the public's interest in an orderly society. Similarly, there are few defendants charged with crime, few indeed, who fail to hire the best lawyers they can get to prepare and present their defenses. That government hires lawyers to prosecute and defendants who have the money to hire lawyers to defend are the strongest indications of the widespread belief that lawyers in criminal courts are necessities, not luxuries. The right of one charged with crime to counsel may not be deemed fundamental and essential to fair trials in some countries, but it is in ours. From the very beginning, our state and national constitutions and laws have laid great emphasis on procedural and substantive safeguards designed to assure fair trials before impartial tribunals in which every defendant stands equal before the law. This noble idea cannot be realized if the poor man charged with crime has to face his accusers without a lawyer to represent him. ... The Court in *Betts v. Brady* departed from sound wisdom upon which the Court's holding in *Powell v. Alabama* rested. Florida, supported by two other States, has asked that *Betts v. Brady* be left intact. Twenty-two states, as friends of the Court, argue that *Betts* was "an anachronism when handed down" and that it should now be overruled. We agree. ... Reversed.

To qualify for appointed counsel, the defendant does not have to be financially destitute. It need only be shown that the defendant's financial situation will prevent him or her from being able to retain an attorney. An indigent defendant does not have a right to choose the appointed attorney; this decision falls within the discretion of the trial court.

Effective Assistance of Counsel

Defendants are entitled not only to have an attorney, but also to the "effective assistance of counsel." On appeal, defendants may challenge their convictions claiming that at a lower level (trial or appellate) they did not have effective counsel.

To be successful with such a claim, two facts must be shown. First, the representation must be extremely inadequate. Second, the defendant must show that he or she was actually harmed by the lack of adequate counsel. So, if an appellate court determines that a defendant would have been convicted with the best of attorneys, the defendant's claim of inadequate counsel fails.

A Sixth Amendment claim of ineffective assistance of counsel can take many forms. Incompetence of counsel is often claimed, but rarely successful. Attorneys are expected to make the legal and tactical decisions of the defense. The fact that defense counsel rendered incorrect legal advice is not determinative. The issue is whether the defendant's representation was shockingly substandard.

A defendant has a right to the "undivided loyalty" of defense counsel. Hence, it is common to have ineffective assistance of counsel claims where one attorney is representing co-defendants. In *Cuyler v. Sullivan,*[34] it was held that an ineffective assistance of counsel claim based upon an alleged conflict of interest will be successful only if the defendant can show that the conflict "adversely affected" his or her rights.

Also, the accused has a right to confer with counsel to prepare a defense. If a court denies a defendant access to his or her counsel, a Sixth Amendment claim may be made.

Governmental eavesdropping on a defendant's conversation with his or her counsel is also improper and violative of the Sixth Amendment.

The Right to Self-Representation

In *Faretta v. California,*[35] the right to self-representation was established. The Supreme Court recognized that the assistance of trained legal counsel is essential to preparing and presenting a defense. However, in balance, the Court found that a defendant's right of choice is of greater importance. Therefore, defendants may choose to act as their own counsel (pro se), even though the decision increases the probability of a conviction.

The record must clearly show that a defendant who has chosen to proceed pro se has done so voluntarily and knowingly. The defendant "must be made aware of the dangers and disadvantages of self-representation." Whether the defendant possesses any legal training or education is not relevant.

Trial judges are permitted to appoint "standby counsel" for trial. This attorney attends the trial and is available to counsel the defendant or take over the defense, if necessary. The Court later approved the practice of appointing standby counsel over the objection of the defendant. This is routinely done in felony cases in which the defendant has opted to proceed pro se.

The right to self-representation is not absolute. A defendant who engages in disruptive behavior during the proceeding may be relieved of pro se status. Standby counsel, if appointed, may be ordered to complete the trial.

The Scope of the Right

Through *Gideon,* the right to counsel in criminal prosecutions was extended to the states. *Argersinger* made it clear that counsel must be provided in all cases in which the defendant is sentenced to actual imprisonment. But when does the right begin?

The United States Supreme Court has stated that the Sixth Amendment right to counsel applies to all critical stages of a criminal prosecution. This definition requires that a "prosecution" be initiated before the right to counsel, under the Sixth Amendment, attaches. Accordingly, the Sixth Amendment does not apply to juvenile proceedings, nor to administrative hearings such as parole determination and revocation.

The right starts whenever the "adversary judicial proceeding" is initiated. Police contacts prior to the initiation of an adversary judicial proceeding are not covered by the Sixth Amendment.

In determining what constitutes a critical stage, courts focus on "whether substantial rights of the defendant may be affected." The greater the contact between the prosecutor and the defendant, the more likely the event is at a critical stage.

The first critical stage is normally the initial appearance or the arraignment. Courts have also determined that a defendant may be entitled to counsel at a police lineup, sentencing, preliminary hearing, and during a probation revocation hearing. Once charges are filed, all interrogations of the defendant by the government are critical stages. See Figure 11-1.

The Sixth Amendment is not the only constitutional provision assuring counsel. The Fifth Amendment's right to be free from self-incrimination also guarantees counsel in some instances, as does the Fourteenth Amendment's equal protection and due process clauses.

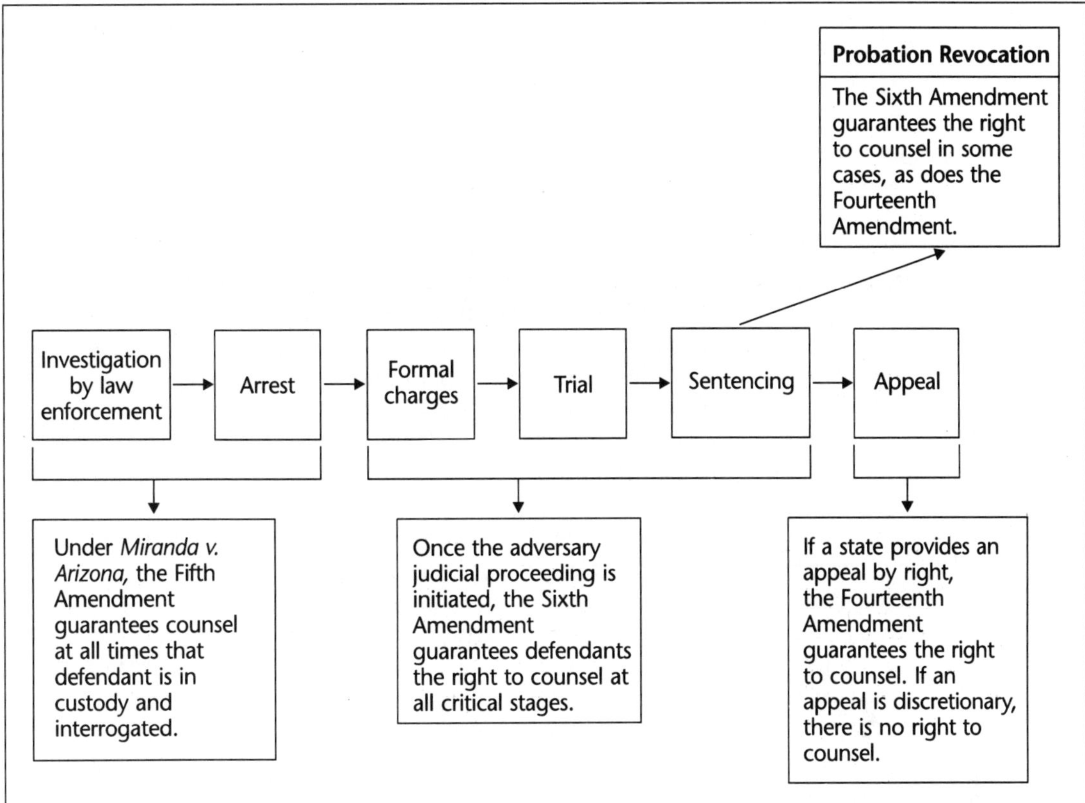

FIGURE 11-1 The Right to Counsel

Double Jeopardy

The Fifth Amendment to the United States Constitution provides that "no person shall be subject for the same offense to be twice put in jeopardy of life or limb." The principle of not punishing someone twice for the same act can be found back as far as Blackstone's Commentaries.[36] The **double jeopardy** clause applies only to criminal proceedings.

There are actually two prohibitions in the double jeopardy clause. The clause prevents: (1) a second prosecution for the same offense and (2) a second punishment for the same offense.

Often the question is whether a prior "jeopardy" occurred. It is generally held that a person has been put in jeopardy once a plea of guilty

TERMS

double jeopardy A rule originating in the Fifth Amendment that prohibits a second punishment or a second trial for the same offense. It is sometimes referred to as *former jeopardy* or *prior jeopardy*.

has been entered and accepted by a court. An unapproved plea will not suffice, and a subsequent prosecution will not be prohibited by the double jeopardy clause. In jury trials, jeopardy attaches once a jury has been selected and sworn. States treat bench trials differently, although the prevailing view is that jeopardy attaches once the first witness has been sworn.

Once jeopardy attaches, the defendant may not be tried again. However, there are a few exceptions. A defendant may be retried if the first trial was terminated by a properly declared mistrial. Mistrials may be declared for a variety of reasons. Death of the trial judge or one of the participating attorneys would likely result in a mistrial. If a witness blurts out an answer to a question before the judge has an opportunity to sustain an objection to the question, and the answer is extremely prejudicial, a mistrial may be declared. The causes of a mistrial are endless. Note that the mistrial must be proper. That is, if an appellate court later determines that a mistrial should not have been declared, the defendant has been put into jeopardy. It is always proper to retry a defendant whose prior trial was declared a mistrial upon the defendant's motion. If a defendant objects to a government motion for a mistrial, there must be a "manifest necessity" (darn good reason) for the mistrial.[37]

It is also not a violation of the Fifth Amendment to prosecute a defendant who was previously charged, but whose charges were dismissed prior to jeopardy attaching. Additionally, if a defendant appeals a conviction and prevails, the defendant may be retried, unless the appellate court finds that insufficient evidence exists to retry the defendant. However, if a defendant is acquitted on a serious charge and convicted on a lesser and then prevails on appeal, he or she may be retried only on the lesser. It is violative of the Fifth Amendment to retry the defendant on the more serious offense.

The Fifth Amendment only forbids retrial for the same offense. Determining whether two acts constitute the same offense is not always an easy task. Two offenses are the same unless one requires proof of a fact that the other does not.[38] This is the "same evidence test."

The double jeopardy clause is fully applicable to the states through the Fourteenth Amendment. However, the clause does not prevent second punishments for the same offense by different sovereigns. For example, a person who robs a federally insured bank may be prosecuted by both the state where the bank resides and the United States. This is true even though the offenses are the same. Although the double jeopardy clause does not prohibit two sovereigns from prosecuting for the same offense, many states prohibit this by statute. In practice, and sometimes by policy, most prosecutors do not pursue a defendant who has been previously prosecuted in another jurisdiction for the same crime. The Model Penal Code incorporates this approach in certain circumstances.[39] Municipalities are not independent beings; they owe their existence not to the Constitution of the United States, but to a state. Accordingly, prosecutions by cities are treated as being brought by the state, and it is a violation of the double jeopardy clause for a state and city to punish one for the same offense.

Finally, several lower courts have set aside acquittals and allowed retrial of defendants when fraud was used to obtain an acquittal, such as when a judge is bribed to enter a not guilty verdict. The Supreme Court has not addressed this issue.[40]

Self-Incrimination and Immunity

The Fifth Amendment also states that no person "shall be compelled in any criminal case to be a witness against himself." The following passage explains why the framers of the Constitution included a privilege against self-incrimination.

> Perhaps the best-known provision of the Fifth Amendment is the clause against forced "self-incrimination," whose origin goes back to England where persons accused of crimes before ecclesiastical courts were forced to take an ex officio oath. That is, they had to swear to answer all questions even if the questions did not apply to the case at trial. This requirement was later adopted by the Court of Star Chamber. One of the victims of the Court was a printer and book distributor named John Lilburne, charged in 1637 with treason for importing books "that promoted Puritan dissent." Lilburne told his accusers, "I am not willing to answer you to any more of these questions because I see you go about by this examination to ensnare me. For seeing the things for which I am imprisoned cannot be proved against me, you will get other material out of my examination; and therefore if you will not ask me about the thing laid to my charge, I shall answer no more. ... I think by the law of the land, that I may stand upon my just defense." Lilburne was convicted, fined, whipped, pilloried, and gagged, and imprisoned until he agreed to take the oath. ...
>
> One notorious instance of forced self-incrimination in the American colonies occurred in the Salem witch trials. In 1692, Giles Corey, an elderly Massachusetts farmer, was accused of witchcraft. He knew whether he pleaded guilty or not guilty he would be convicted, executed and his property confiscated. So to assure that his heirs inherited his property, he refused to plead and thus could not be convicted. The judges ordered him strapped to a table, and stones were loaded upon his chest to force the plea out of him. Corey's final words were "more weight." Then his chest caved in.[41]

John Bradshaw, John Lilburne's attorney, stated it best when he said that "It is contrary to the laws of God, nature and the kingdom for any man to be his own accuser."

Generally, the Amendment prohibits the government from compelling people to testify when incrimination is possible. Most people have heard of "pleading the Fifth." However, if immunity from prosecution is granted to a witness, he or she may be compelled to testify. If a witness refuses to testify because of the fear of self-incrimination, the government may offer the witness immunity from prosecution so that the testimony may be compelled. There are two types of immunity: transactional and derivative use.

Transactional immunity shields the witness from prosecution for all offenses related to his or her testimony. For example, if a witness testifies concerning a robbery, the government may not prosecute the witness for that robbery, even though the government may have evidence of guilt independent of the witness's testimony. Transactional immunity gives more protection to the witness than required by the Constitution, so when it is granted a witness may be ordered to testify.

The minimum immunity that must be provided a witness to overcome a Fifth Amendment claim is derivative **use immunity.** This prohibits the government from using the witness's testimony or any evidence derived from that testimony to prosecute the witness. However, all evidence that is independently obtained may be used against the witness.

Use immunity only prohibits the government from using the witness's testimony against him or her. Statutes that provide only for use immunity are unconstitutional, as derivative use is the minimum protection required by the Fifth Amendment.

States vary in how immunity is granted. Some permit the prosecutor to give the immunity; others require both the request of the prosecutor and the approval of the trial judge.

A person may also waive the Fifth Amendment privilege against self-incrimination. Generally, once a person testifies freely, the privilege is waived as to the subject discussed during the same proceeding. A witness (or defendant) may not testify selectively concerning a subject. It is often said that testifying to a fact waives to the details. This prevents a witness from testifying only to the information beneficial to one party and then refusing to testify further, even though he or she may have omitted important facts. However, a witness may not be compelled to testify if there is a chance of incriminating himself or herself beyond the original testimony.

TERMS

transactional immunity A guaranty given a person that if he or she testifies against others he or she will not be prosecuted for his or her own involvement in the crime (i.e., the "criminal transaction") to which his or her testimony relates.

use immunity A guaranty given a person that if he or she testifies against others, his or her testimony will not be used against him or her if he or she is prosecuted for his or her involvement in the crime.

The fact that a witness may waive the Fifth Amendment privilege against self-incrimination on one occasion does not mean it is waived forever. First, a defendant (or witness) may speak to the police during the investigative stage and later refuse to testify at trial, provided such testimony may be incriminating. Second, it is generally held that a person who testifies before a grand jury without claiming the Fifth does not waive the right to raise the defense at trial. Third, even within the same proceeding a person may invoke the Fifth Amendment privilege against self-incrimination if the two hearings are separate and distinct. For example, a defendant may testify at a suppression hearing without waiving the privilege not to testify at trial.

Finally, the Fifth Amendment applies to all proceedings, whether civil, criminal, or administrative.[42] Therefore, a person called to testify in a civil proceeding may invoke the Fifth Amendment's privilege and refuse to testify.

The First Amendment prohibits the government from calling the defendant to testify. The Supreme Court has said that requiring a defendant to plead the Fifth Amendment in front of a jury is too prejudicial. Once a defendant chooses to testify, however, the prosecutor is allowed to cross-examine.

§ 11.2 Trial Procedure

Voir Dire

The first stage of trial is the **voir dire**. This is a French phrase that translates "look speak" (to speak the truth). Voir dire is also known as *jury selection*.

The process of selecting a jury differs among the jurisdictions. In all jurisdictions, prospective jurors are asked questions bearing upon their individual ability to serve fairly and impartially. Each state differs in how this information is obtained. In many, the judge is responsible for asking most of the questions. In others, the judge only makes a few brief inquiries, and the lawyers do most of the questioning.

TERMS

voir dire examination Examination of a potential juror for the purpose of determining whether he or she is qualified and acceptable to act as a juror in the case. A prospective juror who a party decides is unqualified or unacceptable may be challenged for cause or may be the subject of a peremptory challenge.

There are two ways of eliminating a juror. First, if one of the attorneys believes that a juror could not be fair and impartial, the juror can be **challenged for cause.** If the judge agrees, the juror is released. An unlimited number of jurors may be eliminated for cause.

In addition to challenges for cause, a juror may be eliminated by a party using a **peremptory challenge**. Each party is given a specific number of peremptory challenges at the start of the trial and may strike jurors until that number is exhausted. A party is free to eliminate, without stating a reason, any potential juror. However, a juror may not be eliminated because of race.[43]

In the federal system, both defendant and prosecutor have twenty peremptory strikes in death cases and three in misdemeanors; in non-capital felony cases the defendant gets ten and the government six.[44] States have similar rules.

Preliminary Instructions

The next stage in the trial proceeding is for the judge to give preliminary instructions to the jury. The trial judge explains to the jury what its obligation is and gives a brief introduction to the law and facts of the case. The judge may read the formal charge verbatim to the jury or may summarize its contents.

The presumption of innocence is explained, and the judge admonishes the jury not to discuss the case prior to deliberating. Jurors are told not to read newspaper articles or watch television reports concerning the trial. In rare cases, it may be necessary to keep the jurors' identities secret and to conduct the voir dire in private. Threat to the safety of the jurors is an example of such an instance. This method is to be used cautiously, as it encroaches upon First Amendment rights of media and of the defendant to a public trial. Moreover, when used, the trial judge should be careful not to prejudice the jury. If the reason for secrecy is a perceived threat, the judge should instruct the jury as to another reason, such as concern over pretrial publicity.[45]

Opening Statements

After the judge has given the preliminary instructions, the parties address the jury. These statements are commonly known as *opening*

TERMS

challenge for cause An objection, for a stated reason, to a juror being allowed to hear a case.

peremptory challenge A challenge to a juror that a party may exercise without having to give a reason.

statements. The purpose of opening statements is to acquaint the jury with the basic facts of the case. Opening statement is not the time for counsel to argue the law; only the facts expected to be presented should be mentioned.

In some cases the defense attorney may be permitted to wait until after the prosecution has put on its case before giving an opening. Because the purpose of opening statements is to present the facts surrounding the charge to the jury, opening statements are often waived in bench trials.

The Prosecution's Case in Chief

Because the government has brought the charges, it puts its case on first. This consists of calling witnesses to testify and producing exhibits.

All jurisdictions have rules of evidence that govern procedure and the admissibility of evidence. The Federal Rules of Evidence are used in the federal courts, and many states have modeled their rules after the federal ones.

Many evidentiary questions can be resolved prior to trial through a motion **in limine**. Those arising during trial are handled through **objections.** Any time an attorney believes that a question, statement, or action of the opposing lawyer is improper, he or she may object. The court will then rule on the objection, and the trial will continue. In some instances the attorneys will want to argue the objection outside the hearing of the jury. In such cases a **sidebar** may be held, or the judge may order that the jury be removed until the matter is resolved.

The confrontation clause assures the defendant the right to cross-examine the prosecution's witnesses. Normally, cross-examination is limited to matters raised during the prosecution's direct examination. The defense also has the right to review an exhibit before it is shown to the jury.

TERMS

in limine [Latin for] "at the outset." Appears in the context of *motion in limine,* a motion made before the commencement of a trial which requests the court to prohibit the adverse party from introducing prejudicial evidence at trial.

objection The customary method, during a trial or hearing, of calling the attention of the judge or hearing officer to some aspect of the proceeding which one believes to be illegal or improper, and of seeking a ruling on the matter.

sidebar A term applied to a private discussion between the judge and the attorneys for the parties during the course of a trial. The conversation takes place at the bench, beyond the jury's hearing.

Directed Verdict and Judgment of Acquittal

After the government has rested (finished its case), the defendant may move for a directed verdict or, as it is also known, a judgment of acquittal. Upon such motion the trial judge reviews the evidence presented by the government. If the evidence to support a conviction is insufficient, the judge will enter a directed verdict favoring the defendant. A directed verdict may never be entered favoring the government.

The prosecution's evidence is insufficient if reasonable persons could not conclude that the defendant is guilty. If the trial court grants a motion for directed verdict, the jury never deliberates and is discharged. Directed verdicts are rarely granted, as most judges prefer to have the jury return a verdict.

The Defense Case

If the motion for directed verdict is denied, the defense may put on its case. The defendant is not required to put on a defense, and juries are instructed to not infer guilt by the absence of a defense.

If a defendant chooses to present a defense, the rules are the same as for the prosecution. The defendant may call witnesses and introduce exhibits, as limited by the rules of evidence. Defense witnesses are subject to cross-examination by the prosecutor. Defendants do not have to testify, but may choose to do so. If a defendant does testify, he or she is subject to cross-examination by the prosecutor.

Rebuttal

After the defense has concluded, the prosecution may call rebuttal witnesses in an effort to disprove the evidence of the defense. No new issues may be raised during rebuttal. The defense is then permitted to rebut the prosecution's rebuttal evidence.

Closing Arguments

After the evidentiary stage of the trial has concluded, the parties present their closing arguments. The length of closing arguments is left to the discretion of the trial judge.

Attorneys may argue both the facts and the law during closing arguments. However, an attorney may not argue law different from that the judge will express to the jury as controlling in the case. Closing arguments give the parties an opportunity to summarize the evidence and explain their positions to the jury.

Attorneys must not make incorrect factual or legal statements to the jury. Objections to such statements may be made. If sustained, the jury will be instructed by the judge to disregard the statement. Prosecutors must be especially careful not to make inflammatory remarks about the defendant or defense counsel. Such remarks, if extreme, can lead to mistrial.

Final Instructions

After closing arguments are completed, the judge will instruct the jury. Through these instructions the judge explains the law to the jury. The information contained in the judge's instructions includes the prosecutorial burden, the standard of proof, the elements of the charged crime, how to weigh and value evidence, and rules for reaching a verdict.

Jury Deliberations and Verdict

After receiving its instructions, the jury goes into deliberations. Jury deliberations are secret in all cases.

Generally, no person has contact with the jury when it is deliberating. If the jury has a question for the judge, it is escorted into the courtroom where all the parties may hear the question. Some judges, but not all, permit juries to take the exhibits and instructions with them into the jury room. Although not constitutionally required, many jurisdictions require juries to be sequestered during deliberations. If a jury is not, the trial judge must admonish them not to discuss the case with any person and not to read or listen to media reports concerning the case.

On occasion, a jury may communicate to the judge that a verdict cannot be reached. Some courts will then give the jury an "Allen charge," an instruction encouraging jurors in the minority to re-examine their position. The charge gets its name from *Allen v. United States,*[46] wherein the Supreme Court approved its use. Courts must be careful with such charges, but they are not violative of the United States Constitution. However, some states have banned the Allen charge.

In the event of a **hung jury**, the court will declare a mistrial and set a new trial date. Because of the expense and inconvenience of trying cases a second time, plea bargains are often reached.

If a verdict is reached, the parties are summoned to the courtroom and the jury verdict is read. The parties may request that the jury be

TERMS

hung jury A jury that cannot reach a unanimous verdict.

polled. **Polling the jury** involves asking each juror how he or she voted. If there has been an error, the judge may order the jury to return to deliberations or may declare a mistrial.

Jurors have an obligation to follow the law, as interpreted by the trial judge, when rendering a verdict.[47] Trial judges instruct jurors in this obligation. Further, the trial judge is not to instruct the jury, nor the parties to encourage the jury in closing arguments, to disregard the law. This rule affects defense, not prosecution. That is, if a law (defining a crime or punishment) is harsh or unfavorable, defendants have an interest in arguing that a jury should disregard the law and acquit, notwithstanding guilt. This is not permitted in most, if not all, jurisdictions. Accordingly, a defendant has no right to insist that a jury be instructed that it has the authority to nullify the law.[48]

In reality, though, juries can and may disregard the law. When a jury retires, its deliberations are secret, and each juror, while feeling bound by the law, also feels bound by personal conscience. A jury does not have to support its verdict with a statement of its findings and conclusions. An acquittal, even if the result of nullification, is valid. Accordingly, although the trial judge may comment on the evidence to the jury before it retires to deliberate, a judge may not instruct a jury that the government has met its burden and that the jury must return a guilty verdict.[49]

JNOV and New Trial

If the jury returns a verdict of guilty, the defendant may move for a judgment notwithstanding the verdict or JNOV. This is similar to a directed verdict, in that the defendant is asserting that the evidence is insufficient to support a guilty verdict.

In addition to JNOV, a defendant may file a motion for a new trial. The common-law equivalent of a motion for a new trial was the *writ of error coram nobis. Coram nobis* is still recognized in a few states.

This motion is different from the JNOV because the defendant is not claiming that the evidence was insufficient, but rather that the trial was flawed. For example, if a defendant believes that evidence was admitted that should have been excluded and that he was denied a fair trial because of the admission of the evidence, he may file a motion for new trial. A motion for new trial may also be made because of new evidence, discovered after trial.

TERMS

polling the jury Individually examining the jurors who participated in a verdict to ascertain whether they unanimously support the verdict.

Review Questions

1. What rights are encompassed by the Confrontation Clause?
2. What is the standard of proof in criminal cases? Define that standard.
3. How soon after arrest must a defendant be tried to comply with the Sixth Amendment's speedy trial clause?
4. What is jury nullification? May a prosecutor ask a jury to nullify? May defense counsel?
5. Distinguish challenging a prospective juror for cause from using a peremptory challenge.
6. Does a defendant have a right to self-representation?
7. What must a defendant show on appeal to be successful with a claim of ineffective assistance of counsel at trial?

Review Problems

1–4. Does each of the following defendants have a right to a jury trial? Explain your answer.

1. A juvenile delinquency proceeding has been initiated against John because of his involvement with drugs. For more than a year he has been dealing drugs, a crime punishable by as much as five years in prison in his state.
2. Jane is charged with simple assault. In her state that crime is punishable by a maximum fine of $2,500 and twelve months imprisonment. However, the judge assigned to her case has never sentenced a person to more than four months and customarily suspends that sentence to probation.
3. Nick is sixteen years old. He is charged with murder in state trial court. Murder in his state is punished with life imprisonment or death.
4. Norm, an officer in the military, has been charged with raping a female officer. Rape is punished with ten years to life imprisonment in the military.

Notes

1 *Baldwin v. New York,* 399 U.S. 66 (1970).

2 *McKeiver v. Pennsylvania,* 403 U.S. 528 (1971).

3 *Williams v. Florida,* 399 U.S. 78 (1970).

4 *Burch v. Louisiana,* 441 U.S. 130 (1979).
5 390 U.S. 570 (1968).
6 *Strauder v. West Virginia,* 100 U.S. 303 (1880).
7 273 U.S. 510 (1927).
8 *Ward v. Monroeville,* 409 U.S. 57 (1972).
9 *Mayberry v. Pennsylvania,* 400 U.S. 455 (1971).
10 381 U.S. 532 (1965).
11 384 U.S. 333 (1966).
12 *Id.* at 335.
13 *Globe Newspaper v. Superior Court,* 457 U.S. 596 (1982).
14 *Chandler v. Florida,* 449 U.S. 560 (1981).
15 *Smith v. Illinois,* 390 U.S. 129 (1968).
16 *Maryland v. Craig,* 497 U.S. 836 (1990).
17 *Cumbie v. Singletary,* 991 F.2d 715 (11th Cir. 1993).
18 *Washington v. Texas,* 388 U.S. 14 (1967).
19 *Chambers v. Mississippi,* 410 U.S. 284 (1973).
20 *Brooks v. Tennessee,* 406 U.S. 605 (1972).
21 *Johnson v. Louisiana,* 406 U.S. 356 (1972).
22 *Estelle v. Williams,* 425 U.S. 501 (1976).
23 *Stewart v. Corbin,* 850 F.2d 492 (9th Cir. 1988).
24 *Barker v. Wingo,* 407 U.S. 514 (1972).
25 *United States v. Marion,* 404 U.S. 307 (1971).
26 18 U.S.C. § 3161.
27 18 U.S.C. § 3162.
28 21 Am. Jur. 2d 225 (1990); *State v. Borucki,* 505 A.2d 89 (Me. 1986).
29 287 U.S. 45 (1923).
30 *Betts v. Brady,* 316 U.S. 455 (1942).
31 304 U.S. 458 (1938).
32 *Argersinger v. Hamlin,* 407 U.S. 25 (1972).
33 *Burgett v. Texas,* 389 U.S. 109 (1962).
34 446 U.S. 335 (1980).
35 422 U.S. 806 (1975).
36 21 Am. Jur. *Criminal Law* 243 (1978).
37 *Arizona v. Washington,* 434 U.S. 497 (1978).
38 *Blockburger v. United States,* 284 U.S. 299 (1932).
39 Model Penal Code § 1.10.
40 *See Illinois v. Aleman,* 1994 WL 684499 (Ill. Cir. Ct. 1994).
41 Passage taken from a 1991 calendar prepared by the Commission on the Bicentennial of the United States Constitution, Washington, D.C.

42 *Pillsbury v. Conboy,* 459 U.S. 248 (1983).

43 *Batson v. Kentucky,* 476 U.S. 79 (1986).

44 Fed. R. Crim. P. 24(b).

45 *United States v. Locascio,* 6 F.3d 924 (2d Cir. 1993).

46 164 U.S. 492 (1896).

47 *See United States v. Avery,* 717 F.2d 1020 (6th Cir. 1983).

48 *United States v. Newman,* 743 F. Supp. 533 (M.D. Tenn. 1990).

49 *See Sparf v. United States,* 156 U.S. 51 (1895); *United States v. Martin Linen Supply Co.,* 430 U.S. 564 (1977).

CHAPTER 12

SENTENCING AND APPEAL

CHAPTER OUTLINE

I'm here because I'm guilty. ... I'm willing to pay according to the laws of Texas because I know I'm guilty.

Eliseo Moreno, convicted murderer

§ 12.1 Sentencing: Introduction

After conviction, sentence must be imposed. For many misdemeanors and nearly all infractions, sentence is imposed immediately. For felonies and some misdemeanors, a future sentencing date is set.

In most cases sentence is imposed by the trial judge. A few jurisdictions provide for a jury sentence recommendation, and an even fewer number actually permit the jury to impose sentence. Although not constitutionally required, the jury always plays a role in deciding whether death should be imposed.

The legislature determines how a crime should be punished. Legislatures normally set ranges within which judges may punish violators. In recent years there has been a substantial movement to limit the discretion of judges. This has been done in the federal system and many states.

The right of the legislative branch in this area is curbed by the Eighth Amendment, which prohibits "cruel and unusual punishment." The protection of the Eighth Amendment has been extended to state proceedings through the Fourteenth Amendment. However, legislatures enjoy wide discretion in deciding how to punish criminals.

§ 12.2 Sentencing Procedure

The Presentence Investigation/No Right to Counsel

After a defendant is determined guilty, a sentencing date is set. For most felonies and misdemeanors the date will be set far enough in the future to permit the probation officer to complete a presentence investigation.

The investigation typically begins with an interview of the defendant. Information concerning the defendant's drug habits, criminal history, family, employment history, education, medical and psychological problems, and personal finances is obtained. The defendant is also permitted to give his or her version of the facts surrounding the offense. There appears to be no right to counsel during this interview,[1] although most courts and probation officers permit attorneys to attend. The Seventh Circuit Court of Appeals held that the Sixth Amendment right to counsel does not apply at presentence interviews by probation officers. The court reasoned that because probation officers are neutral judicial employees, and not law enforcement officers, interviews conducted by them are not critical stages of an *adversarial* proceeding.[2] The Seventh Circuit, like other courts that have considered the issue, thus determined that the presentence interview is a neutral, nonadversarial meeting between the probation officer and the defendant. This is so even though the defendant may be in custody and admissions could lead to greater punishment.

Three facts support the conclusion that there is no right to counsel during a presentence investigation interview. First, the objective of the interview is to gather information to assist the sentencing court, not to establish that the defendant committed a crime. Second (and related to the first), a probation officer is not, strictly speaking, a law enforcement officer. Third, the questions asked at the interview are routine and defense counsel can properly advise the client of his or her rights before the interview occurs.

In addition to conducting an interview of the defendant, the probation officer will obtain copies of vital documents, such as the defendant's "rap sheet" and relevant medical records. The probation officer will attempt to verify the information provided by the defendant through these documents and other investigatory processes.

When the probation officer has completed the investigation, a presentence report is prepared. This report reflects the information discovered during the investigation and is used by the court in determining what sentence should be imposed. Often, the prosecutor and law enforcement officers involved in prosecuting the defendant, family members of the defendant, and the victim of the crime are permitted to make statements that are incorporated into the report.

There is no constitutional right to the preparation of a presentence report; however, most jurisdictions have followed the lead of the federal government, which requires a presentence report unless "there is in the record information sufficient to enable the meaningful exercise of sentencing discretion."[3]

In the federal system, the defendant is entitled to review the presentence report prior to sentencing. This is true in most states as well, but right is not absolute. For example, the recommendation of the probation officer is kept confidential.[4]

At the sentencing hearing, the defendant may disprove factual statements contained in the report. To this end witnesses may be called and exhibits introduced.

The Sentencing Hearing

The next stage in the process is the sentencing hearing. Sentencing hearings are adversarial. Witnesses may be called, other evidence introduced, and arguments made. In most instances the hearing is before a judge, not a jury, and accordingly the rules of evidence are relaxed. When before a jury, such as in capital cases, the rules of evidence are fully effective. This is a critical stage under the Sixth Amendment, and therefore there is a right to counsel.

One issue that has received considerable attention, and contradictory treatment, from the Supreme Court in recent years is the use of **victim impact statements** at sentencing. A *victim impact statement* is an oral or written statement to the sentencing judge explaining how the crime has affected the victim and, possibly, the victim's family. In 1987 the Supreme Court handed down *Booth v. Maryland,*[5] wherein it invalidated a state statute requiring sentencing judges to consider victim impact statements in capital cases. The Court determined that the use of victim impact statements could prejudice the proceeding by injecting irrelevant, but inflammatory, evidence into the sentencing determination.

Only four years later, though, the Supreme Court overruled *Booth* in *Payne v. Tennessee.* Thus, victim impact evidence may be admitted, even if it is not related to the facts surrounding the crime. The decision concerning admissibility must be made on a case-by-case basis, and it is a violation of due process to admit evidence that is so prejudicial that the sentencing becomes fundamentally unfair.

On the other side of the coin, defendants are generally allowed to present nearly any evidence at sentencing. This is constitutionally mandated in capital cases; the Supreme Court has said that a state cannot preclude a defendant from proffering evidence in support of a sentence less than death.[6]

TERMS

victim impact statement At the time of sentencing, a statement made to the court concerning the effect the crime has had on the victim or on the victim's family.

PAYNE v. TENNESSEE 501 U.S. 808 (1991)

In this case we reconsider our holdings in *Booth v. Maryland* ... that the Eighth Amendment bars the admission of victim impact statement evidence during the penalty phase of a capital trial.

The petitioner, Pervis Tyrone Payne, was convicted by a jury on two counts of first-degree murder and one count of assault with intent to commit murder in the first degree. He was sentenced to death for each of the murders, and to 30 years in prison for assault.

The victims of Payne's offenses were 28-year-old Charisse Christopher, her 2-year-old daughter Lacie, and her 3-year-old son Nicholas. The three lived together ... across the hall from Payne's girlfriend, Bobbie Thomas. On Saturday, June 27, 1987, Payne visited Thomas's apartment several times in expectation of her return from her mother's house in Arkansas, but found no one at home. One visit, he left his overnight bag, containing clothes and other items for his weekend stay, in the hallway outside Thomas's apartment. With the bag were three cans of malt liquor.

Payne passed the morning and early afternoon injecting cocaine and drinking beer. Later, he drove around the town with a friend in the friend's car, each of them taking turns reading a pornographic magazine. Sometime around 3 P.M., Payne returned to the apartment complex, entered the Christophers' apartment, and began making sexual advances toward Charisse. Charisse resisted and Payne became violent. A neighbor who resided in the apartment directly beneath the Christophers heard Charisse screaming, " 'Get out, get out,' as if she were telling the children to leave." The noise briefly subsided and then began "horribly loud." The neighbor called the police after she heard a "bloodcurdling scream" from the Christopher apartment. ...

When the first police officer arrived at the scene, he immediately encountered Payne, who was leaving the apartment building, so covered with blood that he appeared to be "sweating blood." The officer confronted Payne, who responded, "I'm the complainant." ... When the officer asked, "What is going on up there?" Payne struck the officer with the overnight bag, dropped his tennis shoes, and fled.

Inside the apartment, the police encountered a horrifying scene. Blood covered the walls and floor throughout the unit. Charisse and her children were lying on the floor in the kitchen. Nicholas, despite several wounds inflicted by a butcher knife that completely penetrated through his body from front to back, was still breathing. Miraculously, he survived ... . Charisse and Lacie were dead.

Charisse's body was found on the kitchen floor on her back, her legs fully extended. ... None of the 84 wounds inflicted by Payne were individually fatal; rather, the cause of death was most likely bleeding from all of the wounds. She had suffered stab wounds to the chest, abdomen, back, and head. The murder weapon, a butcher knife, was found at her feet. Payne's baseball cap was snapped on her arm near her elbow. Three cans of malt liquor bearing Payne's fingerprints were found near her body, and a fourth empty was on a landing outside the apartment door.

Payne was apprehended later that day ... .

[T]he jury returned guilty verdicts against Payne on all counts.

During the sentencing phase of the trial, Payne presented the testimony of four witnesses, his mother and father, Bobbie Thomas, and Dr. John T. Huston, a clinical psychologist specializing in criminal court evaluation work. Bobbie Thomas testified that she met Payne at church, during a time when she was being abused by her husband. She stated that Payne was a very caring person, and that he devoted much time and attention to her three children, who were being affected by her marital difficulties. She said that the children had come to love him very much and would miss him, and that he "behaved just like a father that loved his kids." She asserted that he did not drink, nor did he use drugs, and that it was generally inconsistent with Payne's character to have committed these crimes. ...

The State presented the testimony of Charisse's mother, Mary Zvolanek. When asked how Nicholas had been affected by the murder of his mother and sister, she responded:

> He cries for his mom. He doesn't seem to understand why she doesn't come home. And he cries for his sister Lacie. He comes to me many times during the week and asks me, Grandma, do you miss Lacie. And I tell him yes. He says, I'm worried about my Lacie.

In arguing for the death penalty during closing argument, the prosecutor commented on the continuing effects of Nicholas's experience, stating:

> But we do know that Nicholas was alive. And Nicholas was in the same room. Nicholas was still conscious. His eyes were open. He responded to the paramedics. He was able to follow their directions. He was able to hold his intestines in as he was carried to the ambulance. So he knew what happened to his mother and baby sister. ...
>
> Somewhere down the road Nicholas is going to grow up, hopefully. He's going to want to know what happened. And he is going to know what happened to his baby sister and mother. He is going to want to know what type of justice was done. He is going to want to know what happened. With your verdict, you will provide the answer. ...

In the rebuttal to Payne's closing argument, the prosecutor stated:

> You saw the videotape this morning. You saw what Nicholas Christopher will carry in his mind forever. When you talk about cruel, when you talk about atrocious, and when you talk about heinous, that picture will always come into your mind, probably throughout the rest of your lives.
>
> * * *
>
> No one will ever know about Lacie Jo because she never had a chance to grow up. Her life was taken from her at the age of two years old. ... His mother will never kiss [Nicholas] good night or pat him as he goes off to bed, or hold him and sing him a lullaby. [Petitioner's attorney] wants you to think about a good reputation, people who love the defendant and things about him. He doesn't want you to think about the people who loved Charisse Christopher, her mother, and daddy who loved her. The people who loved little Lacie Jo, the grandparents who are still here. The brother who mourns for her every single day and wants to know where his best little playmate is. He doesn't have anybody to watch cartoons with him, a little one. These are the things that go into why it is especially cruel, heinous, and atrocious, the burden that child will carry forever.

The jury sentenced Payne to death on each of the murder counts. The Supreme Court of Tennessee affirmed the conviction and sentence. ...

We granted certiorari ... to reconsider our holdings in *Booth* ... that the Eighth Amendment prohibits a capital sentencing jury from considering "victim impact" evidence relating to the personal characteristics of the victim and the emotional impact of the crimes on the victim's family. ...

Under our constitutional system, the primary responsibility for defining crimes against state law, fixing punishments for the commission of these crimes, and establishing procedures for criminal trials rests with the States. The state laws respecting crimes, punishments, and criminal procedure are of course subject to the overriding provisions of the United States Constitution. ...

Within the constitutional limitations defined in our cases, the States enjoy their traditional latitude to prescribe the method by which those who commit murder should be punished. ... The states remain free, in capital cases, as well as others, to devise new procedures and new remedies to meet felt needs. Victim impact evidence is simply another form or method of informing the sentencing authority about the specific harm caused by the crime in question, evidence of a general type long considered by sentencing authorities. [The] *Booth* Court was wrong in stating that this kind of evidence leads to the arbitrary imposition of the death penalty. In the majority of cases, and in this case, victim impact evidence serves entirely legitimate purposes. In the event that evidence is introduced that is so unduly prejudicial that it renders the trial fundamentally unfair, the Due Process Clause of the Fourteenth Amendment provides a mechanism for relief. ... Courts have always taken into consideration the harm done by the defendant in imposing sentence, and the evidence adduced in this case was illustrative of the harm caused by Payne's double murder.

We are now of the view that a State may properly conclude that for the jury to assess meaningfully the defendant's moral culpability and blameworthiness, it should have before it at the sentencing phase evidence of the specific harm caused by the defendant. "[T]he State has a legitimate interest in counteracting the mitigating evidence which the defendant is entitled to put in, by reminding the sentencer that just as the murderer should be considered an individual, so too the victim is an individual whose death represents a unique loss to society and in particular to his family." ... By turning the victim into a "faceless stranger at the penalty phase of a criminal trial" ... *Booth* deprives the State of the full moral force of its evidence and may prevent the jury from having before it all the information necessary to determine the proper punishment for a first-degree murder.

The present case is an example of the potential for such unfairness. The capital sentencing jury heard testimony from Payne's girlfriend that they met at church, that he was affectionate, caring, kind to her children ... . Payne's parents testified that he was a good son, and a clinical psychologist testified that Payne was an extremely polite prisoner and suffered from a low IQ. None of this testimony was related to the circumstances of Payne's brutal crimes. ... The Supreme Court of Tennessee in this case obviously felt the unfairness of the rule pronounced in *Booth* when it said "[i]t is an affront to the civilized members of the human race to say that at sentencing in a capital case, a parade of witnesses may praise the background, character and good deeds of the defendant (as was done in this case), without limitation as to relevancy, but nothing may be said that bears upon the character of, or the harm imposed, upon the victims." ...

We thus hold that if the State chooses to permit the admission of victim impact evidence and prosecutorial argument on that subject, the Eighth Amendment erects no per se bar.

§ 12.3 The Objectives of Punishment

You have already learned that the general goal of criminal law is to prevent behavior determined by society to be undesirable. The criminal justice system uses punishment as a prevention tool. Many theories support punishing criminal law violators. Although some people focus on one theory and use it as the basis for punishment, a more accurate approach, in this author's opinion, is to recognize that many theories have merit and that when a legislature establishes the range of punishment applicable to a particular crime, many theories were involved in motivating individual legislators. It is unlikely that every member of a legislature will be motivated by the same objective. It is also unlikely that an individual legislator will be motivated by one theory only. Rather, all of the following objectives influence legislative decision making to some degree.

Specific and General Deterrence

Specific deterrence seeks to **deter** individuals already convicted of crimes from committing crimes in the future. It is a negative reward theory. By punishing Mr. X for today's crime, we teach him that he will be disciplined for future criminal behavior. The arrest and conviction of an individual show that individual that society has the capability to detect crime and is willing to punish those who commit crimes.

General deterrence attempts to deter all members of society from engaging in criminal activity. In theory, when the public observes Mr. X being punished for his actions, the public is deterred from behaving similarly for fear of the same punishment. Of course, individuals will react differently to the knowledge of Mr. X's punishment. Individuals weigh the risk of being caught and the level of punishment against the benefit of committing the crime. All people do this at one time or another. Have you ever intentionally run a stoplight? Jaywalked? If so, you have made the decision to violate the law. Neither crime involves a severe penalty. That fact, in addition to the likelihood of not being discovered by law enforcement agents, probably affected your decision. Presumably, if conviction of either crime was punished by incarceration (time in jail), then the deterrent effect would be greater. Would you be as likely to jaywalk if you knew that you could spend time in jail for such an act? Some people would; others would not. It is safe to assume, however, that as the punishment increases, so does compliance. However, one author observed that it is not as effective to increase the punishment as it is to increase the likelihood of being punished.[7] It is unknown how much either of these factors influences behavior, but it is generally accepted that they both do.

Incapacitation

Incapacitation, also referred to as *restraint,* is the third purpose of criminal punishment. Incapacitation does not seek to deter criminal conduct by influencing people's choices, but prevents criminal conduct by restraining those who have committed crimes. Criminals who are restrained in jail or prison, or in the extreme, executed, are incapable of causing harm to the general public. This theory is often the rationale for long-term imprisonment of individuals who are believed to be beyond rehabilitation. It is also promoted by those who lack faith in rehabilitation and feel that all criminals should be removed from society to prevent the chance of repetition.

TERMS

deter To discourage; to prevent from acting.

Crimes that are caused by mental disease or occur in a moment of passion are not affected by deterrence theories, because the individual does not have the opportunity to consider the punishment that will be inflicted for committing the crime before it is committed. Deterrence theories are effective only for individuals who are sufficiently intelligent to understand the consequences of their actions, who are sane enough to understand the consequences of their actions, and who are not laboring under such uncontrollable feelings that an understanding that they may be punished is lost.

Rehabilitation

Rehabilitation is another purpose of punishing criminals. The theory of rehabilitation is that if the criminal is subjected to educational and vocational programs, treatment and counseling, and other measures, it is possible to alter the individual's behavior to conform to societal norms. Another author noted that:

> To the extent that crime is caused by elements of the offender's personality, educational defects, lack of work skills, and the like, we should be able to prevent him from committing more crimes by training, medical and psychiatric help, and guidance into law-abiding patterns of behavior. Strictly speaking, rehabilitation is not "punishment," but help to the offender. However, since this kind of help is frequently provided while the subject is in prison or at large on probation or parole under a sentence that carries some condemnation and some restriction of freedom, it is customary to list rehabilitation as one of the objects of a sentence in a criminal case.[8]

The concept of rehabilitation has come under considerable scrutiny in recent years, and the success of rehabilitative programs is questionable. However, the poor quality of prison rehabilitative programs may be the cause of the lack of success of these programs.

Retribution

Retribution, or societal vengeance, is the fifth purpose. Simply put, punishment through the criminal justice system is society's method of avenging a wrong. The idea that one who commits a wrong must be punished is an old one. The Old Testament speaks of an "eye for an eye." However, many people question the place of retribution in contemporary society. Is retribution consistent with American values? Jewish or Christian values? The question is actually moot, as there are few instances in which retribution stands alone as a reason for punishing someone who did not comply with the law. In most instances society's desire for revenge can be satisfied while fulfilling one of the other purposes of punishment, such as incapacitation.

It has also been asserted that public retribution prevents private retribution.[9] That is, when the victim (or anyone who might avenge a victim) of a crime knows that the offender has been punished, the victim's need to seek revenge is lessened or removed. Therefore, punishing those who harm others has the effect of promoting social order by preventing undesirable conduct by victims of crimes. Retribution in such instances has a deterrent effect, as victims of crimes are less likely to seek revenge. This is a good example of how the various purposes discussed are interrelated.

§ 12.4 Forms of Punishment

The legislature determines what type of sentence may be imposed; judges impose sentences.

Capital Punishment

Clearly the most controversial punishment is the death penalty. In early American history, capital punishment was commonly used. During the nineteenth century, use of the death penalty greatly declined. Today, more than half the states provide for the death penalty, and its use has regained popular support. Although the number of inmates actually executed every year is small, the number is increasing. (See Figure 12-1 for a sample death warrant.)

The contention that the death penalty is inherently cruel and unusual and therefore violative of the Eighth Amendment has been rejected. However, the Court has struggled, as have state courts and legislatures, with establishing standards for its use.

In *Furman v. Georgia,*[10] the Court held that the death penalty cannot be imposed under a sentencing procedure that creates a substantial risk of being implemented in an arbitrary manner. It found that Georgia's law permitted arbitrary decisions and so declared it void. *Furman* required that the sentencer's discretion be limited by objective standards to eliminate unfairness—specifically, to eliminate racial and other bias from death sentence decisions.

States responded to *Furman* in a variety of ways. Some chose to eliminate discretion entirely by mandating capital punishment for certain crimes. The Supreme Court invalidated mandatory capital punishment laws in *Locket v. Ohio.*[11] In *Locket* the Court held that individualized

FIGURE 12-1
Ted Bundy Death Warrant

DEATH WARRANT
STATE OF FLORIDA

WHEREAS, THEODORE ROBERT BUNDY, did on the 9th day of February, 1978, murder Kimberly Diane Leach; and

WHEREAS, THEODORE ROBERT BUNDY was found guilty of murder in the first degree and was sentenced to death on the 12th day of February, 1980; and

WHEREAS, the Florida Supreme Court upheld the sentence of death imposed upon THEODORE ROBERT BUNDY on the 9th day of May, 1985, and Certiorari was denied by the United States Supreme Court on the 14th day of October, 1986; and

WHEREAS, it has been determined that Executive Clemency, as authorized by Article IV, Section 8(a), Florida Constitution, is not appropriate; and

WHEREAS, attached hereto is a copy of the record pursuant to Section 922.09, Florida Statutes;

NOW, THEREFORE, I, BOB MARTINEZ, as Governor of the State of Florida and pursuant to the authority and responsibility vested by the Constitution and Laws of Florida do hereby issue this warrant directing the Superintendent of the Flórida State Prison to cause the sentence of death to be executed upon THEODORE ROBERT BUNDY on some day of the week beginning noon, Monday, the 23rd day of January, 1989 and ending noon, Monday, the day of 30th, 1989, in accord with the provisions of the laws of the State of Florida.

IN TESTIMONY WHEREOF, I have hereunto set my hand and caused the Great Seal of the State of Florida to be affixed at Tallahassee, the Capitol, this 17th day of January, 1989.

GOVERNOR

ATTEST:

SECRETARY OF STATE

sentencing was constitutionally required. The Court stated that any law prohibiting a sentencer from considering "as a mitigating factor, any aspect of a defendant's character or record and any circumstances of the offense that the defendant proffers as a basis for a sentence less than death" creates an unconstitutional risk that the "death penalty will be imposed in spite of factors which may call for a less severe penalty."[12]

However, Georgia's new death penalty legislation was upheld in *Gregg v. Georgia.*[13] The new law provided that the jury must find, in a sentencing hearing separate from the trial, an aggravating circumstance before the death penalty could be imposed. The statute enumerated possible aggravating circumstances. By requiring a jury to find an aggravating circumstance, arbitrariness is believed to be lessened.

Furman, Gregg, Locket, and their progeny stand for the principle that a sentencing statute cannot totally eliminate discretion, nor grant so much discretion that the death penalty can be imposed arbitrarily. These concepts of individualized sentencing and minimized discretion in sentencing are somewhat antithetical. The Supreme Court itself recognizes that a tension exists between the two goals and has struggled to establish procedures and standards to successfully implement them. "Experience has shown that the consistency and rationality promised in *Furman* are inversely related to the fairness owed the individual when considering a sentence of death. A step toward consistency is a step away from fairness."[14]

The death penalty issue has been divisive to the Court. Some Justices have so strongly believed that the death penalty is unconstitutional (either inherently or as administered) that they have refused to acquiesce to notions of *stare decisis* on the issue. Justice Thurgood Marshall, for example, dissented in every capital punishment case, including both denials of petitions of certiorari and cases under review, because of his firmly held belief that capital punishment was unconstitutional.

Until 1994, Justice Blackmun held that the death penalty was not inherently unconstitutional. However, in *Callins v. Collins*, he made the following statement:

> Courts are in the very business of erecting procedural devices from which fair, equitable, and reliable outcomes are presumed to flow. Yet, in the death penalty area, this Court, in my view, had engaged in a futile effort to balance these constitutional demands, and now is retreating not only from the *Furman* promise of consistency and rationality, but from the requirement of individualized sentencing as well. Having virtually conceded that both fairness and rationality cannot be achieved in the administration of the death penalty ... the Court has chosen to deregulate the entire enterprise, replacing, it would seem, substantive constitutional requirements with mere aesthetics, and abdicating its statutorily and constitutionally imposed duty to provide meaningful judicial oversight to the administration of death by the States.

> From this date forward, I no longer shall tinker with the machinery of death. For more than 20 years I have endeavored—indeed, I have struggled—along with a majority of this Court, to develop procedural and substantive rules that would lend more than the mere appearance of fairness to the death penalty endeavor. Rather than continue to coddle the Court's delusion that the desired level of fairness has been achieved and the need for regulation eviscerated, I feel morally and intellectually obligated simply to concede that the death penalty experiment has failed. It is virtually self-evident to me now that no combination of procedural rules or substantive regulations ever can save the death penalty from its inherent constitutional deficiencies. The basic question—does the system accurately and consistently determine which defendants "deserve" to die?—cannot be answered in the affirmative. It is not simply that this Court has allowed vague aggravating circumstances to be employed ... relevant mitigating evidence to be disregarded ... and vital judicial review to be blocked. ... The problem is that the inevitability of factual, legal, and moral error gives us a system that we know must wrongly kill some defendants, a system that fails to deliver the fair, consistent, and reliable sentences of death required by the Constitution. ... Perhaps one day this Court will develop procedural rules or verbal formulas that actually will provide consistency, fairness, and reliability in a capital-sentencing scheme. I am not optimistic that such a day will come. I am more optimistic, though, that this Court eventually will conclude that the effort to eliminate arbitrariness while preserving fairness "in the infliction of [death] is so plainly doomed to failure that it—and the death penalty—must be abandoned altogether." ... I may not live to see that day, but I have faith that eventually it will arrive. The path the Court has chosen lessens us all. I dissent.[15]

One of the decisions of the Court that bothered Justice Blackmun was *McCleskey v. Kemp,*[16] wherein the Court refused to set aside a death sentence even though the defendant presented reliable statistical data supporting the conclusion that race continues to be a significant factor in the application of capital punishment. The Court held that statistical evidence could not be used to invalidate an entire sentencing scheme; rather, the burden falls on each individual defendant to prove that race was a factor in his or her sentence. Justice Blackmun argued that the Court was thereby abandoning the *Furman* requirement of consistency and rationality.

Capital Punishment in the United States

In 1993, thirty-six states and the federal government permitted capital punishment. Alaska, Hawaii, Iowa, Kansas, Maine, Massachusetts, Michigan, Minnesota, New York, North Dakota, Rhode Island, Vermont, West Virginia, and Wisconsin were the states without the death penalty. Also, there was no death penalty in the District of Columbia.

By the end of 1993, there were 2,716 people awaiting execution. Hundreds of new inmates sentenced to death are added to the total every year. A total of thirty-eight were executed in 1993, the largest number since the Supreme Court reinstated capital punishment in 1976. Texas executed the most (seventeen). The next closest was Virginia, where five inmates were executed. Between 1977 and 1992, 226 executions took place in the United States. Since 1930, 4,085 persons have been executed by the states and federal government, in addition to 160 executed by the military during that period.

Electrocution and lethal injection are the primary methods of execution, but state laws also provide for gassing, hanging, and firing squad. Among prisoners executed between 1977 and 1992, the average time between imposition of the most recent sentence and the execution was seven years and ten months. However, the length of time appears to be increasing. The average length of time for the inmates executed in 1993 was more than nine years.

Source: Capital Punishment 1993 (Bureau of Justice Statistics, December 1994).

The definition of cruelty is an evolving concept. Electrocution, lethal injection, hanging, and shooting are all approved methods of executing a prisoner. Other methods, such as starvation, would not pass constitutional muster.

The Eighth Amendment has been interpreted to prohibit sentences that are disproportionate to the crime committed. In this vein, the Supreme Court has held that capital punishment may not be imposed for the crime of raping an adult woman.[17] Similarly, a person may not be put to death for aiding in a felony that results in murder, unless there was an intent to kill.[18]

In 1986, the Supreme Court stated that defendants who are incapable of understanding why they are being executed because of insanity may not be executed until they regain their faculties.[19]

SIDEBAR

Executive Clemency, Pardons, and Reprieves

In most states and the federal government, the chief executive (i.e., the governor or the president) possesses several powers concerning criminal convictions and sentences. One such power is executive clemency. To forgive or, more commonly, to reduce a punishment is clemency. To reduce a prisoner's sentence from death to life imprisonment is clemency. The reduction of a sentence is also known as **commutation of sentence.** Commutation is used when the executive believes a person guilty, but also believes the sentence is too harsh. In 1993 the Supreme Court ruled that prisoners sentenced to death who claim to have new evidence of their

TERMS

commutation of sentence The substitution of a less severe punishment for a more severe punishment.

innocence do not possess the right to federal review in all instances. The Court indicated that executive clemency is the "fail-safe" to guard against unwarranted executions.

The **pardon** is similar to commutation of sentence in that both relieve a person of punishment. However, the pardon is different in one important respect: it also relieves the defendant of the conviction. With the pardon, the conviction is erased and treated as though it never occurred. Pardons are used when the executive believes there was an error concerning the defendant's guilt.

Finally, a **reprieve** is a stay or delay of execution of sentence. Reprieves are used to give the executive or a court the opportunity to further review the case.

The governor has the sole authority to grant clemency in thirty-one states. In ten states, clemency boards have the final authority. In seven states, clemency boards make recommendations to their respective governors. In Rhode Island, the governor can grant clemency only with the consent of that state's senate.

Sources: Janice Brown, "Note: The Quality of Mercy," 40 *U.C.L.A. L. Rev.* 327 (1992), citing Deborah Leavy, "Note, A Matter of Life or Death: Due Process Protection in Capital Clemency Proceedings," 90 *Yale L.J.* 889, 895–96 (1981).

Corporal/Physical Punishment

The Eighth Amendment limits the use of physical punishment. Punishment is not, however, unconstitutional simply because it involves pain. The issue is whether the pain is excessive. Pain is excessive when it exceeds the quantity necessary to achieve a legitimate penological purpose, such as rehabilitation or retribution. Generally, hard labor is not per se cruel.[20] If the labor is beyond the physical limits of the inmate, or involves unnecessary pain, it is unconstitutional.

Whipping has been held both constitutional[21] and unconstitutional[22] by lower courts. The Supreme Court has not decided the issue.[23]

Solitary confinement may be used in some circumstances, such as when a prisoner is disruptive or is highly dangerous. The use of prolonged solitary confinement for other prisoners is of questionable constitutionality.

The basic medical and nutritional needs of inmates must be satisfied by the government. Deliberately disregarding the medical or nutritional

TERMS

pardon An act of grace by the chief executive of the government, ... relieving a person of the legal consequences of a crime of which he or she has been convicted. A pardon erases the conviction.

reprieve The postponement of the carrying out of a sentence. A reprieve is not a commutation of sentence; it is merely a delay.

needs of inmates, or in some other manner imposing cruel or unusual punishment, can lead to liability under 42 U.S.C. § 1983.

The Supreme Court has said that the Eighth Amendment is to be interpreted consistent with society's evolving standards of decency. Therefore, although some courts have approved sterilization, and many states are considering chemical castration of men who commit sexual assault, there is a possibility that such practices could be found inconsistent with the Eighth Amendment.

Incarceration

Restraint is an effective method of dealing with dangerous persons. Incarceration serves this purpose, and in some cases the offender is also rehabilitated. Regrettably, because rehabilitation is rare and (contrary to popular belief) prison conditions are often poor, many offenders leave prison angry, no more educated or employable, and occasionally more dangerous.

Nevertheless, incarceration continues to be the most common method of punishing violent offenders. Offenders may be committed to prisons, camps, or local jails. Those sentenced to short terms (one year or less) are usually housed in a local jail. Individuals sentenced to longer terms are committed to prisons.

§ 12.5 Sentencing

Indeterminate and Determinate Sentencing

The **indeterminate** sentence gives corrections officials the greatest amount of control over an inmate's sentence. Under an indeterminate sentence, the judge sets a minimum and maximum period to be served and the corrections agency determines the actual date of release. Once common in the United States, indeterminate sentencing has fallen into disfavor.

TERMS

indeterminate sentence A prison sentence that is for no less than a minimum period and no more than a maximum period, its exact duration to be determined by the prison or parole authorities based upon behavior in prison or similar considerations.

In **determinate sentencing** schemes, the sentencing judge is given discretion to set a fixed sentence from within a range set by the legislature. The determinate sentence is fixed and there is no possibility of early release.

Definite and Indefinite Sentencing

Unlike determinate sentencing, with definite sentencing the sentencing judge has no discretion. Rather, the legislature establishes the specific penalty to be imposed for each crime and there is no possibility of early release. Definite sentencing reduces sentencing disparity. However, it is criticized for not allowing the particular facts of each case to be taken into consideration.

Indefinite sentencing incorporates both judicial and corrections agency discretion. It is the antithesis of definite sentencing. The sentencing judge is given a range from which to impose sentence and the corrections agency is delegated the authority to grant early releases.

Presumptive Sentencing

In many instances, when a legislature gives the sentencing judge discretion, it also establishes a *presumptive sentence*. That is, the legislature states what sentence should be imposed from within a range, absent **aggravating** or **mitigating circumstances**. Circumstances upon which the judge relies to increase the presumptive sentence are aggravating; those used to justify a sentence below a presumption are mitigating.

If a judge deviates from a presumptive sentence, the aggravating or mitigating circumstances justifying the departure must be made part of the record. For example, an assault statute may call for one to three years' punishment with a presumptive sentence of eighteen months. If the judge sentences the defendant to more or less than eighteen months, the reasons must be reflected on the record. Of course, even

TERMS

determinate sentence 1. A sentence whose duration is set by statute and cannot be reduced by a parole board based upon apparent rehabilitation, behavior in prison, or other considerations. 2. A sentence whose duration is set by statute and can be modified by the sentencing judge only in very special circumstances.

aggravating circumstances Acts or conduct which increase the seriousness of a criminal act or the gravity of its effect. Courts often impose more severe sentences when there are aggravating circumstances.

mitigating circumstances Circumstances that lessen blame or reduce the degree of civil or criminal responsibility.

when deviating from a presumption, the sentencing judge must remain within the statutory limits.

What constitutes an aggravating or mitigating circumstance is often expressed in the statute. Examples of aggravating circumstances are: injury, torture, or death of the victim; use of a weapon during commission of the crime; whether the crime involved a child; and whether the defendant violated a trust. Examples of mitigating circumstances are: physical disability of the defendant; the defendant's having dependents; a crime committed in a nonviolent manner; and the defendant's acting in good faith.

Suspended Imposition of Sentence

For some misdemeanors and infractions, judges are sometimes permitted to *suspend imposition of sentence* (SIS), also known as *diversion*. SIS is one of many forms of community-based correction, a term that refers to several varieties of nonincarceration correctional programs, such as probation, restitution, halfway houses, and parole. (Some of these other forms of community-based correction are discussed later.)

SIS is different from suspended sentencing. In SIS, a judge not only withholds sentencing the defendant, but also refrains from entering a judgment of conviction until some future date. If the defendant complies with imposed conditions until that date, the prosecution is dismissed and the defendant is freed from having a criminal record. Suspended sentences, in contrast, involve conviction and imposition of sentence, but the defendant is relieved of actually serving the sentence so long as conditions are satisfied.

Where available, SIS is usually limited to nonviolent misdemeanors and infractions and is available to first-time offenders only.

Concurrent and Consecutive Sentencing

If a defendant is already serving a sentence for another crime, or is convicted of two related crimes, the sentencing judge may impose **concurrent** or **consecutive sentences.** If two sentences are concurrent, it is said that they "run together." That is, a defendant who receives two

TERMS

concurrent sentences Two or more sentences of imprisonment for crime in which the time of each is to run during the same period as the others, and not consecutively.

consecutive sentences Sentences of imprisonment for crimes in which the time of each is to run one after the other without a break.

five-year sentences will actually spend five years incarcerated. If the sentences are consecutive, the defendant will spend a total of ten years incarcerated.

Parole

After committing a defendant to a correctional institution, the judge loses control and responsibility over that defendant, unless a statute provides otherwise. In many states, parole is available to prison inmates. **Parole**, an early release from prison, is used to encourage inmates to stay out of trouble and engage in rehabilitative efforts while in prison. Parole decisions are made by corrections officials (i.e., a parole board). Similar to probation, an offender must comply with certain conditions while on parole. Conditions routinely include not possessing a gun; not contacting witnesses, judge, jurors, or prosecutors associated with the offender's conviction; and not becoming involved in further criminal activity. Violation of a condition of parole may result in recommitment to prison.

Parole has fallen into disfavor in recent years. The result has been to limit the availability of parole in many situations. Parole has been eliminated for those convicted of crimes against the United States.

The Federal Guidelines

In November 1987, the Federal Sentencing Guidelines became effective. The guidelines are a milestone in federal criminal law. Their purpose is twofold: (1) to reduce sentencing disparity and (2) to achieve "honesty in sentencing."[24] Prior to the Guidelines, judges were given a large penalty range from which a defendant could be sentenced. The result of this discretion was that defendants similarly situated were often sentenced very differently. One goal of the Guidelines is to reduce such disparity in sentencing.

TERMS

parole The release of a person from imprisonment after serving a portion of his or her sentence, provided he or she complies with certain conditions. Such conditions vary, depending upon the case, but they generally include stipulations such as not associating with known criminals, not possessing firearms, and not leaving the jurisdiction without the permission of the parole officer. Parole is not an act of clemency; it does not set aside the sentence. The parolee remains in the legal custody of the state and under the control of her parole officer [and] may be returned to prison if he or she breaches the specified conditions. However, due process requires that parole cannot be revoked without a hearing.

The second goal, honesty in sentencing, concerns parole. Prior to the Guidelines, defendants could be released on parole, in some cases, after only one-third of the imposed sentence had been served. In addition, prisoners complained that parole was arbitrarily and inconsistently applied. Accordingly, Congress eliminated parole, and the guidelines now reflect the time that will be served, less fifty-four days of good time that may be earned yearly (after the first year).

To achieve the first goal—the reduction of sentencing disparity—the Guidelines greatly limit the discretion of the judge in sentencing. To determine what sentence should be imposed, the offender's criminal history category and offense level must be determined. The criminal history category is simply determined by the number of prior convictions of the offender.

Finding an offender's offense level is more complex. First, the crime is assigned a base offense number. That number is then increased by "specific offense characteristics." Adjustments to this figure are then made for mitigating or aggravating circumstances. This final figure is the offense level.

Once the criminal history category and offense level are determined, the court looks to the sentencing table. This table provides a small range (the top figure never exceeds 25 percent of the bottom figure) from which the judge is to sentence the defendant. Only in rare instances may a judge deviate from the proscribed sentencing range.

The Guidelines continue to permit judges to suspend sentences to probation for offenses at the low end of the sentencing table. For offenses just above the probation cutoff, judges may sentence an offender to probation, provided some form of confinement is ordered, such as house arrest or community confinement. There is also a third layer of offenses for which the judge may order a "split sentence." This is where one-half or more of the sentence must be served in prison, and the remaining amount may be served in another form of confinement.

SIDEBAR

A Sentencing Story

Sentencing a defendant today is much different from years ago, as evidenced by the following sentence imposed upon a defendant in the Federal District of the Territory of New Mexico. The sentence was imposed by a United States judge, sitting in Taos, in an adobe stable used as a temporary courtroom.

"Jose Manuel Miguel Xavier Gonzales, in a few short weeks it will be spring. The snows of winter will flee away, the ice will vanish, and the air will become soft and balmy. In short, Jose Manuel Miguel Xavier Gonzales, the annual miracle of the year's awakening will come to pass—but you won't be here.

"The rivulet will run its purling course to the sea, the timid desert flowers will put forth their tender roots, the glorious valleys of this imperial domain will blossom as the rose—still you won't be here to see.

"From every treetop some wild woods songster will carol his mating song, butterflies will sport in the sunshine, the busy bee will hum happily as it pursues its accustomed vocation, the gentle breeze will tease the tassels of the wild grasses, and all nature—Jose Manuel Miguel Xavier Gonzales—will be glad but you. You won't be here to enjoy it because I command the sheriff or some other officer or officers of this country to lead you out to some remote spot, swing you by the neck from a nodding bough of some sturdy oak, and let you hang until you are dead.

"And then, Jose Manuel Miguel Xavier Gonzales, I further command that such officer or officers retire quickly from your dangling corpse, that the vultures may descend from the heavens upon your filthy body, until nothing shall remain but the bare, bleaching bones of a cold-blooded, copper-colored, blood-thirsty, throat-cutting, sheep-herding, murdering son of a bitch."

The Guidelines have been the subject of much controversy. Federal judges themselves have been very critical of the Guidelines. Many contend that the reason judges are complaining is simply their loss of authority. Though this may be true, there also appear to be problems caused by the rigidity of the Guidelines.

The drafters of the Guidelines knew that all factors which should be considered in sentencing could not be anticipated (or quantified). As such, provisions are made permitting deviation from the Guidelines. However, deviation is rarely permitted. This has led to some absurd results. For example, one twenty-one-year-old honor student, with no prior record, was sentenced to ten years in prison for his involvement in one drug transaction.[25] At least one federal district judge has resigned because of dissatisfaction with the guidelines. Whether the guidelines will become more flexible remains to be seen.

The federal government was not the first to enact guideline sentencing. At least two states, Minnesota and Washington, were using guidelines when the federal version became law. It is probable that more jurisdictions will contemplate similar reform in the future.

Prisons in the United States

Lack of space in United States prisons is an ever-increasing concern. Most prisons are overcrowded, often housing double or triple the intended capacity; this leads to serious problems for both prison administrators and inmates. If prison conditions are extremely bad, an inmate may succeed in an Eighth Amendment lawsuit against prison authorities.

The total number of state and federal prisoners reached a record high of 948,881 in 1993. In 1989, the number was approximately 700,000. Since 1980, the number of prisoners has increased 188 percent; the growth from 1992 to 1993 was 7.4 percent. During that year, the rate of increase in number of federal prisoners was greater than that of state prisoners (13.2 percent versus 7 percent).

Increases in imprisonment of women and blacks continue to outpace that of men and Caucasians. Incarceration for drug offenses is increasing more than any other crime. Stiffer penalties and mandatory prison time for drug cases are largely responsible for the increase in the federal system. In 1980, 22.7 percent of the federal prison population consisted of drug offenders. By 1990, this group made up 47.8 percent of the federal inmate population.

These numbers do not capture the total story, however. Many persons are also housed in local jails, which also suffer from overcrowding. In 1992, an average of 445,000 persons were committed to jail. Nationwide, jails were at 99 percent of rated inmate capacity.

A stunning 1 in 428 persons are in jail on any given day. Blacks constitute 44 percent of jail population; whites, 40 percent; Hispanics, 15 percent; and others, 1 percent. These figures do not include combined prison-jail systems used in Alaska, Connecticut, Delaware, Hawaii, Rhode Island, and Vermont, nor commitments to drunk tanks and other facilities that hold inmates for less than forty-eight hours.

Source: Jail Inmates (Bureau of Justice Statistics, Aug. 1993); *Prisoners in 1993* (Bureau of Justice Statistics, June 1994).

Probation and Revocation

A popular alternative to incarceration is probation (also known as a **suspended sentence**). Probation is not always an alternative and is rarely available for crimes that are punished with life imprisonment or death. While on probation, the defendant is released from custody, but must comply with conditions imposed by the court during the probationary period. Each defendant is placed under the supervision of a probation officer during this period. The probation officer is an officer of the court, not of the corrections system.

Typical conditions of probation include a requirement of steady employment, refraining from other unlawful conduct, not carrying a firearm or other weapon, and not leaving the jurisdiction of the court. A judge may tailor conditions to fit the circumstances of each case. For example, a child molester may be prohibited from obtaining employment that requires working around children.

Some judges make consent to search by a probation officer a condition of probation. This may include search of the person as well as property. In some cases, judges impose the search requirement independently; in others, the defendant and prosecutor stipulate to the searches through a plea agreement. In either situation, are there limits to this authority? May a probation officer search a probationer at any time, in any manner, and without any cause to believe that mischief is afoot? Further, can a defendant who is facing incarceration as an

TERMS

suspended sentence A sentence imposed after conviction of a crime, the carrying out of which is stayed.

alternative give meaningful consent to such a condition? This is the subject of the *Consuelo-Gonzalez* case, in which the court decided that probationers are entitled to full Fourth Amendment protection as to law enforcement officers generally. Searches by police officers of probationers must satisfy the usual Fourth Amendment requirements.

UNITED STATES
v.
CONSUELO-GONZALEZ
521 F.2d 259 (9th Cir. 1975)

Consuelo-Gonzalez appeals from a conviction under 21 USC §§ 841(a)(1) for possession of heroin with intent to distribute. We reverse.

Between November 15, 1972, and December 18, 1972, agents of the Federal Bureau of Narcotics and Dangerous Drugs received information from four different sources that Virginia Consuelo-Gonzalez was actively engaged in the importation and sale of heroin. A check of the records at the United States Attorney's Office on December 12, 1972, revealed to the agents that Virginia Consuelo-Gonzalez had previously been convicted of heroin smuggling under the name of Virginia Cardenas and was currently on probation. At this time, the agents were also apprised that it was a condition of Consuelo-Gonzalez's probation that she submit her person and property to search at any time upon request by a law enforcement officer. On December 14, 1972, an independent verification was made of the fact that Virginia Cardenas and Virginia Consuelo-Gonzalez were one and the same person; and on December 19, 1972, the agents reconfirmed the probationary status and condition that she submit to search.

On the morning of December 19, 1992, ... federal and local law enforcement officers approached the Consuelo-Gonzalez residence for purposes of conducting a search of the premises. When they arrived, they found the front door of the house ajar. The agents knocked on the door and waited for Consuelo-Gonzalez to appear. When she did so, the lead agent showed her his identification, informed her that he was aware of her probation and the conditions which had been attached to it, and indicated his intention to enter the residence and conduct a search. Consuelo-Gonzalez responded to his request by stepping back and saying "Sure, search my purse." Upon entering the house, the lead agent made a cursory search of her handbag to determine whether it contained weapons. None were found. The handbag was then placed beside a chair in which Consuelo-Gonzalez was asked to sit.

A thorough search of Consuelo-Gonzalez's person and residence was then commenced. In the bedroom, the agents found a narcotics injection outfit in a dresser; and on a shelf in the living room they discovered a paper sack containing a bundle of notebook papers with brown debris on them. Both of these items were seized. A second search of Consuelo-Gonzalez's handbag revealed two coin purses, inside of which the agents found two white paper bundles and seven rubber condoms containing a total of 11.7 grams of brown powder, later proven to be heroin. This evidence was also seized, and subsequently used to provide the basis for the present conviction.

In a timely and appropriate manner, counsel for Consuelo-Gonzalez moved to suppress this evidence. However, the trial judge denied the motion to suppress, relying specifically upon the authorization to search which had been made a condition of the probation ... . Thereafter, defendant was found guilty of possession of heroin with intent to distribute ... .

In this appeal, defendant asserts that the trial court erred in failing to suppress the evidence on the ground that the condition of probation requiring her to "submit to search of her person or property at any time when requested by a law-enforcement" officer was improper and thus could not serve to make the search lawful. It is argued that the Fourth Amendment requires this result.

While we are not prepared to embrace the full reach of defendant's argument, we do believe that the condition employed in the instant case is not in keeping with the purposes intended to be served by the Federal Probation Act. It is our view that, even though the trial judge has very broad discretion in fixing the terms and conditions of probation, such terms must be reasonably related to the purposes of the Act. In determining whether a reasonable relationship exists, we have found it necessary to give consideration to the purposes sought to be served by probation, the extent to which the full constitutional guarantees available to those not under probation should be accorded probationers, and the legitimate needs of law enforcement. Having done so, we have concluded that Consuelo-Gonzalez could have been required to submit her person and property to search by a probation officer. We have further concluded that any search made pursuant to the condition included in the terms of probation must necessarily meet the Fourth Amendment's standard of reasonableness. ...

Although it is doubtful that any formulation of a condition relating to the search of a probationer's person or property can be drafted that will provide unambiguous guidance to both the probationer and the probation officer, it is suggested that the following condition would properly reflect the views expressed herein:

> That she submit to search of her person or property conducted in a reasonable manner and at a reasonable time by a probation officer.

... [W]e hold that the search in this case was improper and that the motion to suppress should have been granted. ...

The guiding principle which has emerged in construing the Probation Act is that the only permissible conditions are those that, when considered in context, can reasonably be said to contribute significantly both to the rehabilitation of the convicted person and to the protection of the public. ...

This guiding interpretive principle plainly suggests the manner in which the Act's administration should be accommodated to the constitutional guarantees of the Bill of Rights. While it must be recognized that probationers, like parolees and prisoners, properly are subject to limitations from which ordinary persons are free, it is also true that these limitations in the aggregate must serve the ends of probation. ... [I]t is necessary to recognize that when fundamental rights are curbed it must be done sensitively and with a keen appreciation that the infringement must serve the broad purposes of the Probation Act. This burden cannot be avoided by asserting either that the probationer has voluntarily waived his rights by not objecting in a proper manner to the conditions imposed upon him or that he must accept any condition the court "deems best" as a consequence of being "in custody."

Turning to the Fourth Amendment rights that Consuelo-Gonzalez insists were infringed, two things are obvious. The first is that some forms of search by probation officers are not only compatible with rehabilitation, but, with respect to those convicted of certain offenses such as possession and distribution of narcotics, are also essential to the proper functioning of a probationary system. The second is that the condition imposed on Consuelo-Gonzalez literally permits searches which could not possibly serve the ends of probation. For example, an intimidating and harassing search to serve law enforcement ends totally unrelated to either her prior conviction or her rehabilitation is authorized by the terms of the condition. Submission to such searches should not be the price of probation. A probationer, like the parolee, has the right to enjoy a significant degree of privacy. ...

Probation authorities also have a special and unique interest in invading the privacy of probationers. This special and unique interest does not extend to law enforcement officers generally. ... Inasmuch as the search of Consuelo-Gonzalez's residence and handbag occurred neither during the course of a probation visit by a probation officer nor pursuant to a proper warrant, the evidence must be suppressed.

... [I]t may well be necessary during the course of a probation visit to conduct a pat-down search for weapons or contraband, to examine the probationer's arms to ascertain whether drugs are being used, or take the probationer into custody. When done reasonably and humanely by probation officers, no question concerning the appropriateness of their actions should arise. Moreover, a thorough search of a probationer's residence incident to, or following, a probation visit is not dependent upon the establishment of probable cause. A reasonable belief on the part of the probation officer that such a search is necessary to perform properly his duties is sufficient. As we said [in a prior case], this belief may be based on a "hunch" having its origin in what the probation officer has learned or observed about the behavior and attitude of the probationer.

Probationers are also protected by the Fourth Amendment's reasonableness requirement in regard to searches by probation officers. However, the standards are lowered, as the public has a greater interest in searching the probationer and the probationer has a lessened expectation of privacy. Also, probation officers do have a penal objective; in fact, they should have the welfare of their probationers in mind.

Therefore, probation officers may search a probationer's person or property with reasonable grounds; no warrant is required, although the search must be conducted in a reasonable manner. These conclusions have also been reached by the Supreme Court.[26] As a condition of probation, a search condition must be reasonably related to the probation, or it is invalid. Therefore, if a person is convicted of embezzlement, a condition providing for searches of the person would be unreasonable. The result would, of course, be different if the offense were possession of a firearm or drugs.

Finally, any other condition of probation that encroaches upon a constitutional guarantee is suspect. For example, a condition that restricts free speech is unconstitutional in most circumstances.[27] However, the right to travel freely and to bear arms are examples of constitutionally preserved rights that are commonly restricted during probation and parole.

A defendant who violates a condition of probation may be disciplined. Generally, the decision about whether any action should be taken for a violation is made by the probation officer. If a violation is extreme, the probation officer may file a petition to revoke probation. The sentencing court then holds a **revocation hearing**. If granted, the defendant is taken off probation and incarcerated.

TERMS

revocation hearing The due process hearing required before the government can revoke a privilege it has previously granted.

At the revocation hearing, the defendant may be entitled to counsel. As a general rule, the right is not found in the Sixth Amendment, as the "critical stages" of trial have passed. In one rare case, the Supreme Court held that a Sixth Amendment right to counsel did exist at a revocation hearing. In *Mempa v. Rhay,*[28] the trial judge withheld sentencing, placed the defendant on probation, and did not pronounce sentence until after the defendant violated his probation and then had it revoked. Because the revocation hearing turned out to be the defendant's sentencing hearing, where there is a right to counsel under the Sixth Amendment, the Court found that the Sixth Amendment applied.

The due process clauses of the Fifth and Fourteenth Amendments may also provide a right to counsel at a revocation hearing. If a substantial question of law or fact must be resolved at the hearing, counsel must be appointed for the indigent defendant so that the issues can be fully explored and developed. If revocation is obvious, though, counsel need not be allowed.

Community Service

One alternative to incarceration for nonviolent offenders is community service. In such a program, a defendant's sentence is suspended and the completion of a stated number of community service hours is a condition of the defendant's probation.

In most instances, the probation officer works with the probationer to find an appropriate job. However, the judge may require that a specific job be performed.

The requirements of community service range from unskilled to professional. For example, a judge may require that a professional, such as a physician or attorney, work in a clinic that provides services to the poor. The same person may be expected to pick up trash from local roads. Clearly, the former makes best use of the defendant's skills and benefits the community the most.

Restitution

The purpose of restitution is to compensate the victim, not to punish the offender. As such, restitution is not a substitute for other forms of punishment.

Restitution is limited to the actual amounts resulting from the offenses convicted.[29] Said another way, restitution is limited to losses resulting from the specific conduct that formed the basis of the conviction.[30] However, an agreement between the government and the defendant to pay a higher amount may be constitutional.[31]

Restitution may be made a condition of probation. A probationer's refusal to pay restitution can result in a revocation of probation. However, when a fine or restitution is imposed as a condition of probation, and "the probationer has made all reasonable efforts to pay ... yet cannot do so through no fault of his own, it is fundamentally unfair to revoke probation automatically without considering whether adequate alternative methods of punishing the defendant are available."[32]

Fines

Different from restitution, the purpose of a fine is to punish the offender. Accordingly, restitution monies are paid to victims and fines end up in the public treasury. Fines are a very common method of punishing misdemeanants. Serious crimes are frequently punished with both a fine and incarceration. Any fine imposed must be reasonable, that is, the amount must be within the financial means of the offender. Excessive fines are prohibited by the Eighth Amendment.

It is a violation of equal protection to sentence individuals without means to pay a fine to longer periods of incarceration than those who can pay a fine. In *Williams v. Illinois,*[33] a defendant was sentenced to a maximum one year in prison and a $500 fine for petty theft. Illinois statute provided that if at the end of the year, the fine (and court costs) were not paid, the defendant was to remain in jail for a time to satisfy the debt. This was calculated at $5.00 per day. The Court found that because Williams was indigent, the statute violated the equal protection clause by improperly sentencing defendants according to economic status. Of course, a defendant who has the financial means to pay a fine, and does not, may have probation revoked or incarceration increased.

Forfeiture

Forfeitures are similar to fines, in that they involve the taking of property and money to punish defendants. A forfeiture is, however, not directed at the defendant's pocketbook in general, as is a fine. Rather, forfeiture focuses on taking the property owned by a defendant that is in some manner connected with the crimes. Automobiles, airplanes, or boats used to transport drugs are an example. Forfeiture has become an increasingly popular tool amongst law enforcement agencies.

Procedurally, forfeiture may occur within and as part of a criminal proceeding. In addition, many laws permit forfeiture to occur in a separative in rem civil proceeding. Most statutes allow law enforcement officers to make seizures based upon probable cause, to be immediately followed by the filing of a forfeiture proceeding.[34] Of course, seizure can also occur later in the proceedings. Under federal law, if a seizure was proper (i.e., based upon probable cause), the burden of proof falls on a claimant to establish that the property is not subject to seizure. The claimant must prove this by a preponderance of the evidence.[35]

Under federal law, forfeiture is provided for in several instances, including violations of the Racketeer Influenced and Corrupt Organizations Act (RICO) and under the so-called drug kingpin statute, the Continuing Criminal Enterprise law.[36]

There are limits to the use of forfeiture. In *United States v. James Daniel Good Real Property,*[37] the Supreme Court determined that the due process clause requires the government to provide notice and a preseizure hearing when it intends to forfeit real property, unless exigent circumstances justify an immediate seizure. There is no requirement of preseizure notice in cases where property can disappear. The Court stated that in cases where property is movable, immediate seizure, without notice or a hearing, is necessary to "establish the court's jurisdiction over the property" and to guard against someone absconding with the property.

A critical issue concerns the relationship between the crime and the property forfeited. Forfeiture of all property associated with a crime can be troubling. Forfeiting a boat that was purchased with drug money and is used to transport drugs from Colombia to the United States is not problematic. But is it constitutionally sound to forfeit a home because one joint of marijuana is discovered inside? Does the Eighth Amendment's Excessive Fines Clause limit the use of forfeitures? In *Austin*, the Supreme Court examined this issue.

The *Austin* Court held that the Eighth Amendment's excessive fines clause applies to civil in rem forfeiture proceedings. Accordingly, a forfeiture must be proportional to the offense. A fine or forfeiture that is grossly larger than the underlying offense is excessive and violative of the Eighth Amendment.

Similarly, even though forfeiture may be characterized as civil, the exclusionary rule applies to bar illegally seized evidence in quasi-criminal forfeiture cases.[38] This is contrary to the rule that the exclusionary rule is not applied in civil and administrative cases.

Modern Sentencing Alternatives

In recent years, many new alternatives to incarceration have been developed. Such alternatives are actually forms of probation, and, as such, are administered by courts and probation officers.

For the nonviolent criminal, work release is an alternative. While in these programs the offender lives in a jail, but is permitted to leave jail to work. Work release has many advantages. The defendant continues

AUSTIN
v.
UNITED STATES
113 S. Ct. 2801 (1993)

In this case, we are asked to decide whether the Excessive Fines Clause of the Eighth Amendment applies to forfeitures of property under 21 U.S.C. §§ 881(a)(4) and (a)(7). We hold that it does and therefore remand the case for consideration of the question whether the forfeiture at issue here was excessive.

On August 2, 1990, petitioner Richard Lyle Austin was indicted on four counts of violating South Dakota's drug laws. Austin ultimately pleaded guilty to one count of possessing cocaine with intent to distribute and was sentenced by the state court to seven years' imprisonment. On September 7, the United States filed an in rem action in the United States District Court for the District of South Dakota seeking forfeiture of Austin's mobile home and auto body shop under 21 U.S.C. §§ 881(a)(4) and (a)(7) [these laws provide for the forfeiture of property in drug cases]. Austin filed a claim and an answer to the complaint.

On February 4, 1991, the United States made a motion, supported by an affidavit from Sioux Falls Police Officer Donald Satterlee, for summary judgment. According to Satterlee's affidavit, Austin met Keith Engebretson at Austin's body shop on June 13, 1990, and agreed to sell cocaine to Engebretson. Austin left the shop, went to his mobile home, and returned to the shop with two grams of cocaine which he sold to Engebretson. State authorities executed a search warrant on the body shop and mobile home the following day. They discovered small amounts of marijuana and cocaine, a .22 caliber revolver, drug paraphernalia, and approximately $4,700 in cash. In opposing summary judgment, Austin argued that forfeiture of the properties would violate the Eighth Amendment. The District Court rejected this argument and entered summary judgment for the United States.

The United States Court of Appeals for the Eighth Circuit "reluctantly agree[d] with the government" and affirmed. ... Although it thought that "the principle of proportionality should be applied in civil actions that result in harsh penalties, ... and that the Government was "exacting too high a penalty in relation to the offense committed ... the court felt constrained from holding the forfeiture unconstitutional." ...

Austin contends that the Eighth Amendment's Excessive Fines Clause applies to in rem civil forfeiture proceedings. ... In [an earlier case] we held that the Excessive Fines Clause does not limit the award of punitive damages to a private party in a civil suit when the government neither has prosecuted the action nor has any right to receive a share of the damages. ... The Court concluded that both the Eighth Amendment and §§ 10 of the Bill of Rights of 1789, from which it derives, were intended to prevent the government from abusing its power to punish ... and therefore "that the Excessive Fines Clause was intended to limit only those fines directly imposed by, and payable to, the government." ...

We found it unnecessary to decide ... whether the Excessive Fines Clause applies only to criminal cases. ... The United States now argues that

> any claim that the government's conduct in a civil proceeding is limited by the Eighth Amendment generally, or by the Excessive Fines Clause in particular, must fail unless the challenged action, despite its label, would have been recognized as a criminal punishment at the time the Eighth Amendment was adopted.

* * *

It further suggests that the Eighth Amendment cannot apply to a civil proceeding unless that proceeding is so punitive that it must be considered criminal ... .

Some provisions of the Bill of Rights are expressly limited to criminal cases. ... The text of the Eighth Amendment includes no similar limitation.

Nor does the history of the Eighth Amendment require such a limitation. Justice O'Connor noted in *Browning-Ferris*: "Consideration of the Eighth Amendment immediately followed consideration of the Fifth Amendment. After deciding to confine the benefits of the Self-Incrimination Clause of the Fifth Amendment to criminal proceedings, the Framers turned their attention to the Eighth Amendment. There were no proposals to limit that Amendment to criminal proceedings ... ."

The purpose of the Eighth Amendment, putting the Bail Clause to one side, was to limit the government's power to punish. ... The Cruel and Unusual Clause is self-evidently concerned with punishment. The Excessive Fines Clause limits the Government's power to extract payments, whether in case or in kind, "as punishment for some offense." ... "The notion of punishment, as we commonly understand it, cuts across the division between civil and criminal law." ... "It is commonly understood that civil proceedings may advance punitive and remedial goals, and conversely, that both punitive and remedial goals may be served by criminal penalties." ... Thus, the question is not, as the United States would have it, whether forfeiture ... is civil or criminal, but rather whether it is punishment.

In considering this question, we are mindful of the fact that sanctions frequently serve more than one purpose. We need not exclude the possibility that a forfeiture serves remedial purposes to conclude that it is subject to the limitations of the Excessive Fines Clause. We, however, must determine that it can be explained as serving in part to punish. ... We turn, then, to consider whether, at the time the Eighth Amendment was ratified, forfeiture was understood at least in part as punishment and whether forfeiture under §§ 881(a)(4) and (a)(7) should be so understood today.

Three kinds of forfeiture were established in England at the time the Eighth Amendment was ratified in the United States: deodand, forfeiture upon conviction for a felony or treason, and statutory forfeiture. ... Each was understood, at least in part, as imposing punishment.

* * *

The First Congress passed laws subjecting ships and cargos involved in customs offenses to forfeiture. ... Indeed, examination of those laws suggests that the First Congress viewed forfeiture as punishment. ... It is also of some interest that "forfeit" is the word Congress used for fine. ...

We turn next to consider whether forfeitures under 21 U.S.C. §§ 881(a)(4) and (a)(7) are properly considered punishment today. We find nothing in these provisions or their legislative history to contradict the historical understanding of forfeiture as punishment. ...

The legislative history of §§ 881 confirms the punitive nature of these provisions. When it added subsection (a)(7) to §§ 881 in 1984, Congress recognized "that the traditional criminal sanctions of fine and imprisonment are inadequate to deter or punish the enormously profitable trade in dangerous drugs." ... It characterized the forfeiture of real property as "a powerful deterrent." ...

We therefore conclude that forfeiture under these provisions constitutes "payment to a sovereign as punishment for some offense," ... and, as such, is subject to the limitations of the Eighth Amendment's Excessive Fines Clause.

to earn a living. This is particularly important if the defendant has dependents. Also, it is good for the self-esteem of offenders; they continue to feel a useful part of the community. The final advantage is true of many sentencing alternatives: the cost to the public is lower because the offender is often required to pay, in whole or part, for participation in the program.

For those convicted of some alcohol and drug offenses, courts have turned to alcohol and drug treatment over imprisonment. These programs vary greatly. For first-time drunk driving convictions, offenders may be required to do one or more of the following, in addition to traditional conditions of probation:

1. Participate in an alcohol treatment program, such as Alcoholics Anonymous
2. Report for periodic urine or blood tests to detect the presence of alcohol
3. Take Antabuse, a drug which makes a person ill if alcohol is ingested
4. Participate in a defensive/safe-driving school.

If a defendant has a previous drunk driving conviction, he or she is likely to receive some "executed time" or jail time, in addition to some or all of the previously listed conditions. A few courts have tried a form of shock treatment. For example, a defendant may be required to meet with drunk drivers who are responsible for killing someone and discuss that experience. In another example, at least one judge has required that a drunk driver work in a hospital emergency room so that the defendant would be exposed to alcohol-related injuries and deaths.

First-time drug users may also be placed on probation, subject to conditions similar to those previously listed: periodic urinalysis or blood screening and drug counseling and treatment. This form of probation is not available to drug dealers.

Two other forms of probation that may be used independently or mixed with one or more of the others are house arrest and halfway houses. If a defendant is sentenced to house arrest, he or she may not leave the home without prior permission of the probation officer, except in emergencies.

Today, the use of electronic shackles makes enforcement of house arrests easier. These devices are attached to the probationer's leg, and through the transmission of a radio signal it can be determined if the defendant is at home.

Halfway houses are minimum security homes located in the community. Generally they serve two groups of offenders: those making the transition from prison to the community and those who need some confinement, but not jail or prison.

Halfway houses are commonly used in conjunction with work release programs. The residents are given some freedom to leave the home, but

TERMS

halfway house A facility in which persons recently discharged from a rehabilitation facility or prison live for a time and are given support and assistance in readjusting to society at large.

are restricted in their travel. Often such homes provide drug and alcohol counseling and treatment and vocational training.

Yet another community-based correction program is the boot camp or "shock incarceration" program. Boot camps are gaining in popularity as a method of reforming youthful offenders. As of early 1994, nearly thirty states were operating prison boot camps.[39]

The typical boot camp experience involves 90 to 180 days of "rigid military-training atmosphere followed by intensive community supervision." Boot camp programs are usually limited to first-time offenders who have been sentenced to a term of imprisonment. Most programs are designed to accommodate individuals sentenced to prison, but a growing number of jails are using boot camps as an alternative to traditional confinement.[40]

This is not by any means an exhaustive list of alternative punishments. The list is limited only by the Constitution and the imagination of judges. For example, one Florida judge required those convicted of drunk driving to place bumper stickers on their cars warning of their convictions. This requirement was upheld by the Florida Court of Appeals.[41]

SIDEBAR

Another Sentencing Story

Willie Smith was convicted of the extortion and assault of a ninety-three-year-old woman confined to a wheelchair. He was also convicted of resisting arrest, counterfeiting food stamps, and mugging.

During sentencing, the trial judge told the defendant that he was irritated by the defendant's constant claims of police brutality and left the bench, approached the defendant, and punched him in the nose. While the defendant was on the floor of the courtroom, the judge kicked and punched him. The judge then returned to the bench and stated to the defendant, "That, Mr. Smith, is a sample of real, honest-to-goodness police brutality."

Habitual Offender Statutes

The career criminal or repeat offender is now subject to extreme penalty in most jurisdictions. These statutes are referred to as *recidivist* or **habitual offender laws.**

TERMS

habitual offender statutes State statutes that impose a greater punishment for a second or subsequent conviction than for the first.

Most statutes provide for an increased penalty if a defendant has been convicted of a stated number of felonies, often three, within a certain period of time, such as ten years.

To prevent unfair prejudice to the defendant, the jury usually does not know about the habitual criminal charge until it has reached a verdict in the underlying charge. So, if Pam is charged with murder and of being a habitual criminal, the jury would initially know only of the murder charge. If the jury comes back with an acquittal, the habitual criminal charge is dismissed. If the verdict is guilty, the jury is then told that it must also determine if the defendant is an habitual criminal. This is known as a *bifurcated procedure.*

To prove the habitual criminal charge, the prosecutor will introduce court records reflecting the prior convictions and, in some instances, call the prosecutors involved in the prior convictions to attest that the defendant was indeed convicted.

Habitual criminal laws have been attacked as violative of the double jeopardy clause. Such claims have not been successful, as they are not considered a second punishment of one of the earlier offenses. Rather, evidence of a criminal record provides a reason to increase the penalty for the most recent offense.

§ 12.6 Postconviction Remedies: Appeal

Technically, motions for new trials are postconviction remedies. Other than such motions, there are two major methods of attacking a conviction or other decision at the trial level: appeal and habeas corpus.

The Constitution of the United States does not expressly confer a right to appeal.[42] Regardless, every state provides for appeal either through statute or constitution. Once a state establishes a right to appeal, the United States Constitution requires that appellate procedure not violate the Fourteenth Amendment's due process or equal protection clauses.

Appeals from federal district courts go to the United States Courts of Appeals (circuit courts). From there, appeal is taken to the Supreme Court of the United States. In state cases, appeal is taken to the state intermediate appellate court, if any. Appeal from that court is taken to the state high court, usually named the Supreme Court of the state. All issues, federal and state, are heard by those courts. Issues of state law may not be appealed any further. If the defendant wishes to appeal a decision of the state high court concerning an issue of federal law, the appeal is taken to the United States Supreme Court.

Filing the Appeal

Because the right to appeal is purely statutory, it may be lost if it is not timely filed. The federal rules require that appeals be filed within ten days of the date of judgment.[43] The government is given thirty days in those instances where it may appeal. Appeals from state courts to the United States Supreme Court must be filed within ninety days of the entry of judgment.[44]

Procedures vary, but it is common to require the appellant to file a number of documents to begin the appeal. The first document is a notice or petition of appeal. This simply informs all the parties, as well as the trial judge, that the case is being appealed. A designation of record will also be filed by the parties. Through this document, the parties select the portions of the trial record that they desire to be sent to the appellate court. A statement of issues that must be resolved on appeal may also be filed by the appellant. Finally, a filing fee must be paid. Appellants who cannot afford it may seek relief from the filing fee requirement.

After the necessary documents are filed, the parties brief the issues for the appellate court. The appellate court, in its discretion, may hear oral arguments.

Because the penalty for untimely filings is harsh (dismissal of the appeal), most courts recognize constructive filings. This is particularly true for incarcerated defendants who rely on counsel or prison officials in preparing or filing an appeal.

Note that most jurisdictions provide for the possibility of bail pending appeal. This is most often available in misdemeanor cases; however, it may be granted in felony cases also.

Release During Appeal

State and federal statutes provide for the release of convicted defendants during appeals. Like pretrial release, not all defendants are entitled to release. A judge may deny release if a defendant appears to be a threat to the public or if it appears that the defendant will flee. The merit of the appeal is also considered in making the bail decision. The decision on whether to release a defendant pending appeal is usually made by the trial judge, but the appellate court may render the final decision in some circumstances.

Release may be granted on the offender's recognizance or upon the posting of bail or securing a bond. As is true of pretrial release, the court will establish conditions of release, such as prohibiting contact with the prosecutor, victim and witnesses and limiting the geographical area over which the defendant may travel.

The Scope of Review

To avoid unnecessary delay, only **final orders** may be appealed. Therefore, erroneous pretrial decisions are not corrected until appeal is taken, after the case is completed. Orders that may not be reviewed until after final judgment are those relating to the suppression of evidence, discovery, and the sufficiency of the charging instruments.

There are a few exceptions to the final judgment rule. The most prominent exception is the collateral order doctrine. Under this doctrine, orders that are independent of the criminal case may be immediately appealed. The appeal proceeds concurrently with the underlying criminal case.

Appeals taken from ongoing litigation (where no final order has been issued) are called **interlocutory appeals**. Orders holding a defendant incompetent to stand trial, denying bail, and denying a defendant's double jeopardy claim have been held collateral and immediately appealable.[45] Certain orders that occur after judgment, such as revocation of probation, are also immediately appealable.

Remember, cases are not retried on appeal. Appellate courts review the record for errors of law, not fact. That means the appellate court will not examine the evidence and substitute its judgment for that of the trial court (or jury). However, the court will examine the record to make sure that sufficient evidence exists to support the judgment. So long as sufficient evidence can be found, the appellate court will not reverse, even if it would have decided the case differently. Issues of law are reviewed anew (de novo).

Not every error warrants reversing the trial court. Only when an error prejudices the defendant is reversal required. An error is prejudicial if there is a possibility that it changed the outcome of the case. If not, it was **harmless error**. The appellant bears the burden of proving that he or she was prejudiced by the error of the trial court.

TERMS

final judgment (order) A judgment that determines the merits of the case by declaring that the plaintiff is or is not entitled to recovery. For purposes of the doctrine of res judicata, any judicial decision that is not conditional or subject to change in the future by the same court. For purposes of appeal, a judgment that terminates the litigation between the parties on the merits and leaves nothing to be done but to enforce what has been decided.

interlocutory appeal An appeal of a ruling or order with respect to a question that, although not determinative of the case, must be decided for the case to be decided.

harmless error Trivial or merely formal error; a ruling or other action by a judge in the trial of a case which, although erroneous, is not prejudicial to substantial rights, does not affect the final outcome of the case, and does not form a basis for appeal.

Some error is so violative of the Constitution that it is irrebuttably presumed prejudicial, so reversal is automatic. An order denying defense counsel at trial is never harmless error.[46]

Prosecution/Defense Appeals

Because of the double jeopardy clause, defendants have a broader right to appeal than does the government. A defendant who is tried and convicted is free to appeal any factual or legal error. However, this right may be limited by a requirement of *preservation*. To satisfy this rule, the defendant must raise the issue at the trial level. This gives the trial judge an opportunity to avoid error.

Failure to raise the issue results in a waiver. For example, a defendant who does not challenge the sufficiency of an indictment at the trial level may not raise the issue for the first time before the appellate court. The same is true of evidentiary matters. The defendant must object to the admission of evidence that he or she believes should be excluded, so as to preserve the issue for appeal.

The prosecution has a limited right to appeal. Because of the prohibition on trying a person twice for the same offense, the government has no right to appeal acquittals. However, most states permit the government to appeal certain orders issued before jeopardy attaches. Orders dismissing charging instruments, suppressing evidence prior to trial, and releasing the defendant before trial may be appealed. These interlocutory appeals do not violate the Fifth Amendment's double jeopardy clause because jeopardy does not attach until a jury has been impaneled or the first witness is sworn in a nonjury trial.

The Right to Counsel on Appeal

There is no Sixth Amendment right to counsel on appeal. The Sixth Amendment right begins once a defendant is charged and continues, at all critical stages, through trial and sentencing. In some instances, it is in effect at probation revocation. It does not ever include appeals.

The right to counsel on appeal can be found, however, in the equal protection clause of the Fourteenth Amendment. The Supreme Court said, in *Douglas v. California*,[47] that indigent defendants convicted of a felony have a right to appointed counsel on appeal, provided that the appeal is by right. *By right* means that the defendant's appeal must be heard by the appellate court. Most, if not all, states have provided for appeal by right.

If an appeal is discretionary, the equal protection clause of the Fourteenth Amendment does not compel the state to provide counsel. The *Ross* case illustrates this point.

ROSS v. MOFFITT 417 U.S. 600 (1974)

MR. JUSTICE REHNQUIST delivered the opinion of the Court.

[This case involved two defendants from North Carolina. Both were provided counsel at trial, but were denied counsel in discretionary appeals, one to the North Carolina Supreme Court and the other to the United States Supreme Court. They appealed the decisions not to provide counsel.]

* * *

This Court, in the past 20 years, has given extensive consideration to the rights of indigent persons on appeal. In *Griffin v. Illinois,* the first of the pertinent cases, the Court had before it an Illinois rule allowing a convicted criminal defendant to present claims of trial error to the Supreme Court of Illinois only if he procured a transcript of the testimony adduced at his trial. No exception was made for the indigent defendant, and thus one who was unable to pay the cost of obtaining such a transcript was precluded from obtaining appellate review of asserted trial error. ... The Court in *Griffin* held that this discrimination violated the Fourteenth Amendment.

Succeeding cases invalidated similar financial barriers to the appellate process, at the same time reaffirming the traditional principle that a State is not obliged to provide any appeal at all for criminal defendants. ...

The decisions discussed above stand for the proposition that a State cannot arbitrarily cut off appeal rights for indigents while leaving open avenues of appeal for more affluent persons. In *Douglas v. California,* however, ... the Court departed somewhat from the limited doctrine of the transcript and fee cases and undertook an examination of whether an indigent's access to the appellate system was adequate. The Court in *Douglas* concluded that a State does not fulfill its responsibility toward indigent defendants merely by waiving its own requirements that a convicted defendant procure a transcript or pay a fee in order to appeal, and held that the State must go further and provide counsel for the indigent on his first appeal as of right. It is this decision we are asked to extend today. ...

The precise rationale for the *Griffin* and *Douglas* lines of cases has never been explicitly stated, some support being derived from the Equal Protection Clause of the Fourteenth Amendment, and some from the Due Process Clause of that Amendment. Neither Clause by itself provides an entirely satisfactory basis for the result reached, each depending on a different inquiry which emphasizes different factors. "Due process" emphasizes fairness between the State and the individual dealing with the State, regardless of how other individuals in the same situation may be treated. "Equal protection," on the other hand, emphasizes disparity in treatment by a State between classes of individuals whose situations are arguably indistinguishable. We will address these issues separately in the succeeding sections.

* * *

We do not believe that the Due Process Clause requires North Carolina to provide respondent with counsel on his discretionary appeal to the State Supreme Court. At the trial stage of a criminal proceeding, the right of an indigent defendant to counsel is fundamental and binding upon the States by virtue of the Sixth and Fourteenth Amendments. ... But there are significant differences between the trial and appellate stages of a criminal proceeding. The purpose of the trial stage from the State's point of view is to convert a criminal defendant from a person presumed innocent to one found guilty beyond a reasonable doubt. To accomplish this purpose, the State employs a prosecuting attorney who presents evidence to the court, challenges any witnesses offered by the defendant, argues rulings of the court, and makes direct arguments to the court and jury seeking to persuade them of the defendant's guilt. Under these circumstances "reason and reflection require us to recognize that in our adversary system of criminal justice, any person haled into court, who is too poor to hire a lawyer, cannot be assured a fair trial unless counsel is provided for him." ...

By contrast, it is ordinarily the defendant, rather than the State, who initiates the appellate process, seeking not to fend off the efforts of the State's prosecutor but rather to overturn a finding of guilt made by a judge or jury below. The defendant needs an attorney on appeal not as a shield to protect him against being "haled into court" by the State and stripped of his presumption of innocence, but rather as a sword to upset the prior determination of guilt. This difference is significant for, while no one would agree that the State may simply dispense with the trial stage of proceedings without a criminal defendant's consent, it is clear that the State need not provide any appeal at all. ... The fact that an appeal *has* been provided does not automatically mean that a State then acts unfairly by refusing to provide counsel to indigent defendants at every stage of the way. ... Unfairness results only if indigents are singled out by the State and denied meaningful access to the appellate system because of their poverty. That question is more profitably considered under an equal protection analysis.

Language invoking equal protection notions is prominent both in *Douglas* and in other cases treating the rights of indigents on appeal. The Court in *Douglas,* for example, stated:

> "[W]here the merits of *the one and only appeal* an indigent has as of right are decided without benefit of counsel, we think an unconstitutional line has been drawn between rich and poor."

* * *

Despite the tendency of all rights "to declare themselves absolute to their logical extreme," there are obviously limits beyond which the equal protection analysis may not be pressed without doing violence to principles recognized in other decisions of this Court. The Fourteenth Amendment "does not require absolute equality or precisely equal advantages," ... nor does it require the State to "equalize economic conditions." ... It does require that the state appellate system be "free of unreasoned distinctions," ... and that indigents have an adequate opportunity to present their claims fairly within the adversary system. ... The State cannot adopt procedures which leave an indigent defendant "entirely cut off from any appeal at all," by virtue of his indigency, ... or extend to such indigent defendants merely a "meaningless ritual" while others in better economic circumstances have a "meaningful appeal." ... The question is not one of absolutes, but one of degrees. In this case we do not believe that the Equal Protection Clause, when interpreted in the context of these cases, requires North Carolina to provide free counsel for indigent defendants seeking to take discretionary appeals to the North Carolina Supreme Court, or to file petitions for certiorari in this Court.

* * *

The facts show that respondent, in connection with his Mecklenburg County conviction, received the benefit of counsel in examining the record of his trial and in preparing an appellate brief on his behalf for the state Court of Appeals. Thus, prior to his seeking discretionary review in the State Supreme Court, his claims had "once been presented by a lawyer and passed upon by an appellate court." ... We do not believe that it can be said, therefore, that a defendant in respondent's circumstances is denied meaning access to the North Carolina Supreme Court simply because the State does not appoint counsel to aid him in seeking review in that court. At that stage he will have, at the very least, a transcript or other record of trial proceedings, a brief on his behalf in the Court of Appeals setting forth his claims of error, and in many cases an opinion by the Court of Appeals disposing of his case. These materials, supplemented by whatever submission respondent may make *pro se,* would appear to provide the Supreme Court of North Carolina with an adequate basis for its decision to grant or deny review.

We are fortified in this conclusion by our understanding of the function served by discretionary review in the North Carolina Supreme Court. The critical issue in that court, as we perceive it, is not whether there has been "a correct adjudication of guilt" in every individual case, ... but rather whether "the subject matter of the appeal has significant public interest," whether "the cause involves legal principles of major significance to the jurisprudence of the State," or whether the decision below is in probable conflict with a decision of the Supreme Court. The Supreme Court may deny certiorari even though it believes that the decision of the Court of Appeals was incorrect, ... since a decision which appears incorrect may nevertheless fail to satisfy any of the criteria discussed above. Once a defendant's claims of error are organized and presented in a lawyerlike fashion to the Court of Appeals, the justices of the Supreme Court of North Carolina who make the decision to grant or deny discretionary review should be able to ascertain whether his case satisfies the standards established by the legislature for such review.

This is not to say, of course, that a skilled lawyer, particularly one trained in the somewhat arcane art of preparing petitions for discretionary review, would not prove helpful to any litigant able to employ him. An indigent defendant seeking review in the Supreme Court of North Carolina is therefore somewhat handicapped in comparison with a wealthy defendant who has counsel assisting him every conceivable manner at every stage in the proceeding. But both the opportunity to have counsel prepare an initial brief in the Court of Appeals and the nature of discretionary review in the Supreme Court of North Carolina make this relative handicap far less than the handicap borne by the indigent defendant denied counsel on his initial appeal as of right in *Douglas*. And the fact that a particular service might be of benefit to an indigent defendant does not mean that the service is constitutionally required. The duty of the State under our cases is not to duplicate the legal arsenal that may be privately retained by a criminal defendant in a continuing effort to reverse his conviction, but only to assure the indigent defendant an adequate opportunity to present his claims fairly in the context of the State's appellate process. We think respondent was given that opportunity under the existing North Carolina system.

Much of the discussion in the preceding section is equally relevant to the question of whether a State must provide counsel for a defendant seeking review of his conviction in this Court. ... This Court's review, much like that of the Supreme Court of North Carolina, is discretionary and depends on numerous factors other than the perceived correctness of the judgment we are asked to review.

* * *

We do not mean by this opinion to in any way discourage those States which have, as a matter of legislative choice, made counsel available to convicted defendants at all stages of judicial review. ... Our reading of the Fourteenth Amendment leaves these choices to the State, and respondent was denied no right secured by the Federal Constitution when North Carolina refused to provide counsel to aid him in obtaining discretionary appellate review.

The judgment of the Court of Appeals' holding to the contrary is *Reversed.*

As is true at trial, the defendant is entitled to effective counsel. The appointed attorney has an ethical obligation to zealously pursue the defendant's appeal. Because of the large number of frivolous appeals, the Supreme Court has stated that an appointed attorney may be allowed to withdraw. However, the following must be done: first, the attorney must request withdrawal from the appellate court; second, a brief must be filed explaining why the attorney believes the appeal to be wholly without merit. In that brief, all potential issues must be outlined for the court's review. If the appellate court agrees that there are no valid issues, the attorney may withdraw. If the court finds an issue that has some merit, the lawyer must continue to represent the defendant.

Habeas Corpus

Both the states and federal governments have habeas corpus relief. Here we discuss federal habeas corpus relief, particularly federal habeas corpus in state criminal proceedings. Although habeas corpus relief is available at any stage of a criminal proceeding, most habeas corpus petitions are filed after conviction. The discussion here is limited to such postconviction petitions.

Through habeas corpus proceedings, an individual may attack the lawfulness of confinement, whether it be substantive or procedural in nature. Further, the conditions of confinement and the lawfulness of an imposed punishment may be reviewed by a habeas court.

History

Translated, habeas corpus means "you have the body." In action, the writ is used to order someone who has custody of another to bring that person before the court. Any person who believes that he or she is being detained illegally may use the writ to gain his or her freedom. Because of the significant power of the writ, it has come to be known as the "Great Writ of Liberty."

The writ has ancient origin, dating back as far as the twelfth century. Habeas corpus was often used to enforce provisions of the Magna Carta. The success of the writ in protecting liberty in England influenced the drafters of the American Constitution. The result is Article I, § 9, clause 2, which states: "The Privilege of the Writ of Habeas Corpus shall not be suspended unless when in Cases of Rebellion or Invasion the Public Safety may require it."

Federal habeas corpus is important in criminal law because it is used to challenge state court convictions. That is, if a defendant believes that his or her federal constitutional rights were violated in a state court, he or she may attack the conviction through federal habeas corpus.

Habeas corpus has had congressional authorization since 1789. The first statute made habeas corpus available only to federal prisoners. This was changed by the Habeas Corpus Act of 1867, which extended habeas corpus to any person "restrained of his or her liberty in violation of the constitution, or of any treaty or law of the United States." The 1867 act continues to be in effect, with some modifications.

Scope of Review

The current habeas corpus statutes are found at 28 U.S.C. §§ 2241–2255. Section 2254 provides habeas corpus relief to state prisoners. Under § 2255, federal prisoners are to move to vacate or set aside their sentences, in a procedure nearly identical to § 2254. Relief under this section must be sought before a federal prisoner can bring a habeas corpus action. Even then, the statute states that habeas corpus shall not be issued if the prisoner was unsuccessful with a § 2255 claim, unless that proceeding was "inadequate or ineffective." A biased judge is an example of when habeas corpus may be issued after a § 2255 motion has been denied.

The federal courts continued to have little involvement with state proceedings, even after the 1867 act extended the reach of federal habeas corpus to state prisoners. This was in large part due to Supreme Court decisions limiting the review of federal habeas corpus to questions of jurisdiction.

The scope of review was enlarged in *Brown v. Allen,*[48] in which it was held that federal habeas corpus could be used to relitigate all issues of federal law. This decision significantly increased the power of federal habeas corpus and resulted in increased intervention of federal courts in state criminal proceedings.

The Supreme Court has since narrowed habeas corpus relief by decision. For example, a state prisoner may not use federal habeas corpus to relitigate Fourth Amendment claims (search and seizure), provided the defendant was provided a "full and fair litigation" in state court. Also, the Court has emphasized that the purpose of habeas corpus is to provide relief to persons imprisoned in violation of the laws of the United States, not to relitigate or correct factual errors. Accordingly, a claim of innocence, even when supported by new evidence, is not alone sufficient to confer habeas jurisdiction upon a court. An independent constitutional claim must be made for a court to examine such a petition.[49]

SIDEBAR

Crime in the United States: Felony Case Dispositions

Four percent (36,686 persons) of all felony convictions in 1990 were in federal court. In the same year, 91 percent of all state court felony convictions were the product of guilty pleas; 4 percent of felons in state courts were convicted by a jury and another 3 percent by a judge after a bench trial.

Murder, rape, robbery, and other violent crimes accounted for approximately 18 percent of felony convictions, but 39 percent of all jury trials. Guilty pleas were the most common among defendants charged with larceny or fraud (94 percent) and least common for murder and manslaughter (59 percent).

The mean time from date of arrest to conviction was about six months. The mean time in jury cases was almost eight months. Guilty-plea and bench trial cases were roughly the same, about six months. Not surprisingly, murder cases take the longest time to adjudicate, the mean being approximately ten months.

The mean time from conviction to sentencing was approximately one month. Sentences to jail or prison occurred in 80 percent of all jury cases, 71 percent of bench trial cases, and 70 percent of all guilty-plea cases. Felons convicted by juries were sentenced to an average of nearly fourteen years. Those convicted by bench trial received an average of slightly less than nine years and felons who pleaded guilty averaged less than six years. Forty percent of murderers were sentenced to life imprisonment or death.

Source: National Judicial Reporting Program, 1990 (Bureau of Justice Statistics, Dec. 1993).

Exhaustion of Remedies

Before a state prisoner can seek the aid of a federal court, he or she must satisfy certain procedural requirements. First, the defendant must use all means available in the state system to correct the alleged error. This is the doctrine of **exhaustion** of remedies. Section 2254(b) states:

> An application for a writ of habeas corpus in behalf of a person in custody pursuant to the judgment of a State court shall not be granted unless it appears that the applicant has exhausted the remedies available in the courts of the State, or that there is either an absence of available corrective process or the existence of circumstances rendering such process ineffective to protect the rights of the prisoner.

The remedies that must be exhausted depend on what is available in the state system, such as motions for new trial, state habeas corpus relief, and appeals. Of course, if no remedy is available, the defendant may immediately petition for habeas corpus relief.

If a remedy is available, but it would be futile to exhaust it, habeas corpus may be brought without exhaustion. For example, assume State Supreme Court has previously addressed the legal issue raised by the defendant, and its decision is contrary to the defendant's claim. Unless there is reason to believe that the court will reconsider its decision, there is no need to exhaust this remedy. Excessive delay in the state proceedings may also be a basis for bringing habeas corpus before the state remedies have been exhausted, provided the state does not have a remedy for such delays (e.g., mandamus).

The fact that a defendant has failed to timely appeal (or file a motion for new trial, etc.) does not mean that habeas corpus is unavailable. The

TERMS

exhaustion The doctrine, applicable in many types of cases, that the federal courts will not respond to a party seeking relief until he or she has exhausted her remedies in state court.

question is: Are state remedies available? If a defendant has missed the right to appeal under state law, and no other remedy is available, then habeas corpus may be used to resolve his or her federal constitutional claims. However, defendants who deliberately bypass state procedures may be denied habeas relief.[50]

The Custody Requirement

The Habeas Corpus Act speaks of prisoners "in custody." However, this has been interpreted to include all wrongful restraints of liberty. The Supreme Court has said that persons who are subject to "restraints not shared by the public generally" are entitled to habeas corpus protection, even though they may not be in the physical custody of the government.

Under this interpretation, persons placed on probation and parole have been held to be in custody, as have defendants released on bail.[51] Habeas corpus protection is also available to a defendant who has served his or her entire sentence, because the restraint of liberty includes not only incarceration but also collateral loss of civil liberties (e.g., right to carry a weapon), injury to reputation, and the possibility of an increased penalty for a later conviction.

A defendant who is lawfully detained may use habeas corpus to challenge his or her sentence if he or she believes it is excessive. Also, if he or she was convicted of several crimes and was sentenced to consecutive sentences, he or she need not wait until the lawful sentence expires before petitioning for habeas corpus. It appears that an invalid sentence may be attacked even though it runs concurrently with a valid sentence. Again, the collateral effects of the conviction are the rationale.

Procedure

The following rules were established by the United States Supreme Court to implement 22 U.S.C. § 2254.[52] The petition for habeas corpus relief is filed in the federal district within which the prisoner is being held. The petition shall name the person who has custody of the applicant as the respondent. Indigent persons may file a motion to proceed in forma pauperis, which relieves such persons from paying the filing fee.

Immediately after the petition is filed, the district judge will examine the petition. If the petition is "plainly" invalid, the court will dismiss it. If not, the court will direct the respondent to answer the petition.

Counsel may be appointed and discovery is available, with leave of the district court. After the petition has been answered and appropriate discovery conducted, the district court may hold an evidentiary hearing and issue an opinion or rule from the record without a hearing. Habeas corpus decisions may be appealed.

The Right to Counsel

To date, the Supreme Court has not found a constitutional right to the assistance of counsel in preparing and presenting a petition for habeas corpus.

In some instances the district court may have to hold an evidentiary hearing. It is possible that in such instances a due process right to counsel exists to assure that the hearing is fair. The issue is not of critical importance presently, because federal habeas corpus rules require the appointment of counsel for such hearings. Additionally, the rules give the district court the discretion to appoint counsel earlier, if necessary.

Although there may be no right to counsel, there is a right to "access to the courts." Therefore, prisoners must be furnished with paper, pens, stamps, and access to a law library. Further, unless a prison provides adequate legal assistance to its prisoners, so-called "jailhouse lawyers" may not be prohibited from assisting other inmates in the preparation of legal documents.

Review Questions

1. What is a presentence investigation? Who conducts the investigation and what is its purpose?
2. What are aggravating and mitigating circumstances in sentencing?
3. What is the final judgment rule?
4. Does a defendant have a right to appointed counsel on appeal?
5. What is habeas corpus?
6. Distinguish harmless from prejudicial error.
7. May victim impact evidence be considered by sentencing courts?
8. Which of the following punishments has been held to be inherently cruel and unusual by the Supreme Court?
   a. Death by hanging
   b. Death by starvation
   c. Flogging
   d. Solitary confinement
   e. Imprisonment without lighting or a bed.
9. Differentiate a suspended imposition of sentence from a sentence suspended to probation.

Review Problems

1–4. Kevin, an attorney, has been indicted for embezzlement. After his preliminary hearing, he filed a motion to suppress a confession he believes was illegally obtained. A hearing was conducted and the trial court granted his motion. The evidence was vital to the prosecution.

Kevin's attorney has also requested that the trial be continued because he claims that Kevin is not competent to stand trial. The judge ordered a mental evaluation, held a hearing, and found Kevin competent to stand trial.

The defense also requested that the court order a number of police officers to submit to depositions prior to trial. The court denied the motion.

At trial, the defendant objected to the introduction of a document that he believed was unconstitutionally obtained during a search of his office. The judge overruled the objection and admitted the confession into evidence.

Answer the following questions using these facts.

1. The prosecution strongly believes that the documents that were suppressed are admissible. The prosecutor objects on the record to the judge's order and then appeals the issue after Kevin is acquitted. What should be the outcome on appeal?
2. Kevin disagrees with the trial court finding of competency. What is his remedy?
3. Believing that Kevin cannot have a fair trial without the depositions, his attorney filed an interlocutory appeal seeking an order from the appellate court requiring the trial judge to provide for the depositions. What should be the outcome?
4. Kevin appealed the trial court's decision denying his motion to suppress the document. The appellate court affirmed the trial court, and Kevin filed a habeas corpus petition in federal court claiming that his federal constitutional rights were violated by admission of the evidence. What should be the outcome?

Notes

1 The Supreme Court has not yet definitively answered this question. *See also United States v. Rogers*, 921 F.2d 957 (10th Cir. 1990), *cert. denied*, 111 S. Ct. 113 (1991).

2 *United States v. Jackson*, 886 F.2d 838 (7th Cir. 1989).

3 Fed. R. Crim. P. 32(c)(1).

4 Fed. R. Crim. P. 32(c)(3).

5 482 U.S. 496 (1987).

6 *Eddings v. Oklahoma*, 455 U.S. 104 (1982).

7 *See* E. Puttkammer, *Administration of Criminal Law,* 16–17 (1953).

8 Schwartz and Goldstein, *Police Guidance Manuals* (University of Virginia Press, 1968), Manual No. 3, at 21–32, reprinted in *Cases, Materials, and Problems on the Advocacy and Administration of Criminal Justice* 173 by Harold Norris (unpublished manuscript available in the Detroit College of Law library).

9 *See* Note, 78 *Colum. L. Rev.* 1249, 1247–59 (1978); LaFave and Scott, *Criminal Law* 26 (Hornbook Series, St. Paul: West, 1986).

10 408 U.S. 238 (1972).

11 438 U.S. 586 (1978).

12 *Locket,* 438 U.S. at 604–05.

13 428 U.S. 153 (1976).

14 *Callins v. Collins,* 510 U.S. ___, 114 S. Ct. 1127, 1132 (1994) (Blackmun, J., dissenting).

15 114 S. Ct. at 1129–30.

16 481 U.S. 279 (1987).

17 *Coker v. Georgia,* 433 U.S. 584 (1977).

18 *Enmund v. Florida,* 458 U.S. 782 (1972).

19 *Ford v. Wainwright,* 477 U.S. 399 (1986).

20 *Pervear v. Commonwealth,* 72 U.S. (5 Wall) 475 (1867); *Wing Wong v. United States,* 163 U.S. 228 (1896); *Kehrli v. Sprinkle,* 524 F.2d 328 (10th Cir. 1975).

21 *Delaware v. Cannon,* 55 Del. 587, 190 A.2d 574 (1963).

22 *Jackson v. Bishop,* 404 F.2d 571 (8th Cir. 1968).

23 For a thorough discussion of the constitutionality of whipping, *see* Daniel Hall, "When Caning Meets the Eighth Amendment: Whipping Offenders in the United States," 4 *Widener J. Pub. L.* ___ (1995).

24 Breyer, "The Federal Sentencing Guidelines and the Key Compromises Upon Which They Rest," 17 *Hofstra L. Rev.* 4 (1988).

25 Federal Judges Association, *In Camera* (Dec. 1990).

26 *Griffin v. Wisconsin,* 483 U.S. 868 (1987).

27 *Porth v. Templar,* 453 F.2d 330 (10th Cir. 1971).

28 389 U.S. 128 (1967).

29 *United States v. Green,* 735 F.2d 1203 (9th Cir. 1984).

30 *Hughey v. United States,* 495 U.S. 411 (1990).

31 *Phillips v. United States,* 679 F.2d 192 (9th Cir. 1982).

32 *Bearden v. Georgia,* 461 U.S. 660, 668–69 (1983).

33 399 U.S. 235 (1970).

34 *See,* for example, 21 U.S.C. § 881.

35 19 U.S.C. § 1615.

36 *See* 21 U.S.C. § 853.

37 114 S. Ct. 492 (1993).

38 *One 1958 Plymouth v. Pennsylvania,* 380 U.S. 693 (1965).

39 *The Growing Use of Jail Boot Camps: The Current State of the Art* (National Institute of Justice, Oct. 1993).

40 Belinda McCarthy & Bernard McCarthy, *Community-Based Corrections* 128 (2d ed., Brooks/Cole 1991).

41 *Goldschmitt v. State,* 490 So. 2d 123 (Fla. Dist. Ct. App.), *review denied,* 496 So. 2d 142 (Fla. 1986).

42 *McKane v. Durston,* 153 U.S. 684 (1894).

43 Fed. R. Crim. P. 37.

44 Supreme Ct. R. 11.1.

45 LaFave & Israel, *Criminal Procedure* § 26.2(c) (Hornbook Series; St. Paul, Minn.: West, 1985).

46 *Gideon v. Wainwright,* 373 U.S. 335 (1963).

47 372 U.S. 353 (1963),.

48 344 U.S. 443 (1953).

49 *Herrera v. Collins,* 113 S. Ct. 853 (1993).

50 *Fay v. NOIA,* 372 U.S. 391 (1963).

51 *Jones v. Cunningham,* 371 U.S. 236 (1963); *Hensley v. Municipal Court,* 411 U.S. 345 (1973).

52 *See Rules Governing Section 2254 Cases in the United States District Courts* (Feb. 1989). These rules also contain the forms necessary to petition for habeas corpus relief in the district court of the United States.

APPENDIX

THE CONSTITUTION OF THE UNITED STATES OF AMERICA

We the People of the United States, in Order to form a more perfect Union, establish Justice, insure domestic Tranquility, provide for the common defence, promote the general Welfare, and secure the Blessings of Liberty to ourselves and our Posterity, do ordain and establish this Constitution for the United States of America.

ARTICLE I

Section 1 All legislative Powers herein granted shall be vested in a Congress of the United States, which shall consist of a Senate and House of Representatives.

Section 2 (1) The House of Representatives shall be composed of Members chosen every second Year by the People of the several States, and the Electors in each State shall have the Qualifications requisite for Electors of the most numerous Branch of the State Legislature.

(2) No Person shall be a Representative who shall not have attained to the age of twenty-five Years, and been seven Years a Citizen of the United States, and who shall not, when elected, be an Inhabitant of that State in which he shall be chosen.

(3) Representatives and direct Taxes shall be apportioned among the several States which may be included within this Union, according to their respective Numbers, which shall be determined by adding to the whole Number of free Persons, including those bound to Service for a Term of Years, and excluding Indians not taxed, three fifths of all other Persons. The actual Enumeration shall be made within three Years after the first Meeting of the Congress of the United States, and within every subsequent Term of ten Years, in such Manner as they shall by Law direct. The Number of Representatives shall not exceed one for every thirty Thousand, but each State shall have at Least one Representative; and until such enumeration shall be made, the State of New Hampshire shall be entitled to chuse three, Massachusetts eight, Rhode Island and Providence Plantations one, Connecticut five, New York six, New Jersey four, Pennsylvania eight, Delaware one, Maryland six, Virginia ten, North Carolina five, South Carolina five, and Georgia three.

(4) When vacancies happen in the Representation from any State, the Executive Authority thereof shall issue Writs of Election to fill such Vacancies.

(5) The House of Representatives shall chuse their Speaker and other Officers; and shall have the sole Power of Impeachment.

Section 3 (1) The Senate of the United States shall be composed of two Senators from each State, chosen by the Legislature thereof, for six Years; and each Senator shall have one Vote.

(2) Immediately after they shall be assembled in Consequence of the first Election, they shall be divided as equally as may be into three Classes. The Seats of the Senators of the first Class shall be vacated at the Expiration of the second Year, of the second Class at the Expiration of the fourth Year, and of the third Class at the Expiration of the sixth Year, so that one third may be chosen every second Year; and if Vacancies happen by Resignation, or otherwise, during the Recess of the Legislature of any State, the Executive thereof may make temporary Appointments until the next Meeting of the Legislature, which shall then fill such Vacancies.

(3) No Person shall be a Senator who shall not have attained to the Age of thirty Years, and been nine Years a Citizen of the United States, and who shall not, when elected, be an Inhabitant of that State for which he shall be chosen.

(4) The Vice President of the United States shall be President of the Senate, but shall have no Vote, unless they be equally divided.

(5) The Senate shall chuse their other Officers, and also a President pro tempore, in the Absence of the Vice President, or when he shall exercise the Office of the President of the United States.

(6) The Senate shall have the sole Power to try all Impeachments. When sitting for that Purpose, they shall be on Oath or Affirmation. When the President of the United States is tried, the Chief Justice shall preside: And no Person shall be convicted without the Concurrence of two thirds of the Members present.

(7) Judgment in Cases of Impeachment shall not extend further than to removal from Office, and disqualification to hold and enjoy any Office of honor, Trust or Profit under the United States: but the Party convicted shall nevertheless be liable and subject to Indictment, Trial, Judgment and Punishment, according to Law.

Section 4 (1) The Times, Places and Manner of holding Elections for Senators and Representatives, shall be prescribed in each State by the Legislature thereof; but the Congress may at any time by Law make or alter such Regulations, except as to the Places of chusing Senators.

(2) The Congress shall assemble at least once in every Year, and such Meeting shall be on the first Monday in December, unless they shall by Law appoint a different Day.

Section 5 (1) Each House shall be the Judge of the Elections, Returns and Qualifications of its own Members, and a Majority of each shall constitute a Quorum to do Business; but a smaller Number may adjourn from day to day, and may be authorized to compel the Attendance of absent Members, in such Manner, and under such Penalties as each House may provide.

(2) Each House may determine the Rules of its Proceedings, punish its Members for disorderly Behaviour, and, with the Concurrence of two thirds, expel a Member.

(3) Each House shall keep a Journal of its Proceedings, and from time to time publish the same, excepting such Parts as may in their Judgment require Secrecy; and the Yeas and Nays of the Members of either House on any question shall, at the Desire of one fifth of those Present, be entered on the Journal.

(4) Neither House, during the Session of Congress, shall, without the Consent of the other, adjourn for more than three days, nor to any other Place than that in which the two Houses shall be sitting.

Section 6 (1) The Senators and Representatives shall receive a Compensation for their Services, to be ascertained by Law, and paid out of the Treasury of the United States. They shall in all Cases, except Treason, Felony and Breach of the Peace, be privileged from Arrest during their Attendance at the Session of their respective Houses, and in going to and returning from the same; and for any Speech or Debate in either House, they shall not be questioned in any other Place.

(2) No Senator or Representative shall, during the Time for which he was elected, be appointed to any civil Office under the Authority of the United States, which shall have been created, or the Emoluments whereof shall have been encreased during such time; and no Person holding any Office under the United States, shall be a Member of either House during his Continuance in Office.

Section 7 (1) All Bills for raising Revenue shall originate in the House of Representatives; but the Senate may propose or concur with Amendments as on other Bills.

(2) Every Bill which shall have passed the House of Representatives and the Senate, shall, before it become a Law, be presented to the President of the United States; If he approve he

shall sign it, but if not he shall return it, with his Objections to that House in which it shall have originated, who shall enter the Objections at large on their Journal, and proceed to reconsider it. If after such Reconsideration two thirds of that House shall agree to pass the Bill, it shall be sent, together with the Objections, to the other House, by which it shall likewise be reconsidered, and if approved by two thirds of that House, it shall become a law. But in all such Cases the Votes of both Houses shall be determined by Yeas and Nays, and the Names of the Persons voting for and against the Bill shall be entered on the Journal of each House respectively. If any Bill shall not be returned by the President within ten Days (Sunday excepted) after it shall have been presented to him, the Same shall be a Law, in like Manner as if he had signed it, unless the Congress by their Adjournment prevent its Return, in which Case it shall not be a Law.

(3) Every Order, Resolution, or Vote to which the Concurrence of the Senate and House of Representatives may be necessary (except on a question of Adjournment) shall be presented to the President of the United States; and before the Same shall take Effect, shall be approved by him, or being disapproved by him, shall be repassed by two thirds of the Senate and House of Representatives, according to the Rules and Limitations prescribed in the Case of a Bill.

Section 8 (1) The Congress shall have Power To lay and collect Taxes, Duties, Imposts and Excises, to pay the Debts and provide for the common Defence and general Welfare of the United States; but all Duties, Imposts and Excises shall be uniform throughout the United States;

(2) To borrow Money on the credit of the United States;

(3) To regulate Commerce with foreign Nations, and among the several States, and with the Indian Tribes;

(4) To establish an uniform Rule of Naturalization, and uniform Laws on the subject of Bankruptcies throughout the United States;

(5) To coin Money, regulate the Value thereof, and of foreign Coin, and to fix the Standard of Weights and Measures;

(6) To provide for the Punishment of counterfeiting the Securities and current Coin of the United States;

(7) To establish Post Offices and post Roads;

(8) To promote the Progress of Science and useful Arts, by securing for limited Times to Authors and Inventors the exclusive Right to their respective Writings and Discoveries;

(9) To constitute Tribunals inferior to the supreme Court;

(10) To define and punish Piracies and Felonies committed on the high Seas, and Offenses against the Law of Nations;

(11) To declare War, grant Letters of Marque and Reprisal, and make Rules concerning Captures on Land and Water;

(12) To raise and support Armies, but no Appropriation of Money to that Use shall be for a longer Term than two Years;

(13) To provide and maintain a Navy;

(14) To make Rules for the Government and Regulation of the land and naval Forces;

(15) To provide for calling forth the Militia to execute the Laws of the Union, suppress Insurrections and repel Invasions;

(16) To provide for organizing, arming, and disciplining, the Militia, and for governing such Part of them as may be employed in the Service of the United States, reserving to the States respectively, the Appointment of the Officers, and the Authority of training the Militia according to the discipline prescribed by Congress;

(17) To exercise exclusive Legislation in all Cases whatsoever, over such District (not exceeding ten Miles square) as may, by Cession of particular States, and the Acceptance of Congress, become the Seat of the Government of the United States, and to exercise like Authority over all Places purchased by the Consent of the Legislature of the State in which the Same shall be, for the Erection of Forts, Magazines,

Arsenals, dock-Yards, and other needful Buildings;—And

(18) To make all Laws which shall be necessary and proper for carrying into Execution the foregoing Powers, and all other Powers vested by this Constitution in the Government of the United States, or in any Department or Officer thereof.

Section 9 (1) The Migration or Importation of such Persons as any of the States now existing shall think proper to admit, shall not be prohibited by the Congress prior to the Year one thousand eight hundred and eight, but a Tax or Duty may be imposed on such Importation, not exceeding ten dollars for each Person.

(2) The Privilege of the Writ of Habeas Corpus shall not be suspended unless when in Cases of Rebellion or Invasion the public Safety may require it.

(3) No Bill of Attainder or ex post facto Law shall be passed.

(4) No Capitation, or other direct, Tax shall be laid, unless in Proportion to the Census or Enumeration herein before directed to be taken.

(5) No Tax or Duty shall be laid on Articles exported from any State.

(6) No Preference shall be given by any Regulation of Commerce or Revenue to the Ports of one State over those of another; nor shall Vessels bound to, or from, one State, be obliged to enter, clear or pay Duties in another.

(7) No Money shall be drawn from the Treasury, but in Consequence of Appropriations made by Law; and a regular Statement and Account of the Receipts and Expenditures of all public Money shall be published from time to time.

(8) No Title of Nobility shall be granted by the United States: And no Person holding any Office of Profit or Trust under them, shall, without the Consent of the Congress, accept of any present, Emolument, Office, or Title, of any kind whatever, from any King, Prince or foreign State.

Section 10 (1) No State shall enter into any Treaty, Alliance, or Confederation; grant Letters of Marque and Reprisal; coin Money; emit Bills of Credit; make any Thing but gold and silver Coin a Tender in Payment of Debts; pass any Bill of Attainder, ex post facto Law, or Law impairing the Obligation of Contracts, or grant any Title of Nobility.

(2) No State shall, without the Consent of Congress, lay any Imposts or Duties on Imports or Exports, except what may be absolutely necessary for executing its inspection Laws: and the net Produce of all Duties and Imposts, laid by any State on Imports or Exports, shall be for the Use of the Treasury of the United States; and all such Laws shall be subject to the Revision and Controul of the Congress.

(3) No State shall, without the Consent of Congress, lay any Duty of Tonnage, keep Troops, or Ships of War in time of Peace, enter into any Agreement or Compact with another State, or with a foreign Power, or engage in War, unless actually invaded, or in such imminent Danger as will not admit of Delay.

ARTICLE II

Section 1 (1) The executive Power shall be vested in a President of the United States of America. He shall hold his Office during the Term of four Years, and, together with the Vice President, chosen for the same Term, be elected, as follows:

(2) Each State shall appoint, in such Manner as the Legislature thereof may direct, a Number of Electors, equal to the whole Number of Senators and Representatives to which the State may be entitled in the Congress: but no Senator or Representative, or Person holding an Office of Trust or Profit under the United States, shall be appointed an Elector.

The Electors shall meet in their respective States, and vote by Ballot for two Persons, of whom one at least shall not be an Inhabitant of the same State with themselves. And they shall make a List of all the Persons voted for, and of the Number of Votes for each; which List they shall sign and certify, and transmit sealed to the Seat of the Government of the

United States, directed to the President of the Senate. The President of the Senate shall, in the presence of the Senate and House of Representatives, open all the Certificates, and the Votes shall then be counted. The Person having the greatest Number of Votes shall be the President, if such Number be a Majority of the whole Number of Electors appointed; and if there be more than one who have such Majority, and have an equal Number of Votes, then the House of Representatives shall immediately chuse by Ballot one of them for President; and if no Person have a Majority, then from the five highest on the List the said House shall in like Manner chuse the President. But in chusing the President, the Votes shall be taken by States, the Representation from each State having one Vote; a quorum for this Purpose shall consist of a Member or Members from two thirds of the States, and a Majority of all the States shall be necessary to a Choice. In every Case, after the Choice of the President, the Person having the greatest Number of Votes of the Electors shall be the Vice President. But if there should remain two or more who have equal Votes, the Senate shall chuse from them by Ballot the Vice President.

(3) The Congress may determine the Time of chusing the Electors, and the Day on which they shall give their Votes; which Day shall be the same throughout the United States.

(4) No Person except a natural born Citizen, or a Citizen of the United States, at the time of the Adoption of this Constitution, shall be eligible to the Office of President; neither shall any Person be eligible to that Office who shall not have attained to the Age of thirty five Years, and been fourteen Years a Resident within the United States.

(5) In Case of the Removal of the President from Office, or of his Death, Resignation, or Inability to discharge the Powers and Duties of the said Office, the Same shall devolve on the Vice President, and the Congress may by Law provide for the Case of Removal, Death, Resignation or Inability, both of the President and Vice President, declaring what Officer shall then act as President, and such Officer shall act accordingly, until the Disability be removed, or a President shall be elected.

(6) The President shall, at stated Times, receive for his Services, a Compensation, which shall neither be increased nor diminished during the Period for which he shall have been elected, and he shall not receive within that Period any other Emolument from the United States, or any of them.

(7) Before he enter on the Execution of his Office, he shall take the following Oath or Affirmation:—"I do solemnly swear (or affirm) that I will faithfully execute the Office of President of the United States, and will to the best of my Ability, preserve, protect and defend the Constitution of the United States."

Section 2 (1) The President shall be Commander in Chief of the Army and Navy of the United States, and of the Militia of the several States, when called into the actual Service of the United States; he may require the Opinion, in writing, of the principal Officer in each of the executive Departments, upon any Subject relating to the Duties of their respective Offices, and he shall have Power to grant Reprieves and Pardons for Offenses against the United States, except in Cases of Impeachment.

(2) He shall have Power, by and with the Advice and Consent of the Senate, to make Treaties, provided two thirds of the Senators present concur; and he shall nominate, and by and with the Advice and Consent of the Senate, shall appoint Ambassadors, other public Ministers and Consuls, Judges of the supreme Court, and all other Officers of the United States, whose Appointments are not herein otherwise provided for, and which shall be established by Law: but the Congress may by Law vest the Appointment of such inferior Officers, as they think proper, in the President alone, in the Courts of Law, or in the Heads of Departments.

(3) The President shall have Power to fill up all Vacancies that may happen during the Recess of the Senate, by granting Commissions which shall expire at the End of their next Session.

Section 3 He shall from time to time give to the Congress Information of the State of the Union, and recommend to their Consideration such Measures as he shall judge necessary and expedient; he may, on extraordinary Occasions, convene both Houses, or either of them, and in Case of Disagreement between them, with Respect to the Time of Adjournment, he may adjourn them to such Time as he shall think proper; he shall receive Ambassadors and other public Ministers; he shall take Care that the Laws be faithfully executed, and shall Commission all the Officers of the United States.

Section 4 The President, Vice President and all Civil Officers of the United States, shall be removed from Office on Impeachment for, and Conviction of, Treason, Bribery, or other high Crimes and Misdemeanors.

ARTICLE III

Section 1 The judicial Power of the United States, shall be vested in one supreme Court, and in such inferior Courts as the Congress may from time to time ordain and establish. The Judges, both of the supreme and inferior Courts, shall hold their Offices during good Behaviour, and shall, at stated Times, receive for their Services, a Compensation, which shall not be diminished during their Continuance in Office.

Section 2 (1) The judicial Power shall extend to all Cases, in Law and Equity, arising under this Constitution, the Laws of the United States, and Treaties made, or which shall be made, under their Authority;—to all Cases affecting Ambassadors, other public Ministers and Consuls;—to all Cases of admiralty and maritime Jurisdiction;—to Controversies to which the United States shall be a party—to Controversies between two or more States;—between a State and Citizens of another State;—between Citizens of different States;—between Citizens of the same State claiming Lands under Grants of different States, and between a State, or the Citizens thereof, and foreign States, Citizens or Subjects.

(2) In all Cases affecting Ambassadors, other public Ministers and Consuls, and those in which a State shall be Party, the supreme Court shall have original Jurisdiction. In all the other Cases before mentioned, the supreme Court shall have appellate Jurisdiction, both as to Law and Fact, with such Exceptions, and under such Regulations as the Congress shall make.

(3) The Trial of all Crimes, except in Cases of Impeachment, shall be by Jury; and such Trial shall be held in the State where the said Crimes shall have been committed; but when not committed within any State, the Trial shall be at such Place or Places as the Congress may by Law have directed.

Section 3 (1) Treason against the United States, shall consist only in levying War against them, or in adhering to their Enemies, giving them Aid and Comfort. No Person shall be convicted of Treason unless on the Testimony of two Witnesses to the same overt Act, or on Confession in open Court.

(2) The Congress shall have Power to declare the Punishment of Treason, but no Attainder of Treason shall work Corruption of Blood, or Forfeiture except during the Life of the Person attainted.

ARTICLE IV

Section 1 Full Faith and Credit shall be given in each State to the public Acts, Records, and judicial Proceedings of every other State. And the Congress may by general Laws prescribe the Manner in which such Acts, Records and Proceedings shall be proved, and the Effect thereof.

Section 2 (1) The Citizens of each State shall be entitled to all privileges and Immunities of Citizens in the several States.

(2) A Person charged in any State with Treason, Felony, or other Crime, who shall flee from Justice, and be found in another State, shall on Demand of the executive Authority of the State from which he fled, be delivered up, to be removed to the State having Jurisdiction of the Crime.

(3) No Person held to Service of Labour in one State, under the Laws thereof, escaping into another, shall, in Consequence of any Law or Regulation therein, be discharged from such Service or Labour, but shall be delivered up on Claim of the Party to whom such Service or Labour may be due.

Section 3 (1) New States may be admitted by the Congress into this Union; but no new State shall be formed or erected within the Jurisdiction of any other State; nor any State be formed by the Junction of two or more States, or Parts of States, without the Consent of the Legislatures of the States concerned as well as of the Congress.

(2) The Congress shall have power to dispose of and make all needful Rules and Regulations respecting the Territory or other Property belonging to the United States; and nothing in this Constitution shall be so construed as to Prejudice any Claims of the United States, or of any particular State.

Section 4 The United States shall guarantee to every State in this Union a Republican Form of Government, and shall protect each of them against Invasion; and on Application of the Legislature, or of the Executive (when the Legislature cannot be convened) against domestic Violence.

ARTICLE V

The Congress, whenever two thirds of both Houses shall deem it necessary, shall propose Amendments to this Constitution, or, on the Application of the Legislatures of two thirds of the several States, shall call a Convention for proposing Amendments, which, in either Case, shall be valid to all Intents and Purposes, as Part of this Constitution, when ratified by the Legislatures of three fourths of the several States, or by Conventions in three fourths thereof, as the one or the other Mode of Ratification may be proposed by the Congress; Provided that no Amendment which may be made prior to the Year One thousand eight hundred and eight shall in any Manner affect the first and fourth Clauses in the Ninth Section of the first Article; and that no State, without its Consent, shall be deprived of its equal Suffrage in the Senate.

ARTICLE VI

(1) All Debts contracted and Engagements entered into, before the Adoption of this Constitution, shall be as valid against the United States under this Constitution, as under the Confederation.

(2) This Constitution, and the Laws of the United States which shall be made in Pursuance thereof; and all Treaties made, or which shall be made, under the Authority of the United States, shall be the supreme Law of the Land; and the Judges in every State shall be bound thereby, any Thing in the Constitution or Laws of any State to the Contrary notwithstanding.

(3) The Senators and Representatives before mentioned, and the Members of the several State Legislatures, and all executive and judicial Officers, both of the United States and of the several States, shall be bound by Oath or Affirmation, to support this Constitution; but no religious Test shall ever be required as a Qualification to any Office or public Trust under the United States.

ARTICLE VII

The Ratification of the Conventions of nine States, shall be sufficient for the Establishment of this Constitution between the States so ratifying the Same.

ARTICLES IN ADDITION TO, AND AMENDMENT OF, THE CONSTITUTION OF THE UNITED STATES OF AMERICA, PROPOSED BY CONGRESS, AND RATIFIED BY THE SEVERAL STATES, PURSUANT TO THE FIFTH ARTICLE OF THE ORIGINAL CONSTITUTION

AMENDMENT I (1791)

Congress shall make no law respecting an establishment of religion, or prohibiting the free exercise thereof; or abridging the freedom of speech, or of the press; or the right of the people peaceably to assemble, and to petition the Government for a redress of grievances.

AMENDMENT II (1791)

A well regulated Militia, being necessary to the security of a free state, the right of the people to keep and bear Arms, shall not be infringed.

AMENDMENT III (1791)

No Soldier shall, in time of peace be quartered in any house, without the consent of the Owner, nor in time of war, but in a manner to be prescribed by law.

AMENDMENT IV (1791)

The right of the people to be secure in their persons, houses, papers, and effects, against unreasonable searches and seizures, shall not be violated, and no Warrants shall issue, but upon probable cause, supported by Oath or affirmation, and particularly describing the place to be searched, and the persons or things to be seized.

AMENDMENT V (1791)

No person shall be held to answer for a capital, or otherwise infamous crime, unless on a presentment or indictment of a Grand Jury, except in cases arising in the land or naval forces, or in the Militia, when in actual service in time of War or public danger; nor shall any person be subject for the same offence to be twice put in jeopardy of life or limb; nor shall be compelled in any criminal case to be a witness against himself, nor be deprived of life, liberty, or property, without due process of law; nor shall private property be taken for public use, without just compensation.

AMENDMENT VI (1791)

In all criminal prosecutions, the accused shall enjoy the right to a speedy and public trial, by an impartial jury of the State and district wherein the crime shall have been committed, which district shall have been previously ascertained by law, and to be informed of the nature and cause of the accusation; to be confronted with the witnesses against him; to have compulsory process for obtaining witnesses in his favor, and to have the Assistance of Counsel for his defence.

AMENDMENT VII (1791)

In Suits at common law, where the value in controversy shall exceed twenty dollars, the right of trial by jury shall be preserved, and no fact tried by a jury, shall be otherwise reexamined in any Court of the United States, than according to the rules of the common law.

AMENDMENT VIII (1791)

Excessive bail shall not be required, nor excessive fines imposed, nor cruel and unusual punishments inflicted.

AMENDMENT IX (1791)

The enumeration in the Constitution, of certain rights, shall not be construed to deny or disparage others retained by the people.

AMENDMENT X (1791)

The powers not delegated to the United States by the Constitution, nor prohibited by it to the States, are reserved to the States respectively, or to the people.

AMENDMENT XI (1798)

The Judicial power of the United States shall not be construed to extend to any suit in law or equity, commenced or prosecuted against one of the United States by Citizens of another

State, or by Citizens or Subjects of any Foreign State.

AMENDMENT XII (1804)

The Electors shall meet in their respective states and vote by ballot for President and Vice-President, one of whom, at least, shall not be an inhabitant of the same state with themselves; they shall name in their ballots the person voted for as President, and in distinct ballots the person voted for as Vice-President, and they shall make distinct lists of all persons voted for as President, and of all persons voted for as Vice-President, and of the number of votes for each, which lists they shall sign and certify, and transmit sealed to the seat of the government of the United States, directed to the President of the Senate;—The President of the Senate shall, in the presence of the Senate and House of Representatives, open all the certificates and the votes shall then be counted;—The person having the greatest number of votes for President, shall be the President, if such number be a majority of the whole number of Electors appointed; and if no person have such majority, then from the persons having the highest numbers not exceeding three on the list of those voted for as President, the House of Representatives shall choose immediately, by ballot, the President. But in choosing the President, the votes shall be taken by states, the representation from each state having one vote; a quorum for this purpose shall consist of a member or members from two-thirds of the states, and a majority of all the states shall be necessary to a choice. And if the House of Representatives shall not choose a President whenever the right of choice shall devolve upon them, before the fourth day of March next following, then the Vice-President shall act as President, as in the case of the death or other constitutional disability of the President—The person having the greatest number of votes as Vice-President, shall be the Vice-President, if such number be a majority of the whole number of Electors appointed, and if no person have a majority, then from the two highest numbers on the list, the Senate shall choose the Vice-President; A quorum for the purpose shall consist of two-thirds of the whole number of Senators, and a majority of the whole number shall be necessary to a choice. But no person constitutionally ineligible to the office of President shall be eligible to that of Vice-President of the United States.

AMENDMENT XIII (1865)

Section 1 Neither slavery nor involuntary servitude, except as a punishment for crime whereof the party shall have been duly convicted, shall exist within the United States, or any place subject to their jurisdiction.

Section 2 Congress shall have power to enforce this article by appropriate legislation.

AMENDMENT XIV (1868)

Section 1 All persons born or naturalized in the United States and subject to the jurisdiction thereof, are citizens of the United States and of the State wherein they reside. No State shall make or enforce any law which shall abridge the privileges or immunities of citizens of the United States; nor shall any State deprive any person of life, liberty, or property, without due process of law; nor deny to any person within its jurisdiction the equal protection of the laws.

Section 2 Representatives shall be apportioned among the several States according to their respective numbers, counting the whole number of persons in each State, excluding Indians not taxed. But when the right to vote at any election for the choice of electors for President and Vice-President of the United States, Representatives in Congress, the Executive and Judicial officers of a State, or the members of the Legislature thereof, is denied to any of the male inhabitants of such State, being twenty-one years of age, and citizens of the United States, or in any way abridged, except for participation in rebellion, or other crime, the basis of representation therein shall be reduced in the proportion which the number of such male citizens shall bear to the whole number of male citizens twenty-one years of age in such State.

Section 3 No person shall be a Senator or Representative in Congress, or elector of President and Vice-President, or hold any office, civil or military, under the United States, or under any State, who, having previously taken an oath, as a member of Congress, or as an officer of the United States, or as a member of any State legislature, or as an executive or judicial officer of any State, to support the Constitution of the United States, shall have engaged in insurrection or rebellion against the same, or given aid or comfort to the enemies thereof. But Congress may by a vote of two-thirds of each House, remove such disability.

Section 4 The validity of the public debt of the United States, authorized by law, including debts incurred for payment of pensions and bounties for services in suppressing insurrection or rebellion, shall not be questioned. But neither the United States nor any State shall assume or pay any debt or obligation incurred in aid of insurrection or rebellion against the United States, or any claim for the loss or emancipation of any slave; but all such debts, obligations and claims shall be held illegal and void.

Section 5 The Congress shall have power to enforce, by appropriate legislation, the provisions of this article.

AMENDMENT XV (1870)

Section 1 The right of citizens of the United States to vote shall not be denied or abridged by the United States or by any State on account of race, color, or previous condition of servitude.

Section 2 The Congress shall have power to enforce this article by appropriate legislation.

AMENDMENT XVI (1913)

The Congress shall have power to lay and collect taxes on incomes, from whatever source derived, without apportionment among the several States, and without regard to any census or enumeration.

AMENDMENT XVII (1913)

The Senate of the United States shall be composed of two Senators from each State, elected by the people thereof, for six years; and each Senator shall have one vote. The electors in each State shall have the qualifications requisite for electors of the most numerous branch of the State legislatures.

When vacancies happen in the representation of any State in the Senate, the executive authority of such State shall issue writs of election to fill such vacancies: *Provided,* That the legislature of any State may empower the executive thereof to make temporary appointments until the people fill the vacancies by election as the legislature may direct.

This amendment shall not be so construed as to affect the election or term of any Senator chosen before it becomes valid as part of the Constitution.

AMENDMENT XVIII (1919)

Section 1 After one year from the ratification of this article the manufacture, sale, or transportation of intoxicating liquors within, the importation thereof into, or the exportation thereof from the United States and all territory subject to the jurisdiction thereof for beverage purposes is hereby prohibited.

Section 2 The Congress and the several States shall have concurrent power to enforce this article by appropriate legislation.

Section 3 This article shall be inoperative unless it shall have been ratified as an amendment to the Constitution by the legislatures of the several States, as provided in the Constitution, within seven years from the date of the submission hereof to the States by the Congress.

AMENDMENT XIX (1920)

The right of citizens of the United States to vote shall not be denied or abridged by the United States or by any State on account of sex.

Congress shall have power to enforce this article by appropriate legislation.

AMENDMENT XX (1933)

Section 1 The terms of the President and Vice President shall end at noon on the 20th day of January, and the terms of Senators and Representatives at noon on the 3d day of January, of the years in which such terms would have ended if this article had not been ratified; and the terms of their successors shall then begin.

Section 2 The Congress shall assemble at least once in every year, and such meeting shall begin at noon on the 3d day of January, unless they shall by law appoint a different day.

Section 3 If, at the time fixed for the beginning of the term of the President, the President elect shall have died, the Vice President elect shall become President. If a President shall not have been chosen before the time fixed for the beginning of his term, or if the President elect shall have failed to qualify, then the Vice President elect shall act as President until a President shall have qualified; and the Congress may by law provide for the case wherein neither a President elect nor a Vice President elect shall have qualified, declaring who shall then act as President, or the manner in which one who is to act shall be selected, and such person shall act accordingly until a President or Vice President shall have qualified.

Section 4 The Congress may by law provide for the case of the death of any of the persons from whom the House of Representatives may choose a President whenever the right of choice shall have devolved upon them, and for the case of the death of any of the persons from whom the Senate may choose a Vice President whenever the right of choice shall have devolved upon them.

Section 5 Sections 1 and 2 shall take effect on the 15th day of October following the ratification of this article.

Section 6 This article shall be inoperative unless it shall have been ratified as an amendment to the Constitution by the legislatures of three-fourths of the several States within seven years from the date of its submission.

AMENDMENT XXI (1933)

Section 1 The eighteenth article of amendment to the Constitution of the United States is hereby repealed.

Section 2 The transportation or importation into any State, Territory or possession of the United States for delivery or use therein of intoxicating liquors, in violation of the laws thereof, is hereby prohibited.

Section 3 This article shall be inoperative unless it shall have been ratified as an amendment to the Constitution by conventions in the several States, as provided in the Constitution, within seven years from the date of the submission hereof to the States by the Congress.

AMENDMENT XXII (1951)

Section 1 No person shall be elected to the office of the President more than twice, and no person who has held the office of President, or acted as President, for more than two years of a term to which some other person was elected President shall be elected to the office of the President more than once. But this Article shall not apply to any person holding the office of President when this Article was proposed by the Congress, and shall not prevent any person who may be holding the office of President, or acting as President, during the term within which this Article becomes operative from holding the office of President or acting as President during the remainder of such term.

Section 2 This Article shall be inoperative unless it shall have been ratified as an amendment to the Constitution by the legislatures of three-fourths of the several States within seven years from the date of its submission to the States by the Congress.

AMENDMENT XXIII (1961)

Section 1 The District constituting the seat of Government of the United States shall appoint in such manner as the Congress may direct:

A number of electors of President and Vice President equal to the whole number of Senators and Representatives in Congress to which the District would be entitled if it were a State, but in no event more than the least populous State; they shall be in addition to those appointed by the States, but they shall be considered, for the purposes of the election of President and Vice President, to be electors appointed by a State; and they shall meet in the District and perform such duties as provided by the twelfth article of amendment.

Section 2 The Congress shall have power to enforce this article by appropriate legislation.

AMENDMENT XXIV (1964)

Section 1 The right of citizens of the United States to vote in any primary or other election for President or Vice President, for electors for President or Vice President, or for Senator or Representative in Congress, shall not be denied or abridged by the United States or any State by reason of failure to pay any poll tax or other tax.

Section 2 The Congress shall have power to enforce this article by appropriate legislation.

AMENDMENT XXV (1967)

Section 1 In case of the removal of the President from office or of his death or resignation, the Vice President shall become President.

Section 2 Whenever there is a vacancy in the office of the Vice President, the President shall nominate a Vice President who shall take office upon confirmation by a majority vote of both Houses of Congress.

Section 3 Whenever the President transmits to the President pro tempore of the Senate and the Speaker of the House of Representatives his written declaration that he is unable to discharge the powers and duties of his office, and until he transmits to them a written declaration to the contrary, such powers and duties shall be discharged by the Vice President as Acting President.

Section 4 Whenever the Vice President and a majority of either the principal officers of the executive departments or of such other body as Congress may by law provide, transmit to the President pro tempore of the Senate and the Speaker of the House of Representatives their written declaration that the President is unable to discharge the powers and duties of his office, the Vice President shall immediately assume the powers and duties of the office as Acting President.

Thereafter, when the President transmits to the President pro tempore of the Senate and the Speaker of the House of Representatives his written declaration that no inability exists, he shall resume the powers and duties of his office unless the Vice President and a majority of either the principal officers of the executive department or of such other body as Congress may by law provide, transmit within four days to the President pro tempore of the Senate and the Speaker of the House of Representatives their written declaration that the President is unable to discharge the powers and duties of his office. Thereupon Congress shall decide the issue, assembling within forty-eight hours for that purpose if not in session. If the Congress, within twenty-one days after receipt of the latter written declaration, or, if Congress is not in session, within twenty-one days after Congress is required to assemble, determines by two-thirds vote of both Houses that the President is unable to discharge the powers and duties of his office, the Vice President shall continue to discharge the same as Acting President; otherwise, the President shall resume the powers and duties of his office.

AMENDMENT XXVI (1971)

Section 1 The right of citizens of the United States, who are eighteen years of age or older, to vote shall not be denied or abridged by the United States or by any State on account of age.

Section 2 The Congress shall have power to enforce this article by appropriate legislation.

AMENDMENT XXVII (1992)

No law varying the compensation for the services of the senators and representatives shall take effect, until an election of representatives shall have intervened.

GLOSSARY

accusatory (accusatorial) system The system of criminal justice in the United States. Under the accusatory system, the government must formally accuse a person of having committed a crime and must prove the accusation.

admission A statement of a party to an action which is inconsistent with his or her claim or position in the lawsuit and which therefore constitutes proof against him or her.

adversary (adversarial) system The system of justice in the United States. Under the adversary system, the court hears the evidence presented by adverse parties and decides the case.

affirmative defense A defense that amounts to more than simply a denial of the allegations in the plaintiff's complaint. It sets up new matter which, if proven, could result in a judgment against the plaintiff even if all the allegations of the complaint are true.

aggravating circumstances Acts or conduct which increase the seriousness of a criminal act or the gravity of its effect. Courts often impose more severe sentences when there are aggravating circumstances.

appellate court A higher court to which an appeal is taken from a lower court.

arraignment The act of bringing an accused before a court to answer a criminal charge ... and calling upon him or her to enter a plea of guilty or not guilty.

arrest Detention of a person on a criminal charge.

bail 1. The customary means of securing the release from custody of a person charged with a criminal offense, by assuring his or her appearance in court and compelling him or her to remain within the jurisdiction. 2. The security given for a defendant's appearance in court in the form of cash, real property, or a bail bond.

beyond a reasonable doubt The degree of proof required to convict a person of a crime. A reasonable doubt is a fair doubt based upon reason and common sense, not an arbitrary or possible doubt. To convict a criminal defendant, a jury must be persuaded of his or her guilt to a level beyond "apparently" or "probably." Proof beyond a reasonable doubt is the highest level of proof the law requires.

bill of attainder A legislative act that inflicts capital punishment upon named persons without a judicial trial. Congress and the state legislatures are prohibited from issuing bills of attainder by the Constitution.

bill of particulars In criminal prosecutions, a more detailed statement of the offense charged than the indictment or information provides. A criminal defendant is entitled to a bill of particulars, as part of the discovery process, if the nature and extent of the offense are not alleged with sufficient particularity to allow the preparation of an adequate defense.

burden of going forward (production) The duty of a party, with respect to certain issues being tried, to produce evidence sufficient to justify a verdict before the other party is obligated to produce evidence to the contrary. This burden is also referred to as the *burden of evidence,* the *burden of proceeding,* and the *burden of producing evidence.* The burden of going forward may shift back and forth between the parties during the course of a trial.

burden of persuasion The ultimate burden of proof; the responsibility of convincing the jury, or, in a nonjury trial, the judge, of the truth.

burden of proof The duty of establishing the truth of a matter; the duty of proving a fact that is in dispute. In most instances the burden of proof, like the burden of going forward, shifts from one side to the other during the course of a trial as the case progresses and evidence is introduced by each side.

chain of custody The succession of people who had possession or control of an object, or of the places an object was stored or located, from one point in time to another. In many instances, a chain of custody must be established for physical evidence to be admissible at trial. A chain of custody is sometimes called a chain of possession.

challenge for cause An objection, for a stated reason, to a juror being allowed to hear a case.

commutation of sentence The substitution of a less severe punishment for a more severe punishment.

complaint 1. The initial pleading in a civil action, in which the plaintiff alleges a cause of action and asks that the wrong done ... be remedied by the court. 2. A formal charge of a crime.

concurrent jurisdiction Two or more courts having the power to adjudicate the same class of cases or the same matter.

concurrent sentences Two or more sentences of imprisonment for crime in which the time of each is to run during the same period as the others, and not consecutively.

confession A voluntary admission by a person that he or she has committed a crime.

consecutive sentences Sentences of imprisonment for crimes in which the time of each is to run one after the other without a break.

consent Agreement; approval; acquiescence; being of one mind. Consent necessarily involves two or more persons because, without at least two persons, there cannot be a unity of opinion or the possibility of thinking alike.

court of general jurisdiction Generally, another term for trial court; that is, a court having jurisdiction to try all classes of civil and criminal cases except those which can be heard only by a court of limited jurisdiction.

court of limited jurisdiction A court whose jurisdiction is limited to civil cases of a certain type or which involve a limited amount of money, or whose jurisdiction in criminal cases is confined to petty offenses and preliminary hearings. A court of limited jurisdiction is sometimes called a court of special jurisdiction.

court of record Generally, another term for trial court.

de novo Anew; over again; a second time.

deposition 1. The transcript of a witness's testimony given under oath outside of the courtroom, usually in advance of the trial or hearing, under oral examination or in response to written interrogatories. 2. In a more general sense, an affidavit; a statement under oath.

detainer A writ for the continued detention of a prisoner.

deter To discourage; to prevent from acting.

determinate sentence 1. A sentence whose duration is set by statute and cannot be reduced by a parole board based upon apparent rehabilitation, behavior in prison, or other considerations. 2. A sentence whose duration is set by statute and can be modified by the sentencing judge only in very special circumstances.

discovery A means for providing a party, in advance of trial, with access to facts that are within the knowledge of the other side, to enable the party to better try his or her case. A motion to compel discovery is the procedural means for compelling the adverse party to reveal such facts or to produce documents, books, and other things within his or her possession or control.

discretion The power conferred upon an official to act according to his or her own judgment and conscience, within general rules of law only, uncontrolled by the judgment or conscience of others.

DNA fingerprinting A method for identifying the perpetrator of a crime by comparing tissue ... found at the scene of the crime with similar tissue from the defendant. It is also a method for establishing paternity. DNA (short for deoxyribonucleic acid) is a basic material in all living cells, which transmits the hereditary pattern. DNA evidence is admissible in some jurisdictions in criminal prosecutions and, in most jurisdictions, in paternity suits. Other terms for DNA fingerprinting are HLA testing and genetic marker testing.

double jeopardy A rule originating in the Fifth Amendment that prohibits a second punishment or a second trial for the same offense. It is sometimes referred to as *former jeopardy* or *prior jeopardy.*

ex post facto law A law making a person criminally liable for an act that was not criminal at the time it was committed. The Constitution prohibits both Congress and the states from enacting such laws.

exclusionary rule The rule of constitutional law that evidence secured by the police by means of an unreasonable search and seizure, in violation of the Fourth Amendment, cannot be used as evidence in a criminal prosecution.

exhaustion The doctrine, applicable in many types of cases, that the federal courts will not respond to a party seeking relief until he or she has exhausted her remedies in state court.

extradition The surrender by one nation or state to another of a person accused or convicted of an offense within the territory of the second.

federalism The system by which the states of the United States relate to each other and to the federal government.

final judgment (order) A judgment that determines the merits of the case by declaring that the plaintiff is or is not entitled to recovery. For purposes of the doctrine of res judicata, any judicial decision that is not conditional or subject to change in the future by the same court. For purposes of appeal, a judgment that terminates the litigation between the parties on the merits and leaves nothing to be done but to enforce what has been decided.

fruit of the poisonous tree doctrine The constitutional law doctrine that evidence, including derivative evidence, obtained as the result of an illegal search is inadmissible.

grand jury A body whose number varies with the jurisdiction, never less than 6 nor more than 23, whose duty it is to determine whether probable cause exists to return indictments against persons accused of committing crimes. The right to indictment by grand jury is guaranteed by the Fifth Amendment.

habeas corpus [Latin for] "you have the body." A writ whose purpose is to obtain immediate relief from illegal imprisonment by having the "body" (that is, the prisoner) delivered from custody and brought before the court. A writ of habeas corpus is a means for attacking the constitutionality of the statute under which, or the proceedings in which, the original conviction was obtained. There are numerous writs of habeas corpus, each applicable in different procedural circumstances. The full name of the ordinary writ of habeas corpus is *habeas corpus ad subjiciendum.*

habitual offender statutes State statutes that impose a greater punishment for a second or subsequent conviction than for the first.

halfway house A facility in which persons recently discharged from a rehabilitation facility or prison live for a time and are given support and assistance in readjusting to society at large.

harmless error Trivial or merely formal error; a ruling or other action by a judge in the trial of a case which, although erroneous, is not prejudicial to substantial rights, does not affect the final outcome of the case, and does not form a basis for appeal.

hung jury A jury that cannot reach a unanimous verdict.

in limine [Latin for] "at the outset." Appears in the context of *motion in limine,* a motion made before the commencement of a trial which requests the court to prohibit the adverse party from introducing prejudicial evidence at trial.

incorporation The act of combining one thing with another.

independent source rule Although evidence gained as the result of government misconduct cannot be used in a criminal prosecution, the facts obtained by such conduct are admissible if the government gained knowledge of these facts from an independent source.

indeterminate sentence A prison sentence that is for no less than a minimum period and no more than a maximum period, its exact duration to be determined by the prison or parole authorities based upon behavior in prison or similar considerations.

indictment 1. A charge made in writing by a grand jury, based upon evidence presented to it, accusing a person of having committed a criminal act, generally a felony. It is the function of the prosecution to bring a case before the grand jury. If the grand jury indicts the defendant, a trial follows. 2. The formal, written accusation itself brought before the grand jury by the prosecutor.

inevitable discovery rule The fruit of the poisonous tree doctrine does not bar the introduction into evidence of facts obtained by a search that violates the Fourth Amendment, or a confession secured in violation of the Sixth Amendment, if the facts would have been discovered whether or not the illegal conduct occurred.

inferior court 1. A court of original jurisdiction, as distinguished from an appellate court; a trial court. 2. A court of limited jurisdiction.

information 1. An accusation of the commission of a crime, sworn to by a district attorney or other prosecutor, on the basis of which a criminal defendant is brought to trial for a misdemeanor and, in some states, for a felony. 2. In some jurisdictions, which prosecute felonies only on the basis of indictment by a grand jury, an affidavit alleging probable cause to bind the defendant over to await action by the grand jury.

interlocutory appeal An appeal of a ruling or order with respect to a question that, although not determinative of the case, must be decided for the case to be decided.

interpret To construe; to explain; to draw out meaning.

interrogation 1. The questioning of a criminal suspect by the police. 2. The questioning of any person.

judicial review † 1. Review by a court of a decision or ruling of an administrative agency. 2. Review by an appellate court of a determination by a lower court.

jurisdiction A term used in several senses: 1. In a general sense, the right of a court to adjudicate lawsuits of a certain kind. 2. In a specific sense, the right of a court to determine a particular case; in other words, the power of the court over the subject matter of, or the property involved in, the case at bar. 3. In a geographical sense, the power of a court to hear cases only within a specific territorial area.

lineup A police practice in which a number of individuals, including the criminal suspect, are displayed to the victim of the crime or other witnesses to determine if one of the individuals can be identified as the perpetrator of the offense.

mitigating circumstances Circumstances that lessen blame or reduce the degree of civil or criminal responsibility.

motion An application made to a court for the purpose of obtaining an order or rule directing something to be done in favor of the applicant. The types of motions available to litigants, as well as their form and the matters they appropriately address, are set forth in detail in the Federal Rules of Civil Procedure and the rules of civil procedure of the various states, as well as in the Federal Rules of Criminal Procedure and the various states' rules of criminal procedure. Motions may be written or oral, depending on the type of relief sought and on the court in which they are made.

nolle prosequi [Latin for] "unwilling to pursue." In a criminal case, an entry of record by the prosecutor by which he or she declares his or her intention not to prosecute the case further.

objection The customary method, during a trial or hearing, of calling the attention of the judge or hearing officer to some aspect of the proceeding which one believes to be illegal or improper, and of seeking a ruling on the matter.

pardon An act of grace by the chief executive of the government, ... relieving a person of the legal consequences of a crime of which he or she has been convicted. A pardon erases the conviction.

parole The release of a person from imprisonment after serving a portion of his or her sentence, provided he or she complies with certain conditions. Such conditions vary, depending upon the case, but they generally include stipulations such as not associating with known criminals, not possessing firearms, and not leaving the jurisdiction without the permission of the parole officer. Parole is not an act of clemency; it does not set aside the sentence. The parolee remains in the legal custody of the state and under the control of her parole officer [and] may be returned to prison if he or she breaches the specified conditions. However, due process requires that parole cannot be revoked without a hearing.

per se [Latin for] by itself; in and of itself.

peremptory challenge A challenge to a juror that a party may exercise without having to give a reason.

petty offenses A minor criminal offense, usually tried before a justice of the peace or a magistrate.

plain view doctrine An exception to the search warrant requirement of the Fourth Amendment, which allows warrantless seizure of evidence observed in "plain view" by an officer from a place where he or she had a legal right to be.

plea In criminal cases, a response required by law of a person formally accused of crime, specifically, either a plea of guilty, a plea of nolo contendere, or a plea of not guilty.

plea bargain (plea agreement) An agreement between the prosecutor and a criminal defendant under which the accused agrees to plead guilty, usually to a lesser offense, in exchange for receiving a lighter sentence than he or she would likely have received had he or she been found guilty after trial on the original charge.

police power 1. The power of government to make and enforce laws and regulations necessary to maintain and enhance the public welfare and to prevent individuals from violating the rights of others. 2. The sovereignty of each of the states of the United States that is not surrendered to the federal government under the Constitution.

polling the jury Individually examining the jurors who participated in a verdict to ascertain whether they unanimously support the verdict.

precedent Prior decisions of the same court, or a higher court, which a judge must follow in deciding a subsequent case presenting similar facts and the same legal problem, even though different parties are involved and many years have elapsed.

preliminary hearing A hearing to determine whether there is probable cause to formally accuse a person of a crime; that is, whether there is a reasonable basis for believing that a crime has been committed and for thinking the defendant committed it. If the judge concludes that the evidence is sufficient to hold the defendant for trial, and if the offense is a bailable offense, the court sets bail. If the judge concludes that the evidence is insufficient to bind the defendant over for trial, the defendant is discharged from custody.

probable cause A reasonable amount of suspicion, supported by circumstances sufficiently strong to justify a prudent and cautious person's belief that certain alleged facts are probably true. A judge may not issue a search warrant unless he or she is shown probable cause to believe there is evidence of crime on the premises. A police officer may not make an arrest without a warrant unless he or she has reasonable cause, based upon reliable information, to believe a crime has been or is being committed.

quash To suppress; to set aside; to vacate; to abrogate. Thus, a motion to quash indictment is a motion that asks the court to suppress an indictment that is defective. Similarly, one may quash an information or quash a subpoena.

record 1. A memorial that evidences something written, said, or done. 2. A copy of a document or instrument filed or deposited with a public officer to have it preserved as a public record. 3. An official record.

reprieve The postponement of the carrying out of a sentence. A reprieve is not a commutation of sentence; it is merely a delay.

revocation hearing The due process hearing required before the government can revoke a privilege it has previously granted.

separation of powers A fundamental principle of the Constitution, which gives exclusive power to the legislative branch to make the law, exclusive power to the executive branch to administer it, and exclusive power to the judicial branch to enforce it. The authors of the Constitution believed that the separation of powers would make abuse of power less likely.

show-up A police practice by which a witness to a crime confronts the suspect. Like a lineup, its purpose is to make an identification; unlike a lineup, it involves only the suspect and the witness.

sidebar A term applied to a private discussion between the judge and the attorneys for the parties during the course of a trial. The conversation takes place at the bench, beyond the jury's hearing.

sovereign immunity The principle that the government—specifically, the United States or any state of the United States—is immune from suit except when it consents to be sued.

standing The position of a person with respect to his or her capacity to act in particular circumstances.

standing to sue The legal capacity to bring and to maintain a lawsuit. A person is without standing to sue unless some interest of his or hers has been adversely affected or unless he or she has been injured by the defendant. The term "standing to sue" is often shortened simply to "standing."

stare decisis [Latin for] "standing by the decision." Stare decisis is the doctrine that judicial decisions stand as precedents for cases arising in the future. It is a fundamental policy of our law that, except in unusual circumstances, a court's determination on a point of law will be followed by courts of the same or lower rank in later cases presenting the same legal issue, even though different parties are involved and many years have elapsed.

statute A law enacted by a legislature; an act.

statutes of limitations Federal and state statutes prescribing the maximum period of time during which various types of civil actions and criminal prosecutions can be brought after the occurrence of the injury or the offense.

statutory rape Sexual intercourse with a female under the age of consent, with or without her consent.

subpoena A command in the form of written process requiring a witness to come to court to testify; short for subpoena ad testificandum.

suspended sentence A sentence imposed after conviction of a crime, the carrying out of which is stayed.

transactional immunity A guaranty given a person that if he or she testifies against others he or she will not be prosecuted for his or her own involvement in the crime (i.e., the "criminal transaction") to which his or her testimony relates.

treason The act of transferring one's allegiance from one's own country to the enemy, and giving the enemy aid and comfort.

trial court A court that hears and determines a case initially, as opposed to an appellate court; a court of general jurisdiction.

use immunity A guaranty given a person that if he or she testifies against others, his or her testimony will not be used against him or her if he or she is prosecuted for his or her involvement in the crime.

victim impact statement At the time of sentencing, a statement made to the court concerning the effect the crime has had on the victim or on the victim's family.

voir dire examination Examination of a potential juror for the purpose of determining whether he or she is qualified and acceptable to act as a juror in the case. A prospective juror who a party decides is unqualified or unacceptable may be challenged for cause or may be the subject of a peremptory challenge.

INDEX

D

G

H

I

J

K